Vanguard or Vandals

African Dynamics

VOLUME 4

Vanguard or Vandals

Youth, Politics and Conflict in Africa

Edited by

Jon Abbink
Ineke van Kessel

BRILL
LEIDEN · BOSTON
2005

This book is printed on acid-free paper.

Library of Congress Cataloging-in-Publication Data

Library of Congress cataloging-in-publication data are available on the
Library of Congress website: catalog.loc.gov.

LC control number: 2004059608

ISSN   1568–1777
ISBN   90 04 14275 4

PRINTED IN THE NETHERLANDS

Contents

PART III: INTERVENTIONS: DEALING WITH YOUTH IN CRISIS

Illustrations

Maps

Tables

Photographs

Map indicating the case studies in this book

Being young in Africa:
The politics of despair and renewal

Jon Abbink

The 'problem of youth' in Africa

In his most recent book on Africa, *Négrologie*, the French author Stephen Smith makes a sober assessment of Africa's problems: 'il faut cesser de travestir les réalités de l'Afrique en mêlant ce qui serait souhaitable à ce qui existe .... *le présent n'a pas d'avenir sur le continent*' (2003: Avant Propos). Even if we are less Afro-pessimist than Smith, see more diversity and variety than he does and look for positive aspects, this remark could very well apply to the overall situation of young people in Africa. They are facing tremendous odds and do not seem to have the future in their own hands. While there has been progress in some respects – for example, in education, migration and job opportunities in the urban arena – the exponential population increase and the fierce competition for resources within the contexts of malfunctioning or failing states have led to a relative decline in the well-being and social advancement of young people in Africa. They are growing up in conditions of mass unemployment and are facing exclusion, health problems,[1] crisis within the family due to poverty and the AIDS pandemic, and a lack of education and skills. They also are marginalized in national state policies and have a weak legal position. African youths are over-represented in armed rebel or insurgent movements of various kinds as well as in criminal activities, to which they are so easily recruited. There is no prospect that this situation will change for the better in the near future.

---

[1] This starts early. According to Black, Morris & Bryce (2003: 2226), there was a child mortality rate in 2000 of 176 per 1000 live births in Sub-Saharan Africa (as against 6 per 1000 in developed industrialized countries).

This introduction treats a few key aspects of the question of youth in Africa and is not exhaustive. For instance, little will be said about evidently important subjects such as young refugees, migration and its impact on youth, the culture of street children or the role of youth in the labour force and in labour movements.

It is a paradox that while *children* in Africa are highly valued by adults, the ability, and perhaps even the interest, to care for them declines as they become adolescents. Poverty and destitution, violence, migration, AIDS, and the breakdown of the family also contribute to this. The simple fact is that most of Africa's young people are no longer growing up in the relatively well-integrated societies described in rich detail by anthropologists and historians only one or two generations ago: monographs on, for example, the Nuer, the Dinka, the Murle, the Tiv, the Meru, the Kpelle, the Somali, the Acholi, the Kikuyu or the Karimojong give the impression of another world. Only faint traces of social order and cultural integrity still exist. Most of these societies have transformed into impoverished and internally divided wholes, with many of them caught up in violent conflict and marginalization. Even the last bastion of African society – the (extended) family – seems to have succumbed to the pressure as parents and relatives find it increasingly difficult to foster the young and provide them with a relatively carefree period in which to grow and develop. This transformation has led to a large proportion of youth having no well-defined place in society and being vulnerable and dependent, especially in urban conditions. McIntyre *et al.* (2002: 8) have mentioned the lack of 'constructive social incentives' in society as a key feature that narrows youngsters' possibilities for more or less orderly growth and development, and makes them look elsewhere for survival and opportunities.

The dilemma is how to write about youth in Africa without falling back on the bleak picture of crisis, crime and violence that the available statistics and research reports seem to confirm time and again. And how can one do justice to the many positive exceptions and to the versatility and survival skills of youngsters in such dire straits?[2] It would be a mistake to deny African youth intentionality of action and agency, as has so often happened in Africanist discourse.

While not denying the disturbing facts, it has to be noted that *perceptions* play an important role. Being young in Africa is widely and consistently perceived as problematic in essence. Social analysts, policy makers, NGOs,

---

[2] See Falola (2004). For a moving example, see also Sili, the heroic girl who sells newspapers, in the film *La Petite Vendeuse du Soleil* by Djibril D. Mambéty (Senegal 1998).

governments and international organizations all reiterate that African youth is in deep trouble and enmeshed in violence. While understandable, this view is overburdening and prejudges the issues before understanding them. The assumption that developed Western or other modern industrialized societies can be held up as the example must also be rejected. Both theoretically and empirically one needs to avoid positing 'youth' and generational tension in Africa as an inherently destructive or exceptional factor in the social order. This reveals a kind of Hobbesian worldview applied to Africa. On the contrary, there is a need to *integrate* the youth factor as a necessary element in any social analysis of African societies, thus testing the relative autonomy of youths as actors (re)shaping social relations and power formations. We also need to keep a comparative perspective and recognize that not only youth in Africa face challenges but equally those in many countries in the Middle East,[3] South America, Asia and the developed 'North'.

This book chiefly addresses the political and conflict-generating 'potential' of youth and generational conflict in Africa and describes their societal manifestations and causes. It is now evident that the chronic problems faced by youth – and their responses to them – have clear political implications. By their sheer numbers, their availability, and their eagerness to take up anything that may relieve them of conditions of poverty, idleness or *ennui*, youth are easily recruited by political parties, armed groups or criminal networks. In addition, youths pose their own demands and form their own movements. Here the perception that they are all engaged in socially undesirable or criminal activities, or are unemployable (youth as *lumpen*, as a lost generation, etc.) is erroneous, as the many developments in African popular culture (music, theatre, fashion), religious revival, new indigenous NGOs, the creative appropriation of ICT in Africa, and of course sports make clear: youths are active on all fronts (see Trudell *et al.* 2002). In this, their direct or indirect political role is evident.

The concept of 'generation' is arguably a difficult one, and perhaps not explanatory as such. But apart from recognizing a psycho-biological factor – youths in adolescence want to act, to test the world they are engaging, and do not shun aggression against rivals or those above them[4] – young people and rebellious groups in Africa consistently phrase many of their problems in terms of generational opposition. They often say that they receive too little attention from those in power – both in rural society (chiefs, ruling age grades) and in the cities (political leaders, party bosses, teachers, etc.). We thus take our cue from

---

[3] See the UNDP's 'Arab Human Development Reports' of 2002 and 2003, at: www. undp.org/rbas/ahdr/ahdr1/presskit1/PRExecSummary.pdf and www.undp.org/rbas/ahdr/ ahdr2/presskit/6_AHDR03ExSum_E.pdf.

[4] Cf. Daly & Wilson's study (1993) on the 'young male syndrome'.

this and use 'generation' as a heuristic concept but recognize its connection with other inequalities like class, ethnicity or religious denomination.

Generally speaking, generational tension and change occur anywhere, and are always 'problematic'. The phenomenon is multidimensional (social, psychological and political) and is as old as human society. It is a universal and popular theme reflected in the literary imagination from across the world: the Oedipus myth, Old Testament stories, tribal myths, and great novels like Turgenev's *Fathers and Children* (1862)*, Stendhal's *Vie de Henri Brulard* (1835), Salinger's *The Catcher in the Rye* (1951) or Ellison's *The Invisible Man* (1952).[5] Sigmund Freud made the theme a cornerstone of his psycho-analytic theory and elaborated it in *Totem und Tabu,* a 1913 monograph on cultural history describing the archetypal rivalry between the generations.[6] But the ways in which social systems have dealt with this demographic-biological fact of age and generational difference varies widely. In most modernized industrial societies, generations are informally delineated, boundaries between 'young' and 'old' are fuzzy, and the category 'young' often acquires a curious prestige and aura of desirability not based on social merit or particular achievements, the latter no doubt connected to the new consumer value of youth for commercial companies. Hence, contestation and struggle as to boundaries, symbolism, prestige and power in the public domain of contemporary societies are common.

In Africa, a large number of agro-pastoral societies still have intricate age systems, where the generational problem is formally 'solved' with the assigning of social roles to age groups and maintaining clear ritual boundaries between them, access to which can only be gained by ritual transition and formal confirmation.[7] Sometimes the application of this age principle has led to an age-set system, with fixed, mutually exclusive categories of people of a certain age that are cohesive and move through time as a collective, or to generation sets with alternating ranked categories where parents and children are always members of different opposed groups and have ritual obligations towards each other. They are set in a hierarchical order, each having an expected code of behaviour and a circumscribed public role. Good examples are the *gaada* systems of the Konso, Burji and various Oromo peoples (Guji and Boran) in

---

[5] The Ethiopian masterpiece *Fiqir iske Meqabir* ('Love until the Grave') by Haddis Alemayehu published in 1973 is an African example that describes the gradual emergence of disenchantment and rebellion among Ethiopia's young generation. It was in many ways a prophetic novel: one year later the Ethiopian revolution began.

[6] For some recent views on children and youth in African fiction, see the special issue of *Mots Pluriels* at: www.arts.uwa.edu.au/MotsPluriels/MP2202index.html.

[7] For a classic, formal analysis of the complexities of age systems, see the study by Stewart (1976). For Africa, see Abélès & Collard (1985).

southern Ethiopia (cf. Aguilar 1998, Bassi 1996, Hinnant 1978), the Nyangatom generation system (Tornay 2001), or the age organization of the Kenyan Gusii and Meru (Péatrik 1993, 2003), all of a fascinating ethnographic complexity. While the actual transitions were often marked by rituals and by symbolic resistance or violence, no one fell outside the system and all acquired a clear and recognized social identity. The drawbacks of these systems are that the gerontocratic element is too strong and that they are not always capable of dealing with external changes and shocks (see Simonse this volume).[8] Other types of social organization in Africa are still strongly informed by lineage and clan principles, with youths expected to defer to elders and lineage seniors. While in the post-colonial era these inherited principles of social order are more respected in the breach than in the keeping, many of the underlying ideas of reciprocity, complementarity and mutual obligation (for example via kinship relations) are still present. There is a pattern of moral expectation that many youths in Africa feel is being flouted by the older generation. Religious notions to which they appeal reinforce this. These are ingredients for the emerging struggles between the 'older' and the 'younger' generations in Africa. In explaining the youth experience in Africa, a processual view on the place and role of youth is needed to take into account both these struggles as well as the existing cultural representations on and of youth, recognizing that they are set in a context of faulty modernization, social rupture and inequalities of economic opportunity or power.

Defining 'youth'

Implicit in the above is that we know what we are talking about when using the terms 'youth' and 'youngsters'. When is one young in Africa? Certainly below the age of 14, the largest age group in Africa. But what about people in their thirties or early forties? Several authors include groups, advanced in biological age, in their definition of youth. Obviously, 'youth' is partly a socially con-structed or constituted category, like most social phenomena. Some people who are well into their thirties have not completed their education, have no job, are

---

[8] This was also demonstrated by Eisei Kurimoto in his conference presentation entitled 'War, Displacement and an Emerging New Generation: Pari Youths in South Sudan and Beyond' at the African Studies Centre, Leiden, 24 April 2003. He mentioned that during the upheaval of Päri society during the Southern Sudanese civil war, the age system was destroyed, with youngsters even shooting the members of the incumbent ruling grade, the *mojomiji*. Interestingly, however, the age system was reinstated in exile, although in a different form.

not in a position to raise a family, etc. indeed sociologically resemble the biologically younger people with whom they share a way of life defined by poverty and deprivation. In Africa there are many such people who have had to delay their entry into adulthood: they feel excluded and powerless, and struggle to survive. But despite this there has to be a limit to calling someone a 'youngster': forty-year olds, for instance, are no longer youths but pass into another category, perhaps that of street people, beggars or vagrants. For this tragic category of people, the adage of 'youth possessing the future' or 'having a whole life before them' is vacuous: they are, by local standards, already middle-aged and have effectively *lost* the promise of youth. No strict definition of age limits can be given (see also d'Almeida-Topor 1992). For the above reasons and following statistical custom, we pragmatically limit the category of 'youth' in Africa to the 14-35 age bracket.[9] Under 14, they are children, usually dependent on older people and not accepted as adults, while over thirty-five they are, or were, more or less expected to be socially independent, have a family and have acquired some social status of their own.[10] Finally, youth comprises males and females. The gender dimension, however, is often relegated to second place in studies and policies about youth in Africa. It may be true that young males are dominant in politics, on the street, in the job market, in insurgent movements and as perpetrators of crime and violence, but the same social problems are equally faced by females. Conflict and violence have a particularly dramatic impact on the perception and construction of gender relations, with new, more aggressive formations of masculinity – within already existing patriarchal relations – often leading to more dependency, abuse and subordination of girls and women (see Jok, this volume). The gender perspective is not yet sufficiently integrated in youth studies.

Recent debates

In the post-colonial nation-states of Africa that emerged in the early 1960s, generational tension has become a recurrent feature of politics. This has been

---

[9] Thirty-five is too high for the customary census bureau practices, but in view of conditions in Africa can be defended. The US Population Reference Bureau (see: www.prb.org) takes as the category 'youth' the ten to twenty-four age group. The under-10 group are children. Another commonly used bracket is 14-25.

[10] As a result of the AIDS catastrophe in Africa, many orphaned children under 14 are already the main breadwinners for their younger siblings, effectively running the family. This illustrates the need to take the age boundaries as loose, open borders for the category 'youth'.

fuelled by the young generation that has grown up since independence, who both as an age group and as a socially blocked generation of sons and daughters of the independence or *uhuru* generation, has fared rather badly. In the early years after independence, many young and promising politicians, like Tom Mboya in Kenya, had to be contained by the 'elders' and were manoeuvred out, or eliminated. Forty years of post-colonial history has not shown a takeover of power by the young or a substantial improvement in the life of youth in Africa in general.[11] To be young in Africa came to mean being disadvantaged, vulnerable and marginal in the political and economic sense. A long historical process, shaped by authoritarian colonialism, post-colonial state failure and a generally problematic engagement with material modernity has yielded the conditions of crisis and upheaval under which youths in Africa are growing up. State failure and the peculiar nature of the African bureaucratic bourgeoisie that are living on 'rent-seeking' not productive investment, dubious Cold War alliances, and a lack of economic initiatives have played their role. But in a wider sense, even before independence, much of the traditional social fabric and cultural meaning had been lost, and the socialization of the young and the transmission of social capital or indigenous skills and knowledge were interrupted.[12] Education and employment did not offer alternative routes, or only for a select few. One might metaphorically say that, in a way, the socially and culturally accepted *initiation* of the young into adult society – that in many societies used to be ritually marked by rites of transition and a period of seclusion and training – can no longer be properly accomplished in Africa. This metaphor is apt because youth interpret their problems through a moral prism: they often suggest that adults have given up on them or have reneged on their social and moral obligations towards them. There is also a psychology of humiliation and shame involved.

Globalization and hegemonistic processes emanating from the contemporary world system are now also affecting African societies – politically and economically but also socially and culturally. The continent's assets (minerals, raw materials, wildlife, art objects, etc.) are being siphoned off in a predatory and uncontrolled manner, its productive capacity stunted and caught in relations of persistent inequality in a resurrected *laissez-faire* style of capitalism,[13] and

---

[11] A pioneering collection surveying many of the conditions of youth in Africa was d'Almeida-Topor *et al.* (1992).

[12] The famous novel *Things Fall Apart* by the Nigerian author Chinua Achebe (1958), was a prophetic view of things to come.

[13] The World Bank and especially the IMF have a poor record of success in Africa over the past 20 years. Structural Adjustment Programmes have only rarely achieved anything durable, as they were often based on wrong premises and short-term perspectives.

African norms and values are being declared irrelevant or harmful, in line with a long tradition of alienating discourse on Africa by both the Islamic and the Western world. These processes are often actively supported by the African political elites in place. While globalization and social change offer new opportunities, most of the scientific as well as policy discourse on the subject is preoccupied with crisis-related aspects, fuelled by recent hotly debated issues such as child soldiers (Machel 1996, Stohl 2002, McIntyre *et al.* 2002, Peters & Richards 1998),[14] AIDS orphans (Dane & Levine 1994),[15] child slavery and trafficking (Rossi 2003),[16] female genital mutilation (Gosselin 2000) and the sexual abuse of young children, especially in Southern Africa (Richter, Dawes & Higson-Smith 2004). Recent studies reiterate the fact that the social insertion of the young, i.e. their more-or-less stable and predictable inclusion and incorporation in the wider society during adolescence, is highly precarious.

A number of responses in the academic literature arise from this picture of despair and doom. One is the 'agency' response that emphasizes the active role of youth in finding their own answers to the problems they face, and thus having them shape their own destiny. They are versatile, resilient and make do with whatever they can to survive. They often move into alternative modes of expression but *can* influence policy and local society. The annual 'Day of the African Child' (16 June) commemorates the 1976 Soweto youth revolt on that day, a prime example of a mass youth protest that made a difference.[17] Another telling example of the leverage that youth can have and consciously use is given in Lesley Sharp's study (2002) of Malagasy youth identity politics, historical memory and political change. Her analysis demonstrates that youth, as an intermediate social category, can catalyze processes of change in the wider society. In South Africa, youth was at the forefront of the broad social movement that mobilized anti-apartheid protest and resistance in the 1980s, thus

---

The ideal of trimming down the oversized African state and its huge budget deficits was achieved only at a very high social cost. For a recent critique, see Schatz (2002), also Van de Walle *et al.* (2003).

[14] See also a special website on the subject:
www.essex.ac.uk/armedcon/themes/child_soldiers/default.htm.

[15] See the BBC news item 'AIDS Orphans to Double', at: http://news.bbc.co.uk/1/hi/health/2120449.stm and the article '"Tidal Wave" of AIDS orphans rising', *New Scientist*, 13 July 2004, at: www.newscientist.com/news/news.jsp?id=ns99996143. At present there are an estimated 11 million AIDS orphans in Africa: one child in every 20. See: http://www.oneliferevolution.org/unbelievable/.

[16] See this alarming UNESCO report at:
www.unicef-icdc.org/publications/pdf/insight9e.pdf.

[17] See Smith (2003: 67-68).

laying the foundations for a democratic transition in the 1990s (see Van Kessel 2000).

Part of the agency perspective is to recognize that youth has been equally inclined, especially over the past few decades of social decline, to be actively involved in crime and predatory armed movements.[18] This is often explained by their tangible despair, their search for role models (among males) and a lack of other options (see below). It is well-known that youths are the driving forces in numerous rebel or guerrilla movements (see Young 1997 on the Ethiopian TPLF) and neo-traditional protest movements (see Kanneworff 2004 on the *Mungiki* and Kagwanja this volume), sometimes with a major socio-political impact. The agency approach is usually accompanied by a call to take the study of youth, in Africa and elsewhere, more seriously and to listen to young people's voices. Agency, both on empirical and epistemological grounds, should not – and cannot – be denied. As a meta-concept it is useful to sensitize us to the fact that social structure is an interactive whole where the actions of individuals and minor groups play a role and 'realize' as well as transform structures. Youths are neither universally manipulated nor passive actors in a world designed by others but individuals who are trying to chart their own course. The dynamics of collective movements is incomplete without a realist perspective on individual agency and emergent forms of action. Various chapters in this book provide clear evidence of this (Dorman, Burgess, Marguerat).

A second response is the interventionist one that is based on the premise that, in the face of enduring youth deprivation, remedial policies should be developed and implemented, and that both local and international NGOs should be actively involved in creating programmes and policies designed to help youngsters attain independence, employment, civic representation and social standing. Target groups are often street children, young ex-combatants and chronically unemployed and unskilled youths. On the basis of well-described case studies,[19] national governments are being urged to more actively 'invest in people'[20] and develop education and employment policies that assist youngsters, at the peril of losing them and pushing them into socially subversive activities

---

[18] Compare the various armed groups in the Liberia and Sierra Leone wars, clan-based militias in Somalia, the armed groups in the Democratic Republic of the Congo, the young thug squads organized by Zimbabwe's current government, Nigerian vigilante groups, youth recruitment into the Sudanese state army and rebel movements, and the devastation by the Lord's Resistance Army in northern Uganda.

[19] For one comprehensive collection of studies on Ethiopia, see Habtamu (1996).

[20] See Chapter 4 in the World Bank document *Can Africa Claim the 21st Century?* (Washington, DC, 2000).

or political protest. Even a well-controlled new state like Eritrea, which could count on a high level of commitment from youth in its war of independence against the Ethiopian regime, is faced with youth disenchantment, as Dorman's chapter shows.

Both these responses are closely connected to the 'rights discourse' (see De Waal & Argenti 2002), which develops a normative approach towards youth and its rightful place in society. No one will argue the value of realizing rights and the increased empowerment of children and youth, but apart from the need to define or understand what these rights are or have to be in specific contexts, current conditions in Africa are unfavourable for attaining this goal in the foreseeable future.

A third response is the more descriptive-analytic one, trying to offer historically and sociologically grounded accounts to explain what has been happening with African youth in the past century and to lay out current scenarios. Agency rightfully calls attention to the individual power of actors and their cumulative impact, clarifying what the structural constraints of social and political conditions are on individual behaviour. The actor-oriented perspective associated with the agency approach is productive but only when the interaction with structural elements is taken seriously. The interventionist approach has a laudable ethical dimension and assumes the self-evidence of rights. Rights, however, are the issue of negotiation and political struggle, and cultural perceptions about them differ notably across communities. An analytic perspective, informed by a realist theory of social action that focuses on generative structures explaining social phenomena has a particular interest in the *interaction* of structure, agency and normative or reflexive discourse. Needless to say, therefore, the three approaches are interrelated but an analytic approach seems necessary for initial understanding. In this book, a mix of approaches is found but the analytic one predominates.

The aim of this collection is thus to present, through a variety of cases, a comprehensive overview of all crucial socio-cultural and historical factors involved in the youth experience in contemporary Africa. There is a predictable diversity in theme and approach but all contributions are based on original fieldwork and attempt to address conflict-generating processes, test hypotheses on generational tensions, and assess the political impact of youth problems in society. They intend to provide more general insights that could be taken up by politicians at government level, NGOs and international (donor) organizations. Most of the contributors to this book are historians, sociologists and anthropologists. Some have, on the basis of their scientific work, played a pioneering role in action-oriented research and project implementation in the field of youth problems in Africa (see the chapters by Simonse, McIntyre, Peters and, especially, Marguerat).

Youth and generational tensions then and now

An historical-anthropological analysis of youth and age in Africa reveals that generational conflict, as a socio-cultural phenomenon, has existed for a long time. But due to rapid processes of change related to colonialism, modernization, social upheaval and disturbed demographic trends such as runaway population growth,[21] this phenomenon has assumed crisis proportions, fundamentally different from those in the past. Virtually everywhere on the continent, youth, while forming a numerical majority,[22] are in a situation of dependency, economically marginalized, and feel excluded from formal power and prestige, even when the time has come for them to become part of established society. The dominant power structures and patronage networks are rigid, conservative and often vertically organized with reference to ethnic or religions groups. These function as frameworks of 'extended kinship' or moral community with limited access. In the absence of judicial or state structures guaranteeing some kind of equity or redistribution effect, patronage and power have a tendency to exclude non-insiders. This makes for a politically volatile situation in many African countries (Cruise O'Brien 1996). The sheer numbers involved make it acute as young people form the large majority and exert pressure due to the size of their group. This unprecedented demographic imbalance therefore has a political dynamic of its own.

African societies and politics could be reconsidered in the light of these generational tensions engendered by dramatic population growth in conditions of state stagnation or failure. Inequality and dependency seem to have marked the generational relations in pre-colonial and rural African societies as well, but there may be essential differences in the social organization of inequality and age organization, as well as in their valuation in past and present societies. In

---

[21] Many pre-colonial African societies had certain mechanisms, for example regulating marriage age and birth frequency, that kept population growth in check and in line with economic possibilities. See Legesse (1989) for the example of the traditional Boran system. Today, no African society has yet entered the stage of demographic transition (towards lower fertility and higher life expectancy). The average figure for population growth in Africa is 2.7%, four times the average of industrialized countries. A similar fast growth, though, is seen in some other parts of the world, for example the Middle East.

[22] Youth between ages 0 and 24 in Africa make up a substantial majority; those under age 15 already constitute some 45% of the total Sub-Saharan African population (1999 UNDP figures). According to the US Population Resources Bureau, in 2003 youth between 5 and 24 made up 47% of the total Sub-Saharan African population (See: www.prb.org/template.cfm?template=InterestDisplay.cfm&InterestCategoryID=210). In Western industrial societies, the population under the age of 15 is less than 20%.

many rural, especially pastoral, societies of today, for example in East Africa, this problem can be observed at first hand because seemingly well-integrated age organization societies, where social relations are largely based on a metaphoric use of 'age' as a social distinction and power marker (cf. Turton 1995: 100), have great difficulty in absorbing the challenges and problems of 'modernity'. They are faced with processes of economic exclusion, unmediated commercialization, wrong-headed state policies and so-called development schemes (Fratkin 1998) that do not enhance interaction, cooperation or well-being, but rather the reverse. These societies also face intensified armed conflict, or its members see short-term advantages in resorting to it. The wide availability of arms (particularly automatic rifles) has enhanced this. One could think here of societies like the Karimojong (Dyson-Hudson 1966, see also Simonse this volume), the Nuer (Hutchinson 1996), the Suri (Abbink 1994, 2003, 2004), the Nyangatom (Tornay 2001) or the Päri (Kurimoto).[23]

These generational tensions in the post-colonial age of modernization or, in a wider sense, modernity – as a comprehensive socio-cultural, not only political-economic, phenomenon – have led to the massive recruitment and involvement of youths in revolutionary or insurgent movements, starting in the 1970s. The guerrilla movements in Ethiopia – the Eritrean People's Liberation Front (EPLF) and the Tigray People's Liberation Movement (TPLF) – were clear examples of this, but also the armed movements in Angola, Mozambique, Sierra Leone and Liberia. Youths, mostly males, with no educational or career options in an impoverished or marginalized society see here the opportunity to join an exciting movement in which they are valued as members and fighters, and where there is promise of social change, justice or, at best, loot. While many of these earlier movements (such as the EPLF, TPLF, PAIGC in Guinea-Bissau, NRM in Uganda) had social-revolutionary programmes and partly realized them, in the early 21st century the ideological content of armed insurgent movements is often lost (cf. Mkandawire 2002). As is most evident in Somalia, Congo-Brazzaville (in the 1990s) or in the Democratic Republic of the Congo, many seem to have turned into predatory looting machines that seek not only material booty and destruction but also humiliation though torture and mutilation, terror through the arbitrary killing of innocent individuals, and sexual gratification, as is evident from the large-scale abuse of women and girls in the civilian population. In a mimetic circle of violence and intimidation, national army troops sent to combat insurgents, and often also including child

---

[23] Kurimoto, 'War, Displacement and an Emerging New Generation', see note 8.

soldiers, come to join in such practices.[24] The reinsertion of such combatants in any kind of normal society is fraught with problems (see Peters this volume).

Youth and politics

When looking more closely at African politics in the post-colonial era, one notes that they were marked by immobility and the monopolizing behaviour of the elites in power, sustained by often surrealistic and ruthless methods of intimidation. In much of Eastern and Southern Africa, the generation that secured independence blocked the path of the younger generation in political life and in the state bureaucracy.[25] Robert Mugabe's pathetic and destructive policies in Zimbabwe in the last few years illustrate this graphically. Namibia is another example: incumbent President Sam Nujoma prepared constitutional changes in 1999 that allowed him to extend his increasingly autocratic presidential rule for a third term. Eritrea may be another, as the current president has eliminated any opposition, delayed party formation and elections indefinitely, and insulted or imprisoned youths who contest certain national policies. Power is seen as indivisible and thus the old idea of the prerogative of the senior generation (having 'led the struggle' for independence or freedom) has come full circle.

In the first decades of African independence, young leaders were carefully screened and contained. They were enticed to enter the ranks of the reigning elite, to set themselves against each other, or were banned. As the years went by and the older generations clung on to power, youths became prominently involved in opposition politics, provided they were not co-opted or neutralized by being offered positions in the existing system. Not only were they present in opposition factions within the reigning political parties (often the only ones allowed), they were also involved in the potentially powerful labour unions and in student movements. In addition, they set up or joined armed insurgent

---

[24] The scale and cruelty of such destruction and abuse in Africa – the latest case (2003-2004) being the mass killings, "ethnic cleansing" and scorched-earth campaigns of Sudan's government and it allied militias in Darfur – is often beyond belief.

[25] Witness Kenya, where Mwai Kibaki, a coeval and advisor of the country's first president, Jomo Kenyatta, in the early years of independence, was elected president in the 2002 national elections at the age of 71. His participation in politics, as well as that of anyone else over the age of fifty, was heavily criticized by the *Mungiki* youth movement, which called for a shake-up and generational change in Kenyan politics. Interestingly, as Kanneworff (2004: 88) notes, *Mungiki* youngsters' ideas here referred back to notions of the Kikuyu age-grade system.

movements in the 1970s and 1980s, some of which ultimately successfully took over power (cf. Clapham 1998).

Youth was also at the forefront of democratic agitation in Africa in the late 1980s and 1990s but their success was limited, except in the case of South Africa. The prospects of democratization and socio-economic development that seemed to open up after 1989, the year of the fall of Communist regimes in Eastern Europe and the end of the Cold War, were not realized. New approaches proposed by the World Bank[26] and other international institutions and donors led to economic liberalization and regime pressure in many countries, but these were not sustainable. They were often accompanied by new informal power configurations and criminalized elite activities. Established systems of patronage, endangered by new but often inconsistent demands for 'good governance' and political accountability by donor countries and inter-national organizations, were redefined, allowing many old-style elites (as well as new ones) to reinstate or reshape neo-patrimonial rule. The average citizen, let alone the younger generation, in Africa did not substantially benefit from reforms. In an important and widely read study, Paul Richards (1996) has interpreted the violence in Sierra Leone as issuing from a wider crisis affecting youth in a declining patrimonial state that could not cater to its young population. The country's forest resources, in high demand on the world market, became an issue of competition and violence between state and rebels, and allowed marginalized youth to carve out a domain of alternative careers and self-assertion in line with traditional cultural notions as well new social values acquired in the setting of struggle. No 'natural inclination' of youth to behave violently can explain their presence in socially destructive movements. The breakdown of a socio-political and moral order in the wider society and the degree of governability of a certain type of state are more likely to precipitate this.

In the wake of political and economic changes in the early 1990s and the failure of effective regime changes toward democracy and equity, new armed conflicts have proliferated across Africa, with youth playing a prominent role in them. The part played by university students in ideological contestation (see Arnaut and Konings in this volume) in the absence of strong civil-society organizations, like labour unions, parties, religious groups or local NGOs, is remarkable. A good early example is Imperial Ethiopia, where the students created a new leftist discourse of change and social reordering that had a huge influence on the army officers who took over power in 1974 (cf. Balsvik 1985). Students in Ethiopia have remained active to this day. Another is Madagascar,

---

[26] See *Africa: from Crisis to Sustainable Growth* (1989).

where student uprisings have led to the fall of two governments (Sharp 2002: 10). In the past few decades, Africa has also seen the emergence of relatively powerful student movements in countries like Cameroon, Côte d'Ivoire and Mali. Many insurgent and guerrilla leaders have risen from the ranks of the students, often, as in the case of Ethiopia, steeped in a Socialist/Marxist ideology.

Throughout the post-colonial period, regimes in power have often created youth wings of the ruling party that were not loathe to exercise intimidating violence on opponents (as in Kenya, Cameroon, Malawi and most recently in Mugabe's Zimbabwe). So-called political action here has gradually turned into criminal violence, which shows that young people can easily be manipulated into such movements directed by adult power-holders. The PRESBY group mentioned in Piet Konings's chapter (this volume) is but one example of a violent, unabashedly pro-government militia formed to build a counterweight to democratic and grassroots Anglophone protests against social injustice and political manipulation by the Cameroon elite. The rapid dismantling of Zimbabwe in recent years is a contemporary example that demonstrates how the manipulation of youth into semi-criminal, pro-regime militias can be observed as it happens (Ndlovu 2003). Often, as in northern Nigeria, there is a relationship between youth action and its use for political purposes. No doubt the controversial introduction of Islamic *shari'a* as state law in many northern Nigerian states (which goes against the federal constitution) partly reflects the wish of local people to have speedy and predictable justice in conditions of rising crime, but it also supports the political agenda of elite leaders who have lost or fear losing power and want to build an alternative basis of support among youngsters and are ready to use intimidation and force.[27]

As religious and ethnic antagonisms are being discursively emphasized in the competition for resources and the quest for political power or elite rule (see Atieno-Odhiambo 2004), the young generation will be called upon and be used by power-holders as allies or vanguards in the realization of certain political goals, both peacefully and violently. That youths display agency in the process and can become autonomous forces to be reckoned with, dominating social movements and often setting an agenda of violent action, was evident in South Africa during apartheid, the West African wars, and in the conflict in Southern Sudan (see Jok this volume).

---

[27] Cf. the study by Makiko (2002), and the recent Human Rights Watch report (2004).

Youth and conflict

The dynamics underlying the hardening ethno-regional and political identities mentioned above and their conversion into armed conflicts of alarming proportions are to be explained by, among others, the underlying dynamics of social exclusion and inequality as well as state crisis and economic decline reducing the cake available for division. Political antagonisms and conflict do not only exist on the discursive level but are also produced by demographic and social contradictions that can not be resolved within the conciliation mechanisms of the (post-colonial) African state or in accordance with the tenets of Africa's traditional political cultures.

The conflict between generations and/or age groups in many African countries is now a structural phenomenon in both the social and the political sense. As we saw above, the social problem that will not go away in many African neo-patrimonial countries is that of blocked social mobility. If only on the basis of demographics (the 'overproduction of youth'), finding employment and access to representative positions and political power is Utopian for most youngsters, except for a happy few. The state sector is just too small and too poor a resource to redistribute and to provide for its many needy and ambitious citizens, and neither the formal economy nor the NGO sector – though expanding in many African countries – offer sufficient absorptive capacity. There is often an overproduction of highly educated graduates, at least in view of the very limited absorptive capacity of African economies. This phenomenon of blocked mobility is particularly acute in Africa (see for a discussion of specific examples: Toungara 1995, Abdullah 1997, Richards 1996, Peters & Richards 1998), and will continue to form the background of the growth of opposition movements, criminal networks and armed revolts. Political insurgencies are often rooted in a combination of a structural lack of opportunities and generational antagonism, as exemplified in the leftist urban revolt of the Ethiopian People's Revolutionary Party in the 1970s and the ethno-regional rebellions of the Tigray People's Liberation Front (1975-1991) and the Oromo Liberation Front in Ethiopia, all of which emanated from the Marxist-leaning student protest movement against Emperor Haile Sellassie before 1974.

These examples show that resorting to conflict is one of the most frequent responses to a situation of stagnation and a lack of future prospects. There is also an element of revenge involved. The rebellious young generation, through looting and violence, consciously 'takes back' what they consider was monopolized by the older generation, often even from their leaders and kin relations.[28] For armed insurgencies in countries where the state is not the all-powerful surveillance bureaucracy that exists in the developed West, there is still social and geographical space to develop a separate social domain (for example, experiments with revolutionary reforms in the countryside) and alternative routes to power.

In recent years, youth rebellions and/or generational tensions have developed a new social and political idiom, whereby the impact of new images and signs disseminated through Western or Asian mass media products (radio, TV, video, the Internet and other emerging electronic communication forms) are playing a growing role. Global genres and narratives are eagerly absorbed by youngsters, and local aspirations, desires and ideals are redefined by them (cf. Frederiksen 1999). Factors like ethnicity and cultural difference have been brought into play in recent years with references to ethnic 'oppression' or 'colonization', and with opposition parties, civil-society groups or rival presidential candidates being branded as 'tribalist', 'non-nationals', 'immigrants', 'narrow-nationalist' and 'chauvinist'. Youth militias, for instance in Nigeria, have emerged among specific ethnic groups (Yoruba, Igbo) and declare themselves, under the threat of intimidating violence, the custodians of public order or urban space. Thus, the discourse of autochthony and ethnic exclusionism has entered the politics of generational conflict in Africa.

Youth and violence

Young people are prominently involved in most of the existing armed conflicts and criminal networks on the African continent. The mere facts of demographic generational imbalance and socio-political tensions do not, however, explain why and how patterns of conflict and violence emerge among younger age groups, nor why they show such a remarkably uneven spread and intensity across the continent. For instance, in Tanzania, Botswana, Benin and Ghana we have not seen such cut-throat violence as in Sudan, Rwanda, Nigeria, Zimbabwe, Côte d'Ivoire or Somalia, and some movements, like the strongly disciplined and focused EPLF and TPLF in Eritrea/Ethiopia, have avoided humiliating and killing civilians.

A complex of political and sociological factors seem crucial here: a strong central state tradition, a society used to plurality of beliefs and ethnic identities – i.e. that recognizes difference – and a pattern of values geared to restraint,

---

[28] Bazenguissa (2003: 93) cites a young militia member in Congo-Brazzaville who, when asked why he was looting, put it exactly this way.

cooperation and discursive conflict mediation appear to reduce the escalation of violent practices into brutal forms. It seems certain now that societies with traditional, culturally defined age-group systems or with age and generation grading are not necessarily more resilient to violent tensions (Abbink 2004, Simonse this volume). Cultural discourses of symbolic violence, for example in the context of initiation and secret society membership, can play a role, albeit indirectly (cf. Ellis 2003). The correlation between violence and religion is also unclear. Is it true that Islamic societies – marked by an ideology of 'unity of the believers', gender inequality, authoritarianism and weak educational structures – are more prone to youth violence, especially against the background of the demographic 'youth bulge', as Samuel Huntington claimed on the basis of a statistic analysis (1998: 254-65), and, if so, why?

Another serious question is that of 'cultures of violence', more or less durable, socially rooted patterns of repeated violent practice or performance among certain groups that become integrated in a way of life and that thrive on intimidation and the abuse of power. Obviously, there is a contagious effect to state violence, often applied without measure and quite devastatingly, which may evoke similar practices in response. But still, violent performances by non-state actors and those in alleged liberation or insurgent movements vary widely in nature and intensity. In a culture of violence they become ends in themselves, a source of arbitrary and gratuitous infliction of physical suffering and pain on others – often people from their own communities of origin. Examples are seen in insurgent movements in Sierra Leone, Liberia, Mozambique, Somalia and Sudan. Many such patterns of violence emerge in what are, or were, *political* insurgent movements with, at least initially, a number of political goals (for example, the RUF, NPFL, RENAMO),[29] but also among criminal sub-cultures, of which perhaps the oldest forms are to be found in South Africa.[30] It seems that practices long unknown elsewhere in Africa, such as burning opponents alive, gang rape, the sexual abuse of young children and public torture (mostly of fellow Blacks) were 'invented' in South Africa. The intensity of this violence is often explained by the specific conditions of political-economic repression and the traumatic ruptures in the socio-cultural life of Black South Africans under the colonial and apartheid system. These may have contributed to creating one of the most violently criminal, anomic societies in Africa, as we are still seeing years after the end of apartheid. But still, such acts do not explain this cruelty and humiliating violence and the evident joy that people get from them. The same issues surface time and again in the ongoing debate about the

---

[29] Cf. Mkandawire (2002).
[30] See, for instance, Mokwena (1991) and Glaser (2000).

cruelties by RUF combatants in Sierra Leone against the civilian population. The cases of RENAMO, the Rwandan genocide, or, today (in 2004) the Janjawid militia violence in Darfur, Sudan, present similar problems. As Erik Bähre states in his interesting book *Money and Violence* (2003: 95), a political-economic explanation of such violence simply falls short here. While it is easy to see the strategic advantage of using terror on civilians (to undermine the state), as well as of forcing child combatants to kill their family or members of their own community (to create extremely loyal fighters),[31] violent practice is often pursued well beyond this, especially in the domain of mutilation, gender violence and torture. The element of enjoyment and the sense of impunity are disturbing and have perhaps to be explained in another way (see Baumeister 1996). When considering this matter, it is good to bear in mind comparable cases elsewhere in the world, not only the recent European wars, for example in Bosnia, but also organized crime, such as the intimidating and cruel punishments that the Italian *mafia* inflicted on opponents or detractors (cf. Gambetta 1993).

A good deal has been written on insurgent movements with an agenda of liberation and social reform but which cannot prevent a serious militarization of the society or group they claim to fight for (see Jok this volume). This phenomenon is quite common and is related to the emergence of a fighting caste that lives off violence, accepts military power as the only relevant authority and instils values of aggressive combat and self-assertion that flout ideals of sociality and respect. 'Disciplining' fighters is not only a matter of military leadership and internal cohesion but also of the strength of pre-existing values in the society from which a movement has emerged – religious leadership, gender relations, strength of the family, etc. – and of the way the insurgent movement has defined its relations with the civilian population. In unforeseen ways, the performance of violence undermines the social fabric and thus lays a heavy burden on post-conflict reconstruction.

The lasting impact of unsettling violence on both perpetrators and survivors is important because recent research has shown that the result is usually long-term trauma, dysfunctional family organization and precarious fertility behaviour. Images and practices of violence among both perpetrators and victims (especially when young) become part of a new *habitus* of violence – an internalized mental response pattern anchored in behavioural routines – and also a template in the collective memory of a society. They may thus resurface in new situations of crisis. The reconstitution of society after such phases of

---

[31] Even apart from the general political-philosophical question of whether the use of such means is ever allowed and what end can possibly justify them.

unsettling violence is therefore highly precarious, as Rwanda and Angola show, and is never guaranteed.

Youth and religion

While the closing decades of the 20th century may have shown the massive involvement of African youth in political and violent insurgent movements, the 21st century will perhaps show a remarkable shift towards religious activity. Religion may be seen as an alternative circuit of meaning and dignity after the failure of political engagement (cf. Argenti 2002: 138). Recourse to religion combines the quest for meaning in an insecure world with the creation of a sense of belonging to a wider community, and presents an alternative way of 'knowing' in the absence of access to proper public education and scientific knowledge. Religious groups can provide a new universe of values replacing or superseding the family or ethnic context. There is a notable upsurge in religious life in Africa, with many youths becoming involved in Pentecostal and other Christian churches, with Islamic revivalism, and in some places with neo-traditional indigenous movements (see Kanneworff 2004, Kagwanja this volume). This turn to the religious, however, has a clear link with the political sphere (see Ellis & Ter Haar 2004) and obviously does not preclude militancy and violence, as for instance the activities of several Islamist groups demonstrate. Murray Last's chapter in this volume also provides some historical evidence of this.

Interestingly, what these revivalist Christian and Islamic movements share is a disdain, even a repulsion, of 'traditional' African cultures and values. The leaders of these movements insist on adherents effecting a total break with the past and on a personal 'cleansing' of 'evil forces' seen as being associated with the old culture and its 'harmful' customs like bridewealth, widow inheritance, initiation, scarification, burial practices, and oral performances like praise songs and epics. In itself, this ideological 'anti-heritage' movement accelerates the socio-cultural ruptures that have marked African societies and generational relations over the past century.

Chabal and Daloz, in their controversial book *Africa Works* (1999: 64), have called the domain of the religious in Africa 'the irrational', for which they have been repeatedly criticized. But there is no doubt that the sphere of the supernatural shades into a readiness to succumb to mysticism, witchcraft and erroneous ideas about social causality, illness and morals.[32] In conditions of

---

[32] Cf. also the Comaroffs' (1999) description of the 'occult economy' in South Africa

existential insecurity, destitution and despair among the young, the willingness to believe tends to override questions of factual truth and rational effectiveness. This manner of belief has an enormous social and political impact because it tends to supplant the tangible realities of everyday life (cf. De Boeck 2000: 33). Youths are also involved in inventive frauds, trickster schemes and con games, such as the *feymania* originating in Cameroon in the 1990s.[33] It would, however, be a mistake to see the resort to the imaginary or 'double' world of occult supernatural forces as only an African phenomenon.

In any event, religious thought and its global resurgence among the young have to be taken seriously. For our purposes, the point is that African youth are greatly attracted by the new religious movements and are joining (in large numbers) a discourse of morality and identity that holds out the promise of regeneration and collective power with transnational resonance. These movements will have a big impact on their members' self-image, their view of 'traditions', and on leadership ideals and roles. In addition, the economic dimension of these transnational religious movements is not to be under-estimated. Not only do they receive funds (for example, remittances) from fellow members and related groups overseas, but also subsidies to propagate their faith and build new religious schools,[34] churches and mosques in Africa.[35] As the well-known examples of the Pentecostal churches in Africa or the Islamic Mouride brotherhood in Senegal illustrate, religious movements often function as frameworks of vigorous, joint economic action, promoting a new work ethic and creating new networks of opportunity.

---

steeped in supernatural imagery and violent representations and practices. De Boeck (2000) provides an interesting analysis of the disturbing phenomenon of 'witchcraft children' in the Democratic Republic of the Congo.

[33] For an early study, see Malaquais (2001).

[34] However, they do not impart knowledge useful for improving young people's chances in the labour market.

[35] Some Islamic countries have been the most active here. It is estimated that Saudi Arabia alone has invested tens of billions of dollars in Africa in the past twenty years in 'overseas aid': for the building of mosques and religious schools, the distribution of copies of the Koran, and the training of Islamic teachers and missionaries. See political scientist Alex Alexiev's testimony before the US Senate, on http://judiciary.senate. gov/testimony.cfm?id=827&wit_id=2355, citing the Saudi government newspaper *Ain al-Yaqeen*.

Youth and the reconstitution of African societies

There are high hopes in much of the literature about the potential and promise of youth in Africa and elsewhere. It is not the aim of this book to evaluate this normative issue but care should be taken not to see the young generation by definition as *the* agent of change. In negative as well as positive terms, the role of youth in the reconstitution of future African society is indeed obvious (Trudell 2002). They are both in the vanguard and at the same time vandals, depending on the conjunctures of economic opportunity, power structures and social space. Elements of hope are provided in the emergence of vibrant youth cultures,[36] some with transnational connections such as the undiminished obsession with education, democratic activism, the commitment to family and cooperative values, and the wide response that anti-AIDS campaigns are finding among young people across Africa. The versatility of urban youth with new technologies and the media,[37] and their commitment to open debate, democratic news media and social activism show that, when given the chance, youths can be constructive partners in the reconstitution of African societies. At present, however, these developments are only touching a small minority of African youth. The crucial factors that would allow youth to play a wider role are not determined by them: political stability and equity, an end to corruption and selective neo-patrimonialism, growing ecological problems and resource scarcity fuelled by unabated demographic imbalances, inequalities in the global system, ethnicized elite rule, and violent state repression. Through political and religious action, young people indeed are claiming agency and a greater stake for themselves. The force of arms has sometimes brought them to power, or has yielded huge spoils and benefits. Sometimes, the results of violence itself lead to a reconstitution of society. Religious action has increased collective identity and solidarity, economic advancement (for example, the Pentecostalists and their transnational connections), and political presence.

There remains, however, a fundamental ambiguity in the constitutive role of youth in society. One example is education. Youth in Africa attach great value to education: it is seen as the way out of poverty, and as a passport to employment and perhaps emigration to greener pastures outside the home country. It is a highly contested resource, and access to it can make or break a

---

[36] See Fuglesang's (1994) interesting study of female Swahili youth culture in Lamu, Kenya.

[37] A negative side of globalization is the rapid spread among urban youth in Africa of the worst kind of violent and pornographic video cassettes that are shown in illegal video houses. This phenomenon has already had a demonstrable effect on gender perceptions and practices of sexual abuse.

person's future. But high-school drop-outs or even those with a diploma but no job are forced to sit idly at home with their parents on whom they become a burden, often pushed out onto the streets and drifting into street hawking, crime or a rebel movement. There is also a fundamental division between youngsters: a minority will make it, a majority not. And it often depends on luck. There is no automatic solidarity among youths in any country. For example, the exceedingly rich children of the business and political elite in Kenya have nothing in common with the youths from the slums who are members of *Mungiki*. Youth is thus variously incorporated or co-opted into society or its margins, showing that generations are vertically divided and thus pose no cohesive challenge to an established socio-political order.

While the role of youth as a 'mediating' social force in Africa – connecting tradition and modernity, the past and the present – is often somewhat exaggerated (e.g., De Boeck & Honwana 2000: 11), young people can be seen as 'stakeholders' in the reconfiguration of society and the political project of a nation (cf. also McIntyre and Peters in this volume). Not only after conflict and civil war but also in the regular political process, governments have to deal with youths who claim rights and representation, and previously had *reasons* for joining an armed movement. In this respect, the present generation is more vocal and self-conscious than previous ones, perhaps because they are more aware of the power to contest and disrupt society. In more theoretical terms, youth agency has to be interpreted better as to its temporal and situated nature, referring back to the past and its meanings, as well as to the future seen through the prism of newly emerging ideals and desires.

Relevance and theory

The social relevance of studying youth in order to influence the development policies of donors, state, NGOs and self-organizations is growing. The Convention of the Rights of the Child was adopted by the United Nations in 1990 and is seen as the framework for global policy, although there is doubt about the ability of African governments to implement it. In 2003 the World Bank circulated a draft paper on 'Youth – Strategic Directions for the World Bank' in which it was acknowledged that neglecting youth in development policies is a costly mistake that needs to be redressed. The thought will no doubt find its way into future policy documents and country assistance programmes. It is indeed surprising that it has been absent from donor policy for so long, despite the usual rhetorical references. Social science and African studies have also rediscovered the subject and numerous studies are being made of street children,[38] crime networks, youth movements, gender relations and conflict, the political agency of youths, and young (ex-) combatants (see Peters this volume). This renewed focus is welcome but is as yet still too weakly integrated in theory.

There is a need to develop sound theory for the study of youth and generational conflict, if only to be able to ask the right questions. A unified theoretical perspective is neither likely nor necessary but we think that the following key elements should be addressed in any attempt to develop more general explanations of the youth experience in Africa:

- the historical impact of the ruptures and changes in the political systems of Africa due to colonialism – that brought authoritarian structures, new elites, new borders, new ethnic identities – and the current world system enhancing global economic inequality is a major background factor.
- the post-colonial elites clinging to power and resources, thus blocking the emergent young generations. Thwarted socio-economic and political mobility creates instability and a tendency towards the use of force.
- the huge demographic expansion of the last forty years has put enormous strain on the adult generation and on the post-colonial state and its 'public delivery' structures (education, training, employment, health care, social services). The critical limits are most evident in the inadequate responses to the HIV/AIDS disaster.
- generational tensions in the wider sociological and cultural sense. While many of the traditional age and clan systems are in decline or are unsuccessful at offering solutions for problems engendered by modernity and state encroachment, the associated cultural representations ordering the relations between age groups and generations retain some importance. They are rooted in world-views, social memory, values and ritual performance, and are manifest in, for example, gender relations, deference to elders, initiatory symbolism, and the transformative meaning of (ritual) violence. The cognitive dimension of age and generational difference in African societies is underestimated.
- the crisis or decline of 'neo-patrimonial' state governance itself, with its zero-sum game politics, its exclusivist nature, its 'extraversion', its educational failure, and its repressive policies, is generating marginalization and destitution among social groups, including the young generation.

---

[38] Marguerat (1992: 131, n. 6) notes that the phenomenon of street children is quite new, only emerging in Africa in the 1960s and 1970s.

Despair at survival or social advancement prepares youths for social experiments of all kinds, including deceit, crime and violence, also towards each other (cf. Lebeau 1999). Resource competition in conditions of scarcity, while essentially economic, resonates in group relations and politics, as ethnic and other cultural markers are used to differentiate people into opponents or allies.

- the potential of youth, because of their being young, marginal, not yet adult and established, to construct symbolic counter-discourse that challenges society in a moral and political sense and indicates alternatives. Increasingly, youth can find allies here in transnational global networks, in foreign NGOs, etc. and becomes the nexus and agent of change.
- the logic of violence and armed struggle, especially among youths, can attain a momentum of its own. Sub-cultures of criminal gangs and violent rebel movements claim social space by intimidation and destruction, 'resocialize' youngsters in a self-centred enclave culture, and rearrange power relations and the social order. Youths socialized in such 'cultures of violence' will remain an element of instability in any society trying to reconstitute itself in the post-conflict phase. Depending on the force of common values in the wider society, the presence of positive social incentives, and the legitimacy and efficacy of the political system upholding them, young people will not successfully 'return'.
- the gender dimension. The experience of female youths should not be ignored because of their lower 'nuisance value'.

These elements combine historical conditions with sociological and demographic mechanisms in a setting of cultural meanings to generate youth response. We do not plead for overly social-constructivist theories that relativize the concept of youth as a purely historical, situational category with little comparability across time or space (as Comaroff & Comaroff seem to do, 2000: 91). On the contrary, it is more fruitful to explore, on the basis of a fairly universal psychological model of personal development (of youths into adults) and on that of the structural opposition, in virtually any society, of 'not-yet adults' *vis-à-vis* the preceding generation, the similarities *and* differences in collective representations of youth and in youth agency in conjunctures of crisis and change.

In the end, the three perspectives mentioned above – the agency, the interventionist and the analytic – must come together in a realist understanding of the experiences of youth in Africa. This allows us to recognize their diversity and to reconcile the dialectic of despair and crisis with that of survival and renewal. Research and writing on youth in Africa must also inform public debate and policy formation, and thus contribute to providing youth with the social space and agency that they need. It is hoped that the chapters in this book do this.

The chapters

This book has three parts. In the first part, *Historical Perspectives on Youth as Agents of Change*, the chapters by Murray Last and Thomas Burgess present studies of youth action or agency at critical historical conjunctures. Both in northern Nigeria and in Zanzibar, movements fuelled by youth pathos and activist membership have brought about a significant change in existing power structures. What is notable in both cases is that Islam played a role, but unevenly, and not always as the dominant frame of reference. In the Sokoto *jihad* described by Last, Islam (or opposition to its dominant form) was the ideological idiom of rebellion referred to by the young to oust the older generation; in the case of the British conquest the older generation ruling the Caliphate saw defeat as a sign from God, but the young saw the new political structure as an opportunity. In the generation that planned the military coup of 1966 no religious reference was there, as youth simply grabbed the opportunity to assert themselves under the new conditions of national military power. Last's historical analysis has relevance for the understanding of contemporary – volatile – developments in northern Nigeria.

In the Zanzibar revolution described by Burgess, an African-indigenous majority on the former slave-trader island, on the face of it, overturned Islamic-Arab hegemony in the name of social justice and an end to servitude. But the author, with reference to the historiographical debate, reinterprets the revolution as primarily a generational revolt, also within the population of Arab ancestry, connected to identity struggles and nationalist mobilization. Youth, in particular students, saw themselves as the vanguard that would put Zanzibar on the map as a socialist, developed nation, and for Burgess youth is to be considered as an autonomously functional political identity.

In Part 2, on *State, Crisis and the Mobilization of Youth*, the emphasis is on contemporary dramas of youth as collective actors and as a socially marginal class. The chapters, all based on recent field research and set in the relevant theoretical debates, show that while young people are not in a strong social position, they are being urged to contest and challenge the state as a result of the accumulating problems affecting them. In all the chapters, the crisis of the state in Africa is evident, but also that it is not yet a spent force.

Peter Kagwanja addresses the impact of the intriguing *Mungiki* movement, one of the more original and controversial social youth movements in Kenya, pleading for generational change in Kenyan politics and calling for national renewal on the basis of 'traditional' (Kikuyu) cultural values. This fascinating story shows how the force of 'culture' – be it selectively recovered and applied – can be highly relevant in modern political processes in the post-colony. The *Mungiki* backs this up with a culture of force: violent actions, probably as a response to the widespread violence and displacement by regime-supported youth militias in the 1990s. A recent MA thesis by Kanneworff (2004), based on inside fieldwork with the leaders and regular members of *Mungiki*, also considers this issue. The position of *Mungiki* in the democratic process in Kenya indeed seemed a riddle, with the movement apparently preferring generational change (by rallying behind the young Uhuru Kenyatta, a member of the KANU ruling party of the hated President Moi) to the election of Mwai Kibaki, the senior candidate of the democratic opposition, because he was an old man. But the *Mungiki* leadership was also being pragmatic: it sought any opportunity to gain a share of the power and deliver on promises to its disadvantaged young adherents. When Kibaki and his party won the 2002 elections, a violent self-assertion of *Mungiki*, such as in January 2003, was almost inevitable.

Karel Arnaut analyses in detail the backgrounds of the recent conflict in Côte d'Ivoire, a country where nobody really expected such an explosion of violence and disunity as has been seen in the past few years. But such a statement perhaps underestimates the problems of the patriarchal one-party state that Côte d'Ivoire was under Houphouët-Boigny. Ivoirian youths spearheaded the upheaval and, as in so many cases in Africa, the seedbed of rebellion was a national student movement, the FESCI, founded in 1990. The two new youth movements of recent years, the Young Patriots and the New Forces, claiming primacy because they were the young generation opposed to the one in power, seem to have set much of the political agenda in the country, this time inspired by an autochthony debate about who 'belongs' to the nation and who does not.

The chapter by Piet Konings is a revealing and authoritative study of student politics in Cameroon, highlighting the struggle of a doubly marginalized group, the Anglophone students, on behalf of their region. The aggravating economic and political crisis of the country created a treacherous arena for heightened power struggles and exclusionism by the reigning elite, pursued by all available means. Konings speaks about 'protracted warfare' between state and students, with the authorities unable to see or admit the rights of the young generation, and certainly not when coupled to an Anglophone agenda demanding more representation or autonomy. He also demonstrates the deep divisions existing within the student body due to vertical loyalties of an ethno-regional and political nature, and, thus, underlines a point made above that the young generation, and particularly students *vis-à-vis* the state, have no natural cohesion and commonality of interest.

Jok Madut Jok's important chapter on Dinka communities involved in the long war in Southern Sudan painfully illustrates the pernicious effects of long-term violence on the society from which the combatants, members of the SPLA and fighting for the rights of the Southerners, emerged. The war created a mindset of military supremacy that was very attractive for youngsters who, by enlisting, could escape idleness and circumvent laborious socio-cultural practices. But it negated traditional cultural values on gender relations and respect for women, children or elders, procreation and legitimate authority relations that were bound to the moral universe of the society and not to those of the wider world, thus evoking a internal social crisis in Dinka society of enormous magnitude.[39] Jok, interestingly, also highlights the importance that religious conversion can have for intergenerational tensions due to the distance created between young Christian converts and their non-converted parents. This is a general problem seen in contexts of conversion to certain forms of the Islamic and Christian faiths (for example, Pentecostalism).

Sara Dorman's analysis of the changing role of youth in Eritrea is one of the first of such studies and of interest because of the rapidly changing conceptions of politics and nation-building in this country, only independent (*de facto*) since 1991. Eritrea fought in a war against Ethiopia that was carried out by a young generation of students from the early 1970s onwards, who came of age during the fighting. 'Youth' was always a prime metaphor for the future and the new political order and in the early years there was a remarkable sense of purpose and unity. Eritrea set up one of the most massive youth mobilization efforts ever seen in Africa, with compulsory national service for youth (in this case defined as all those between the ages of 18 and 40), military training, and high-school students spending their last year in classes organized by the Ministry of Defence, but also participating in social projects. Politicians' speeches are replete with references to the obligations of the young generation to the 'martyrs' who secured independence. Dorman shows that, in the stifling political atmosphere in the country, slowly and inevitably cracks emerged in the projected picture of unity and solidarity between the generations. In the eyes of the governing circles, the young generation has no agency and no autonomy but must continue to follow the precepts of nation-building as defined by the leaders.

In the last part, entitled *Interventions: Dealing with Youth in Crisis*, the spotlight is on crisis situations and their aftermath, notably young combatants and their problematic 'return' to a more or less normal, non-war situation. Yves Marguerat's impressive chapter is on the expanding problem of street children

---

[39] Similar developments were seen in Nuer society; see Hutchinson (1996).

in urban Africa, and points to the dangers of an almost self-reproducing 'sub-culture' that is emerging. His case study of Lomé children, sensitive and insightful, is the result of long years of work with these children, and continues a series of remarkable studies that made the author a world authority on the subject.[40]

Simon Simonse describes in perceptive detail a, by now, quite general situation among pastoral people in Africa: the breakdown of social order as exemplified by the age or generation system, and the alarming spread and use of automatic rifles, impacting in unexpected and unintended ways on people's social organization, notably gender relations. In Karamoja, women, as victims of violence (including sexual abuse), are also on the receiving end when faced with the violent deaths of brothers, husbands and children, and become the victims of overburdening rules such as widow inheritance. Women are coming to question not only the massive violence but also their own culture. Many pastoral societies are thus becoming internal war zones and are showing deep divisions that are not going to be solved in the immediate future. As a staff member of an influential Dutch NGO, Simonse is actively working on projects in Uganda (and elsewhere in Africa) trying to change this situation.

McIntyre and Peters address similar issues related to the rehabilitation or resocialization of young ex-combatants in a post-conflict society. The issue is highly relevant, not only because of the large numbers of youngsters involved – and still more to come when, for example, some form of normality returns to Sudan, northern Uganda and Somalia – but also because of the difficulties in reconstituting society in conditions of economic scarcity, disagreement about values and a plurality of political models for the future.

McIntyre proposes properly recognizing the role of young combatants as stakeholders, both in a period of fighting – they were not only simple naïve recruits manipulated by others but also took decisions to become involved – as well as thereafter, in the phase of return to or reconstruction of a civil society, where a sensitive attitude towards their past experience and an understanding of their aspirations are required. The issue takes on special importance in view of the international concern, if not obsession, with child soldiers and their lot.

Peters's chapter is a revealing account about the problematic articulation of wartime values acquired by youths in violent armed movements with those of the society into which they are expected to reintegrate (although some young ex-combatant will have spent their entire lives in the movement). With convincing empirical case material the author shows that those wartime values

---

[40] See Y. Marguerat & D. Poitou (eds), *À l'Ecoute des Enfants de la Rue*, Paris: Fayard (2003).

have reinforced generational, or indeed general, opposition *vis-à-vis* the society of origin of the combatants, precluding an easy 'return'. The author also highlights the underestimated differences that existed within the RUF and other fighting forces in Sierra Leone in terms of the precarious internal organization of factions. Peters's conclusions about the relevance of knowing the motives and backgrounds of ex-combatants in order to make reintegration packages more effective can only be supported. Lastly, while not the focus of his chapter, Peters's account points to the relevance of a wider debate on values in African societies (for example, regarding child-raising, gender roles, the role of the supernatural, kinship, trust, work, relations of authority) and their possible connection with socio-economic development.[41]

Acknowledgements
The editors wish to express their deepest gratitude to Ann Reeves for her valuable editorial assistance. Our sincere thanks also go to Marieke van Winden for her efficient logistical help in organizing the 2003 African Studies Centre conference[42] that provided the basis of this book, to Mieke Zwart for her work on the layout that went beyond the call of duty, and to Nel de Vink for the maps. Finally, we are particularly indebted to the Netherlands Ministry of Foreign Affairs for generously supporting the conference and providing the funds that enabled a number of African colleagues to travel to Leiden.

References

Abbink, J. 1994, 'Changing Patterns of "Ethnic" Violence: Peasant-Pastoralist Confrontation in Southern Ethiopia and its Implications for a Theory of Violence', *Sociologus*, 44 (1): 66-78.

Abbink, J. 2003, 'Ritual and Political Forms of Violent Practice', in T. Young (ed.), *Readings in African Politics*, Oxford: James Currey, pp. 80-89.

Abbink, J. 2004, 'Culture Slipping Away: Violence, Social Tension and Personal Drama in Suri Society, Southern Ethiopia', in A. Rao, M. Böck & M. Bollig (eds), *The Practice of War*, London & Oxford: Berghahn, forthcoming.

Abdullah, I. 1997, 'Lumpen Youth Culture and Political Violence: Sierra Leoneans Debate the RUF and the Civil War', *Africa Development*, 22 (3/4): 171-215.

---

[41] For a controversial but thought-provoking book on the subject, see Harrison & Huntington (2000). Two of its chapters are about Africa. Political correctness codes in academia seem to have inhibited a thorough debate on this Weberian topic of the role of values in development in Africa.

[42] The two-day conference was organized by the ASC's 'Culture, Power and Inequality in Africa' theme group and held in Leiden in April 2003.

Abélès, M. & C. Collard (eds) 1985, *Age, Pouvoir et Société en Afrique Noire*, Montréal/Paris: Presses de l'Université de Montréal/Karthala.

Aguilar, M.I. 1998, 'Reinventing *Gada*: Generational Knowledge in Boorana', in M.L. Aguilar (ed.), *The Politics of Age and Gerontocracy in Africa*, Trenton, NJ & Asmara: Africa World Press, pp. 257-80.

Argenti, N. 2002, 'Youth in Africa: A Major Resource for Change', in A. de Waal & N. Argenti (eds), *Young Africa: Realising the Rights of Children and Youth*, Trenton, NJ/Asmara: Africa World Press, pp. 123-34.

Atieno-Odhiambo, E.S. 2004, 'Ethnic Cleansing and Civil Society in Kenya 1969-1992', *Journal of Contemporary African Studies*, 22 (1): 29-42.

Bähre, E. 2002, Money and Violence. Financial Mutuals among the Xhosa in Cape Town, South Africa, University of Amsterdam, PhD thesis.

Balsvik, R.R. 1985, *Haile Selassie's Students: the Intellectual and Social Background to a Revolution, 1952-1977*, East Lansing: Michigan State University.

Bassi, M. 1996, 'Power's Ambiguity, or the Political Significance of *Gada*', in P.T.W. Baxter, J. Hultin & A. Triulzi (eds), *Being and Becoming Oromo*, Lawrenceville, NJ: Red Sea Press, pp. 150-61.

Baumeister, R.F. 1996, *Evil. Inside Human Cruelty and Violence*, New York: W.H. Freeman.

Bazenguissa-Ganga, R. 2003, 'The Spread of Political Violence in Congo-Brazzaville', in T. Young (ed.), *Readings in African Politics*, Oxford: James Currey, pp. 89-96.

Black, R., S.S. Morris & J. Bryce 2003, 'Where and Why are 10 Million Children Dying Every Year?', *The Lancet*, 361, 2226-34.

Chabal, P. & J-P. Daloz 1999, *Africa Works. Disorder as Political Instrument*, Oxford/Bloomington, Indianapolis: James Currey/Indiana University Press.

Clapham, C. (ed.) 1998, *African Guerrillas*, Oxford/Bloomington, Indianapolis: James Currey/Indiana University Press.

Comaroff, J. & J. Comaroff 1999, 'Occult Economies and the Violence of Abstraction: Notes from the South African Postcolony', *American Ethnologist*, 26 (2): 279-303.

Comaroff, J. & J. Comaroff 2000, 'Réflexions sur la Jeunesse. Du Passé à la Postcolonie', *Politique Africaine*, 80, 90-110.

Cruise O'Brien, D.B. 1996, 'A Lost Generation?: Youth Identity and State Decay in West Africa', in R. Werbner & T. Ranger (eds), *Postcolonial Identities in Africa*, London: Zed Books, pp. 55-74.

D'Almeida-Topor, H., '"Jeune", "Jeunes", "Jeunesse": Réflexions autour d'une Termi-nologie', in H. d'Almeida-Topor, C. Coquéry-Vidrovich, O. Goerg & F. Guitart (eds) 1992, *Les Jeunes en Afrique*, Paris: Éditions l'Harmattan, vol.1, pp. 14-16.

D'Almeida-Topor, H., C. Coquéry-Vidrovich, O. Goerg & F. Guitart (eds) 1992, *Les Jeunes en Afrique*, Paris: Éditions l'Harmattan, 2 volumes.

Dane, B.O. & C. Levine (eds) 1994, *AIDS and the New Orphans: Coping with Death*, Boston: Auburn House.

De Boeck, F. 2000, 'Le "Deuxième Monde" et les "Enfants-Sorciers" en République Démocratique du Congo', *Politique Africaine*, 80, 32-57.

De Boeck, F. & A. Honwana 2000, 'Faire et Défaire la Société: Enfants, Jeunes et Politique en Afrique', *Politique Africaine*, 80, 5-11.

De Waal, A. & N. Argenti (eds) 2002, *Young Africa. Realising the Rights of Children and Youth,* Trenton, NJ & Asmara: Africa World Press.

Dyson-Hudson, N. 1966, *Karimojong Politics,* Oxford: Clarendon Press.

Ellis, S. 2003, 'Violence and History: A Response to Thandika Mkandawire', *Journal of Modern African Studies*, 41 (3): 457-475.

Ellis, S. & G. ter Haar 2004, *Worlds of Power. Religious Thought and Political Practice in Africa,* London: C. Hurst & Co.

Falola, T. (ed.) 2004, *Teen Life in Africa*, Westport & London: Greenwood Press.

Fratkin, E. 1998, *Ariaal Pastoralists of Kenya: Surviving Drought and Development in Africa's Arid Lands*, Boston: Allyn & Bacon.

Frederiksen, B.F. 1999, '"We Need That Life". Global Narratives and Local Aspirations among Youth in a Nairobi Slum', in N.N. Sørensen (ed.), *Narrating Mobility, Boundaries and Belonging*, Copenhagen: Centre for Development Research, Working Paper 99.7, pp. 49-64.

Fuglesang, M. 1994, Veils and Videos. Female Youth Culture on the Kenyan Coast, Stockholm University, PhD thesis.

Gambetta, D. 1993, *The Sicilian Mafia: The Business of Private Protection*, Cambridge: Harvard University Press.

Glaser, C. 2000, *Bo-tsotsi: The Youth Gangs of Soweto 1935-1976*, Portsmouth, NH: Heinemann.

Gosselin, C. 2000, 'Feminism, Anthropology and the Politics of Excision in Mali: Global and Local Debates in a Postcolonial World', *Anthropologica*, 42 (1): 43-60.

Habtamu Wondimu (ed.) 1996, *Research Papers on the Situation of Children and Adolescents in Ethiopia*, Addis Ababa: Addis Ababa University Printing Press.

Harrison, L.E. & S.P. Huntington 2000, *Culture Matters: How Values Shape Human Progress*, New York: Basic Books.

Hinnant, J. 1978, 'The Guji: *Gada* as a Ritual System', in P.T.W. Baxter & U. Almagor (eds), *Age, Generation and Time. Features of East African Age Group Systems*, London: C. Hurst & Co., pp. 207-43.

Human Rights Watch 2004, *"Political Shari'a"? Human Rights and Islamic Law in Northern Nigeria*. New York: HRW.

Huntington, S.P. 1998, *The Clash of Civilizations and the Remaking of World Order*, London & New York: Touchstone Books.

Hutchinson, S.E. 1996, *Nuer Dilemmas. Coping with War, Money and the State*, Berkeley, Los Angeles & London: University of California Press.

Kanneworff, A.B. 2004, '"These Dread-Locked Gangsters…" De Mungiki-Beweging in Kenia: Van Neo-Etnisch Protest naar Politieke Participatie', Vrije Universiteit, Amsterdam, MA thesis.

Kessel, I. van 2000, *'Beyond Our Wildest Dreams': The United Democratic Front and the Transformation of South Africa*, Charlottesville & London: University Press of Virginia.

Lebeau, Y. 1999, 'Permissivité et Violence sur les Campus Nigérians', *Politique Africaine*, 76: 173-80.

Legesse, A. 1989, 'Adaptation, Drought and Development: Boran and Gabbra Pastoralists of Northern Kenya', in R. Huss-Ashmore & S.H. Katz (eds), *African Food Systems in Crisis*, New York: Gordon & Breach, pp. 261-79.

Machel, G. 1996, Impact of Armed Conflict on Children, *New York: United Nations. (also available online at:* http://www.unicef.org/graca/a51-306_en.pdf*)*

Makiko, T. 2002, 'Religion and Politics in Nigeria: The Real Causes of the *Sharia* Conflict in 2000', *Journal of Asian and African Studies*, 64, 217-236.

Malaquais, D. 2001, *Anatomie d'une Arnaque: Feymen et Feymania au Cameroun*. Les Études du CERI 77.

Marguerat, Y. 1992, 'Les *Smallvi* Ne Sont Pas des *Gbevouvi*: Eléments pour une Histoire de la Marginalité Juvénile à Lomé', in H. d'Almeida-Topor, C. Coquéry-Vidrovich, O. Goerg & F. Guitart (eds) 1992, *Les Jeunes en Afrique*, Paris: Éditions l'Harmattan, vol. 1, pp. 130-54.

McIntyre, A., E.K. Aning & P.N.I. Ado 2002, 'Politics, War and Youth Culture in Sierra Leone: An Alternative Interpretation', *African Security Review*, 11 (3): 7-15.

Mkandawire, T. 2002, 'The Terrible Toll of Post-Colonial Rebel Movements in Africa: Towards an Explanation of the Violence Against the Peasantry', *Journal of Modern African Studies*, 40 (2): 181-215.

Mokwena, S. 1991, 'The Era of the Jackrollers: Contextualising the Rise of Youth Gangs in Soweto', Braamfontein: Centre for the Study of Violence and Reconciliation.

Ndlovu-Gatsheni, S.J. 2003, 'Dynamics of the Zimbabwe Crisis in the 21st Century', *African Journal of Conflict Resolution*, 3 (1): 99-134.

Péatrik, A-M. 1993, 'Age, Génération et Temps Chez les Meru, Tigania-Igembe du Kenya', *Africa*, 63 (2): 241-60.

Péatrik, A-M. 2003, 'Arrangements Générationnels: Le Cas Inattendu des Gusii (Kenya)', *L'Homme*, 167-168: 209-34.

Peters, K. & P. Richards 1998, '"Why We Fight": Voices of Youth Combatants in Sierra Leone', *Africa*, 68 (2): 183-210.

Richards, P. 1996, *Fighting for the Rain Forest: War, Youth and Resources in Sierra Leone,* London/Portsmouth, NH: James Currey/Heinemann.

Richter, L., A. Dawes & C. Higson-Smith (eds) 2004, *Sexual Abuse of Young Children in Southern Africa,* Cape Town: Human Sciences Research Council Publishers.

Rossi, A. (ed.) 2003, *Trafficking in Human Beings, especially Women and Children, in Africa*. Florence: UNICEF Innnocenti Research Centre.

Sharp, L.A. 2002, *The Sacrificed Generation. Youth, History and the Colonized Mind in Madagascar*, Berkeley, Los Angeles & London: University of California Press.

Schatz, S.P. 2002, 'Structural Adjustment', in G.C. Bond & N.C. Gibson (eds), *Contested Terrains and Constructed Categories: Contemporary Africa in Focus*, Boulder: Westview Press, pp. 87-104.

Smith, S. 2003. *Négrologie. Pourquoi l'Afrique Meurt,* Paris: Calmann-Lévy.

Stewart, F.H. 1977, *Fundamentals of Age-Group Systems*, New York: Academic Press.

Stohl, R.J. 2002, 'Under the Gun: Children and Small Arms', *African Security Review*, 11 (3): 17-25.

Tornay, S. 2001, *Les Fusils Jaunes. Générations et Politique en Pays Nyangatom (Éthiopie)*, Nanterre: Société d'Ethnologie.

Toungara, J-M. 1995, 'Generational Tensions in the *Parti Démocratique de Côte d'Ivoire*', *African Studies Review*, 38 (2): 11-38.

Trudell, B. 2002, 'Introduction: Vulnerability and Opportunity among Africa's Youth', in B. Trudell *et al.* (eds) 2002, *Africa's Young Majority*, Edinburgh: Centre of African Studies, Edinburgh University, pp. 1-15.

Trudell, B. *et al.* (eds) 2002, *Africa's Young Majority*, Edinburgh: Centre of African Studies, Edinburgh University.

Turton, D. 1995, 'History, Age and the Anthropologists', in G. Ausenda (ed.), *After Empire. Towards an Ethnology of Europe's New Barbarians,* London/San Marino: Boydell Press/Center for Interdisciplinary Research on Social Stress, pp. 95-112.

Walle, N. van de, N. Ball & V. Ramachandran (eds) 2003, *Beyond Structural Adjustment. The Institutional Context of African Development*, New York/Houndmills: Palgrave/Macmillan.

Wilson, M. & M. Daly 1993, 'Lethal Confrontational Violence among Young Men', in N.J. Bell & R.W. Bell (eds), *Adolescent Risk Taking*, Newbury Park: Sage, pp. 84-106.

Young, J.W. 1997, *Peasant Revolution in Ethiopia: The Tigray People's Liberation Front, 1975-1991.* Cambridge: Cambridge University Press.

PART I:
Historical perspectives on youth as agents of change

2

Towards a political history of youth in Muslim northern Nigeria, 1750-2000

Murray Last

Muslim youth have come to power in northern Nigeria quite dramatically on at least four occasions over the last two hundred years: with the Sokoto jihad of 1804-1808, at the time of the British colonial takeover ca. 1900-10, in the 1950s with the advent of party politics in the run-up to independence, and recently when local government councils and the enforcement of shari'a law started being largely run by 'the young'. There might seem to be a pattern to this: every forty years or so, yesterday's youth, who have finally grown old, are replaced by tomorrow's young. But 'youth' in Hausaland is not just biological: it is both a style of behaviour and matter of status in a society where seniority plays an important role. The question today is whether the 'old' have been removed permanently from power. The chapter also considers the role of the military government, Nigeria's extensive oil revenues and the current politico-cultural skew created by the sudden access to such an unparalleled 'tap' of unearned money.

Northern Nigeria would be considered by many people, I would suggest, as a 'traditional' gerontocratic society – if not a patriarchy – with wealth, authority and legal control vested in the senior man of the household and his senior wife. Only at prayer or in the mosque is society egalitarian (and even then not for women). Individuals are valued differently otherwise. Similarly, the norm is for the young, if they disagree with the old, not to confront an elder; they should simply move away. Strangers to Hausa society are apt to call it feudal. Yet at certain conjunctures over the last two centuries some young men have successfully ousted the old from positions of power. Despite the gerontocratic norm, these young men are revered in the communal memory, at least in retrospect; the old are considered to have failed the societies they led. Hence the failure of the old can be as significant an issue as the success of the young.

In this chapter I look at three of these conjunctures in the belief that they illustrate rather distinct logics within this otherwise gerontocratic society. Although a core argument of this chapter is that the political role of youth is nothing new, in fact one might put forward the counterargument that it is the nature of today's politics that is fundamentally different in that the young *then* were tools in the hands of elders, whereas *today* the young are both mastermind and tool. Indeed one could go further and add that today an elder if he wishes to be politically effective in contemporary politics has to act like a youth: he has to be seen doing things and heard saying things that normally no elder would conceivably do or say. Such violence and volume, such apparent cheating and lies, however necessary they may be for current politicking, remain antithetical to being 'an elder'.

But first let us consider what age has meant in Hausa society recently. The data are based on my experiences in urban Sokoto, Zaria and Kano, as well as in rural southern Katsina during the last forty years (1961-2003), first as a young man (and student), then as a man growing old but not always behaving – so I was told – as an old man should! Reprimands are instructive.

Age in Hausa society

Age, *biological* age, is central to social awareness, so central and taken-for-granted that it scarcely needs overt expression. Seniority of brother over brother, sister over sister, is strict; there is even seniority between twins.[1] Optimally, in a marriage, the husband should be, say, ten years his wife's senior so that the relationship mimics father-daughter rather than brother-sister bonds; the authority of the husband is 'generational'. (Hence, on marriage a woman moves, for her care and control, from the hand of one father into the hands of another.) In childhood, elder brothers and sisters exercise discipline over their

---

[1] Paradoxically perhaps, the senior twin is the one born second. It is characteristic of his seniority that he sends his junior out from the womb first, to see that all is well outside. Similarly, a 'big man' has people going ahead of him, as if clearing the path. (Cf. the way Psalm 116 verse 9 was translated into the English of 1611: 'I will *walk before the Lord* in the land of living'.)

younger siblings and it is they who may administer even a beating.[2] Children of co-wives share a common ranking by birth order, whatever their mother's status. In a palace, the son of a concubine, if he is his father's first-born son, is the preferred heir to his father's throne (the very lack of maternal kin is seen as an advantage), though the senior wife's first-born may try and make claims based on his maternal kin (who may well be the ruler's first cousins). Thus, even though annual birthdays are never celebrated, an individual's biological age-ranking – as an important part of social knowledge – is widely known.

Secondly, Hausa society (as is commonplace elsewhere) is broadly divided into *yara* (the young) and *dattijai* (the elders). (The extremely old/senile are a different category, as are the very young, the under-seven year olds.) The line that divides the two categories is based partly on age, partly on behaviour and character. You can behave like a *dattijo* when quite young (in your early twenties) but it is not until their mid-thirties or early forties that men really become *dattijai*. They may mark it by taking a second wife at this time.[3]

Finally, *yara* include all those of low status, whatever their biological age. Slaves, for example, or free-born servants remain *yara*, especially in a large, powerful household; they are a 'son of the house'. But *yara* of a royal house may be of higher status than an ordinary free man; the latter's greater age, though, might protect him in a dispute.[4] In a large family it is possible for an uncle to be younger than his nephew, in which case age can sometimes trump generation. Senior women can be *dattijai*. A senior wife has an authority over junior wives, as has the senior concubine over other concubines – seniority matters practically, as junior wives do certain chores for the group. But seniority here is according to the order in which you married the husband and not biological age.

The implication is that *dattijai* make the decisions (often collectively, either as brothers or with advice), and the young carry them out. Elders are expected to meet and discuss matters regularly – in the afternoon or evening, the younger elders gather in the house or at the door of a senior elder who is known to be wise and alert (and not a 'witch' [*mai dodo*] or in any way sinister). Elders thus mediate disputes or find ways of solving them. Their role is to maintain the harmony of the house or the local community both socially and spiritually – literally, as they engage with ancestors and with spirits.

---

[2] On the use and refusal to use beating for disciplining children in Hausa society, see Last (2000a).

[3] The second marriage may, of course, be at the instigation of the first wife who wants the help of a co-wife in servicing a demanding husband. In which case she too is gaining more status by becoming 'the senior wife'.

[4] On the powerful *yara* of a royal house, see Stilwell (2004).

Hence if the young take decisions on their own, let alone reject their elders' advice, it is a kind of rebellion *(fitna)*. 'Rebellion' is not as uncommon as it might seem: it takes the form of moving away – for a wife, it is temporary separation *(yaji)* leading to possible divorce; for an adult son, it is to move out and start a new household of his own on a distinct site (not necessarily far away, as he will build on his own or some kinsman's field or buy a plot of land); for a younger boy, it is to live with an uncle or another friendly adult (boys often select such an adult as a kind of 'patron'). Finally, a young person might leave home for the town or big city and only re-establish contact many years later by revisiting his father's house. But whoever is initiating the contact, there is rarely confrontation by the junior.

A key point is that 'junior' status is temporary, except for slaves, and that there are always people junior to you (unless you are the last wife or the last child, and then you are a 'favourite'). You become an adult by having a dependant: a boy becomes a man when he takes a wife; a girl becomes a woman when she has a baby. A *dattijo* has a whole household *(gida)* dependent upon him; it is hard to imagine a *dattijo* living alone – such a man would be simply 'old' *(tsoho)*. Rebellion by the young, therefore, is merely a premature attempt to move up-status, to escape one's temporary dependent status sooner than expected. But such independence does not by itself make you a *dattijo* – far from it, you may simply be considered a *dan iska*, a 'child of the wind' who is unattached, always in motion. By contrast, a *dattijo* is stable, centred on his house; he rarely moves around (he may well not even go to market) and often is not seen. But these days, when household labour is scarce and hired hands are in short supply, he may well do some light farming in his fields beside the house.

In this context, then, it is the *yara* who are active in politics, in arguments and conflicts. It is they who travel and trade, who migrate for seasonal work, who flock to market-places and court girls, or contest elections. Hence an older man who wishes to remain a political activist has in effect to behave like a 'youth', or at least as a 'commander of youths' (and such a commander [*amir*; *sarki*] still counts as a 'youth'). Traditionally in Hausa communities there was an assembly of youths that mimicked the adult title system and the manners of elders' institutions (including courts). It was 'fun' *(wasa)* and not a serious challenge to the elders, but *dattijai* still sometimes carry into old age the 'play title' they had as a youth. Though such youth assemblies *(kallonkowa*; *fada)* have died out as formal occasions in most places, there is often a local organization of the young. Nowadays it is the football team or club (which exist in both urban and rural areas), or a registered 'association' for local or social development, or even a religiously based vigilante group *(hisba)*. Similarly there were urban 'ward' gangs that fought against other 'wards' in almost ritual aggression, sometimes quite bloodily.

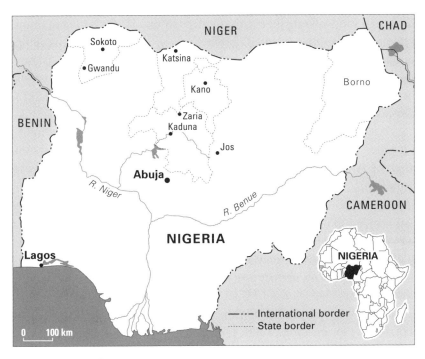

Map 2.1: Nigeria

In short, there are the social structures which make it easy for the young of a locality to act collectively – even to disarm or kill a dangerously violent madman or to beat to death a thief caught red-handed in the market-place. Nor is it difficult, if you have the right connections, to raise a crowd of youth from villages in the area, a crowd that could act as 'party supporters' and demonstrate, or even riot and loot. Their 'fee' is the loot they can gather, but they risk being wounded or even dying in the conflict. There are no 'talking drums' (at least not now) to raise the alarm; it used to be word of mouth until the autumn of 2002 when for the first time a riot was 'raised' through the use of text messages. This was in Kaduna, a large city of young workers away-from-home and where, thanks to two competing southern African companies, mobile phones are a new phenomenon among the young. (Before then, they were an elite possession limited to senior government officials.)

Youth activism 1750-2000

On at least three occasions in the last 250 years in what is now northern Nigeria, youths have collectively acted as the transformative element in society. I am sure there were earlier occasions but the evidence is less detailed. There will have been occasions too, when action by youths was defeated or aborted before it grew powerful. Some of these cases are known but the details remain obscure.

1804-1808
The first of these 'power inversions' was the Sokoto *jihad* that was fought across a series of emirates between 1804 and 1808. In this *jihad*, there were two distinct sets of young men involved. One group was made up of those under the spiritual leadership of a shaikh (the title used for a serious Muslim scholar about 40 years old or older)[5] and who were mainly his own professional students and young converts to Islam (often runaway slaves) who had sought refuge close to him. Such students were neither armed nor trained in weaponry and were meant to be outside war, like a 'caste'.[6] The other set of young men were independent youths from Fulani pastoralist families who had lost their cattle. (There had been epizootics, for example, south of Borno as well as around Gobir, it seems.) Individual Fulani youths had long gravitated towards Hausa courts (as at Kano) as mercenaries and would-be palace retainers in order to earn a livelihood outside the pastoralist economy. Around 1800 these military-minded youth owed allegiance to no one but seem to have been willing to serve as Fulani under Muslim Fulani leadership. But they had a will of their own: on at least one occasion, when stopped from taking the booty of war when on campaign,

---

[5] The title does seem to be associated with seniority and age, and not just with learning. Apart from the Shehu 'Uthman b. Fudi, there were other shaikhs preaching reform in Hausaland whose skill was primarily oral rather than literary. There were also scholars who were never associated with the title of 'shaikh'. It seems to be a matter of prominence, of having a following and possibly a community (e.g. a *tsangaya*) of which the shaikh was the head. There was appropriate behaviour for a shaikh: he did not lead an army or fight, for example.

[6] Only hunters would traditionally be skilled either with spears or with bows. A prominent adult male might have a sword and a knife but the classic weapon for the average person was a stick. Given that there were lions, leopards and hyenas in the countryside at the time, as well as monkeys that could be aggressive towards farmers and travellers, some defensive weapon was imperative even for Qur'anic students – and the stick, cheap as it is, was the weapon of choice. This meant that the transition to being armed for serious *jihad* fighting was a major risk.

they threatened the life of their own Muslim commander, the shaikh's son Muhammad Bello.[7]

In the *jihad* of 1804-1808 in Sokoto, the fighting was sparked off by young hotheads or hooligans (*sufaha'*, in a contemporary's phrase) living in the Muslim community of the Shaikh 'Uthman; they attacked a passing column of government troops to rescue some fellow Muslim prisoners. As the war developed and the Muslim students (keen but poorly trained soldiers) found martyrdom, the *jihad* army came to be dominated by the young military-minded Fulani on whom it was hard to impose the original ideals and discipline of Islamic *jihad*. The senior shaikhs stepped aside and many older scholars retired to Gwandu, away from Sokoto which was the main camp for the war. The commanders left in charge were men in their late twenties and early thirties – they were 'youth', not shaikhs. Once the *jihad* was successful and a new state had been formed (ca. 1812), these young commanders took territorial command and governed their emirates for the next thirty years.[8] In time, then, the caliphate became ruled by 'elders', and political control passed back from the young to the old. In the period 1845-55, many of these old rulers died, creating a crisis. By and large, succession passed to other elders and not to the young, but during the crisis there was political and religious turbulence in many areas, and a major emigration eastwards by young men and their families.[9] In other words, the 'rebellious' young moved away.

A second means for the young to escape their elders' control within this new *jihadi* state was to set up a frontier fort (*ribat*) or even a small emirate from which they could nominally continue to wage *jihad* and raid their pagan neighbours for slaves. Merchants camped close behind raiding armies to recycle their spoils of war. (Ransoms were one source of useful revenue.) Young princes who misbehaved at home in the centre could therefore be despatched to the frontier, and expect to do well for themselves. These frontier zones constituted a very different world from that of the centre that was dominated by scholars and by a formal Islamic culture in which military activity was of low status and more the métier of slaves, mercenaries and the common man. The frontier, by contrast, was less concerned with Islam: pagan neighbours were not

---

[7] Muhammad Bello, *Infaq al-maisur* (Whitting 1957: 100).

[8] For a table of ages of these commanders/emirs, see Last (1993).

[9] The crisis involved a major revolt by Hadejia. But there was intellectual ferment too, with scholars coming out openly for the Tijaniyya (and leaving the Qadiriyya) and moving to Adamawa to avoid trouble at home and to be nearer Mecca should a *hijra* eastwards become necessary. (The road east via Adamawa was deliberately kept open and secure for this purpose.) But the mass emigration around 1855 (which ended in disaster) did not take this route.

converted to the faith, let alone absorbed into Hausa society and culture. Instead, they were kept as a reservoir, a 'farm' providing a crop of captives, property or other payments which sustained the Muslim frontier elite. Today the relationship is sanctified by the term *amana* (peace agreement; but it is not the formal *sulh* of Islamic law); *amana* is a new reading on what was a relationship of exploitation, a euphemism that reflects the new politics. Had the frontier elite wanted their neighbours to convert to Islam there is little doubt that many, if not most, of the young would have done so. If that had happened, there would have been no northern Christians today, and a major contentious element in contemporary Nigerian politics would never have come into existence. In short, the 'youth culture' of the Sokoto Caliphate's frontier regions shaped today's politics, while the formal ideologies of the elders, who formed the caliphate's core, remain the 'myth' that sustains a common regional identity.

Finally, what enabled these young *jihadi* men to be so organized and disciplined that they initially won militarily against all odds, then were able to form a new government over a huge area, and lastly maintained an ascendancy over vast numbers of captives who were settled as slaves on farms and in towns – slaves who outnumbered the free initially by as many as perhaps thirty to one? The answer I think is (i) conversion to an intense practice of Islam which was embodied in (ii) the new system of Sufi brotherhood, the *tariqa*, which offered in group recitation (*dhikr*) both a novel religious experience and a strict discipline under a shaikh. (Islam, unlike traditional religious practice, specifically targets the young through its Qur'anic education.) Thus young men were empowered with new knowledge (Islam and the Arabic language) and new organizational practice, both of which connected them to other similar youths across boundaries of region and ethnicity and gave them, for the first time, a common (albeit sacred) language. It was a radical, new technology of power that made their elders' stumbling efforts at Muslim culture seem not only a failure but morally dangerous – the sinfulness of elders promised hellfire for all unless it was put right! The *jihadi* young created a new state to do just that, and to do it urgently as many of them were told to expect that the world's end was soon to come (which in a way it did ca. 1903).[10]

1903

The second turning-point relates to the conquest, just a century ago, of the northern emirates by Hausa forces controlled, armed and financed by

---

[10] The Shehu told his son to announce to the men appointed as flag-bearers that the end of the world was soon due. Other reports tell of the Shehu prophesying the *jihadi* state would last a hundred years. In the latter half of the century many belonged to the Mahdiyya and awaited the call to make the *hijra* east.

Christians/the British. British officers deposed most of the elderly (or not so elderly) emirs that remained and appointed younger men in their places. (Some of these emirs emigrated eastwards rather than remain under Christian over-rule.) British colonialism was effectively a government by the young: not only were the British officials themselves young men but the 'native administrations' they set up were also staffed by young men. Distaste about serving under Christians led many senior emirate officials to retire or else to act as simply nominal heads of a bureaucratic department.[11]

Again, the young who refused to collaborate with the new system or to live under it emigrated, eastwards to the Sudan where they came under a version of Christian rule but they saw themselves as just 'passing through', as 'permanent pilgrims' rather than as colonial subjects. The emigration was a hard, prolonged trek and only the relatively young and fit (and their wives, many of whom gave birth en route) were able to survive the journey.[12] By moving away, these young 'rebels' did not have to confront their elders' acquiescence in Christian rule. And again, those other young men who had decided to collaborate with the new administrators and stayed put grew old in their jobs, so that once again, forty years on, the northern emirates were ruled by elders, senior emirs and their councillors and district heads. Only the British officials remained relatively young, being regularly rotated and retired at an early age.

The change in regime, however much a notional 'colonial caliphate' sustained the image of continuity, required very different ways of administration: offices and office hours, careful book-keeping, the beginnings of a formal bureaucracy. It involved new styles of enforcing justice, within the framework of a modified *shari'a* law. It involved writing Hausa not in Arabic but Roman script, using 'Arabic' numerals (and not the numerals Arabs use) and new methods of mathematics. And there were new modes of transport, new notions for calculating space and time.

Initially, much of the British side of the administration was run by English-speaking Christian clerks from southern Nigeria, whereas the 'Native Authority' (NA) side required young Hausa men to learn the new skills and everyday

---

[11] The most notable exception was the aged and virtually blind Waziri of Sokoto, Muhammad Bukhari, who was persuaded to return home after the battle outside Sokoto on 15 March and help run the new system under the invaders' supervision. He was, of course, not alone. Many could not think of making the long *hijra* towards Mecca in the late dry season, and the common strategy was to split the family, some to stay with the elderly and weak, and some of the young to go east.

[12] Many died on the horrendous journey, which included battles against the British as well as brigands en route. Scholars such as Prof. Abu Manga in Khartoum and Dr Bawa Yamba (1995) have recorded accounts of the epic journey.

methods. It was an enormous transformation from the manners of the pre-colonial palace administration with its Arabic correspondence, its slaves and servants, and its more personalized fiscal administration. In addition, the new training opened up huge fields of new knowledge – world geography and history, astronomy, and the sciences of medicine, agriculture, botany and zoology. It was 'mind-blowing' for some, who read and talked to teachers and discussed with fellow students. In short, the new world was a young man's world. Alongside it was another world, of increased interest in Sufism and brotherhoods (the 'reformed' Tijaniyya and Qadiriyya mainly), and an extension of Qur'anic (primary) education to groups of children and categories (such as ex-slaves) who had not had access to it before.

Finally, there were new careers for the former military class – the young princes, the royal slaves and the various retainers who in the past had been used to raiding and training for war on the frontier. With their type of war now banned (and the new army not being recruited from the old warrior class), the young princes were put into local administration. They became district and village heads, posted out to the areas they administered and they resided in the countryside, not in the capital any more. There they had new work to do: collecting taxes, measuring land, and maintaining the peace (there was brigandage, and the roads were not always safe for traders). As support they could draw upon the new NA police force: as a novel 'state' institution, the force was not personal in the way late-19th century private armies had been, nor was it recruited from an official's own household (though it was usually commanded by an emir's young son). It was armed with staves or truncheons. (The colonial British had their own, non-local Hausa troops in separate barracks, under British officers and NCOs, with modern weaponry.)

Effectively, then, early colonial rule empowered the young, giving them both new authority and knowledge, and disempowered the old except insofar as the old still carried the morality and integrity of the once independent Islamic state. I do not mean to suggest that the newly powerful young did not behave as good Muslims; rather their faith was so integral to their identity that they could safely engage with the new ideas. Very few converted to Christianity – a few in Zaria did so where there was an Anglican mission; elsewhere in the Muslim north the missions were banned.

This time, then, the new organizational system was the Native Authority that required and enforced a new discipline on the young appointees, along with the notion that there was a 'state' that not only owned property but hired staff – and persisted beyond the lifetimes or offices of individuals. Now, in the name of the state, young officials could take away the houses of the old *masu sarauta* and allocate them as official residences, as state property. The former system had depended on lineages in which offices were vested, and posts and the sites (such as houses, court-rooms, prisons, palaces) associated with those posts were held as personal (and hence, lineage) property. As such, the original caliphate became in time a gerontocracy. The notion of a state, by contrast, was age-free. The state freed, at least in principle, its officials from their parents and other elders, and it was in this way like a Sufi brotherhood, which had shifted the allegiance of the young away from their fathers to the *tariqa's* shaikh. Similarly the new knowledge – this time 'modern' learning and its related skills, its new ways of thinking and being – disempowered the old. The old had singularly failed: above all, they had not been able to resist the incursion of Christians. Earlier their political system had been riven by civil strife and the killing of fellow Muslims, by exploitation and the domination of free men by royal slaves. The old world had indeed seemed near its end. It was time for the young to take over this new-style world, and they did.

The stability of the colonial regime for fifty years meant, however, that this cadre of youth grew old in their jobs, and in time recreated, yet again, a kind of gerontocracy. The Native Authorities recruited the young, of course, and trained them, but seniority was reaffirmed along with the hierarchy of emirs, title-holders and councillors.[13] It was this colonial gerontocracy that a new cohort of the young challenged, not in the name of youth-power but of anti-colonialism.

The 1950s

The third turning-point is the young's rebellion against these elders in the late 1940s and 1950s. In the political parties formed to unite progressives demanding independence from Britain were the new young, school teachers and others with modern education. The young's opportunity came with the worldwide movement against colonial regimes – but first they had to topple the powerful Native Authority system that had been in control for some fifty years. Leaders of these political parties were not necessarily young in years but they had to behave with some of the stridency of the young, talking over-much at public rallies and making jokes in a way no elder would. Politics was a young man's occupation, a trade that brought an income (and travel) – it involved telling lies, it might often involve violence. It is this identification of politics with youth – and the low status it has in many people's eyes – that has remained until today. Once again, forty years on, there are old men at the top of the system – as president, ministers, senators – but the behaviour of most of them is not

---

[13] For an account of 'the colonial caliphate' and the significance of the age patterns of the emirs who ran the various Native Authorities, see Last (1997).

traditionally that of an elder, not least in their pursuit of worldly wealth and their display of affluence.[14]

The new young of the 1950s came from a different milieu from those of the early colonial period. In the 1950s they were also from provincial – even rural – backgrounds and had been able to use the widening school system to escape the limits of their background. Furthermore, they tended to know English and functioned politically on a wider plane, responding to global trends as well as to trends (and tensions) within Nigeria as a whole. Theirs was a world of radios and newspapers, and relatively easy travel within the country. Numerically, they formed a much larger cadre, with its factions and alliances. Not only was the scale new, so too were the actual processes of debate and angry argumentation.

Most importantly perhaps, theirs was a world where freedom and national independence beckoned. Whereas the young of 1910 had (had they known it) a colonially shaped career ahead of them, the young of 1950 could expect to control their own destinies and that of their region or country; and that destiny included such new ideas as 'democracy' and 'modernity' as against the old, stable authoritarianism of their elders' regime. The element of excitement and drive (as well as the thrill of political risk-taking) is evident in the writings of the time.

The most remarkable consequence of this identification of modern politics with the young came in the 1990s with the election of the chairmen for the Local Government Areas (LGA). These LGAs had a huge monthly income coming directly from the oil account of the central government and, with it, considerable power. Yet almost without exception it was young men in their twenties, some unmarried and with at most some secondary-school education, who took control and were in a position to order around their social seniors, the emir or district head in their locality. Some such senior men were deliberately humiliated in public. Elsewhere in Nigeria the LGA posts were won by middle-aged men, often leaders within their communities; but in the far north it was entirely different. The image of a feudal north could scarcely have been further from the truth. Elections as a process are archetypically 'young' in style and in operation: for an older man to run against youth would itself be demeaning, whilst the abuse and lies he would be subjected to would be humiliating. It was better to support a youth as his 'front' man. But where, in one case I know, that happened, the winning youth turned his back on his patron and took all the money, month after month, and shared it out among some of his young mates for their personal use.

---

[14] On this period of NAs and political parties, see Yahaya (1980), Yakubu (1996) and Reynolds (1999).

When it is a military and not a civilian regime that is in power, the issue is clearer still. Military men are by definition 'youths' in style if not always in age; even generals, particularly generals actively in power, are not elders. Many of them retire into civilian life (and are very rich on pensions at full pay), some look for traditional titles and convert themselves in this way into elders, building up an informal political constituency and seeking to influence selection processes and policies. But once they are elders, they cease to be 'politicians'.

Once again, then, there was a new organizational system that gave the young a novel source of power – the concept of a political party which imparted its own disciplines and potentially freed its activists from the elders both in the Native Authority at the centre and in the districts and villages where 'traditional authorities' held sway as agents of the NA. Political parties generated too their own corps of party supporters or thugs (*yan banga*) that were a match for the NA police in any surprise confrontation. The new knowledge that the 1950s young had access to was more a way of thinking and talking: it was the new anti-colonial politics and its associated anti-elite radicalism calling for equality, justice and education for all. But it was also generated in the new schools and colleges built in the 1950s in which the English language was used (whereas Hausa had been the standard language of administration for both Nigerians and the British). Again, this *lingua franca* enabled the young to speak to each other across boundaries – this time to the southern Nigerian activists who, for a decade or two, had been campaigning against colonial rule. It was the language of change. Once again, the elders had been seen to fail – they had collaborated in colonial/Christian rule and in exploiting the peasants for alien interests – and once again, their failure had strong moral implications: there was corruption and oppression (*zalunci*) in ways castigated in Islamic law. In the minds of the young, the legitimacy of the elders' power was once again in question.

Post-1970s

It is tempting to see the rise of military rule, first in January 1966 and then gradually consolidated through the civil war and period of reconstruction, as another 'youth coup'. There was a new organizational system and discipline – the army – and a new set of knowledge and skills (the use of various new weapons, the optimal deployment of force, logistics). The military are, by definition in Hausa, young; the fact that the 1966 coup was led by young officers accentuated the role of youth even within a young army. But in many ways I see military government more as a substitution for rule by political party – indeed the army could be considered as a kind of party – than as a wholly new phase. Admittedly the army does not have elections but, by its very nature, the army through its rank-and-file soldiery has close links to the grass roots of everyday life: soldiers have kin who usually live in the less wealthy parts of the nation, and the army's composition makes for friendships, even marriage alliances, across social and/or regional boundaries.

One could argue, too, that those who ran the 1950s 'youth takeover' were by the mid-1960s being criticized as failures. The NA system of the 'colonial caliphate' had been transformed into a 'party-political caliphate' with the Sardauna of Sokoto as its leader. The old NAs were still in place as were the *Alkalai* who ran the courts but who, in many instances, had been cajoled into acting as enforcers for the government party, the NPC (Northern People's Congress). The army sought to correct these failures by quickly proceeding to abolish the NAs and to rename and reorganize the *Alkali* courts. In a way, I would suggest the military takeover in 1966 was carrying through the kind of reforms that the 1950s youth takeover had initially argued for. In short, I prefer to include the military as part of a single yet diverse phase that started in the 1950s. There remains the issue of whether that phase is now over, with the military's gradual but deliberate breaking-up of the authority once held by emirs and district heads; even the Sultan, *Sarkin Musulmi*, now has less clout than his revered father used to have. The Muslim *umma* is not as united or as single-minded as it once was. I date the end of any kind of 'caliphate' to the early 1990s: the young today are no longer growing up in the shade of that once capacious 'tree'.[15]

Conclusion

One question we need to discuss is how far today's politics are simply a continuation of the 1950s. In one sense, the language of elections, democracy, rights and justice are common to both the 1950s and the early years of the 21st century. But I would suggest that a significant element of each of the three 'power inversions' described – 1804-1808, 1903, and the 1950s – was the need to recreate a stable regime, albeit in a new radical style, whether *jihadi* idealism, colonial bureaucratic efficiency or modern self-government. What is new today is not the role of youth in taking control at moments of deep structural change, but the way no stability has (yet) ensued from contemporary changes. It is as if

---

[15] Today, in a large, powerful emirate such as Kano, many of the district heads are now ex-civil servants or professionals in the fields of accountancy, law or health. Their links are with the elite of modern Nigerian society and they have access to Abuja in a way no traditional district head ever had. His links were much closer to 'his' people in the district, for good or ill. Similarly, over a hundred village heads in Kano now have undergraduate degrees: their eyes focus on a different, more distant horizon than their fathers' did.

frequent easy change is now part of the system itself; and the young therefore have retained, as never before, an integral and continuing part in bringing about these many, varied changes.

A major factor in promoting this change-based system is the existence of a single source of 'unearned' wealth: Nigeria's massive oil revenue. Competition for access, if only briefly, to this revenue legitimates almost any means to achieve temporary political change. Since this wealth is privatisable (and rarely recovered by one's successors), any group within Nigeria not to compete for access to it would be mad: it will determine the status of one's descendants (as 'elite' or proletariat) for generations to come, quite apart from any current pleasure such wealth might bring personally. Furthermore, once one has had access to it for a while, letting others have a period of access is more acceptable. Interestingly, vast oil revenues have not led to any investment in a stable system of government or institutions that might more evenly distribute the benefits of such a massive national income.

The fact that the primary object of politics today is the acquisition of wealth (and not, say, the creation of stable or effective institutions whether local or central) confirms to people that it is appropriately a young man's pursuit. Even for a young man, what is bizarre about this oil-derived wealth at the local-government level is that it requires no work except during the hectic period of politicking at election time. After that, it is the spending (on himself and his friends) that constitutes the local-government chairman's work. It is hard to see this as 'politics' in the conventional sense. It is person-centred politics. If he cannot accumulate and invest his windfall wealth, his road to being a national *dattijo* is in jeopardy.

To close, I will summarize some of the different logics I see as underlying the three power inversions I have mentioned in this chapter.

(i) Islam, unlike traditional religion, empowers the young and gives them a special expertise and experience (especially if they are part of Sufi *daira*, as Shaikh 'Uthman's students were). Certain readings of Islam require them to take power in the face of oppression (*zulm*). In the case of the Sokoto *jihad*, the Muslim reformers largely lost control of the movement and compromises proved necessary. It was these compromises that persistently provoked sections of radical Muslim youth into 'moving away', either on pilgrimage to the east or to sectarian communes in the deep countryside. This politico-religious protest has resurfaced regularly over the last two centuries. In a quietist form, it is seen in much-increased piety (fasting, prayers, reading of the Qur'an) in ordinary households, whereas more overtly it has been manifested in student protest and pressure groups, some more vocal (as the Yan Izala still are), some violent (as the Yan Tatsine were). The latest of these were the 'Taliban' who, mainly university students or graduates, briefly tried to establish a commune in northern Borno in the dry season of 2003-2004. Underlying all this was the local radical recognition that Muslim students could and should be armed in order to fight a serious *jihad*. Empowerment had now its military as well as its mystical dimension.[16]

(ii) 1903 saw an externally generated opportunity to reject the oppressive aspects of the Caliphal regime that were giving rise to some vicious civil wars, to the extent that the Christian conquest was, paradoxically perhaps, seen by some Muslims as part of Allah's will to reform his Muslim community. But the major item was the establishment of a wholly new institution, the Native Authority, that gave the young a range of roles: the NA was stable and predictable in its operation, and it offered its young employees a certain independence *vis-à-vis* their traditional elders in the countryside or (to a less extent) in the city. In addition, the new concept of the age-free, impersonal 'state' weakened the bonds of the lineage; it also generated a new kind of 'state' force, the NA police. Finally the new modern education (*boko*) empowered the 1903 generation as reformist Islam had done a century before.

(iii) The 1950s saw, once again, an externally articulated and legitimated rationale for the young to take over the existing political structures. Once again, the young were offered both an entirely new institution – the political party – and the novel idea of an organized opposition to those ruling locally. The ability of the young not only to have their voice heard but also to contest elections as an organized group was essential to the political credibility of the young as an active political category. The fact that this system was cut short by a coup by *young* army officers (of the rank of major and captain, all alien to the 'north') when it might have achieved a degree of stability, suggests that the regular pattern of quasi-caliphal organization was coming to an end after some 160 years. The army regimes have systematically since broken up what foci of power there were in the old caliphal system so that there are no alternative stable institutions with power. In the face of such a policy, the emirs have largely abdicated any active political function, though some retain considerable grass-roots authority out of a popular sense of tradition.

---

[16] The campaign to re-establish *shari'a* law in its complete form is (and was) more a grass-roots, youth-backed movement than a product of elite politics. It was intended, perhaps, as a means to bring about another 'power inversion'. It certainly established its own force – the vigilantes (who were all young) – and various extra institutions such as the *hisba* committees and the *shari'a* commissions. For a brief discussion of *shari'a*, see Last (2002, 2000b).

(iv) In all this, it is interesting how important external stimuli have been, whether the Fulbe, the British or the southern Nigerians, to the coming-to-the-fore of politically active youth in northern Nigeria, and how important too, the creation has been – usually via outside inspiration – of new institutions (or the destruction of old institutions) to the viability of youth politics being stable enough to transform itself into an administration. Though there is a rough temporal pattern to change in northern Nigeria – approximately every forty to fifty years, as if it was 'generational' – there are clearly other decisive factors at work. The traditional transmission of power and authority from elder to younger brother before it passes to a son sets up a pattern, as well as an ultimate frustration among the young, so that people can periodically 'read' (and treat as legitimating) the radical change in which the young, at last, oust the old.

(v) A final, early item in this political history of youth. Until the mid-18th century throughout the West African Sahel, Islamic specialists – whether scholars, their students or the new breed of Sufis – constituted an unarmed, non-violent caste sitting aloof from warfare, while a political aristocracy mono-polized militarism as a warrior caste. (There were also other castes: craftsmen, slaves, as well as merchants.) The various movements we know under the general label of *jihad* in 18th-19th century West Africa converted this Muslim 'caste' into warriors and political leaders, displacing (or sometimes absorbing) the existing warrior caste. And as a new caste, they proved themselves to be both effective and legitimate. What happened, however, in Hausaland was that, instead of caste, it was biological age that became the criterion of differ-entiation. The new 'warrior caste' were the young, whilst the elders took on the role of the 'caste' of Islamic specialists. Growing up could thus mean moving from one caste to another. But it is not quite as simple as this, as there remained (and still remains) among the young a cadre of men training to be professional scholars: some are militant but many are not. Broadly speaking however, it is this caste-like formalization of 'youth' and 'elders' that has begun to fall apart just as, 200 years ago, the demarcation between 'Muslim' and 'warrior' did. Both were major structural shifts – powerful new political ideas – that were not confined to a single area or to a single culture. So, for comparison's sake, are other political histories of youth possible?

References

Last, M. 1993, 'The Power of Youth, Youth of Power: Notes on the Religions of the Young in Northern Nigeria', in H. d'Almeida-Topor, C. Coquery-Vidrovitch, O. Goerg & F. Guitart (eds), *Les Jeunes en Afrique*, Paris: L'Harmattan, pp. 375-99.

Last, M. 1997, 'The "Colonial Caliphate" of Northern Nigeria', in D. Robinson and J-L. Triaud (eds), *Les Temps des Marabouts: Itinéraires et Stratégies Islamiques en Afrique Occidentale Française v. 1880-1960*, Paris: Karthala, pp. 67-82.

Last, M. 2000a, 'Children and the Experience of Violence: Contrasting Cultures of Punishment in Northern Nigeria', *Africa*, 70 (3): 359-93.

Last, M. 2000b, 'La Chari'a dans le Nord-Nigeria', *Politique Africaine,* 79: 141-52.

Last, M. 2002, 'Notes on the Implementation of *Shari'a* in Northern Nigeria', *FAIS Journal of Humanities* (Bayero University, Kano), 2 (2): 1-17.

Reynolds, J.T. 1999, *The Time of Politics (Zamanin Siyasa): Islam and the Politics of Legitimacy in Northern Nigeria 1950-1966*, Lanham, MD: University Press of America.

Stilwell, S. 2004, *Paradoxes of Power: The Kano 'Mamluks' and Male Royal Slavery in the Sokoto Caliphate, 1804-1903*, Portsmouth, NH: Heinemann.

Whitting, C.E.J. (ed.) 1957, *Infaku'l Maisuri*, London: Luzac & Co. Ltd.

Yahaya, A.D. 1980. *The Native Authority System in Northern Nigeria: A Study in Political Relations with Particular Reference to the Zaria Native Authority*, Zaria: Ahmadu Bello University Press.

Yakubu, A.M. 1996, *An Aristocracy in Political Crisis: The End of Indirect Rule and the Emergence of Party Politics in the Emirates of Northern Nigeria*, Aldershot: Avebury.

Yamba, C.B. 1995, *Permanent Pilgrims: The Role of Pilgrimage in the Lives of West African Muslims in Sudan*, Edinburgh: Edinburgh University Press.

3

Imagined generations: Constructing youth in revolutionary Zanzibar

G. Thomas Burgess

Although scholars have discussed the Zanzibari Revolution as primarily an expression of racial, ethnic and/or class struggle, this chapter argues that generational identities were at the very centre of nationalism and revolution in Zanzibar for over two decades. Two distinct forms of youth identity emerged. Vanguard youth defined themselves as a distinct historical cohort with unique access to resources of extraversion in the late colonial world. Client youth defined themselves instead in reference to 'timeless' principles of patronage and patriarchy. For both vanguards and clients, 'youth' as an identity bequeathed individuals a sense of dignity and recognized position in nationalist discourse and public life. Their status as youth had meaning in either local or global discourses of power.

The Zanzibari Revolution in 1964 brought a permanent end to Arab political and economic hegemony in the islands, as well as the death or exile of between a third and a half of the Arab population,[1] in a wave of violence that was

---

[1] For a range of estimates of revolutionary casualties, see Sheriff (2001: 314). Don Petterson (2002: 191), serving as American Vice Consul in Zanzibar, estimated that by the summer of 1965 'Zanzibar's pre-revolution Arab population of 50,000 had been halved'. The CIA offered the same estimate (CIA Special Report, 'United Republic of Tanzania', Vol. II, 2/65-12/68, Box 100, National Security/Country File/ Africa: Tanganyika, Lyndon Baines Johnson Library, Austin Texas). The revolutionary government's own census in 1967 recorded the number of Zanzibaris living on Unguja who claimed Arab identity as having declining to 8 per cent, half the pre-revolutionary figure. On Pemba, which had not experienced nearly the same level of violence, the

'genocidal in proportions' (Sheriff 2001: 314-15).[2] Scholars have disagreed mostly over the extent to which the uprising was motivated by race or class divisions in Zanzibari society. Michael Lofchie (1965: 269-70) argued that Zanzibar's political parties 'were separated by elemental and irreducible racial fears'. Africans feared 'perpetual economic servitude and political subjection to a racial minority … the end of their hope for a better life'. On the other hand, Abdul Sheriff (1991: 7) asserted that racial identities in Zanzibar were only 'skin deep', even lamenting that they appear to have 'mesmerized' historians.[3] In the same volume, B.D. Bowles (1991: 84) claims that the study of Zanzibari history 'depends on thinking of workers as they actually were, that is, workers, rather than mainlanders or Africans, and to think of employers as employers and not as Zanzibaris or Arabs and Asians. To do otherwise is to write the history of images.'

Sheriff and Bowles's arguments have not discouraged more recent researchers from continuing to emphasize the islands' troubled racial relations, despite their alleged ephemeral reality. Jonathon Glassman's work reconstructs nationalist newspaper debates that were responsible for the emergence of mutually exclusive notions of racial identity. In an attempt to prove which community was the true 'sons of the soil' (Glassman 2000: 409), each side engaged in 'reciprocal dehumanization that culminated in bloodshed. … Discourses of civilization and of race informed and fed off one another, as if locked in a deadly embrace' (Glassman forthcoming).

The origins of the Zanzibari Revolution are located not only in the structure of the islands' social and economic relations, or in the inflammatory rhetoric of the era, but in the nature of nationalist mobilization, which both simplified and complicated the issue of identity. Islanders living in an era of mass politics maintained their previous identities, or they chose to adopt new multiple identities as they observed or participated in nationalist mobilization. What

---

number remained virtually the same as in the post-war era, namely 25 per cent. See also Amory (1994: 125).

[2] The mortality figures place the Zanzibari Revolution in the same category as the Mau Mau Emergency in Kenya, which has attracted considerably more scholarly attention.

[3] However, writing a decade later Sheriff held a different view: 'the primary contradiction in the Zanzibari society on the eve of independence was neither race nor class exclusively, but a complex combination of the two', a position not far removed from Lofchie's original thesis quoted in Sheriff (2001: 313). Jan-Georg Deutsch (2002) recently contributed another assessment that foregrounds inequality in Zanzibar in terms of access in the post-war years to the commodities, ideas and practices of modernity. In a highly cosmopolitan society, people readily articulated their differences in terms of unequal access to material, cultural and political resources; the revolution may be considered mobilized resistance to the 'modernity of the few'.

were once in the colonial world often 'private and individual' choices regarding identity now came to be of immense political significance. Colonial subjects reconsidered their position in a society deeply divided over the question of who should and should not be considered true 'sons of the soil'. Nationalists for their part freely borrowed from one another and from overseas as they experimented with various mobilization techniques. They framed their messages in terms of identities that possessed widely varying degrees of local currency. They did not hesitate to employ identities arranged by their own imagination and subjective reading of history. By provoking local debate, articulating aspirations, identifying common enemies, referring to a common historical heritage, introducing key terms, and founding new associations, nationalists employed identities that were both substantive and ephemeral, but which attained at least a passing public reality during nationalist mobilization. Identities in nationalist Zanzibar were 'precarious articulations', unbound by any sense of historical inevitability (Laclau & Mouffe 2001: 68).

Thus, parallel to the politics of race and class in Zanzibar there was a fairly systematic effort to exploit generational identities for purposes of nationalist mobilization. Nationalists regarded youth as necessary for the strength of any successful political coalition. They targeted them for recruitment and gave them official status with the formation of youth associations attached to the leading nationalist parties. The construction of elaborate networks of youth branches served as a key measure of party vitality and strength. Nationalists articulated generational identities in order to energize volunteers and to distribute power, tasks and responsibilities within their parties. By the late 1950s the need to recruit youth had become an unquestioned given in conventional nationalist wisdom in Zanzibar. The following, then, is a narrative of the Zanzibari Revolution in which I have ordered historical materials in a way that will make legible the story of how islanders imagined generation, the position of youth in public discourse, and the role they played in the Zanzibari Revolution.

A vanguard generation

In Zanzibar, youth as an identity had both recent and ancient origins. Young people came to participate in politics as either vanguards or clients, for whom generational identity meant very different things. For some, their generation was an historical cohort formed by the unique terrain of the late-colonial world, permanently setting them apart from other generations older or younger.[4] Access

---

[4] According to Karl Mannheim's classic definition, historical cohorts are so shaped by

to western education was very much a part of that unique landscape. As late as 1939, 60 per cent of all adult males on Zanzibar island were literate in Swahili written in Arabic script, while only 2 per cent were literate in the Roman script (Wilson 1978: 229, Fair 1994: 239). Then in the 1940s the British introduced Qur'anic education into their school curriculum and in so doing gained for the first time the interest and support of Zanzibari parents. Numbers of students multiplied as western education spread rapidly, especially through the capital. By 1959, 35 per cent of boys and 22 per cent of girls on the islands were studying in colonial primary schools, learning the Roman alphabet and English as a second language (Bennett 1978: 244). Furthermore, between 1955 and 1961 secondary school enrolment in the colony rose from 442 to 984 for boys and from 185 to 526 for girls (Cameron & Dodd 1970: 129). Graduates of Zanzibari secondary schools in the 1950s were able to go on as never before to higher education overseas. In 1949 there were 21 Zanzibari students overseas; and by 1963 there were over 300 Zanzibari students in the United Kingdom alone on government scholarships or subsisting on private funding sources.[5] These numbers indicate the extent to which the British became interested in the post-war era in preparing Zanzibaris, Arabs in particular, for careers in their islands' civil service.[6]

Meanwhile, beginning in 1958 the Zanzibar Nationalist Party (ZNP) and the Afro-Shirazi Party (ASP) also organized hundreds of overseas scholarships for purposes of youth mobilization and recruitment. The two parties in fact could not find enough qualified students to accept all the scholarships offered by nations such as Egypt, China, the Soviet Union and East Germany, which were intent on influencing a generation of Zanzibari leaders reaching maturity at the height of the Cold War. Such politically inspired patronage gave Zanzibari youth able to meet minimum educational requirements far more concentrated access to universities than any other community in East Africa. In the 1950s travel became an initiatory experience for many young Zanzibaris and a new form of secular pilgrimage. They gained in Northern universities crucial

---

their particular historical experiences that they retain their separate generational identity for the rest of their lives. They define themselves in opposition or even hostility to other generations that have not passed through comparable historical circumstances. See also Roseman (1995: 7).

[5]   Zanzibar National Archives (hereafter ZNA) AD 32/27 List of Zanzibar Students Studying Abroad, 1956-63, "Zanzibar Students Studying in the United Kingdom." 4/9/63.

[6]   See Rhodes House Library, Oxford (hereafter RHL), Mss. Afr. Mss. Afr. s. 2249, interview of J.R. Naish, Oxford, 16 October 1971, by J. Tawney. See also Cooper (1987: 138, 168) and Lofchie (1965: 63, 77, 90).

resources of extraversion, such as new consumer tastes and leisure styles; they were now conversant in a world of modernist images, signs and commodities.

In some instances, as in the life of Abdulrahman Muhammed 'Babu', they absorbed new vocabularies, political doctrines and training. In the mid-1950s, Babu was active in London among a network of Zanzibari and East African students and workers, some of whom, like himself, came to identify themselves as socialists. Recruited by the ZNP in 1957 to serve as that party's Secretary General, Babu returned to the islands and soon became, along with Ali Muhsin, the ZNP's leading strategist. Despite his socialist convictions he embraced the ZNP as then the only expressedly multi-racial, anti-colonial party in Zanzibar. He almost immediately set about recruiting youth into the party by establishing the Youth's Own Union (YOU) as the party's semi-independent youth wing. For the next five years the YOU came to play a central role in the ZNP's mobilization efforts. It started a newspaper in 1958, *Sauti ya Vijana* (Voice of Youth),[7] and opened a bookshop in the ZNP party headquarters that distributed party newspapers and various socialist political texts. The YOU established three different 'societies', for education, drama, and debate, and organized frequent demonstrations to put young people on the streets to perform ritualized demands for more secondary schools, to demand an end to racial discrimination, or to show support for the Algerian liberation struggle.[8] YOU members paraded in red and white uniforms, drilled in a small 'Guard of Honour', and performed in their own travelling brass band. Probably the YOU's most ambitious project was a massive literacy campaign that reportedly reached several thousand pupils who met in local ZNP party offices.[9]

YOU activities foregrounded youth in the political struggles of the time. A seemingly endless succession of fundraisers, rallies, debates, demonstrations, performances and service projects encouraged many youth to imagine themselves as a vanguard generation in the history of their islands. Such shared

---

[7] One of at least ten newspapers affiliated with the ZNP during the nationalist period. Unfortunately copies of this newspaper were unavailable to this researcher. The Zanzibar National Archives houses an extensive but incomplete collection of some of these pre-revolution newspapers. See also Hamdani (1981: 42-45, 51).

[8] Public Records Office (hereafter PRO) CO 822, 1377, British intelligence report, November 1957; PRO CO 822, 1377, British intelligence reports, March-June 1958. According to Babu, the ZNP also developed a 'clear-cut international stand' against apartheid in South Africa, for the Palestinian liberation struggle, for the People's Republic of China's admission to the United Nations, and the unification of Korea and Vietnam. See also Babu (1991: 227).

[9] RHL, MSS. Brit. Emp. s. 390., Clarence Buxton papers, Box 5, 'Commission of Inquiry into Civil Disturbances', Ali Muhsin testimony, 10/6/61; *Dawn in Zanzibar*, #3, July-August 1961, 19.

events encouraged a sense that theirs was a generation 'moving [together] onward through calendrical time' (Anderson 1991: 27). The British, meanwhile, closely monitored the YOU, considering it 'an attempt, and a successful one, to attract to its ranks the youths of Zanzibar'.[10] It was 'clearly following the pattern of militant youth movements that had caused such trouble in other parts of the world'.[11] YOU activism earned praise, however, in an editorial in the ZNP-affiliated newspaper *Mwongozi*. The editors effused:

> It is remarkable that whenever a country is in a transition to political maturity its youths tend to get more and more militant. Political parties with more progressive platforms invariably attract larger numbers of the younger element, who in turn adorn the older parties with their youthful spirit.
> It is an established fact that the older people ... are notoriously sceptical about independence. ... at least they [the youth] are more realistic than the older generation which faces the future with its head permanently turned to the past. (*Mwongozi*, 11 April 1958)

YOU programmes generally served to enhance nationalist mobilization without necessarily promoting any specific socialist agenda. Nevertheless, according to his personal statements, it was Babu's intention that YOU exercises would ultimately encourage youth to grasp that non-racialism should not only be defined by Islamic principles, but also by socialist commitment. Babu wanted young people to turn to socialism as a means of transcending the intense racial conflicts of their islands, and as a model for nation building. Confident young 'intellectuals' were most able to discern the correct path of national development and they, in partnership with 'workers', were to play a vanguard role in Zanzibar's anti-colonial struggles.[12] To cultivate vanguard young, Babu collaborated with Ali Sultan Issa, a close friend, fellow socialist and London-veteran,[13] to obtain scholarships to colleges, universities and institutes throughout the socialist world.[14] This was in addition to the approximately 800

---

[10] PRO CO 822, 1377, General intelligence report on ZNP.
[11] PRO CO 822, 1377, British Resident to Secretary of State of Colonies, 29 March 1959.
[12] Interview, Abdulrahman Muhammed Babu, Dar es Salaam, 24 August 1995.
[13] Ali Sultan Issa joined the British Communist Party in 1954, and attended the Moscow Youth Festival in 1957 at his own expense. He returned to Zanzibar in 1958 and was appointed a member, like Babu, of the ZNP's Executive Committee. See his forthcoming memoirs, *Walk on Two Legs: A Memoir of the Zanzibari Revolution*, edited by the author.
[14] In his memoirs, Ali Sultan Issa claims they sent as many as 600 students to socialist countries. British intelligence placed the number somewhat lower at around 116. PRO CO 822 2070, E56ii, Appreciation of Zanzibar Central Intelligence Committee Report,

Zanzibaris who attended schools and colleges in Egypt from 1958 to 1963, a ZNP scholarship programme initiated by Ali Muhsin.[15]

Whether in Cuba, Egypt, China or Eastern Europe the Zanzibari students overseas nurtured a sense of their own importance in the political struggles back home. The conference resolutions of the All Zanzibar Students' Association meeting in Prague in September 1963 stated:

> We, as true sons of our people, feel that we have a great role to play in the present developments that are unfolding in our country. We have always been at the forefront of our people's struggles against colonialism and imperialism. We will continue with this good tradition of ours until all the forces of oppression, reaction and capital are wiped out completely from the face of our motherland. (*ZANEWS*, 17 September 1963, 26 September 1963)

Thus by the early 1960s, Babu and Ali Sultan, who were still in their thirties and who had only preceded the flood of student travellers by a few years when they themselves arrived in London in the early 1950s, were now patrons and 'elders' over their own growing network of scholarship routes for party youth. It was especially worrisome to the British and ZNP conservatives when students returning to Zanzibar commonly came to associate with Babu's faction within the ZNP, depending often on where they had studied. Babu's success marked him in the eyes of the British Resident in Zanzibar as having a dominant 'hold over the frustrated, unemployed youth of the ZNP'.[16] He observed 'the building up within the country of a measurable body of young people, who, even if they do not become card-carrying Communists, at least become so imbued with the doctrines of Communist subversion that they must constitute a threat to future security'.[17]

In the early 1960s 'youth' emerged as an identity in a new era of mass politics in reference to the first cohort in the islands in large numbers with access to bilingual fluency. They attached a deep significance to their youth,

---

July 1962.

[15] Such patronage was part of Nasser's general interest in making Cairo the international capital of African anti-colonial movements by providing their representatives free office space, salaries, unlimited air travel, and scholarships. By 1964 there were in total about 2,000 African students in Cairo. See A.M. Barwani, 'Conflict and Harmony in Zanzibar', (unpublished memoirs), 98-105; PRO CO 822 1378, British intelligence report, May 1959; PRO CO 822, 1382, British intelligence report, October 1958; Bennett (1978: 194-95), Mansfield (1965: 100-101).

[16] PRO CO 822, 2047, British Resident to Secretary of State, Zanzibar security situation, 23 June 1962.

[17] PRO CO 822 2070, British Resident to Colonial Office, 6 October 1962.

appreciated their unique historical endowment, and the differences between themselves and their seniors and country cousins. 'Youth' possessed most currency in the physical and intellectual context of Zanzibar Town, where young people in the ZNP had most access to all of the shared events that together combined to encourage generational identity in the nationalist period: parades and demonstrations, debates and party volunteer work, schools and scholarships. As youth followed the nationalist contests in Zanzibar and other colonial territories, in the newspapers and on the radio they discussed the content and meaning of independence, and reflected on local political dramas in the context of a world stage.[18] Youth emerged as an imagined generation comparable to and in rhetorical relationship with elders, workers, women, and racial terms employed in the partisan discourse of the time. They nurtured a sense of purpose as a generation and they fantasized about the prospects of the years to come. The sum total of hundreds of separate student diasporas was a keen awareness among youth of the opportunities of a moment 'of considerable mobility and category jumping' (Cooper 1994: 1519). In their reading of history, youth imagined themselves members of an emerging vanguard generation with the ideas and skills necessary to place Zanzibar in its rightful position on a world map of modernizing nations, and in the irreversible historical march towards socialism.[19]

The Umma Party

The British Resident, Sir George Mooring, noted in July 1961 for the first time growing friction between Babu and Ali Muhsin over the distribution of scholarships to communist countries.[20] Oral sources suggest the colonial state placed increasing pressure on Muhsin, informing him that the ZNP would not be permitted to inherit power if Babu remained in the party leadership.[21] Mooring considered Babu a 'menace to the peaceful development of Zan-

---

[18] Some sense of this may be derived from Gurnah (1996: 65-66).
[19] See an excellent study of two generations of Ethiopian intellectuals educated abroad in pre-World War II Ethiopia in Bahru Zewde (2002).
[20] PRO CO 822 2046, British Resident to Secretary of State, 13 July 1961.
[21] Interviews, Hussein Kombo, Zanzibar Town, 7 July 1996; Ali Sultan Issa, Zanzibar Town, 4 July 1996; Muhammed Abdullah Baramia, Zanzibar Town, 22 August 1996; Shafi Adam Shafi, Dar es Salaam, 26 June 1996; Khamis Abdallah Ameir, Zanzibar Town, 15 May 1998. Pressure may have also come from Mohammed Shamte and other conservative ZPPP leaders. Babu claims that they required 'the ZNP purge its radical and socialist elements' as a precondition for agreeing to a political alliance in 1961. See Babu (1991: 233).

zibar'.[22] Chief Secretary P.A.P. Robertson regarded Babu not just 'a thorn in the flesh' but 'the most sinister man in Zanzibar ... an evil genius'.[23] Muhsin appears to have been compromised between desires to maintain ZNP unity and keeping Babu on his side, while demonstrating to the British and his conservative base that the ZNP was not a socialist party intent on overthrowing the Sultan or making Zanzibar a communist satellite state. When the British imprisoned Babu in mid-1962 for sedition, Ali Sultan Issa openly accused Muhsin and other party officials of complicity and was expelled from the ZNP. After Babu's release in early 1963, there was a decisive confrontation between him and Muhsin at a party conference in June; Babu formally resigned from the party over a dispute over which candidates to nominate for the elections.[24] Immediately following his resignation, Babu and his faction founded the Umma Party, which soon developed into a well-organized party far more influential than its relatively small numbers might immediately suggest.[25] Babu wrote rather prosaically in the early 1990s that:

> The youth of all parties who were beginning to be demoralised and disenchanted with the political atmosphere were immediately charged with new enthusiasm. The first mass rally of the new party on the second day of its formation attracted several thousand young people, especially young workers from all political parties. The first week of the party's existence saw the registration of masses of youth as card-carrying members. (Babu 1991: 237-38)

Umma held most interest among youth in the capital, finding virtually no support among the old, in the rural areas of Unguja, or anywhere on Pemba.[26] According to Umma's former Secretary-General, the other parties were too strong, and 'the youth didn't know'. Furthermore, there was not enough time before independence to 'awaken the people'.[27] The party evoked hostility among Zanzibaris for whom Umma members were atheists, communists and infidels. Umma identified with a set of political doctrines of at least partial

---

[22] PRO CO 822, 2166, Secret file on Babu; RHL, MSS.Afr.S.1446; R.H.V. Biles interview.

[23] RHL, East Africa, MSS.Afr.S.2250, 'Zanzibar Symposium', tape recording of interview at Oxford University by Alison Smith, 16 October 1971.

[24] See Burgess (in press) for a more detailed narrative of the split within the ZNP.

[25] In its six-month existence Umma reportedly signed up approximately 3,000 members. Interviews, Saed Baes, Zanzibar Town, 8 July 1996; Ali Sultan Issa, Zanzibar Town, 13 July 1996; anonymous, Zanzibar Town, 8 July 1996.

[26] Unguja and Pemba are Zanzibar's two principal islands. Zanzibar Town is located on Unguja.

[27] Interview, Abdul Razak Mussa Simai, Paje, 23 July 1996.

foreign ancestry that did not organically emerge from the dominant nationalist debates that Glassman (2000) describes. The party also suffered from the stigma of race: more youth from the ASP would have joined the new party had Umma not been identified by many as another 'Arab' party.[28] Leading Umma intellectuals (Babu, Ali Sultan, Khamis Abdallah Ameir, Salim Ahmed Salim, Ali Mafoudh, Ahmed Abubakar Quallatein) were all of at least partial Arab ancestry. In Zanzibar such mixed origins commonly translated into identification as 'Arabs' rather than as 'Africans' or the adoption of a distinct Creole identity.

The appeal of the party was, therefore, limited to a relatively small number of youth of heterogeneous backgrounds who participated in the currents of socialist discourse that Babu and his colleagues attempted to foster in Zanzibar Town and among students overseas. Umma sought to define itself through a series of printed manifestos as the friend of the poor African majority, for whose class interests party cadres struggled. According to 'A People's Programme', Umma sought to replace colonialism with socialism, the only system that could ensure the 'dignity' of the individual. In this task, the new party was 'a conscious vanguard of the oppressed people of Zanzibar. It represents the broad interests of the African people who today are bearing the brunt of economic oppression.' As participants in a vanguard movement, it was necessary for each member of Umma 'to be strictly disciplined' and 'to endeavour to raise the level of his consciousness and to understand the fundamentals of socialism and the theory of African revolution'.[29] In 'A Programme of People's Youth', Umma propagandists described their party's youth wing as 'a serious and conscious youth movement', and 'a forefront in the battle of the oppressed and exploited masses of the African youth of Zanzibar'. Its object was 'to win the young generation for the democratic and socialist regeneration … [when] the younger generation's mental and physical development will enjoy boundless opportunity'.[30]

Some young people, however, gravitated towards Umma not so much out of an identification with socialism but as a system of patronage alternative to that of other parties. Some were interested in education and jobs and saw Babu as being most in a position to help. Umma intellectuals nonetheless imagined themselves belonging to a vanguard generation, despite the identity's demographic imprecision and shifting theoretical foundations. They were 'substitute

---

[28] See Lofchie (1965: 260-65), Clayton (1981: 59-61) and Bennett (1978: 264).

[29] RHL, Mss. Brit. Emp. s. 390, Clarence Buxton Papers, Box 3, 'A People's Programme'.

[30] RHL, Mss. Brit. Emp. s. 390, Clarence Buxton Papers, Box 3, 'A Programme for People's Youth'.

proletarians' (Riviere 1977: 230), privileged agents compelled by their times and their travels to pull Zanzibar into the progressive transnational march towards socialism. Umma's rank and file members were neither wholly African nor Arab, were neither poor nor rich, but they were young and they supported propaganda that criticized colonialism, feudalism and capitalism. They established cooperative networks that crossed the frontiers of race, class and neighbourhood among youth wanting to bring down the old order represented by the ZNP.

A client generation

Although the Afro-Shirazi Party claimed to represent the large majority of Zanzibaris of African descent, party leaders were forced to respond to the growing threat posed by effective ZNP grass-roots organization. In response to the expanding institutional profile of the YOU, ASP Chairman Abeid Karume and other party elders founded the Youth League, or ASPYL, in May 1959. According to official ASP history, 'while giving advice to the young people, Mzee Karume and other ASP leaders stressed the need for a firm unity among themselves and also informed them that all the eyes and the strength of the leaders were focused on the youth' (Afro-Shirazi Party 1973: 92). The ASPYL was intended as a recruiting mechanism and it established an extensive network of branches throughout the islands parallel to that of the ASP. Under Chairman Seif Bakari, the Youth League came to embody Karume's most unified and extensive network of support within a party increasingly paralyzed by chronic factionalism.

The ASPYL did not, like the YOU, cultivate an image of vanguard youth parading, performing and protesting across the national stage. Especially in Zanzibar Town it was an organization far less visible and less interested in scholarships, debates and literacy campaigns. Bakari was less concerned than Babu with working out a Youth League stand on distant anti-colonial conflicts, sending youth overseas or securing foreign patronage. From oral testimonies it appears that the Youth League operated according to a different logic altogether. While for some in the YOU, youth was a new identity shaped by a generational cohort's unique access in the post-war era to valuable resources of extraversion, for those with less access to such resources youth was instead an old identity with its origins in pre-colonial African age-relations. In such discourse, generations were determined not so much by their distinctive formative circumstances as by what position they occupied within the life cycle between birth and death, with youth possessing its own characteristics as a generation, and having its own separate social and political roles to play.

It has become a commonplace in a vast anthropological literature to suggest that age has to varying extents historically determined men's access in rural African societies to authority, status, women and ritual power. Age has served as a prominent distinction in male society between economic autonomy and dependency. Despite endless local variations, it was normal for age to 'assume a pre-eminent role as a principle of social structure' (Bernardi 1985: 2). Deeply conservative senior men dominated village politics, and legal and religious systems. Male initiation rites commonly reinforced age-deference as a principle necessary for social stability. Despite social and economic hierarchies based on age, generational identities also commonly ensured reciprocity in community relationships. While they institutionalized stratification, they also typically guaranteed eventual advance. Public ceremonies formally transferred power between the generations and ensured corporate mobility and promotion; they also gave acceptable and controlled public expression of generational antagonisms.[31] Young men achieved promotion corporately in the case of more formalized age grade systems, or individually through the institution of marriage. In societies where elders' capacity to control land and production was severely limited, they instead sought to exercise their control over the reproductive capacities of the community.[32] Until they had established themselves as independent householders, juniors were sometimes called upon to perform labour service for their elders.[33]

While anthropologists have described how generational identities have determined social rank and authority, historians have shown less interest in examining how generation endures as an identity in urban environments or in post-colonial Africa. Despite John Iliffe's contention that 'conflict between male generations [has been] one of the most dynamic and enduring forces in African history' (Iliffe 1995: 95), historians have devoted limited attention to the manner in which, for example, nationalist agendas revived, expressed or sought to manipulate or diffuse these age-old conflicts.[34] In Zanzibar, both conflict and cooperation between generations were at the centre of nationalist

---

[31]   See Moore & Puritt (1977: 74, 126), Gulliver (1963: 34ff), Wilson (1959: 49ff, 96, 160, 218) and Raum (1940).

[32]   See, for example, Geschiere (1982: 49, 91-93, 125).

[33]   In polygynous societies, junior-senior conflicts over access to cattle, women and land were, however, complicated by female agency. All-male generational disputes were sometimes forgotten when women sought to renegotiate their rights as wives and daughters. Junior and senior men formed alliances when their control over wives and daughters was threatened. See Lovett (1996).

[34]   Mamadou Diouf (1996) represents a notable exception. Jean-Francois Bayart (1993) has also given youth some attention as both an 'ancient' and post-colonial identity.

agitation, revolution and the construction afterwards of a socialist society. The ASP under Karume appropriated historical memories of generational deference in order to cement party unity, and to distribute power and responsibilities. The Youth League recruited members who were generally male, somewhere beyond childhood and before serious physical decline, and who had usually not yet become heads of large households. Their status within the party commonly reflected their junior social status in their private lives; social juniors were not by definition considered in a position to dispense patronage, and, therefore, were considered to belong on the margins of decision-making circles in the party. They volunteered to perform whatever tasks their party seniors saw fit to assign them. Client youth sought to earn merit, anticipating opportunities in the future to call upon their elders' patronage and to obtain generational mobility. Thus although the very name of the Afro-Shirazi Party suggests politics based on race or ethnicity, the party was also founded on a generational alliance between elders and youth, patrons and clients. Youth carried out the will of party elders who devised strategies and gave orders (see also Burgess 1999). Such arrangements in nationalist practice nevertheless derived their power from memories of patriarchy and cherished cultural consensus, now 'petrified in a synchronic picture', 'reduced to folklore' (Hountondji 1996: 160).

The Youth League remained loyal to Karume as the ASP underwent a series of defections and electoral defeats. In 1959 the contest was between ASP politicians of 'mainlander' identity and 'Shirazi' identity. Such terms referred respectively to communities of shorter or longer historic residence in Zanzibar and which, particularly on Pemba Island, represented serious cultural differences between relative newcomers and those who regarded themselves as true sons of the soil. Leading Shirazi politicians left the ASP to form a third party, the Zanzibar and Pemba People's Party (ZPPP), which in 1961 formed an alliance with the ZNP (Lofchie 1965: 195, Mrina & Mattoke n.d. 68-69). The ASP then suffered electoral defeats to the ZNP-ZPPP alliance that resulted, upon the final withdrawal of the British in December 1963, in the installation of an independent ZNP-ZPPP government. At this juncture the ASP was deeply demoralized and divided between mutually hostile factions. Kassim Hanga and Hassan Nasser Moyo, leaders of the party's trade union movement, publicly recorded their disenchantment with Karume and began to openly cooperate with leaders of the Umma Party (Lofchie 1965: 261), with whom they shared a common socialist identity and the experience of studying in or visiting socialist countries. A further blow came on 2 January 1964 when four of the most educated and respected senior ASP leaders (Othman Shariff, Hasnu Makame, Idris Wakyl and Saleh Saadalla) formally resigned from the ASP in protest at Karume's failed leadership, due in part, they claimed, to his lack of formal education (Clayton 1981: 92).

The political lives of young party volunteers residing in rural districts or in poor urban neighborhoods of Unguja were, however, relatively unaffected by such divisions. They remained mobilized within local branches of the Youth League, whose chairman, Seif Bakari, shared with Karume the status of a relatively less-educated mainlander. As Karume prepared to submit to the reduced role of leader in parliament of a fractured and weakened opposition, Youth League leaders refused to accept their party's latest electoral defeat. Without assistance from party elders they mobilized hundreds of men through the elaborate structure of Youth League branches throughout Unguja. In January 1964 they executed an insurrection not in defiance of ASP elders but in order to seize power on their behalf through extra-constitutional means party seniors were unwilling to endorse, and who, for the most part, remained in hiding until success was assured.[35]

The revolutionaries appointed Karume as president, and reserved for themselves seats on a new 32-member Revolutionary Council. This council was indeed revolutionary, composed as it was of individuals who a few weeks earlier were for the most part social and political juniors, moving and working on the margins of urban society. Their claim on power and public reverence rested solely on their participation in the revolution. Before assuming seats on the Council they were not members of the urban elite society in Zanzibar, which claimed superior social status according to wealth, numbers of clients, piety, 'manners', ancestry, and scholarship. Their sudden ascension to privilege demonstrates the extent to which the revolution inverted a social pyramid and swept away hegemonic standards of culture and civilization that had been present on the islands since the 19th century. The contrast between their obscure origins and their inclusion after the revolution in the new ruling oligarchy was a vivid illustration of what the Zanzibari Revolution was supposed to be about.

---

[35] Despite the revolution's long shadow, who was actually responsible for its planning and execution remains a matter of controversy. See Babu (1991) and Mapuri (1996). While these two authors both give credit to the ASPYL, they disagree regarding the contribution of the Umma Party in the execution of the revolution. The author's own research (Burgess 2001), based upon extensive oral history data, suggests members of the Umma Party played a significant role in revolutionary events, but only in Zanzibar Town, and only after the key initial seizure of weapons by the ASPYL was already complete.

Revolution

For the youth leaders who organized the uprising, the idea was to seize power and to retaliate against a myriad of past offences. They possessed no fundamental text, guidebook or historical model on how to establish a new nation. This was keenly understood by Umma youth who joined the revolution within a few hours of its inception. After the Umma Party formally dissolved and merged with the ASP, Umma youth continued to regard themselves as a distinct faction within the emerging ruling establishment. They not only denied involvement in the most serious forms of racial violence recently taking place, they also claimed to possess 'new political ideas' necessary to give socialist meaning to the insurrection. 'For us we joined the Revolution because we thought they had manpower but no idea about how to organize and develop'[36] is a representative comment. The common distinction drawn in these memories is between young vanguard intellectuals, who were capable of exercising restraint and who spoke the modern language of socialism, and the lumpen 'illiterates of the ASP', without such a vocabulary and for whom the revolution had different meanings. Such Leninist distinctions appear in Babu's writing, even in the very title of his essay, 'The 1964 Revolution: Lumpen or Vanguard?' (1991: 240ff).[37]

During the brief '100 days' of the People's Republic of Zanzibar, Babu assumed a position of power in the Revolutionary Council second only to Karume himself, and Umma youth came to occupy influential positions in the new army and bureaucracy as officers and junior ministers. Their overseas training and education were essential to a new government serious about replacing a colonial civil service overwhelmingly staffed by British expatriates, Arabs and Asians. Ali Sultan recalled that 'we had to get our [Umma] boys in the administration, depending on their qualifications … if you get a chance to put someone in you are pushing your ideas as well. Mind you, the idea was to revolutionize the mind.'[38]

Relative unity among Umma comrades in the new government dramatically enhanced their capacity to shape public policy and encourage the growing socialist orientation of the revolutionary regime. They believed in socialist tradition as a set of ruling strategies and techniques to address the perceived 'backwardness' of Zanzibari society.[39] Like Ethiopian students in the 1960s and

---

[36] Interview, anonymous, Zanzibar Town, 8 July 1996.
[37] See also Wilson (1989: 12-3).
[38] Interview, Ali Sultan Issa, 18 July 2001.
[39] See Donham (1999: xviii). The problem of 'backwardness' in Ethiopian society was a defining issue for Ethiopian intellectuals from the beginning of the 20th century onwards (Bahru Zewde 2002: 99ff, 209).

1970s, they were drawn to the newly discovered global discourse not only for its 'Utopian vision of human liberation', but as 'a story of how a weak and backward collection of nationalities, located outside of Western Europe, attained unity, wealth, and international respect: the allegory of the Russian and, later, the Chinese, revolution' (Bahru Zewde 2002: 123). Socialist nations possessed comparable revolutionary narratives, were not compromised by associations with past regimes, and they spoke a common language of development and anti-colonialism. China, East Germany and the Soviet Union were also quick to offer aid and advice in order to make Zanzibar a showcase for socialist development in the region.

As a 'unifying code' (Bayart 1993: 173) and a set of discursive references, socialism also provided ideological sanction for the imperative of completing the African revolution in Zanzibar, revised as the triumph of workers and peasants over capitalist exploitation. As an imported discourse of universal improvement, socialism lent its prestige and distinguished provenance to local desires to overthrow Africans' unequal historical relationship to Zanzibar's minority communities, now recast as feudalists and capitalists. Although a 'derivative discourse' (Chatterjee 1986), it was the most coherent and systematic option. Once wedded to nationalist aspirations and readings of history, socialism soon lost its alien origins in a complex African reformulation of the meaning of progress, citizenship and modernity.

All of this represented the temporary realization of Babu's theories of a vanguard generation. While western observers nervously witnessed the emergence of a growing socialist consensus among Zanzibari political elites, Julius Nyerere initially looked upon these developments quite favourably. American Ambassador William Leonhart quoted Nyerere as saying:

> Karume had mass support but for him the fact that African revolution had been successful was enough.
> Left to himself he would merely replace Arabs with Africans in the same feudal structure. This is not enough. If real social reform did not come, Communists would take over. Babu had ideas necessary for thoroughgoing social reform. Zanzibar had to be modernized and no regime there could remain in power unless social change was rapid and effective.[40]

The prominence of Babu and his faction within the government in 1964 and the perception that their influence would continue to grow until they either

---

[40] Telegram, Leonhart to Secretary of State, 1/20/64, #6, National Security File, Country File, Africa – Zanzibar, Box 103, Zanzibar Cables and Memos, Vol. I, 1/64, LBJ Library.

overthrew or sidelined the more moderate Karume caused great anxiety among western observers. American representatives considered Babu to be personally at the epicentre of the 'communist virus' in East Africa. Eventually Nyerere himself was alarmed and pressured Karume to accept a political federation. The Tanganyika-Zanzibar union agreement announced in April 1964 should and has been considered then as an attempt to neutralize Babu's cohort of young socialists in a much larger sea of moderation (Wilson 1989). The federation between the mainland and islands of Tanzania gave Karume the full backing of Nyerere's police and armed forces in order to transfer Babu and other leading Umma figures to positions on the mainland and into political exile from Zanzibar.[41] Despite such developments, Leonhart reported in August 1964 that 'UMMA types have built themselves into second echelon all strategic ministries and organizations and will not be dislodged without fight'.[42] The CIA reported the following month: 'Babu and his colleagues have brought Zanzibar further under Communist influence, or at least for the time being, than has been the case in any other African country'.[43]

In the following years, while cadres of Umma ancestry continued to serve the revolutionary regime in various posts, the Youth League – mentored by advisors from the Eastern Bloc – expanded in terms of its mandate and institutional reach in Zanzibari society. For over a decade the Youth League was the primary instrument through which the post-colonial state sought to impose revolutionary discipline on the populace. The principle of generational deference and cooperation demonstrated in the events of the revolution gradually became the framework for national power relations afterwards. Youth sustained a prominent position in official discourse as the key constituency necessary for building the nation and enforcing conformity to the regime's rather demanding standards of citizenship. Karume and Bakari collaborated in an attempt to reconfigure society according to the patriarchal relationships of an imagined pre-colonial world. They believed that after the distortions of colonialism and capitalism, the revolution made possible the resurrection of generation as a fundamental organizing principle of the state. Generational identities promised eventual promotion within a society that claimed to have rid itself of all permanent class and ethnic divisions. Everyone could now find

---

[41] Dean McHenry (1994: 201-10) discusses the extent of Zanzibari socialists' influence in Nyerere's union government in the 1960s.
[42] Telegram, Leonhart to Secretary of State, 8/6/64, #52, United Republic of Tanganyika/Zanzibar, Zanzibar Cables, Vol. I, 4/64-1/65 [1 of 2], National Security File, Country File-Africa-Tanganyika, Box 100, LBJ Library.
[43] CIA memorandum, 9/29/64, URT-Zanzibar memos, Vol. I, 4/64-1/65, National Security File, Africa-Tanganyika, Box 100, LBJ Library.

inclusion if they were willing to cooperate in the assumed affectionate and deferential relations of the ancient past, rediscovered in the alliance within the ASP between juniors and seniors, and now enacted at a national level. The revolutionary state thus did not simply maintain colonial institutions intact; it sought to explore 'deeper currents' of its own history to find means by which to exercise power (Ellis 2002: 11). In an engagement between village discourse and the national apparatus left behind by the colonial regime, generational identities emerged as a primary idiom through which the state sought to order its affairs.

The politics of generation after the revolution were at the same time inclusive and exclusive: the state recruited, celebrated and foregrounded the vitality of youth on the public stage, and granted a measure of local power to its most committed cadres. And yet the state also excluded from its notions of citizenship images of youth that appeared to conflict with the nationalist imperative of building the nation and its selective invocation of African traditions.[44] Imagining the post-colonial state as a pre-colonial family in which clients affectionately serve their seniors inevitably provoked quarrels. Youth were supposed to serve as the vigilant defenders and enforcers of the new order, yet they were also accused of some of its most flagrant transgressions. Nationalist discourse reminded youth they were the inheritors of a revolutionary heritage: the very possession of such an inheritance – encompassing land, freedom and equality – implied the indebtedness of all juniors to the elders of the revolution. This sense of indebtedness served to legitimate subjection and to justify state intervention in the world of work, leisure and consumption in order to cultivate the social discipline considered necessary for nation building (Burgess 2002).

By the end of the 1960s, Karume and Bakari had constructed an elaborate security apparatus that empowered Karume to rule virtually by personal decree. Many former Umma observers in Tanzania, still retaining their own networks of 'comrades', were increasingly frustrated by what they considered to be Karume's betrayal of the principles of the revolution. In 1972 they launched a failed coup attempt that resulted in Karume's assassination and the imprison-ment of approximately seventy of their own number, including Babu and Ali Sultan.[45] Their years of imprisonment and their individual diasporas following release ended forever the political influence of the Umma cohort in Zanzibar.

---

[44]   Mamadou Diouf's assessment of Senegalese politics of generation is rather more bleak. He argues (1996: 225-26) that the '… logics of exclusion based on tradition, like those of the postcolony's treatment of the young, render public space as an adult terri-tory off limits to youth at the same time that it denies them a private space'.
[45]   See, for example, Chase (1976).

And yet, as recently as 1991, the vanguard imagined by Babu was still generational. After a lengthy description of the untrustworthiness of the petit bourgeoisie and the difficulties in the early 1960s of recruiting workers and peasants to a genuine liberation movement, Babu concludes his essay with a clear enunciation of what was to him the fundamental lesson of the Zanzibari Revolution. It 'brought about an atmosphere of revolt in which the revolutionary potential of the Zanzibar youth revealed itself with a dramatic impact' (Babu 1991: 245).

Generation and class

Recognizing that 'to enumerate is never an innocent operation' (Laclau & Mouffe 2001: 62), an appropriate concern appears to be how to identify Zanzibari historical actors. Are politically mobilized young people to be known as 'youth' or by some other name? The few Africanists who have ventured into this debate have tended to base their assumptions on whether or not 'youth' can be employed as a term signifying a discrete and homogeneous social category, with shared political or material interests that they pursue as a collective whole. In other words, they ask whether or not youth behave as classes are conventionally understood to behave.[46] Or, according to Bowles, identities of race (and for that matter, generation) are merely 'images' that need not concern historians. What ought to be recognized, however, are the considerable ambiguities involved in attempting to distinguish between class and generation in Africa. Bernardo Bernardi's employment of the term 'age class systems' suggests to what extent they have historically been conflated in Africa. If Marx defined classes according to their access to modes of production, anthropologists have described how access to women and reproduction determined men's generational status. For this reason it cannot be maintained in Africa that generation is a term ungrounded in material realities, or that it has only had an episodic historical role, without a legible history. The manner in which juniors in Africa have historically been cast as clients in relation to their elders has been as real as class divisions between workers and capitalists in Europe.

The ambiguity between generation and class may also be seen within the world's leading revolutionary tradition of the 20th century, which certainly made its influence felt in Zanzibar in the 1960s. Lenin did not always share Marx's convictions regarding the revolutionary potential of workers. In one of his most significant revisions of Marxism, Lenin (1962: 98) argued that the working

---

[46] See Seekings (1993), Allman (1993, 1990) and Rathbone (1991).

class, 'exclusively by its own effort', was unable to develop revolutionary consciousness; they depended on the 'educated representatives of the propertied classes', the 'intelligentsia'.[47] Lenin's lack of confidence in the potential of 'spontaneous' trade unionism to initiate revolutionary struggle explains his willingness to imagine a vanguard party drawing strength from youth of diverse social backgrounds. His writings in fact betray his pragmatic interest for over two decades in mobilizing youth for revolution and in canalizing into his revolutionary cause 'spontaneous' student protest that, in the last decades of Tsarist rule, had become a repetitive feature of the political landscape.[48] In 1905 Lenin wrote in a letter:

> We need young forces. I am for shooting on the spot anyone who presumes to say that there are no people to be had. The people in Russia are legion; all we have to do is to recruit young people more widely and boldly, more boldly and widely, and again more widely and again more boldly, *without fearing them*. This is a time of war. The youth – the students, and still more so the young workers – will decide the issue of the whole struggle. (ibid: 122)[49]

Lenin's views on youth were not derived from any theoretical text but emerged instead out of tactical necessity and his own reading of the concrete political circumstances of the time. Nor does it appear that Lenin advanced any specific theories of a vanguard generation other than to suggest students were 'the most responsive section of the intelligentsia', and therefore worthy of consideration as 'substitute proletarians' (Riviere 1977: 230). Soviet scholars in the 1970s sought to paper over the contradictions between Lenin's tactics and Marxist theory (Desyaterik & Latyshev 1977: 8). Since classical Marxism espoused the doctrine of the working class as the single *a priori* privileged agent of revolutionary struggle, it was not acceptable for credit to be granted to other identities assuming historical tasks specifically reserved for the working class. Post-Marxists, such as Ernesto Laclau and Chantal Mouffe, recognize, however, that the working class is not 'a privileged point of access to "the truth", which can be reached only by a limited number of subjects' (Laclau & Mouffe 2001: 192). In their efforts to both reappropriate and transcend Marxist intellectual tradition, Laclau and Mouffe argue that politics is not 'a rationalist game in

---

[47] A number of authors have remarked on Lenin's rejection of the working class as privileged agents of revolution. See Scott (1998: 149-57).
[48] For the best collection of Lenin's essays, speeches and letters that feature discussion of youth, see Lenin (1970).
[49] See also pp. 128-30, 142.

which social agents, perfectly constituted around interests, wage a struggle defined by transparent parameters' (ibid: 104).

The key issue, I believe, is whether or not the *process* wherein an identity such as generation gains local currency, despite its improvisational character, should be regarded worthy of historical research. If a local identity appears to scholars as neither discrete nor homogeneous, is it still historically significant? Should scholars consider African memories, vocabularies and categories of thought as valid tools by which to understand their strategies of dissent? Can we assume all social identities are equally pre-existent in African societies and that none emerge instead as 'a cultural label, a projection or repository' (Roseman 1995: 9) or as a result of nationalist discourse and practice?

Finally, why must we assume an identity emerges around certain shared interests rather than as a unique group of historical actors capable of serving a diversity of interests and causes? This last question helps to explain why generation has been buried in so much analysis on nationalism and revolution in Africa and elsewhere. The history of socialism in the 20th century, for example, reveals repeated instances where socialist strategists like Lenin and Babu poured considerable thought and energy into the mobilization of youth from heterogeneous class backgrounds. They targeted youth not in order to appeal to their material interests *per se*, but because of their observed characteristics as a generation which, local wisdom asserted, justified their status as privileged actors. The architects of the Umma Party sought to establish a 'conscious and disciplined' youth movement composed of recruits who, in some cases, were willing to abandon the supposedly monolithic interests of their race and/or class to serve the cause of African revolution. Such willingness to depart from the logic of dialectical materialism was, ironically, one of the imagined characteristics of their generation that justified their vanguard role in history.

Conclusion

The politics of generation in Zanzibar were at the centre of how nationalists first obtained and then exercised power. Despite the reality of ethnic and class conflicts in Zanzibar, generation functioned as an autonomous political identity, defying submersion. Nationalists called generation into official existence as one of several privileged agents, each with uncompleted historical tasks and responsibilities to fulfil. Youth nurtured a sense of their own importance in their nation's history as either a vanguard generation or as clients entrusted with the task of carrying out the will of party elders. Generational identities emerged through the unique circumstances of the post-war era, or as a result of the application to mass politics of pre-colonial ways of ordering the world. Before the revolution young people assumed political roles in reference to an imagined transnational cohort of vanguard youth, or to historical memories of patterns of social control. While among some youth there was an emerging conviction that their generation was endowed by history to occupy a position on the front line of progressive social change, others defined their role with respect to timeless 'natural' principles of patriarchy and clientalism. For both vanguards and clients, 'youth' as an identity bequeathed individuals a sense of dignity and recognized position in nationalist mobilization. Their status as youth had meaning in reference to either local or global discourses of power.

References

Afro-Shirazi Party 1973, *The Afro-Shirazi Party: A Liberation Movement*, Zanzibar: Government Printer.

Allman, J-M. 1990, 'The Young Men and the Porcupine: Class, Nationalism and Asante's Struggle for Self-Determination, 1954-57', *Journal of African History*, 31: 263-79.

Allman, J-M. 1993, *The Quills of the Porcupine*, Madison: University of Wisconsin Press.

Amory, D. 1994, 'The Politics of Identity on Zanzibar', Stanford University, PhD thesis.

Anderson, B. 1991, *Imagined Communities: Reflections on the Origin and Spread of Nationalism*, (revised edition), London: Verso.

Babu, A.M. 1991, 'The 1964 Revolution: Lumpen or Vanguard?', in A. Sheriff & E. Ferguson (eds), *Zanzibar Under Colonial Rule*, London: James Currey, pp. 220-48.

Bahru Zewde 2002, *Pioneers of Change in Ethiopia: The Reformist Intellectuals of the Early Twentieth Century*, Athens, Ohio: Ohio University Press.

Bayart, J-F. 1993, *The State in Africa: The Politics of the Belly*, translated from French by M. Harper, C. and E. Harrison, London: Longman.

Bennett, N. 1978, *A History of the Arab State in Zanzibar,* Cambridge: Methuen & Co.

Bernardi, B. 1985, *Age Class Systems: Social Institutions and Politics Based on Age*, Cambridge: Cambridge University Press.

Bowles, B.D. 1991, 'The Struggle for Independence, 1946-63', in A. Sheriff & E. Ferguson (eds), *Zanzibar Under Colonial Rule*, London: James Currey, pp. 79-106.

Burgess, T. 1999, 'Remembering Youth: Generation in Revolutionary Zanzibar', *Africa Today*, 46 (2): 29-52.

Burgess, T. 2001, 'Youth and the Revolution: Mobility and Discipline in Zanzibar, 1950-80', Indiana University, PhD thesis.

Burgess, T. 2002, 'Cinema, Bell Bottoms and Miniskirts: Struggles Over Youth and Citizenship in Revolutionary Zanzibar', *International Journal of African Historical Studies*, 35 (2): 287-314.

Burgess, T. in press, 'An Imagined Generation: Umma Youth in Nationalist Zanzibar', in G. Maddox, J. Giblin & Y.Q. Lawi (eds), *In Search of a Nation: Histories of Authority and Dissidence From Tanzania: Essays in Honor of I.M. Kimambo*, London: James Currey.

Cameron, J. & W. Dodd 1970, *Society, Schools and Progress in Tanzania*, Oxford: Pergamon Press.

Chase, H. 1976, 'The Zanzibar Treason Trial', *Review of African Political Economy*, 6 (3): 14-33.

Chatterjee, P. 1986, *Nationalist Thought and the Colonial World: A Derivative Discourse?* Tokyo: Zed.

Clayton, A. 1981, *The Zanzibar Revolution and its Aftermath*, London: C. Hurst & Co.

Cooper, F. 1987, *From Slaves to Squatters*, New Haven: Yale University Press.

Cooper, F. 1994, 'Conflict and Connection: Rethinking Colonial African History', *American Historical Review* 99 (5): 1516-45.

Desyaterik, V. & A. Latyshev 1977, *Lenin: Youth and the Future*, Moscow: Progress Publishers.

Deutsch, J-G. 2002, 'Jazz at the Goan Club: The Making of Modern Zanzibar c.1945-1964', paper presented at the African Studies Association Conference, Washington, DC.

Diouf, M. 1996, 'Urban Youth and Senegalese Politics: Dakar 1988-1994', *Public Culture*, 8: 225-49.

Donham, D. 1999, *Marxist Modern: An Ethnographic History of the Ethiopian Revolution*, Berkeley: University of California Press.

Ellis, S. 2002, 'Writing Histories of Contemporary Africa', *Journal of African History*, 43: 1-26.

Fair, L. 1994, 'Pastimes and Politics: A Social History of Zanzibar's Ng'ambo Community, 1890-1950', University of Minnesota, PhD thesis.

Geschiere, P. 1982, *Village Communities and the State: Changing Relations Among the Maka of South-Eastern Cameroon since the Colonial Conquest*, London: Kegan Paul International.

Glassman, J. 2000, 'Sorting Out the Tribes: The Creation of Racial Identities in Colonial Zanzibar's Newspaper Wars', *Journal of African History*, 41: 395-428.

Glassman, J. forthcoming, 'Slower than a Massacre: The Intellectual Origins of Racial Nationalism in Colonial Zanzibar, 1927-1957'.

Gulliver, P.H. 1963, *Social Control in an African Society*, Boston: Boston University Press.

Gurnah, A. 1996, *Admiring Silence*, New York: The New Press.

Hamdani, M.M.A. 1981, 'Zanzibari Newspapers, 1902 to 1974', University of Dar es Salaam, MA thesis.

Hountondji, P. 1996, *African Philosophy, Myth and Reality*, translated by H. Evans, Bloomington: Indiana University Press.

Iliffe, J. 1995, *Africans: The History of a Continent*, Cambridge: Cambridge University Press.

Laclau, E. & C. Mouffe 2001, *Hegemony and Socialist Strategy: Towards a Radical Democratic Politics*, London: Verso.

Lenin, V.I. 1962, *What is to Be Done?*, translated by J. Fineberg & G. Hanna, New York: Penguin Books.

Lenin, V.I. 1970, *On Youth*, Moscow: Progress Publishers.

Lofchie, M. 1965, *Zanzibar: Background to Revolution*, Princeton: Princeton University Press.

Lovett, M. 1996, 'Elders, Migrants and Wives: Labor Migration and the Renegotiation of Intergenerational, Patronage and Gender Relations in Highland Buha, Western Tanzania, 1921-1962', Columbia University, PhD thesis.

Mansfield, P. 1965, *Nasser's Egypt*, Baltimore: Penguin Books.

Mapuri, O.R. 1996, *Zanzibar: The 1964 Revolution: Achievements and Prospects*, Dar es Salaam: Terna Publishers.

McHenry, D. 1994, *Limited Choices: The Political Struggle for Socialism in Tanzania*, London: Lynne Rienner Publishers.

Moore, S.F. & P. Puritt 1977, *The Chagga and Meru of Tanzania*, London: International African Institute.

Mrina B.F. & W.T. Mattoke n.d., *Mapambano ya Ukombozi Zanzibar*, Dar es Salaam: Tanzania Publishing House.

Petterson, D. 2002, *Revolution in Zanzibar: An American's Cold War Tale*, United States: Westview Press.

Rathbone, R. 1991, 'The Young Men and the Porcupine', *Journal of African History*, 32: 333-38.

Raum, O.F. 1940. *Chagga Childhood: A Description of Indigenous Education in an East African Tribe*, Oxford: Oxford University Press.

Riviere, C. 1977, *Guinea: The Mobilization of a People,* Ithaca, NY: Cornell University Press.

Roseman, M. 1995, 'Introduction: Generation Conflict and German History, 1770-1968', in M. Roseman (ed.), *Generations in Conflict: Youth Revolt and Generation Formation in Germany, 1770-1968*, Cambridge: Cambridge University Press, pp. 1-46.

Scott, J.C. 1998, *Seeing Like a State: How Certain Schemes to Improve the Human Condition Have Failed*, New Haven: Yale University Press.

Seekings, J. 1993, *Heroes or Villains? Youth Politics in the 1980s*, Johannesburg: Ravan Press.

Sheriff, A. 1991, 'Introduction: A Materialist Approach to Zanzibar's History', in A. Sheriff & E. Ferguson (eds), *Zanzibar Under Colonial Rule*, London: James Currey, pp. 1-8.

Sheriff, A. 2001, 'Race and Class in the Politics of Zanzibar', *Afrika Spektrum*, 36 (3): 301-318.

Wilson, A. 1989, *US Foreign Policy and Revolution: The Creation of Tanzania,* London: Pluto Press.

Wilson, F.B. 1978 (Zanzibar, 1939), 'A Note on Adult Literacy amongst the Rural Population of the Zanzibar Protectorate', as cited in N. Bennett, *A History of the Arab State in Zanzibar,* Cambridge: Methuen & Co.

Wilson, M. 1959, *Community Ritual Among the Nyakyusa*, Oxford: Oxford University Press.

PART II:
State, crisis and the mobilization of youth

4

Clash of generations? Youth identity, violence and the politics of transition in Kenya, 1997-2002

Peter Mwangi Kagwanja

This chapter examines the marginality of youth in Kenyan politics and their efforts to recapture and refashion power. Conceiving youth in political rather than biological terms, their visible powerlessness is traced genealogically to the imperatives of the patrimonial politics of the Kenyatta (1963-1978) and the Moi (1978-2002) eras when constitutional encumbrance, 'public executions' or assassinations and cooptation disempowered and marginalized youth. In the multi-party era, the Moi state recruited ethnic militias, vigilantes and 'Majeshi ya Wazee' (Armies of the Elders) to terrorize and disenfranchise opponents, ushering in a lumpen moment in Kenyan politics. From the margins, the Mungiki youth movement crusaded for a new moral order and realignment of the generational balance of power in favour of youth empowerment. This chapter employs the Gramscian concept of hegemony to understand the dynamics of generational tensions and to problematize the concept of youth within the broader canvas of democratic transition in Kenya.

Introduction

It is a paradox that change to political pluralism in Kenya in the early 1990s marginalized the youth in politics and entrenched the hegemony of the dominant elders in the ruling and opposition parties alike. Members of the political old guard like Daniel Moi, Oginga Odinga and Mwai Kibaki, who dominated Kenya's political arena from the 1950s onwards, assumed the leadership of their respective parties in multi-party politics. Politically eligible youths – widely taunted as 'Young Turks' – were rendered powerless and kept in the service of their respective elders. This marginality of Kenyan youth in the multi-party era resonates forlornly with Cruise O'Brien's (1996: 55) apt remarks: '[T]hese young people are very poorly equipped to make their opposition effective: with their limited resources they are easily manipulated by their elders'. However, as the politics of the Moi succession gathered momentum in the run-up to the 2002 elections, public discourse in Kenya started to clamour for a generational transfer of power to young politicians. President Moi's capitulation to public demands to pave the way for a young generation of politicians was a salutary step. However, the process of the transfer of power was shrouded in deep suspicion as the dominant elders were thought to be manipulating the discourse of youth power to perpetuate their hegemony by enthroning youth proxies. These suspicions were given weight by a curious government trend that allowed public displays of violence by youths aligned to the ruling party. The culture of vigilantism, banditry, urban criminality and general youth violence, which marred the multi-party elections in 1992 and 1997, gave rise to the widespread prediction that Kenya would descend into an inferno of violence in the wake of the crucial elections scheduled for December 2002 (Rutten *et al.* 2001, Throup & Honsby 1998). The peace that marked the transition from the Moi regime to that of a new coalition of parties that went under the acronym of NARC (National Rainbow Coalition) poured cold water on this 'prophesy of doom'. But the celebration of NARC's victory was shattered by a fresh wave of youth violence that bedevilled Kenya's post-election political environment.

This new orgy of violence was identified with a group called *Mungiki*. In January 2003 alone, its followers killed nearly fifty people in different parts of Kenya, sparking off a bloody confrontation between the group's followers and the security forces, which continued in the following months. Grace Wamue's seminal study of the *Mungiki* identified it as a revivalist religious-political movement that had sprouted among Kenya's most populous ethnic group, the Kikuyu (Wamue 2001). The *Mungiki*, she argued, did not only signify a return to Kikuyu traditional culture and religious beliefs, but the group also had a long ideological pedigree in the militancy of the Mau Mau movement that had waged an armed struggle against the British in the 1950s. In a perceptive article, David Anderson (2002: 531-55) shifted the debate from Wamue's religion-centred approach to a political analysis of *Mungiki*, situating it within the broader social political canvas of the breakdown of public order and the emerging culture of vigilantism, youth criminality, and extortion in Kenyan politics. Writing in 2002 against the backdrop of the gathering electoral storm in Kenya, he underlined *Mungiki*'s 'stridently ethnocentric' character and its agenda of reviving 'Gikuyu values in the "Kingdom of Kirinyaga"', which 'implies a political restoration of Gikuyu power through the removal of the oppressive Nyayo regime of President

Moi'. *Mungiki*, Anderson argued, was a voice and vehicle of 'Gikuyu political unity and cultural consolidation' whose redemptive message 'is for the Gikuyu, not the Kenyan, nation' (ibid: 535-36). In a previous article, this author (Kagwanja 2003a: 25-49) traced *Mungiki's* descent from a pristine movement that embraced a pan-Kenyan ideology and crusaded for a new moral order into a criminal and opportunistic 'gang for hire' under the thumb of the then-ruling elite.

Mungiki's post-election violence raised serious questions relating to youth identity, culture and violence in the context of generational tensions within and between Kenya's ethnic groups. One of the most intriguing aspects is that, in spite of *Mungiki's* virulently anti-Moi political stance, the movement supported lock, stock and barrel Moi's hand-picked candidate, Uhuru Kenyatta, a son of Kenya's first president, Jomo Kenyatta. It is highly instructive that Uhuru Kenyatta ascended to power on a generational discourse and amid mounting pressure on the aging Moi to endorse a youthful successor.[1] Arguably, the nomination of Mwai Kibaki – a Kikuyu – as the flag-bearer of the opposition's presidential bid would under normal circumstances have complicated *Mungiki's* political choices. Their support for the youthful Uhuru against Kibaki – who was in his early seventies – seems to have been determined more by generational than ethnic considerations. But there was also an ideological touch stemming from intra-Kikuyu politics. While Kibaki's consistent gentlemanly politics increasingly made him the candidate of choice across Kenya's ethnic rainbow, his 'soft' politics never endeared him to the militant political opinion held by Kikuyu lumpen youth, including *Mungiki*.[2] Perhaps more significantly, *Mungiki* embraced a vision of generational transfer of power based on a traditional Kikuyu system called *Ituika* ('break'), which guaranteed a transfer of power from the elders to the younger generation. Their single electoral agenda in 2002 was to ensure such a generational break (*Ituika*). Thus, although *Mungiki's* post-election violence lacked ethnic rationale, in Anderson's sense, because it was directed against the 'Kikuyu government', President Mwai Kibaki and pre-dominantly against the Kikuyu population, its rationale was a lethal combi-nation of generational clash and a legacy of opportunistic youth violence of the Moi era. This analysis raises a fundamental problem. How do we reconcile

---

[1] In a strange twist, the Uhuru candidacy sparked off a debilitating protest within the ranks of the ruling party (KANU) and, eventually, triggered a mass defection from KANU to the opposition of some of the 'Young Turks' with ethnic clout like Raila Odinga, Kalonzo Musyoka and Kipruto Kirwa who dramatically increased the electoral chances of the opposition.

[2] In 1992, Kikuyu lumpen youth voted overwhelmingly for Kibaki's ethnic challenger, Kenneth Matiba, who became Moi's closest rival.

Mungiki's vision of political transition from the gerontocratic orthodoxy of the Moi era to a new democratic dispensation that empowers youths and social movements, on the one hand, and its reactionary violence, on the other? This chapter attempts to address this question.

Thinking through youth politics and violence
From the early 1990s, the wind of change in favour of democratic transition that swept through Africa turned the intellectual spotlight on social movements as embodiments of the spirit of resistance against all forms of tyranny and efforts to liberate and democratize the African 'public sphere'. The phenomenal stalling of the democratic project throughout the continent, the implosion or withering away of the African state, and the consequent upsurge of civil wars, urban gangsterism, vigilantism, banditry and diverse forms of criminal violence engendered a rethinking of social movements. This led to a shift from the more traditional social movements conceived and organized around class and national issues to social movements based on 'identity'. As Cohen (1985: 667) aptly remarked, the identity-centred social movements 'target the social domain of "civil society" rather than the economy or the state, raising issues concerned with democratization of structures of everyday life and focusing on forms of communication and social identity'. Moreover, the focus on identity-based social movements was given a new lease of life by perspectives that stress the agency of subaltern categories and the cultural discourse(s) that inform their action (Werbner & Ranger 1996). The position of social movements of youths in the deepening African crisis became a subject of increasing intellectual curiosity.

In his study of youth politics in South Africa in the 1980s, Jeremy Seekings rightly observed that although youth is a transitory category between childhood and adulthood, in the context of sweeping social change in African childhood such social markers as rituals of initiation or rites of passage from youth to adulthood are de-emphasized and the 'distinction between them blurred' (Seekings 1993: 1). By the same token, confronted with the dilemma of setting clear biological markers between youth and adulthood, many analysts have insisted on defining 'youth' 'in political rather than biological terms' (Cruise O'Brien 1996: 55). The youth category occupies the extreme end of the generational divide between youths and elders as political categories contesting political power. The construction of the African youth is marked by a Manichean dichotomy between an 'emancipatory' youth that is militant and politicized and an 'apocalyptic' youth that is destructive and rebellious (Sitas 1992: 3, Seekings 1993: 2). However, this Manichean conception tends to project the youth in society as a unified rather than a differentiated category.

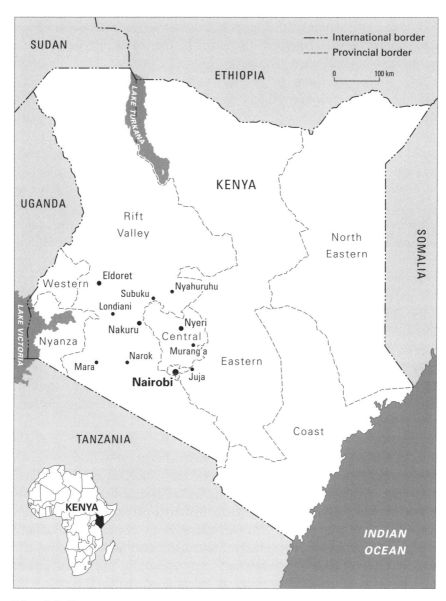

Map 4.1: Kenya

Thus, young people constitute different 'publics', to borrow Michael Warner's (2002) term, articulating different political discourses rather than being a unified 'public' with a common discourse. In the nationalist movement and under the post-colonial state, two groups of youths became clearly discernible: the 'elite' youths and 'lumpens' recently defined by Ibrahim Abdullah (1997: 73) as 'the largely unemployed and unemployable youths, mostly male, who live by their wits or who have one foot in ... the informal or underground economy'. The best examples of lumpen youth in politics are the *veranda* boys of the Convention People's Party in Ghana – who were not violent – and the urban support of the Mau Mau movement in Kenya (which was violent).

In contrast, there are groups of well-financed youth elites in trade-union politics, such as the youthful Tom Mboya and his Kenya Federation of Labour, which were central in the politics of decolonization. However, in the context of generational conflict, the youth category, in all its diversity, constitutes a powerless 'counter-public' to the hegemony of the elders. Nancy Fraser, contributing to the debate on Jürgen Habermas's 'public sphere' (Habermas 1998), identified 'counter-publics' with 'subalterns'.[3] In a similar vein, Cruise O'Brien (1996: 55), echoing Jean-François Bayart and others, rightly defines 'youth politics' as politics 'from below'. This implies that the study of youth politics in Africa within the broader context of generational conflict amounts to a study of 'the politics of powerlessness' (Bayart et al. 1992: 40). It is also a study of the rise of the counter-hegemony of powerless youths against the hegemonic elders who dominate the state, political parties and other instruments of power.

The question of empowering the youth within the framework of generational conflict in Africa is illuminated by the Gramscian concept of hegemony, which clearly defines relations of power between the state and civil society. The primary task of the youths' struggle for power is to establish the hegemony of civil society, which Gramsci defines as the realm of public opinion and culture. Anderson (1976/77) underlines a stable state as being central to the Gramscian idea of the hegemony of civil society. 'Although autonomous of the state', he writes, 'this life [of civil society] cannot be independent of it, for the guarantor of the autonomy of the civil society can be none other than the state.' Youth violence and the consequent instability of the state in Africa are hindrances to the establishment of the hegemony of a youth-led civil society.

---

[3] See also Fraser (1992) whose identification of counter-publics with subalterns has been rightly questioned by Michael Warner and Craig Calhoun, among others, who posit that many groups not clearly in subaltern positions can also challenge the dominant culture or institutions and constitute a counter-public opposed to the dominant patterns in the public sphere.

Confronted with proliferating youth violence in Africa, theorists have revisited Frantz Fanon's (1967) dichotomy between the violence of the colonizer and the violence of the colonized. The former, Fanon argued, is devoid of any iota of moral justification and dehumanizes the colonized subject. This view is echoed in Hannah Arendt's (1975) 'dehumanizing' state violence against its citizens typified by the Holocaust in Nazi Germany or, more recently, spates of ethnic cleansing in the former Yugoslavia and the 1994 genocide in Rwanda. In contrast, the violence of the colonized people is considered emancipatory and humanizing, and therefore justified. Commentaries by Jeremy Seekings (1993) and Monique Marks (2001) eulogize youth violence against the apartheid regime in South Africa as 'liberatory' violence. Between these two extremes is a form of violence that Mahmoud Mamdani (2001, 2002) has defined as 'non-revolutionary' and 'senseless' violence because it is reactionary and lacks an emancipatory agenda. Intellectuals and publics have increasingly identified this kind of violence with 'nationalism', a term that is now widely used to describe the sensibilities linked to culture, ethnicity and/or religion (Anderson 1992). This form of nationalism, Hobsbawm (1990) argues, has acquired a quite different, and reactionary, form to that of the emancipatory nationalism of the 19th century which was strongly associated with the struggle for national democratization. In African studies, this nationalism finds its best articulation in Bruce Berman's (1998) 'uncivil nationalism', which is about identity politics or claims to power on the basis of identity labels – Croat, Serb, Hindu, Kalenjin or Tutsi.

The resurgence of this form of reactionary nationalism has given rise to what Mary Kaldor (1999) christens 'new wars' – new because they lack 'the geopolitical or ideological goals of earlier wars' and the liberatory character of earlier wars of de-colonization, and they are largely internal or civil wars. As Patrick Muana (1997) has clearly shown, violence in such countries as Sierra Leone and Liberia is based on youth culture that, although laying claim to an emancipatory agenda, is completely opportunistic. Of the youth violence in Africa, Abdullah (1997: 73) writes that 'the new movements – with the sole exception of Museveni's NRM – are more concerned with having people who could wield weapons in the name of "revolution"'. Studies of youth culture and violence in relatively stable states such as South Africa and Kenya have focused on vigilantism that thrives on reinvented traditional or tribal cultures (Anderson 2002). Researchers have linked this form of youth violence to the ubiquitous phenomenon of 'informal repression' (Kirschke 2000). The idea of 'informal repression' as an aspect of youth violence is clearly captured by the concept of 'marionette politics' which refers to the pervasive use of 'tribal authorities, institutions and militias in as diverse countries as Nigeria, Cameroon, Malawi, South Africa and Kenya to repress the opposition', undermine the democratic process and sustain the ruling elite (Kagwanja 2001). This chapter argues that youth involvement in this culture of violence has tended to de-legitimize their politics and claims to power and entrench the hegemony of the dominant elders.

Youth and generational conflict in Kenya: An historical overview

The involvement of youth in politics and in political violence in Kenya, as elsewhere in Africa, is not new. Lumpens consisting of unemployed and unemployable youths and idle young African soldiers laid off after the Second World War formed the bulk of the support for the militant labour strikes in the heady politics of the pre-emergency period (1942-1952). In a sense, these lumpens were to the Kenya African Union (KAU) what the *veranda* boys were to Kwame Nkrumah's Convention People's Party in Ghana. However, youth politics grew increasingly violent with the arrival of the Mau Mau on the scene. The lumpen youth, mostly Kikuyu, belonging to the *Riika ria forty* (forty age-group or those initiated in 1940) formed the rank and file of the Kenya Land and Freedom Army, while some young ex-servicemen provided its leadership (Kaggia 1975). Historiography on the politics of decolonization has tended to give pride of place to class, racial, ethnic and, more recently, gender struggles within and between political parties, and to obscure the equally important generational conflict between elders and youths. Tension between elders and youths in Kenyan politics has a long historical pedigree in the gerontocratic politics of the nationalist struggle that was overlaid with the generational conflicts of the post-colonial era. Although the youth never formed a unified category, in the context of generational conflict they tended to forge a common front.

In addition to the lumpen youth, a category of relatively educated, employed but militant elite youth emerged in the 1940s. This multi-ethnic, multi-racial category of militant elite youths consisted of such nationalist icons as Bildad Kaggia, Paul Ngei, Fred Kubai and the indomitable Makhan Singh and Pio Gama Pinto. They mobilized around a workers' identity using the platform provided by the emergent trade-union movement to challenge the pervasive hegemony of gerontocratic chiefs in local authorities and that of elders in the Kenya African Union (KAU), thus radicalizing nationalist politics and paving the way for the Mau Mau armed struggle in the 1950s (see Singh 1969, Kaggia 1975, Clough 1990). The Declaration of Emergency in 1952 and the subsequent detention of elderly politicians and militant youths in the KAU and the trade-union movement created a leadership vacuum that was gradually filled by young moderate politicians like Tom Mboya, Daniel Moi and Ronald Ngala and by elderly militant leaders such as Oginga Odinga and James Gichuru. These youths cooperated with the dominant elders in the KAU on issues of common nationalist concern, but relations revealed sharp generational tensions. The young politicians constituted a counter-hegemonic force to the elders' hegemony in the public sphere. However, while the counter-public of the lumpen youth including the *Riika ria forty* fits in Fraser's subaltern classification, the counter-public of the elite youth, like Kubai, Kaggia or Tom Mboya, was not subaltern. David Goldsworthy (1982a, 1982b), Tom Mboya's biographer, has eloquently narrated the long-drawn-out generational rivalry between Mboya and Oginga Odinga. In an earlier comment on the Odinga-Mboya rivalry we made the argument that:

> While Mboya rose to national politics on the wings of 'politics of utility' in an urban constituency, Odinga scaled to the top on the 'politics of identity' in the rural environment in Luo Nyanza. But Mboya's differences with Odinga were based more on personal, cultural and ideological grounds than on diametrically opposed opinions on the nationalist project. Younger than Odinga, Mboya did not share in his gerontocratic worldview, particularly on leadership. Therefore, he was not prepared to cool his heels and allow the elderly Odinga to call the shots in … politics. Odinga was never enchanted with Mboya's drum-major instinct, but at the same time he never ceased to acknowledge that Mboya was a talent. (Kagwanja 1999)

Young Mboya made successful moves to clip Odinga's political wings. Manipulating Cold War ideological politics, he portrayed Odinga as a communist protégé and, with a nod from President Jomo Kenyatta, eventually manoeuvred him out of power in 1966.[4] As the powerful Minister for Justice and Constitutional Affairs, the Secretary-General of Kenya's ruling party (KANU), the leader of Kenya's only legal trade-union body (COTU), a key mover in pan-Africanist politics and a compatriot of such pan-African icons as Kwame Nkrumah and Julius Nyerere, and a friend of influential American leaders including J.F. Kennedy, Mboya, in his mid-thirties, was undisputedly the most powerful youth on the African continent. Paradoxically, Mboya's political triumph and the threat that his trans-ethnic and transnational political stature, constituency and connections posed to the politically embedded elders and his young contemporaries in the Kenyatta patrimony were to haunt youth politics in post-colonial Kenya. Tom Mboya's is a tragic narrative of the rise, decline and marginalization of the youth in Kenyan politics.

---

[4] In a highly controversial party convention in 1966, Odinga was stripped of his vice-presidential powers. Angry and seething with feelings of betrayal by his old friend and compatriot Jomo Kenyatta, Odinga tendered his resignation from the government and political party, leaving Mboya as the unchallenged leader and man after the aging and sickly Kenyatta's mantle.

Discipline and punishment: Assault on youth politics

The patrimonial Kenyatta and Moi states relied heavily on violence to discipline and punish errant youth politicians. Elders' violence against politically delinquent and ambitious youth in post-colonial Kenya had a distinct similarity with what Michel Foucault (1977) graphically described as public executions in 18th-century Europe with their emphasis on the body as the object of punishment and punishment as a public spectacle. Pio Gama Pinto, a militant young nationalist and parliamentarian of Asian descent who was eulogized by Odinga (1967) in his autobiography as the chief strategist for the Kenyan left in the ideologically turbulent 1960s, fell to an assassin's bullet on a sunny morning in February 1964. Tom Mboya was gunned down in the centre of Nairobi at high noon on 5 July 1969, sparking a wave of ethnic violence between the Kikuyu and Luo groups.

The most grisly and perfect case of 'public execution' of rebellious youth politicians was that of Josiah Mwangi Kariuki, a wealthy and youthful ex-Mau Mau detainee and populist Kikuyu politician who was murdered, mutilated and dumped in the Ngong Forest on 2 March 1975. If Mboya's assassination sparked off a wave of ethnic violence in Nairobi and Kisumu, then Kariuki's horrific and brutal death precipitated nationwide protests resulting in 2 March becoming a day of riots and violent clashes between university students and security forces for decades. Against the backdrop of mounting pressure on the government to introduce political pluralism, political leaders from all walks of life filed past the charred remains of Dr Robert Ouko, Kenya's popular foreign minister who was brutally murdered in October 1990. Whatever impact these ghastly 'public executions' had on Kenya's public psyche, they deprived the country of its best crop of youthful leaders and blazed the trail for the complete marginalization of the younger generation in politics. Throughout the one-party era, youths became pawns in the chess game of the dominant elders in Kenyatta and Moi states.

'Majeshi ya Wazee': Violence against lumpen youth

The multi-party era was indelibly associated with the phenomenon that came to be called *Majeshi ya Wazee* (Armies of the Elders). The culture of state-sponsored *majeshi* or militias evolved as part of the manipulation of youth by the hegemonic elders in the single-party politics. Hard on the heels of the imposition of a *de jure* one-party state in 1982, the KANU Youth Wing (KYW) was formed as a tool to monitor, silence and even punish dissents, especially the lumpens in urban and rural Kenya. The revival of the KANU Youth Wing was a move to get Kenya's growing lumpen youth under control. KANU youths were deployed to markets, workplaces, bus stations and *matatu* (taxi) termini to assert KANU's authority. The cruelty of the KYW elicited violent responses from

Kenyan youths, resulting in spiralling bloody confrontations with the lumpens, including touts, shoeshine and parking boys, vendors and hawkers. *Matatu* operators staged numerous protests against the harassment of touts and their workers, and extortion by members of the KANU youth wing. There were reports galore of injuries and occasional deaths arising from these confrontations. In 1989, a clash between KANU youths and hawkers, touts and shoeshine boys reportedly led to deaths in Nairobi, forcing the government to warn the KYW against the excessive use of violence in their duties. So brutal and powerful was the KANU Youth Wing that it overshadowed the police in its use of force against real and perceived 'anti-Nyayos' (anti-Moi supporters) among the youths in Kenya's rural areas and urban slums. Moreover, the dominant elders engaged the services of KANU youths to terrorize their youthful opponents. In the mounting clamour for a multi-party system in the early 1990s, the KANU Youth Wing was allowed to use violence to hunt down and silence multi-party advocates and their supporters. KANU youths worked in tandem with the dreaded General Service Unit (GSU) to break up meetings of multi-party advocates. They also joined forces with city council *askaris* (guards) in violent operations to demolish the shanty homes and kiosks of lumpen supporters of political pluralism in Kenya's main urban areas (African Rights 1997, Ndolo 1990).

Kenya's return to political pluralism witnessed the fizzling out of the KANU youth wing and the proliferation of different forms of youth violence in the service of the ruling gerontocracy. From 1991, mysterious tribal militias such as 'Kalenjin warriors' and 'Maasai *morans*' appeared in President Moi's Rift Valley Province. By November 1993, these roving warrior bands had killed nearly 2,000 people and displaced over 300,000 others in Kenya's Nyanza, Western and Rift Valley Provinces. A parliamentary committee set up in May 1992 to probe the causes of violence in parts of Kenya accused high-ranking Kalenjin and Maasai politicians in the Moi government of recruiting and funding warriors who carried out the attacks on non-Kalenjins. According to the report: 'The fighters were on hire and were paid sums ranging from Ksh 500 [US$6.50] for safe return from the clash front, Ksh 1,000 [US$13] to Ksh 2,000 [US$26] for killing one person or burning a grass-thatched house and Ksh 10,000 [US$128] per permanent house burned' (Republic of Kenya 1993: 75).

KANU leaders also openly deployed Maasai youths (*morans*) in public places to deal with opposition. In March 1993, a group of Maasai *morans* dressed in traditional costume attacked opposition supporters at the state opening of parliament. The KANU Secretary-General Joseph Kamoth admitted that the *morans* were part of a 3,000-strong youth squad hired by KANU for the occasion to deal with opposition supporters.[5] Even more bizarrely, Maasai *morans* accompanying a senior cabinet minister to the World Conference on Human Rights in Vienna in June 1993 vandalized an exhibition of photos on ethnic violence mounted by a prominent environmentalist, Prof. Wangari Maathai.[6] In the 1992 and 1997 elections, Kalenjin warriors and Maasai *morans* in the Rift Valley and Digo warriors at the coast terrorized, displaced and killed populations suspected of voting for the opposition, disenfranchising thousands of voters and seriously compromising the credibility and fairness of the electoral process (African Rights 1997, Mazrui 2001: 275-95). Rural-based ethnic militias in the service of elders appeared in other parts of Kenya. Among these were the *Chinkororo* (sing: *Enkororo*) and the *Amachuma* ('a piece of metal') youth gangs among the Abagusii community in western Kenya. The *Sungu Sungu* militia also emerged in western Kenya among the Kuria community (Kagwanja 2003b).

A new culture of urban-based vigilantism started with the formation of the infamous *Jeshi la Mzee* (Old Man's or President Moi's army) by senior KANU operatives in April 1997.[7] *Jeshi la Mzee* was a refurbished KANU Youth Wing reinforced by a freshly recruited army of jobless urban youth. It also became a generic term for a plethora of private militias and hit squads organized and funded by KANU bigwigs across the country. Among the private militias that went under the rubric of *Jeshi la Mzee* were numerous hit squads organized by KANU leaders such as *Jeshi la Mbela* (Mbela's army) at the coast, *Jeshi la Embakasi* in Nairobi, and *Jeshi la King'ole* in eastern Kenya (Kenya Human Rights Commission 1997: 51). These 'armies of elders' disrupted opposition rallies and terrorized those agitating for constitutional change.

Opposition leaders also organized youth squads to protect themselves from the violence of the 'Armies of the Elders'. The most publicized of the opposition's armed groups is the Runyenjes Football Club in Embu in eastern Kenya.[8] Before being outlawed by the government, the Runyenjes Football Club is said to have played a role similar to Winnie Mandela's football club, which doubled up as an entertainment group and a protection unit. There also sprung up within the urban environment of Nairobi youth groups that came to represent the vigilante phenomenon in urban Kenya. Among these groups was the *Taliban*, which emerged in Nairobi's Kariobangi area in response to growing

---

[5] 'Morans: Speaker Wants Kamotho to Explain', *Daily Nation*, 2 April 1993, 'A Convoluted Affair', *Weekly Review*, 9 April 1993.
[6] 'Maathai's Vienna Stand Raided', *Daily Nation*, 20 June 1993.
[7] *Mzee* is an honorific title used for elders in general but used exclusively for President Kenyatta in the 1970s and for President Moi from the late 1980s onwards.
[8] M. Munene, 'The Force Behind Terror Gangs', *Daily Nation,* 13 March 2002.

insecurity and criminality. The *Taliban* signified a public response to the breakdown, lethargy or corruption of the public security infrastructure and was part of the politics of protection (Anderson 2002: 541). Most of these youth vigilante groups were politicized and hired or co-opted by politicians for electioneering and protection. *Mungiki* emerged from different circumstances and came to represent a different type of youth movement and politics in Kenya.

Politics from below: *Mungiki* and the politics of resistance

According to Wamue (2001), *Mungiki* was formed by a small group of Kikuyu youths in the late 1980s. Its name is etymologically derived from the archaic Gikuyu word *irindi* (crowds) or publics. The name is thus an assertion of the rights of a social class that feels acutely deprived and marginalized in a rapidly globalizing world.[9] *Mungiki* started as a more radical and vibrant movement of youth between the ages of 18 and 40.[10] It draws the bulk of its followers from the lower classes – mostly former street children, unemployed youths, hawkers, artisans, petty traders in the *Jua Kali* (the informal sector) and the alarmingly growing army of urban poor in Nairobi's slums of Githurai, Dandora, Korogocho, Kariobangi, Kawangware, Kibera, Mathare and Kangemi. It also has strong support among the landless, squatters and internally displaced persons in the Rift Valley in areas such as Londiani, Eldoret, Molo, Olenguruone, Elburgon, Subukia, Narok, Nakuru, Laikipia and Nyahururu. It is estimated that the *Mungiki* has between 1.5 and 2 million paid-up members, with at least 400,000 of these being women (Wamue 2001: 454).[11]

The ideological and historical origins of *Mungiki* can be traced from the intricate politics of resistance against British colonial authoritarianism and the tyranny of the post-colonial state (Kagwanja 2003a). *Mungiki* leaders imagined themselves as heirs to the militant politics of the Mau Mau movement that waged an armed struggle against the British in the 1950s (Wamue 2001: 456). However, they also believed that the movement did not achieve its goals of obtaining total liberation, explaining economic backwardness and susceptibility

---

[9] J. Githongo, 'Why Won't the State Clip Them Dreadlocks?' *East African Standard*, 15 November 2000.

[10] A recent police crackdown on the movement revealed that it has followers among primary-school children and the elderly. See 'Six Pupils in Court Over Mungiki Chaos', *Daily Nation*, 13 March 2002.

[11] In the wake of *Mungiki*'s entry into active electoral politics, it has revised these numbers upwards to a hugely inflated figure of between 3.5 and 4 million.

to forces of economic globalization to the failed Mau Mau project.[12] In this regard, *Mungiki* initially forged alliances with other social movements, and civil society organizations in Kenya such as the Kimathi Movement and *Muungano were Wanavijiji* for the purpose of 'completing' the Mau Mau mission (Turner & Brownhill 2002). As a religious sect, *Mungiki* is also an heir to a long tradition of religio-political resistance identified with groups such as *Dini Ya Msambwa*, *Legio Maria*, *Akorino* and, more recently, *Hema ya Ngai wi Mwoyo* (Tent of the Living God) which acted as counter-publics to the hegemony of the colonial and successor states. Finally, *Mungiki* has some of its roots in the radical politics of the late 1970s and the 1980s identified with such underground movements as *Mwakenya* and radical intellectuals like Ngugi wa Thiong'o and Maina wa Kinyatti, and evokes the continuities and discontinuities between the earlier and later patterns of resistance.[13]

However, *Mungiki* is widely viewed as a resurgence of a Gikuyu identity, traditional culture and religion (Kenyatta 1938, Atieno-Odhiambo 1996). It has been argued that the glorification of Gikuyu culture in the writings and activities of Gikuyu intellectuals, particularly Jomo Kenyatta and Ngugi wa Thiongó, has conferred an ethnically exclusive cultural radicalism on *Mungiki* (Barasa 2002). Others have attributed this influence to Ngugi's literary works, chiefly *The River Between* and *Weep Not Child* that render a distinct ideological slant to Kikuyu culture. Anderson isolates the portrayal of the prophecy of Mugo wa Kibiru, the Gikuyu diviner and seer of the late 19th century, as the ideological wind that drives *Mungiki*'s 'stridently ethnocentric' sail. Through reading Mugo wa Kibiru as depicted in Kenyatta's and Wa Thiong'o's writings, *Mungiki* leadership has become radicalized. As a result, it has blamed Kenya's woes on European colonialism and virulently advocated the restoration of Gikuyu traditional practices as an indigenous refuge in the face of 'the yoke of colonial mental slavery' of the mainstream churches and marginalization by the corrupt and materialistic evangelical churches (Anderson 2002). He sees in the writings of Kenyatta and Wa Thiongó a trigger of *Mungiki's* bifurcated vision: that of re-establishing a *Kirinyaga* Kingdom and the 'restoration of Gikuyu power through the removal of the Moi regime and capturing state power'. Anderson's account does not shed light on how these two visions – one 'primordial' and the other 'modernist' – are to be reconciled. Further, it casts a larger-than-life image of Waruinge who also appears as *Mungiki*'s undisputed ideological Czar and *Mungiki* as a homogenous movement driven by a singular traditional vision

---

[12] *Daily Nation*, 23 October 2000.
[13] Interview with Willy Mutunga, Executive Director, Kenya Human Rights Commission, May 2002.

encapsulated in Mugo's prophecy. Evidence points to the fact that Mugo wa Kibiro occupies a less central place in *Mungiki's* ideology than Anderson suggests. As Wamue (2001: 456) states: 'the educated *Mungiki* members consult books on Gikuyu history *as well as other writings by heroes like Marcus Garvey and Martin Luther [King]*'. As a research associate with the Kenya Human Rights Commission,[14] I interacted in meetings, public demonstrations and private intellectual discussions with *Mungiki* members who fervently identified with a range of radical viewpoints, ranging from Marxist ideas to those of Marcus Garvey, Kwame Nkrumah, Steve Biko and, more pervasively, Che Guevara. Aside from the ideas derived from these sources, most *Mungiki* members read newspapers and magazines, watch films and videos, and interact with university students and activists in Kenya's vibrant civic society.

Mungiki has also forged a strategic alliance with the Islamic movement in Kenya.[15] On 2 September 2000, thirteen of its leaders converted to Islam. *Mungiki* members claimed there is common ground between their beliefs and Islamic tenets that made their conversion easy: 'Islam means submission to God, while *Mungiki* means the masses'. They also believed that conversion to Islam would 'hasten the realization of the movement's goal' of fighting corruption, bad governance, poverty, immorality and diseases such as AIDS among Kenyans.[16] Besides these goals and *Mungiki*'s strong anti-Christian stance, the other reason why these leaders converted to Islam was to gain inclusion in a more universalized non-communitarian faith and to shed the 'tribal' stigma that the state was using to rationalize its harassment of *Mungiki* followers.[17] This conversion to Islam was a strategic political step that guaranteed *Mungiki* the support of a larger and more militant constituency in the face of state persecution rather than a strict adherence to the Islamic faith.[18] Not surprisingly, some moderate Muslims accused the movement of using Islam as a 'hideout'.[19]

Closer scrutiny of Kenya's history reveals that resistance movements resorted to Islam as a strategy of self-camouflage in the face of repression. During the repressive state of emergency in the 1950s, many ordinary Kikuyus

---

[14] I served as a consultant with the Kenya Human Rights Commission from 1996 to 1998 and as a research associate between February 2001 and August 2002.
[15] N. Njuguna, '*Mungiki* Men in Bid to Join Islam', *Daily Nation*, 1 June 2000.
[16] *Daily Nation*, 6 September 2000.
[17] This strategy of converting to Islam to escape state repression dates back to the days of the Mau Mau in the 1950s.
[18] P. Mayoyo, 'Outcry on Mungiki Converts', *Daily Nation,* 6 September 2000.
[19] '*Mungiki* Members Censured', *Daily Nation*, 21 December 2000.

and Mau Mau leaders converted to Islam and migrated in large numbers from their villages to *Mijini* (separate settlements for Muslims) located in the Nyeri, Murang'a, Maragua and other towns in Central Province. In light of this, and *Mungiki's* claim to the Mau Mau mantle, it is tempting to attribute a degree of historical self-knowledge to the recent islamization of *Mungiki*. However, interviews with its leaders tend to support the view that this was a circumstantial and natural political choice available to the sect for self-camouflage in Kenya's radical Islamic wing that has also been facing similar political repression by the Kenyan state. Indeed, many Mungiki informants have tended to stress the political rather than the cultural and religious motives behind *Mungiki's* islamization.[20] It is instructive that *Mungiki* converted to the radical *Shiites* order of the Kenyan Islamic movement. In the multi-party politics, Sheikh Balala, the fiery Muslim preacher, emerged as the icon of radical Islam and its political flagship, the Islamic Party of Kenya (IPK).[21] Like the *Mungiki*, the IPK and its members have encountered severe repression by the Kenyan state.[22]

Mungiki political militancy has its origins in the ethnic violence in the Rift Valley in the 1990s. *Mungiki* youths offered protection to the displaced population of mostly Kikuyu in the Rift Valley. Aside from its task of defending the displaced, *Mungiki* has revitalized the traditional values of generosity and charity to facilitate the return, rehabilitation and social support of its displaced members. Turner and Brownhill (2002) have lauded *Mungiki* for the part it played in supporting the displaced farmers in the Rift Valley in 1992 and 1998. One way *Mungiki* has supported its members is by helping them acquire and establish farms in several areas in the Rift Valley, such as Ng'arua where they grow maize and potatoes, and keep livestock. Beyond the sinister ring of unbridled radicalism that surrounds the movement, it is said that on *Mungiki* farms 'the spirit of harmony, hard work and unity is evident' (Wamue 2001: 466).

---

[20] Interviews carried out in July-August 2002.

[21] Most Kenyan Muslims adhere to the Suni branch of Islam. Others branches of Kenyan Muslims include the Agha Khan, Bola and Almadia orders. The Shiites, who are also connected with the Shiites in Iran, form a small but politically active group of Kenyan Muslims. I am indebted to Willy Mutunga and Hassan Omar for this information on Islam in Kenya.

[22] Since Kenya's return to multi-party politics, this group has been quite controversial. This controversy reached its apogee when the government stripped Sheikh Balala of his Kenyan citizenship while on a trip to Germany, creating a diplomatic stand-off with Yemen, his alleged country of citizenship.

After 1997, *Mungiki* intensified its moral crusade aimed at restoring justice and rebuilding wrecked communities, especially in Nairobi's suburbs and shanty towns where its members live. As a result, even its most ardent critics concede that its crusade against drunkenness, drug addiction, broken families, prostitution, sexually transmitted diseases and HIV/AIDS has been highly successful.[23] It has also flushed out thugs and juveniles, and eliminated criminal activities such as theft, rape, the sale of drugs, and murder in some of Nairobi's suburbs where it has virtual control, such as in the Kasarani area. *Mungiki* has teamed up with community-based movements in Nairobi such as *Muungano wa Wanavijiji* (Movement of the Villagers) in organizing protests against corrupt land-grabbers and oppressive landlords who arbitrarily raise rents. It has also supported a people-driven constitutional reform since 1997. In view of its largely effective struggle for social justice, Turner and Brownhill (2001) have celebrated *Mungiki* as one of the groups that form the anchors of 'globalization from below'.

However, these laudatory accounts of *Mungiki* by Wamue (2001), and Turner and Brownhill (2001, 2002) obscure the fact that some of its unorthodox approaches to social justice have worsened rather than reduced social disorder. Mungiki's takeover of *matatu* (private taxi) routes in Nairobi, which its leaders defend as a way of restoring order, routing out extortionist cartels and stabilizing fares for the benefit of the poor, has been immensely successful on the Githurai and Kamiti routes. But similar attempts to take over routes in other parts of Nairobi and Nakuru have led to bloody clashes with other youths resulting in police intervention. In October 2000, attempts by *Mungiki* to take over the Dandora route in Nairobi's Eastlands provoked clashes between its members and the vested interests of, for example, the *Kamjesh* militia. Similar violence has been reported in Nakuru. This sparked off a public outcry and demands for the government to rein in the militias, including the *Mungiki*.[24] Turner and Brownhill create a glowing picture of *Mungiki* as Robin Hood, stealing from the rich landlords and land-grabbers to give to the poor. However, on several occasions *Mungiki* has defended the interests of landlords in Kibera and Kariobangi. This has been the case when it views demands for rent reductions as being politically driven. Moreover, in the politics of the Moi succession in 2002, *Mungiki*'s crusade for a new moral order was eclipsed by the co-optation of its leader by the KANU elite. Its image has been tarnished by allegations of killings in Nairobi's Kariobangi suburb, of its followers stripping

---

[23] David Mageria, 'Kenyan Sect Banned by State but Defiant', Reuters, 19 April 2002; *Daily Nation*, 23 October 2000.
[24] Bob Odalo, '*Mungiki* Members Jailed', *Daily Nation*, October 2000.

women in Kayole, and of killings in the post-election period. Yet it is imperative that we examine *Mungiki*'s idea of a generational transfer of power.

Tradition in the service of modernity: The idea of *Itwika* and multi-party politics

Mungiki's vision of succession in multi-party politics in 2002 was derived from a reworked version of the pre-colonial Kikuyu generational transfer of political authority from elders to the young generation. This system of transferring power was itself based on the system of governance that emerged from a cumulative process of youth resistance to the tyranny of the elders. In his short monograph, *My People of Kikuyu*, Jomo Kenyatta lists four phases of Kikuyu history. The most remote period is known as *Tene* and *Agu*, about which little is remembered. The second is *Ndemi* and *Mathathi*. *Ndemi* ('those who cut') is the generation that cleared the forests for cultivation, thus marking the transition from hunter-gatherer to sedentary farmers. The *Mathathi* ushered in the age of warriorhood and possibly the conquest of the neighbours. As Kenyatta put it, they were the first to paint their warriors with ochre (*thathi, ma* being the prefix for 'people'). 'It was these,' Kenyatta writes, 'who introduced the art of making soup and mixing it with stimulating herbs which made warriors fearless.' It is also *Ndemi* and *Mathathi* that introduced the gerontocratic, but democratic, system of government.

Kenyatta identifies two levels of revolutionary change of governments in the traditional Kikuyu system which ushered in what he characterizes as a new 'democratic system of government'. The first was the overthrow of matriarchy (women power) that predominated. 'Long ago,' the Kenyan writer of this myth, Ngugi wa Thiong'o, claimed, 'women used to rule this land and its men. They were harsh and men began to resist their hand hard. So when all the women were pregnant, men came together and overthrew them' (wa Thiong'o 1965: 14). Although the *Mungiki* proclaims to believe in the rights of women, its ideas about the place of women in politics is largely informed by this patriarchal myth. The trope of resistance and revolutionary change dominates the narrative of Kikuyu pre-colonial politics and is the most enduring legacy to *Mungiki* politics. The fall of matriarchy resulted in an oligarchy or a system based on the chieftainship of a mythical leader called 'Kikuyu', which turned increasingly repressive towards the youth. According to Kenyatta, the ambitious Chief Kikuyu set up warrior camps and a standing army and forced the youth into prolonged military service, undermining family life and food production. This, Kenyatta argues, 'gradually made the whole tribe share in the warriors' discontent. Finally, the *Iregi* [revolutionaries] generation of warriors planned and carried out a revolution and the despotic chief Kikuyu was dethroned.'

In the aftermath of the revolution, the warriors and elders met and drew up a plan for a better government. According to this system, after initiation to youthhood through circumcision at the age of fourteen or fifteen for boys and ten to twelve for girls, every youth was entitled to some commensurate responsibility and power. The society was governed along gerontocratic lines by a council of elders (*Kiama*) supported by strong councils of fighting warriors (*Njama*). The council was ushered in and sanctified by a huge ceremony known as *Ituika* meaning the 'dissolving of the revolution' or the 'relinquishing' of power or simply a 'break'. Henceforth, leadership was to be passed on from one generation to the next every thirty or forty years when the *Ituika* ceremony was performed. The generation that spearheaded the revolt against the former tyrant was given the name *Mwangi* ('one who captures, conquers, triumphs or gathers together'). The next generation to have the task of consolidating a democratic tradition came to be called *Irungu* (taken from the verb *runga* which means 'to put straight'). The *ituika* system, therefore, produced a political dispensation in which the whole Kikuyu nation was divided into two generations, the older one in power and the younger one waiting in the wings. The strength of the *ituika* system was its predictability and its promise of power to the elders as well as the youth.

Father Constanzo Cagnolo in his book *The Akikuyu* writes: 'When we [the Consolata Missionaries] came to Kikuyuland in 1902, the Maina class was ruling but was about to retire. The *Mwangi* succeeded them and is still ruling in 1932. … After the famine of 1917 during the Great War, the *Irungu* class began to pay tribute and today 1932 they are ousting the *Mwangi*, who will shortly surrender their seats.' In his *Kikuyu-English Dictionary*, T.G. Benson, under the term *ituike*, says: 'The *Maina* generation handed over to the *Mwangi* about 1900; the latest, the *Irungu* or *Maina Kanyi* [generation] set, which is said to have been preparing to succeed the *Mwangi* sometime between 1925-1932, was prevented by social and political changes brought about by Europeanizing influences and by prohibition of ceremonies by Government.' In an interview with Edmondo Cavicchi after the Second World War, Father Cagnolo observes that although the *Ituika* took place in 1932, many of the elders of the *Irungu* generation refused to 'redeem the country for themselves from the out-going generation by paying one goat or sheep' (Cavicchi 1977: 207-8).

This narrative provided the political text for *Mungiki* youths in their interpretation of politics in the multi-party era. The *Mungiki* began to imagine Kenya as a country immersed in a generational struggle between the dominant elders and youths. They accused the generation of elders of perpetuating themselves and staying in power for too long, repressing the youth and looting the Kenyan nation. They invoked the corruption and land-grabbing that reached huge proportions in multi-party Kenya to support the claim that the '*Mwangi* and *Irungu* generations have betrayed the country and, therefore, have to get out of power'.[25] *Mungiki* invoked the trope of youth rebellion signified by the *Iregi* generation when preparing its followers for a takeover of power if the elders refused to step down. They argued that the *Mwangi* and *Irungu/Maina* generations failed to ensure a smooth transfer of power in 1932 and thus disrupted the traditional generational order of things. Therefore, the youth had to go back to the drawing-board and restore the generational system. The process begins with the youth (*Mungiki*) assuming the role of the *Iregi* generation of old and initiating the revolution that will usher in the *Mwangi* generation to power. 'We are neither *Mwangi* nor *Irungu*', declared one youth informant, 'we are *Iregi*.' The concept of *Iregi* is extended not only to generational politics of power at the national level but also to the international realm to capture its resistance to 'the slavery of the Christian church' and the exploitative financial orthodoxy of forces of globalization and westernization. The *Iregi* ideology of resistance forms part of an extended liturgy and routine self-introduction by *Mingiki* adherents. *Mungiki* youths have assumed the name *njama* (singular: *munjama*) which can be translated as 'warrior class' and 'warrior' respectively. Their conversations and ceremonies are punctuated with a distinct language of combat. Self-introduction or contribution by a *munjama* during a public gathering of *Mungiki* members is referred to as *guikia itimu* or 'throwing a spear'. The food of choice by the *njama* is meat and milk, also the preferred food of Kikuyu warriors especially when they are preparing for or are at war. '*Njama ndiriaga marenge*' ('warriors do not feed on pumpkins'), declared one of my informants citing a Kikuyu saying.

Mungiki's vision of a youth leadership in post-Moi Kenya was equally based on Kikuyu prophesy by Mugo wa Kibiru, which is distinctly a redemptive message of the youth. 'A [young] man [shall] rise and save the people in their hour of need. He shall show them the way he will lead them,' Ngugi reminisces on Mugo's prophesy (wa Thiong'o 1965: 19). In 2002, *Mungiki* leadership saw this man in Uhuru Kenyatta, whom they adoringly referred to as *kamwana* (the youth). The *Mungiki* viewed Uhuru[26] as the 'liberatory' youth in Mugo's prophesy, in spite of his evidently conservative political stance and association with Moi. They shared Mugo's frustration when the majority of the Kikuyu population turned its face on 'the youth'.

---

[25] Interview with Gacheke Gachihi, August 2002.
[26] *Uhuru* is the Kiswahili word for freedom. It is the name Jomo Kenyatta chose for his son in anticipation of independence in 1963.

The seer was rejected by the people of the ridges. 'They gave him no clothes and no food. He became bitter and hid himself, refusing to tell them more…'. (wa Thiong'o 1965: 20)

'We Support the Youth': The Uhuru candidacy and post-election violence

In its fanatical crusade for the *ituika* and youth power, *Mungiki* jumped into the fray of the Moi succession politics. Long before the 2002 elections, President Moi, partly succumbing to public pressure to pave the way for younger leaders, embarked on giving his party (KANU) and his government a new and youthful look. He appointed young leaders like Raila Odinga, Ruto, Julius Sunkuli, Cyrus Njirongo and Uhuru Kenyatta to his cabinet and elevated those already in the government, like Kalonzo Musyoka and Katana Ngala. Some of the youth in the KANU's new inter-generational pantheon, such as Njirongo and Ruto, had strong credentials as former leaders of Youth for KANU-1992 (YK 92), a youth lobby that played a supremely important part in President Moi's 1992 electoral victory. Uhuru, Oginga and Ngala were sons of Kenya's nationalist heroes and founding fathers of the independent Kenyan nation, Jomo Kenyatta, Jaramogi Oginga Odinga and Ronald Ngala, respectively. KANU moved to irreversibly change its face by passing on power to the youth. At its delegates' meeting held on March 18, the party elected Uhuru, Raila, Katana and Kalonzo as vice-presidents and Raila as the party's Secretary-General. However, Moi retained the crucial seat of party chairman, whose powers had been dramatically increased. To many, this was a ploy by the Moi patrimony to give token powers to the youth and to retain its hegemony in national politics.

Mungiki had thrown its support behind Uhuru in the lobbying that preceded the KANU party elections. Its national spokesman, Ndura Waruinge, announced that the sect would back the KANU and Uhuru Kenyatta during the 2002 general elections. About 3,000 *Mungiki* followers urged him to go for the top seat. By the same token, Waruinge criticized the National Opposition Alliance (NAC) which Mwai Kibaki, Charity Ngilu and Wamalwa Kijana had formed to unite the fledgling opposition. The NAC, he predicted, was doomed to fail because each one of them was hungry for power. 'We would rather vote President Moi and KANU back to power than the doomed opposition alliance,' he added.

The *Mungiki* sect, which had long acted as a social movement, immersed itself in electoral politics on a platform of youth power.[27] On 3 March 2002, the movement invited Uhuru Kenyatta to be Guest of Honour at a *harambee* (fund raiser) it was organizing in Nyahururu, Laikipia District. The *harambee* turned

---

[27] 'Mungiki Sect to Support KANU, Saitoti and Uhuru in Poll', *East African Standard*, 4 March 2002.

into a campaign rally as 10,000 *Mungiki* members launched a campaign to support the young Kenyatta. During the rally, *Mungiki*'s National Chairman, Maina Njenga, also declared that he would contest the Laikipia seat on a KANU ticket. Waruinge disclosed that *Mungiki* would field over 150 parliamentary candidates throughout the country. He said the movement was only waiting to see the outcome of the KANU party elections on 18 March to decide who to back as presidential candidate. Waruinge warned Kenyans not to underrate the sect as it had the people and resources to change politics in Kenya. To drive this point home, the sect reportedly spent over Ksh 1 million (US$13,000) on organizing the Nyahururu function. Although Mr Kenyatta did not attend the *harambee*, he sent a huge donation of Ksh 300,000 (about US$4,000).

It was at this precise moment that *Mungiki* as a youth movement was covertly co-opted by the KANU. On 13 March 2002, the MP for Ndaragwa in Nyandarua District, Thirikwa Kamau, told parliament that President Moi was hosting members of the *Mungiki* sect and holding discussions with them on an undisclosed agenda. The MP was wondering who really owned and funded *Mungiki*.[28] In the light of this revelation, suspicion was rife that the dominant elders in the Moi regime were planning to manipulate *Mungiki* to chip away at the electoral basis of the opposition and to shape the outcome of the elections in the Kikuyu-dominated areas of Nairobi, Central Province and the Rift Valley.

Kikuyu parliamentarians accused the government of sponsoring hooliganism to terrorize the public and of encouraging the committing of crimes, putting the blame on *Mungiki* as a political ploy to demonize the Kikuyu community. They linked this to KANU's grand plan to use *Mungiki* youths to dismantle Mwai Kibaki's electoral base and undermine his chances of becoming president. They saw an uncanny parallel between this and the tribulations of the former leader of the opposition, Kijana Wamalwa. The MP for Gatanga in Central Province, David Murathe, argued that from 1992 to 1997, when Wamalwa Kijana, the Ford-Kenya chairman, was the official leader of the opposition, the government had clandestinely sponsored a militant youth group, the February Eighteen Revolutionary Army (FERA), which it claimed had bases in Mr Wamalwa's strongholds in Western Province. In the guise of routing out FERA followers, the government infiltrated and dismantled Wamalwa's electoral base by harassing and intimidating his supporters ahead of the 1997 general elections. The legislator concluded that during the tenure of Mwai Kibaki as the official leader of the opposition (1997-2002), KANU was criminalizing and using the *Mungiki* to intimidate the Kikuyu, to clip Kibaki's political wings and destroy

---

[28] 'Government Blamed for Hypocrisy Over Mungiki', *East African Standard*, 14 March 2002.

its political base prior to the 2002 general elections.[29] This view became ubiquitous when *Mungiki* supported Uhuru Kenyatta, who was endorsed as the KANU's presidential candidate and President Moi's successor, against Mwai Kibaki, the opposition's presidential flag-bearer. Speaking in parliament in March, Embakasi MP David Mwenje accused President Moi and Mr Kenyatta of bankrolling the sect. However, the sect insisted that the movement did not rely on handouts from anyone and that its activities were funded by contributions from its 4 million members.

Mungiki made public its choice of Uhuru Kenyatta as its presidential candidate during the presidential nominations in August 2003. This choice was based on generational rather than ethnic concerns. '*Mungiki*'s political agenda,' said *Mungiki* chairman, Njenga Maina, 'is to campaign for youthful leaders and phase out the older generation. That is why we have been supporting Uhuru since he was young.' On the day of nomination, hundreds of thousands of *Mungiki* youth arrived by bus, minibus and donkey cart, or on foot, descending on to the streets of Nairobi from all directions in a procession that caught many residents of Nairobi by surprise. From the vantage point of his office in Harambee House, an elated President Moi watched the procession of *Mungiki* youth as they thronged Harambee Avenue on their way to Nairobi's Uhuru (Independence) Park to declare their support for the presidential candidacy of Uhuru Kenyatta. Imagining themselves as the *Iregi* warriors of old, these *Mungiki* youths wielded machetes, *rungus* (clubs) and sticks in a dramatic parade that brought back eerie memories of the *Interahamwe* in (post-)genocide Rwanda. The Kenyan press accused the law-enforcement agencies of duplicity for tolerating what it had come to immortalize as anarchic youths. 'The police,' it was said, 'looked like they were actually guiding demonstrators carrying placards and snuff boxes to the venue, where speeches denouncing the Local Government Minister's [Uhuru] political enemies were made.' Attorney-General Amos Wako also censored the police's behaviour as a 'serious dereliction of duty'. Opposition leaders accused the government of double standards in their dealings with all the parties involved. A few days later, supporters of NARC – or simply the Rainbow Alliance – who were opposed to Mr Kenyatta's candidacy were forced to leave Uhuru Park by riot police.

Uhuru Kenyatta's policy swung between covertly soliciting *Mungiki*'s support and publicly distancing his campaign from its activities. It was noted that he sought to distance himself from the demonstration while arguing that 'anybody had the freedom to support whoever he wanted'. However, some of

---

[29] Njeri Rugene, 'Mungiki as Clever Ploy, Charges MP', *Daily Nation*, 2 November 2000.

Uhuru's stanch supporters, like the Mayor of Nairobi Dick Waweru and Juja MP Stephen Ndicho, openly supported the sect. At about the same time, Uhuru Kenyatta defended *Mungiki* from the point of view of the impact of Kenya's economic crisis on the youth, arguing that some of the *Mungiki* adherents were well-educated youths capable of playing an active role in the country's development. 'The majority joined the sect,' he said, 'because they were idle but they are still our brothers and sisters who should not be hated or secluded from the society but encouraged to reform.'[30] He promised to create opportunities for such vulnerable groups should Kenyans elect him as the next president. Uhuru's henchman, Stephen Ndichu, said that 'despite their militancy on some contentious issues, *Mungiki* followers were Kenyans and should be accommodated as they also had a role to play in nation-building'.[31] For his part, *Mungiki*'s spokesman, Nduru Waruinge, told the BBC's 'Focus on Africa' programme in August that Mr Kenyatta was actually a member of *Mungiki*.

Public pressure mounted on the government to rein in *Mungiki*, forcing Uhuru Kenyatta to clearly distance himself from it. Describing *Mungiki* as 'a dangerous organization', one fierce opposition leader, Mr Gumo, challenged Mr Kenyatta to go public about any possible links he might have with *Mungiki* 'because we are told he is a member'. In October, the *Matatu* Welfare Association officials, representing *matatu* (commuter taxi) owners in Nairobi, threatened to go on strike if the government did not act against the *Mungiki* sect members on city routes.[32] 'The government,' the association said, 'must stop the harassment of *matatu* owners and enforce laws impartially. They must also stop unnecessary *matatu* inspection.' Opposition leaders claimed in parliament that members of the outlawed sect enjoyed protection from the government despite their involvement in unlawful activities.[33] The government responded by arresting 23 *Mungiki* followers and recovered an assortment of crude weapons linked to the movement.[34] Seven armed *Mungiki* members were arrested in Nairobi following claims that *Mungiki* was behind acts of violence and thuggery around Nairobi and in several areas in Central Province.[35] In Kerugoya in

[30] Njuguna Waweru & Philip Mwakio, 'Uhuru Now Defends Mungiki Adherents', *East African Standard*, 26 August 2002.

[31] Amos Kareithi, 'Ndichu Now Beats Retreat on Mungiki', *East African Standard*, 26 August 2002.

[32] 'Matatu Owners in Strike Threat over *Mungiki* Invasion', *Kenya Broadcasting Corporation*, 15 October 2002.

[33] 'Uproar as MPs Claim State Protecting *Mungiki*', *Daily Nation*, 18 October 2002.

[34] '23 *Mungiki* Sect Adherents Nabbed by Police', *Kenyan Broadcasting Corporation*, 22 October 2002.

[35] 'City Police Nab Armed Sect Members', *Kenya Broadcasting Corporation*, 15 October 2002.

central Kenya, scores of *Mungiki* followers were charged with touting to obtain passengers for *matatus* and causing inconvenience and annoyance to the public.

The *Mungiki* connection was taking a heavy toll on Uhuru's national campaign. In November, he reiterated that he was not the leader of the proscribed *Mungiki* movement, saying he had nothing to do with *Mungiki* because he was a Catholic by birth. 'There are people,' he said, 'who are tarnishing my name. They are claiming that I am the leader of *Mungiki*. I am a Catholic and so is my whole family.' Uhuru reminded Kenyans that there was no love lost between him and *Mungiki*. Two years before, he claimed the sect members had accused him of being used by the government to harass and intimidate them and had burned his effigy outside his father's mausoleum in Nairobi.[36] Simultaneously, KANU headquarters invalidated the candidature of *Mungiki* chairman Maina Njenga to run for the parliamentary seat in Nyahururu. Njenga had won the nomination with 19,509 votes, against the 1,331 for Mr Muruthi. This step sparked off protest from *Mungiki* followers. Hundreds of *Mungiki* sect followers escorted Mr Njenga in a fleet of 50 vehicles to the ECK offices in Nairobi.[37] In spite of this, *Mungiki* followers continued to support Uhuru's candidacy.

In the December 2002 elections, KANU suffered a devastating loss to the opposition, NARK. Mwai Kibaki, in his seventies, defeated young Kenyatta to become Kenya's third president. This loss was seen by many *Mungiki* followers not just as a political loss but as a generational loss; a defeat of their idea of *Ituika* and the '*Iregi* Revolution'. This provides the context for the widely publicized post-election violence that took place between *Mungiki* followers and the NARK government. In early January *Mungiki* followers killed about 25 people in Nakuru while they slept, and on Nairobi's Dandora Estate they hacked a police officer to death.[38] The new government reacted by cracking down hard on the movement. The government's 'shoot-to-kill' policy provoked a bitter response from human-rights organizations. Hundreds of *Mungiki* followers were arrested and put on trial. Post-election violence has revolved around the government's effort to restore security and public order in the public-transport sector by removing *Mungiki* youths from the *matatu* business. According to the police, more than 50 people died in 2002 in clashes involving the sect and *matatu* owners and touts.[39] However, the government has refocused its attention on the economic rehabilitation of *Mungiki* followers, arguing that the *Mungiki* is primarily a reflection of the economic marginality of the youth.

---

[36] 'Kenya: Presidential Candidate Kenyatta Denies Links with *Mungiki* Sect', *East African Standard*, 11 November 2002.
[37] 'KANU Now Bars Mungiki Aspirant', *East African Standard*, 28 November 2002.
[38] 'Five Killed in Mungiki Mayhem', *East African Standard*, 7 February 2003.
[39] 'Profile: Kenya's Secretive *Mungiki* Sect', BBC, 11 February 2003.

Conclusion: The future of youth politics

This chapter has examined the roots of the powerlessness and marginality of the youth category in politics, and considered violence as an indelible feature of the politics that subordinated the youth to the dominant elders. The narrative shifted historically from a focus on the intensive use of violence by the hegemonic elders against youth leadership in politics to the widespread deployment of 'youth' violence organized around the single political party to monitor and punish dissent within the restive lumpen youth in rural and urban areas. With their hegemony threatened by the onset of political pluralism from the early 1990s, the elders resorted to the recruitment of all genres of youth violence on a massive scale to obstruct and subvert a genuine democratic transition. The *Mungiki* sect, a social movement of youths that rose to political prominence in response to state-sponsored violence and displacement in parts of rural Kenya and the urban slums in the mid-1990s, developed a clear idea of the generational transfer of power based on the pre-colonial Kikuyu culture of politics and agitated for a genuine surrender of power by the elders to the youth. However, in the context of the politics of Moi's succession in 2002, the movement's leadership was co-opted by the dominant elders. The leadership abandoned the moral crusade of the movement and embarked on reckless violence that eventually undermined its legitimacy and influence in the Kenyan public sphere. Its idea of generational conflict provided fodder for the ideological cannon of the dominant elders. Although Kenya has become a relatively democratic order, youth violence continues to haunt democracy. The road to democracy in the future lies in strengthening the social movements of the youth and a break with the prevailing powerlessness and marginality of youth in politics. In a Gramscian sense of hegemony, a political transformation that will restore the power of the youth category has to target both civil society and the state. The *Mungiki* lost in its bid to become part of the state, but it continues its role as a social movement. It is this aspect of the movement that the new government has to protect and support and is part of the empowerment of the lumpen youth.

References

Abdullah, I. 1997, 'Bush Path to Destruction: The Origin and Character of the Revolutionary United Front (RUF/SL)', *Africa Development*, 22 (3/4): 45-76.

African Rights, 1997, 'Violence at the Coast: The Human Consequence of Kenya's Crumbling Institutions', *Witness*, 2, p. 15.

Anderson, B. 1992, 'Long-Distance Nationalism: World Capitalism and the Rise of Identity Politics', Wertheim Lecture, Centre for Asian Studies, Amsterdam.

Anderson, D. 2002, 'Vigilantes, Violence, and the Politics of Public Order in Kenya', *African Affairs*, 101 (405): 531-55.

Anderson, P. 1976/77, 'The Antinomies of Antonio Gramsci', *New Left Review*, no. 100, pp. 115-90.

Arendt, H. 1975, *The Origins of Totalitarianism*, New York: Harcourt Brace.

Atieno-Odhiambo, E.S. 1996, 'Reconditioning the Terms of Fact: Ethnicity, Nationalism and Democracy as Political Vectors', in B.A. Ogot (ed.), *Ethnicity, Nationalism and Democracy in Africa*, Kisumu: Institute of Research and Post-Graduate Studies, Maseno University College.

Barasa, S. 2002, 'The Mungiki Prodigy and Ngugi's Literary Adventures', *East African Standard*, 31 March.

Bayart, J-F., A. Mbembe & C. Toulabor 1992, *Le Politique par le Bas en Afrique Noire: Contribution à une Problématique de la Démocratie*, Paris: Karthala.

Berman, B.J. 1998, 'Ethnicity, Patronage and the African State: The Politics of Uncivil Nationalism', *African Affairs*, 97 (388): 305-41.

Cavicchi, E. 1977, *Problems of Change in Kikuyu Tribal Society*, London: Kegan Paul.

Clough, M.S. 1990, *Fighting Two Sides: Kenyan Chiefs and Politicians, 1918-1940*, Boulder: University Press of Colorado.

Cohen, J. 1985. 'Strategies or Identity: New Theoretical Paradigms and Contemporary Social Movements', *Social Research*, 52 (4): 663-716.

Cruise O'Brien, D.B. 1996, 'A Lost Generation: Youth Identity and State Decay in West Africa', in R. Werbner & T. Ranger (eds), *Post-Colonial Identities in Africa*, London & New Jersey: Zed Books.

Fanon, F. 1967, *The Wretched of the Earth*, London: Penguin Publishers.

Foucault, M. 1877, *Discipline and Punish: The Birth of the Prison*, translated by A. Sheridan, New York: Vintage Books.

Fraser, N. 1992, 'Rethinking the Public Sphere: A Contribution to the Critique of Actually Existing Democracy', in C. Calhoun (ed.), *Habermas and the Public Sphere*, Cambridge: MIT Press.

Goldsworthy, D. 1982a, 'Ethnicity and Leadership in Africa: The "Untypical" Case of Tom Mboya', *Journal of Modern African Studies*, 20 (1): 107-26.

Goldsworthy, D. 1982b, *Tom Mboya: The Man Kenya Wanted to Forget*, Nairobi: Heinemann.

Habermas, J. 1998, 'The Inclusion of the Other: Studies in Political Theory', in P. de Greiff & C. Cronin (eds), *Global Justice and Transnational Politics*, Cambridge: MIT Press.

Hobsbawm, E. 1990, *Nations and Nationalism since 1780: Programme, Myth, Reality*, Cambridge: Press Syndicate of the University of Cambridge.

Kaggia, B. 1975, *Roots of Freedom, 1921-1963: The Autobiography of Bildad Kaggia*, Nairobi: East African Publishing House.

Kagwanja, P.M. 1999, *The Legacy of Tom Mboya: Identity Politics and Social Change in Africa*, Kisumu: Institute of Research and Post-Graduate Studies Seminars, Maseno University College, Series No. 2.

Kagwanja, P.M. 2001, 'Politics of Marionettes: Extra-Legal Violence and the 1997 Elections in Kenya', in M. Rutten, A. Mazrui & F. Grignon (eds), *Out for the Count: The 1997 General Elections and Prospects for Democracy in Kenya*, Kampala: Fountain Publishers, pp. 536-82.

Kagwanja, P.M. 2003a, 'Facing Mount Kenya or Facing Mecca? The *Mungiki*, Ethnic Violence, and the Politics of the Moi Succession in Kenya, 1987-2002', *African Affairs*, 102 (406): 25-49.

Kagwanja, P.M. 2003b, *Warlord Democracy: Militias and the Politics of the Moi Succession in Kenya, 1999-2002*, Nairobi: Kenya Human Rights Commission.

Kaldor, M. 1999, *New Wars and Old Wars: Organized Violence in a Global Era*, Cambridge: Polity Press.

Kenya Human Rights Commission 1997, *Kayas of Deprivation, Kayas of Blood: Violence, Ethnicity and the State at the Coast*, Nairobi: Kenya Human Rights Commission.

Kenya, Republic of, 1993, 'Report of the Parliamentary Select Committee to Investigate Ethnic Clashes in Western Kenya and Other Parts of Kenya', Nairobi: Government Printers.

Kenyatta, J. 1938, *Facing Mount Kenya*, London: Secker & Warburg.

Kirschke, L. 2000, 'Informal Repression: Zero-Sum Politics and the Later Third Wave Transitions', *The Journal of Modern African Studies*, 38 (3): 383-405.

Mamdani, M. 2001, *When Victims Become Killers: Colonialism, Nativism and the Genocide in Rwanda*, Princeton, NJ: Princeton University Press.

Mamdani, M. 2002, 'Making Sense of Non-Revolutionary Violence in Rwanda', lecture at the Centre for African Studies, University of Illinois-Urbana Champaign, November 1.

Marks, M. 2001, *Young Warriors: Youth Politics and Violence in South Africa*, Johannesburg: Witwatersrand University Press.

Mazrui, A. 2001, 'Ethnic Voices and Trans-Ethnic Voting: The 1997 Elections at the Kenya Coast', in M. Rutten, A. Mazrui & F. Grignon (eds), *Out for the Count: The 1997 General Elections and Prospects for Democracy in Kenya*, Kampala: Fountain Publishers, pp. 275-95.

Muana, P.K. 1997, 'The Kamajoi Militia: Civil War, Internal Displacement and the Politics of Counter-Insurgency', *Africa Development*, 22 (3/4): 77-100.

Ndolo, C. 1990, 'The Poor Too Have Rights: We Created the Slums, We Must Let Them Be', *Nairobi Law Monthly*, 28: 16-18.

Odinga, O. 1967, *Not Yet Uhuru*, London: Heinemann.

Rutten, M., A. Mazrui & F. Grignon (eds) 2001, *Out for the Count: The 1997 General Elections and Prospects for Democracy in Kenya*, Kampala: Fountain Publishers.

Seekings, J. 1993, *Heroes of Villains? Youth Politics in the 1980s*, Johannesburg: Ravan Press.

Singh, M. 1969, *History of Kenya's Trade Union Movement to 1952*, Nairobi: East African Publishing House.

Sitas, A. 1992, 'The Making of the 'Comrades' Movement in Natal, 1985-1991', *Journal of Southern African Studies*, 18 (3): 629-41.

Thiong'o, N. wa 1965, *The River Between*, Oxford: Heinemann Educational Publishers.

Throup, D. & C. Hornsby 1998, *Multi-party Politics in Kenya: The Kenyatta and the Moi States and the Triumph of the System in the 1992 Elections*, Oxford: James Currey.

Turner, T. & L.S. Brownhill 2001, '"Women Never Surrender": Mau Mau and Globalization from Below in Kenya, 1980-2000', in V. Bennholdt-Thomsen, N.G. Faraclas & C. von Werlhof (eds), *There is an Alternative: Subsistence and World Resistance to Corporate Globalization*, London, New York & Victoria: Zed Books, pp. 106-32.

Turner, T. & L.S. Brownhill 2002, 'African Jubilee: Mau Mau Resurgence and the Fight for Fertility in Kenya, 1986-2002', *Canadian Journal of Development Studies*, 22: 1037-88.

Wamue, G. 2001, 'Revisiting Our Indigenous Shrines Through *Mungiki*', *African Affairs*, 100 (400): 453-67.

Warner, M. 2002, 'Publics and Counter-Publics', *Public Culture*, 14 (1): 49-90.

Werbner, R. & T. Ranger (eds) 1996, *Post-Colonial Identities in Africa*, London & New Jersey: Zed Books.

5

Re-generating the nation:
Youth, revolution and the politics
of history in Côte d'Ivoire

Karel Arnaut

This chapter analyzes the discourse of generation and youth as it developed in the FESCI student movement of the 1990s in Côte d'Ivoire. The discourse's central elements have been transferred to the present-day Young Patriots movement that is playing a central role in the formulation and imposition of a relatively new political project that can be characterized as autochthony-driven. Generation and youth are argued to be powerful instruments in any politics of history as they ambivalently encompass continuity and rupture, inclusion and exclusion. The FESCI in its time made important claims about the historical trajectory and nationwide importance of its revolutionary struggle and the position of youth. These constructs are now being reclaimed by the Young Patriots in order to redefine their youth struggle in a political project that sees itself as a new stage in the emancipation of the Ivorian people from neo-colonial oppression. However, this time around, the inclusiveness of the vaguely defined category 'Ivorian people' hides the awkward exclusion of an equally ill-defined but strategically broad category of allochthones.

Introduction[1]

> The way is open, the signal has been given, the torch has just been handed over into the young, new, and unarmed hands that have no intention of grabbing a portfolio. (Dadié 2003: 170)[2]
> The new generation, the new youth of Côte d'Ivoire wants, like that is the case in all countries, live freely, live autonomously, live independently in its country; *That* is ours, it is our country, our ancestors have given this to us. (Charles Groguhet, 19 September 2003).[3]

These two quotes – the former from a renowned octogenarian writer and the latter from a militia leader in his thirties – give a taste of the rhetoric of youth and generation that features prominently in Ivorian political discourse these days. As many observers have rightly pointed out, at least since the December 1999 *coup d'état* – sometimes called the *coup d'état des jeunes* (Blé Goudé, 21 February 2000) – which removed President Henri Konan Bédié and his PDCI party (*Parti Démocratique de la Côte d'Ivoire*) from power, youngsters have incessantly manifested themselves as new political actors (Konaté 2002, 2003, Banégas & Marshall-Fratani 2000, Chauveau & Bobo 2003). This became even more apparent when the military insurgency of September 2002 resulted in the formation of two movements whose names strongly evoke rejuvenation: the 'Young Patriots' (*Jeunes Patriotes*) who claim to defend the nation and its president, Laurent Gbagbo, against the rebels of the 'New Forces' (*Forces Nouvelles*) who, in turn, demand the immediate removal of the acting president as well as drastic institutional and constitutional changes.

Reviewing the political situation in mid-2003, one youth leader and prominent member of the Young Patriots' Alliance (*Alliance des Jeunes Patriotes*), Damana Adia Pickas, declared:

> It is our generation that is at the centre of attention these days. There are rebel chiefs who are of our generation, patriot chiefs who are of the same generation, and leaders of youth sections of political parties who provide equally from that generation. You

---

[1] Research for this paper was conducted in Côte d'Ivoire and among Ivorians in Europe (France, UK, Germany, and Belgium). I wish to thank all my interlocutors and the many people who have facilitated my field research, especially Alyoun Badara Sall, Jean-Marie Ahoussou, Koffi Koffi Didier, Jean Dekpai and Raymond Dakoua.

[2] All translations from French are mine.

[3] References in which the exact date is specified refer to statements made in public or in the course of interviews with me (between 2000 and 2003). For reasons of privacy, I use pseudonyms (in italics in the text) for most of my interlocutors, and real names for authors of statements made in public.

can observe with me that the effervescence which reigns in our country today is a feat of that generation. So we have an important role to play not only in the FESCI but also in Côte d'Ivoire. (*Notre Voie*, 2 June 2003)

The loyalist Young Patriots and the insurgent New Forces are led by age-mates, Charles Blé Goudé and Soro Kigbafori Guillaume respectively, both 'young-sters' in their thirties who share the experience of having been militants in the FESCI student union (*Fédération Estudantine et Scolaire de Côte d'Ivoire*) during the 1990s.[4] Although the Ivorian press and many observers regularly point out that the two junior political actors gained celebrity in the legendary FESCI movement, they themselves speak about those years in quite different terms. While Soro Guillaume often distances himself from his past as a student leader to the extent of minimizing the importance of the movement, Blé Goudé – together with many fellow Young Patriot leaders who were FESCI members – publicly cherish the memory of their student activism. As explained elsewhere (Arnaut 2004a), this difference in attitude towards their student past is embedded in differential discourses. The Young Patriots stress their youth-fulness and present themselves as members of 'a new generation' that announces the birth of a new Ivorian nation. In contrast, the New Forces prefer to emphasize their maturity and avoid mentioning any divisions among Ivorian citizens and residents in terms of age, ethnicity, religion or (even) nationality.

This chapter explores the 'youth' and 'generation' rhetoric in Côte d'Ivoire since the early 1990s, particularly in the FESCI student union and among the Young Patriots. It is argued that by galvanizing their historical links with the student union, the Young Patriots are reactivating significations and connect-ions that were construed in the context of the deployment of the FESCI student movement in the 1990s, but inscribe these in a new political project that has all the makings of an autochthony movement.

Two of the features of the current autochthony movement can already be discerned in the opening quotes of this chapter. Both Dadié and Groguhet present the movement in terms of 'young' and 'new' which, as will be seen, is reminiscent of the way the FESCI presented itself in its time. When Bernard Dadié alleges that the 'hands' of the Young Patriots (whose praises he sings in this text) have 'no intention of grabbing a [ministerial] portfolio', he further evokes a series of meanings ranging from selfless commitment over patriotic sacrifice to revulsion against 'affairist' national politicians, which are also of

---

[4] Both Soro Guillaume and Blé Goudé held the highest position in the FESCI, that of secretary-general of the National Executive Bureau (*Bureau Exécutif National* – BEN). Soro Guillaume was secretary-general from 1995 until 1998 when he was replaced by Blé Goudé who stayed on until early 2001.

FESCI provenance. Dadié employs these meanings to characterize the patriotic youth as an anti-political, grass-roots civil-society movement that seeks to express the wishes and anxieties of 'the people' rather than impose itself on them. Charles Groguhet hints more clearly at whose political and economic interests the Young Patriot movement (to which he belongs) is dedicated to defend: those of Ivorians with ancestral connections within the country, in other words, the autochthones.

Whereas in the concluding sections this chapter specifically addresses the revival of FESCI discourse by the Young Patriots and their supporters, the chapter focuses on the construction of 'youth/student' and 'generation' in the context of the FESCI student movement of the 1990s. The material used is from fieldwork among former militants of the student union. This field work, conducted over a discontinuous period of three years, was multi-sited and 'multi-partisan'. I worked with former Fescists in Côte d'Ivoire (mainly Abidjan) as well as with several who have been living in Europe since they left in the FESCI exodus of the mid-1990s. Among the local and dispersed ex-Fescists, Young Patriot enthusiasts as well as fans or even representatives of the New Forces rebel movement are to be found. However, the bulk of my interlocutors are self-consciously struggling to resist this dichotomization and trying to carve out a space for themselves in an attempt to develop a critical perspective on the current predicament of their country, as well as on their past student activism and the FESCI legacy in general.

The oral and printed material which my research yielded is unravelled with the help of an analytic scheme that is presented in the following section. In a review of the sociological and anthropological literature on youth and generation, the way in which both concepts can be used to mark continuities while indicating ruptures can be seen, and suggests inclusiveness while imposing exclusions. Both dimensions are extremely relevant.

Firstly, the issue of constructing continuities and discontinuities invites a look at how a youth movement or a 'new generation' situates itself or is situated in a longer history of political activism or in an 'ideological tradition'. It has been suggested (see for example, Bayart 2003) that the Young Patriots, together with President Gbagbo, need to be situated in a 'nationalist tradition' that harks back to the period of decolonization (1945-1960). However, it is argued here that this claim arises from a politics of history whereby, indeed through their reciprocal association, Gbagbo and the Young Patriots are trying to lay claim to the 'nationalist tradition' not only to gain historical legitimacy for their new political projects but also to deny legitimacy to other 'nationalists', not least the ex-Fescists of the rebel movement, who are presently opposing these projects.

This brings us to the second issue of inclusion/exclusion. 'Youth' and 'generation' refer to age-based cross-sections of a population and when associated with historical movements can serve to stress their 'popular' or 'nationwide' character. However, as Groguhet's quote indicates, this vague all-inclusiveness may cover up certain exclusions (for example, the equally vaguely defined category of 'allochthones'). Together then, these plays on continuities/-discontinuities and inclusiveness/exclusivity feature in hegemonic struggles that consist of political claims on the *vox populi*, attempts to redefine citizenship, and economic options to limit redistribution to particular groups of citizens, for instance, autochthones.

'Youth' and 'generation': The politics of history and hegemonic struggles

In the social sciences, 'generation' is ambivalently defined in terms of alternation and flow, inclusion and exclusion. A textbook definition says that members of the same generation are 'contemporaries *or* [...] descended by the same number of degrees from a common ancestor' (Bacon 1964: 284, author's italics). Under the first condition (contemporaries), one can emphasize 'simultaneity' (Dithey in Marías 1968: 89) or what Ortega (in ibid) calls 'coevalness' and stress intra-generational cohesion, inclusion and solidarity, as well as inter-generational conflict (Eisenstadt 1962/1995, Turner 1998). Under the second condition (descent), the generation's specific location in historical time and social space is taken into account. From there, one can emphasize the fact that a generation constitutes itself or is constituted by events external to it (Mannheim in Bundy 1987: 305). What is more important in that respect is that a generation can include as much as it can exclude coevals such as women, non-initiates or strangers (see Rintala in Marías 1968: 94). In such a conception, one can stress inter-generational 'dependency' (Blaikie 1999: 128) or 'the relations through which successive generations are bound in the reproduction of social life' (Irwin 1998: 307), or, indeed, demand attention for intra-generational inequality and exclusion (Irwin 1996).

Since its early use in anthropology, 'generation' induces research and reflections on social and cultural conceptions of time, more particularly on how social formations (including anthropologists) deal with continuity and discontinuity. In one of the rare anthropological volumes dedicated to generations, age cohorts and social change, Spencer (1990: 18) remarks that 'the perception of time in regard to ageing goes in steps rather than in a smooth flow, for it is embedded in a chequered development of social relationships'. The opposition between time as a continuous flow and as a gradual process, reflects the ideas Leach developed in two related essays – 'Cronus and Chronos' (1953) and 'Time and False Noses' (1955) – in which he distinguishes between 'eternal time' that goes on and on (Chronos) and time conceptualized as zigzagging (Cronus) (in Hugh-Jones & Laidlaw 2000: 177, 181). In the latter case, 'time is experienced as something discontinuous, a repetition of repeated reversal, a sequence of oscillations between polar opposites: night and day, winter and summer, drought and flood, age and youth, life and death' (ibid: 176). Interestingly enough, Leach illustrates this zigzag or pendulum con- ceptualization of time with Radcliffe-Brown's findings about the identification of alternating generations (of grandmother and grandchild). Otherwise, Leach's pendulum conception of time – which he sees as underlying all *rites de passages* – rules out a continuous Chrono(s)-logical time conception (ibid: 183). How- ever, that is precisely the point which Spencer extracts from Van Gennep's and Turner's work on *rites de passage*, namely that 'history is not just concerned with the [eternal] succession of [age] cohorts, but with the symbolic elaboration of [historical, unprecedented] events'. In summary, 'all persons are similarly structured in relation to the historical transitions of their time; and the symbols and myths that compose this structure are interwoven with those of the more personal and routine transitions of life' (Spencer 1990: 22). In general, I think, Spencer's view helps us out of the impossible choice between time as rupture and time as flow. More importantly, it allows us to see how people mobilize the metaphoric of the 'routine transitions of life' – that is birth, youth and age- cohorts, adulthood and death – in the way they label, experience and/or contest 'historical transitions' in terms of rebirth or infantilization, rejuvenation or senescence, and such like.

A differential stress on continuity and discontinuity also affects the way in which youth is dealt with in anthropology, and more particularly how youth agency is valuated. In a review of the anthropological literature on youth, Bucholtz (2002) distinguishes between an approach in terms of 'adolescence' or transition towards adulthood, and an emerging anthropology of youth that stresses the 'here-and-now of young people's experience':

> Youth foregrounds age not as trajectory, but as identity, where *identity* is intended to invoke neither … adolescence as a prolonged 'search for identity', nor [a] rigid and essentialized concept… (Bucholtz 2002: 532; italics in the original)

Here Bucholtz urges us to avoid both 'transition thinking' and reification in favour of accentuating youth agency and identity. Such a view, it could be argued, may have prevented authors from summarizing, for instance, the history of the Senegalese students of the 20th century, in the following phrase:[5]

> The intention of students to be involved in the life of their nation as members of civil society ... does not take into account the fact that they are only in transition, over which they have no control because they have no impact on the socio-economic stakes. So instead of being actors/initiators of this change, they have turned into mere artefacts of this evolution... (Bathily, Diouf & Mbodj 1995: 401)

However, it is easier to be scandalized by the reduction of youth to a residual category (see Federici 2000: 50) than to remedy it without ending up with a view of youth that may crudely overstress youth's impact on society whether as liberators or as destroyers (see Seekings 1993).

This chapter attempts to pave a way out of this dyadic trap by focusing on how youth at particular moments in time is politically, socio-economically and culturally constructed *and* constructs itself in contested discourses of history and society, continuity and rupture (see Burgess this volume). My overall stance concerning the constructedness of 'youth' is aptly expressed in the following quote by Durham (2000: 118) in a review of the anthropological literature on youth in Africa:

> the conceptualization of cohorts and generational experience is deeply embedded in a politics of history. This is a politics of the present. ... Claims to the position of youth, claims about the nature of youth, and moral claims about youth are centrally involved in the reinvention of political and social space. They are used to mobilize similar *kinds* of temporal frameworks, in the negotiations of what kinds of power are available and where they can be exercised, and by whom.

Durham argues in favour of a doubly deconstructive focus on youth or generational 'identities'. Firstly, in a sense Durham could be said to be responding to Bourdieu's (1985: 144) slightly immoderate claim that 'divisions in age cohorts or generations are entirely variable and constitute the object of manipulation' by pointing to the discursive limits/grounds of such manipulability. 'Generation', Durham claims, features in particular activations of 'temporal frameworks' or in what Werbner (1999) calls 'politicized memory'. In this respect, Hall (1990: 225) remarks:

> Far from being grounded in a mere recovery of the past, which is waiting to be found, and which when found, will secure our sense of ourselves into eternity,

---

[5] This quote does not do justice to an otherwise richly documented and properly argued paper.

identities are the names we give to the different ways we are positioned by, and position ourselves within, the narratives of the past.

Secondly, Durham intimates that 'youth' as an identity category is seen as a temporal and local outcome of hegemonic struggles of subjectification and power distribution. The negotiation of historical positions described by Hall takes place, as Roseberry (1996: 77) has put it, 'in the dynamic tension between discursive fields and social fields of force'. Thus, identity constructions are articulated 'within present social reality *to create* a specific route of empowerment' (Van Dijk 1998: 156).

The above digression into the anthropological literature on generation and youth demonstrates what many have hinted at (see for example Comaroff & Comaroff 2000) but only a few (such as Burgess this volume) have taken much further, namely that generation and youth are discursive constructs in a politics of history and in hegemonic struggles. In both, I argue, generation and youth, because of what seems to be their inherent (cosmological?) ambiguity, are powerful instruments to ambivalently encompass continuity and rupture, inclusion and exclusion. In the following sections, how these constructs were strongly articulated in the context of the FESCI student movement in the course of the 1990s is examined. First, the issue of continuity is explored and the way it was articulated in terms of family descent and ideological filiation. In the two subsequent sections, I consider aspects of discontinuity as they are expressed in terms of 'the new (activist-based) family' and 'new (ideology-based) politics'. In the first and last sections, the issue of inclusion/exclusion is addressed by observing how the FESCI ambiguously associated and dissociated itself with regard to the 'populus'.

Narratives of continuity: Reproduction and the emergence of a national generation

The origins of the independent student union FESCI in 1990 are usually situated in the international context of new democratic impulses (South Africa, Germany) and the specific Ivorian context of ongoing economic deterioration and social antagonisms (Akindès 2000, 2001). Within this context, many authors (Loucou 1992: 160, Proteau 2002: 100, Konaté 2002: 780, Bailly 1995: 36) recount the same anecdote about power cuts that prevented students from properly preparing for their exams and that provoked the first student demonstrations on 19 February 1990. The repeated strikes and protest actions that followed gave rise to a number of small student associations that later joined together to form the FESCI federation, which presented itself as an alternative to the official government-controlled student association MEECI (*Mouvement des Etudiants et Elèves de Côte d'Ivoire*). Together with the new student unions, the existing independent teachers' unions SYNARES and SYNESCI, amongst others, demanded multipartyism and democratic elections.[6] In April 1990 the government gave in to the demands of the street and in May it officially recognized more than a dozen political parties and condoned a free press. From October onwards, a series of elections (presidential, parliamentary, and communal) were held, which confirmed the ruling PDCI's power.

When evaluating these rapid and drastic changes in Ivorian political life after more than thirty years of single-party rule, it is tempting to focus on the ferocity of the youth activists as the vanguard of a broad democratization movement. In conversations with former FESCI members on the early history of the student movement, my respondents do not so much play down the avant-garde qualities of the youth but rather historicize them. The overall image that arises from these discussions is that, from the very beginning, the youth movement presented itself as accomplishing a historical mission. The memories and documents of my interlocutors attest to the fact that from the start and throughout much of its later history the FESCI strongly situated itself as being embedded in a reform movement which spanned the entire history of Côte d'Ivoire and concerned its entire people.

In one conversation *Bila Foté,* who was a senior student in 1990, pointed out to me that the February riots were not the kind of spontaneous expression of discontent they appeared to be. He recalled how ten days before the riots started a conference was organized by the writer and anti-Houphouëtist activist Jean-Marie Adiaffi and the Club Cheikh Anta Diop. 'I don't remember the exact theme of the conference', he began by saying, 'but that was not important because conference themes were often a cover-up for voicing our collective protest against Houphouët.' He described how, towards the end of the conference, Professor Goré Bi of the Department of Oral Literature, and later a member of the Social Democratic Party (USD) of Zadi Zaourou, intervened:

---

[6] In 1970 two independent teachers' unions were created. The SYNESCI *(Syndicat National de l'Enseignement Secondaire de Côte d'Ivoire)* was for people working in secondary education, and was first led by the later founder of the RDR, Djéni Kobina. The SYNARES *(Syndicat Africain de Recherche et de l'Enseignement Supérieur)* was for researchers and those working in higher education. It was founded under Francis Wodié and included all other later socialist leaders (Laurent Gbagbo, Bernard Zadi Zaourou, and Bamba Moriféré) among its members at one stage or another.

[Goré Bi] said he was deceived by our attitude: we shouted, we were happy, but that was not what was expected from us. 'All the revolutions in the world,' he said 'were conducted by youngsters' and we were happy to just listen and shout. This has remained in my mind ever since. And in retrospect, I have connected it to the protest which broke out 10 days later, on 19 February 1990. It is true what he said. If you look at the French Revolution, Danton and Robespierre, they were youngsters. What Gore Bi asked of the youngsters was to make the country progress. (*Bila Foté*, 22 September 2003)

If *Bila Foté* makes it sound as if the intervention of Goré Bi provided a kind of 'marching order' for revolutionary students, others among my interlocutors emphasize that even in this early period students claimed a certain agency in deliberating the potential import of their movement, and reflected on their actions as potential revolutionaries.

Sanga Dogon (24 May 2003) – a fellow student activist of *Bila Foté* in the early days of the FESCI – recalled a debate which took place on the evening of 19 February during which students discussed the significance of the power cuts and the street violence. According to *Sanga Dogon*, two opinions divided the assembly. One group saw students as an intermediary class between the elite and the masses. For them, the power cuts signalled the gradual 'pauperization of the intellectual elite [of students], whom were thereby turned into some kind of proletariat'. The second group, whom *Sanga Dogon* considered to be the real revolutionaries, 'considered the power cuts as a symbol of the failure of the political system to cope with the economic recession since the early 1980s'. Arguing that 'we needed a new system altogether, a new social and economic dynamic', the second group, according to *Sanga Dogon,* saw its demands for better working conditions (electricity at night) or for (student) scholarships as appeals to the government to satisfy the minimal conditions for the continued existence of 'students' as 'people who think; who reinvent the future of the nation'.[7] In the debate, the second option won, according to *Sanga Dogon*, and with it the revolutionary ideas of the student union fraction of which he himself as well as *Bila Foté* were members.[8]

---

[7] According to Bailly (1995: 36), in February 1990 the students protested against 'obscurity and obscurantism'. In *Sanga Dogon*'s classification, the first group can be seen reacting against 'obscurity', while the second group protested instead against the 'obscurantism' of the government.

[8] Both *Sanga Dogon* and *Bila Foté* were leading members of CESCOCI, one of the most influential among the proto-Fesci student associations. CESCOCI provided the first two secretaries-general of FESCI, Amos Beugré and Ahipeaud Martial, and received financial support and ideological backing from the opposition heavyweight Bamba Moriféré.

Leaving aside the differences of opinion, this reconstruction of the early history of the student movement captures the central concern of the students with different aspects of their *reproduction*, ranging from the role of students in the rejuvenation of the existing anti-Houphouëtist opposition, to their own reproduction as a class of intellectuals, to the reproduction of society or of the nation as a whole. The few sociological accounts of youth and students in Côte d'Ivoire partly confirm this by considering the issue of reproduction in at least two different ways. In the 1980s several sociologists signalled what has been called 'the accumulation of youngsters' who find it increasingly difficult to become part of adult life and what this implies in terms of regular earnings and family responsibilities (Touré 1985: 287-88, Le Pape 1986; 112). Others have focused on the crisis in the reproduction of educated youngsters and observed how the cuts in education budgets yielded unequal access to education (Le Pape & Vidal 1987: 73) and led to the overall marginalization of young intellectuals in Côte d'Ivoire in the 1990s (Proteau 2002). In the analysis that follows, I examine how youngsters have addressed these issues of reproduction in narratives of family history and in a metaphoric of ideological filiation. These narratives, I argue, give shape to the kind of continuities from which the Fescists of the 1990s have arisen as a 'national generation'.

Several former Fescists situated their juvenile activism in family narratives which in some way or another connect with historical anti-Houphouëtism. They evoked the fact that their fathers or uncles were already opponents of Houphouët-Boigny as early as the 1940s or later. Others have broken off relations with their families because of the latters' clientelist obligations towards the PDCI party. But even if their families had no political history, several former Fescists have recounted the predicament of their forebears as resulting from the despised politics of the ruling party. They portray their parents as poor peasants who had small plantations and whose revenues were scarce because the single-party state paid low prices to (small) planters, received high prices on the world market, and used the money for its own enrichment.[9]

With the help of family stories, the former Fescists have firmly inscribed their student activism in larger narratives that span the entire political and socio-economic history of Côte d'Ivoire since its first steps on the way to independence. This same historical scope can also be found back in the documents which my respondents provided me with. In a sense, these official

---

[9] For reasons of space I cannot include original statements illustrating the family narratives of former Fescists. Quoting and interpreting them requires the presentation of a good deal of contextual and historical information for which there is no space here (see Arnaut 2004a).

Figure 5.1: 1992-1993 FESCI membership card.

documents spell out, in terms of ideological filiation, what the family narratives explicate in terms of kin-based experiences.

In 1995 the FESCI published a booklet that was entirely dedicated to the history of the Ivorian student movement from the 1950s until FESCI's creation in 1990.[10] In the preface the then secretary-general Soro Guillaume claims that:

> There is a certain continuity in the struggle of the student youth for about half a century: this continuity resides in the fact that, apart from its corporatist claims, the youth continues to occupy an avant-garde position in the global movement for the liberation of the Ivorian people. (FESCI 1995: 3)

---

[10]   The 1995 brochure was published at a time when the student union was trying to rebuild itself after (i) many Fescists had already left and were leaving the country, (ii) heavy repression had frightened many militants into hiding or forced them to abandon the struggle, and (iii) internal disputes had divided the FESCI membership. The 1995 publication coincided with (i) the belief that after the unanimous election of Soro Guillaume as secretary-general in February 1995, the student movement could retrieve its past strength, and (ii) the hope that democratic presidential elections (in 1995) could remove President Bédié from office. While the latter hope proved to be an illusion, the former belief largely materialized.

The genealogy which the folder constructs is that between the FESCI and the UGECI, which was created in 1956 and protested heavily against the mounting pro-colonial attitude of the Ivorian leadership.[11] After eight pages of detailed historical reconstruction, the folder concludes that:

> Today, the spirit of UGECI is revived in the spirit of the FESCI which cannot die because it goes in the sense of history. (ibid: 11)

While the family narratives often explicate the position of the youngsters in negative terms (of anti-Houphouëtism), the 1995 brochure is formulated in a more constructive (ideological) way, not least by evoking the ongoing project of the liberation of the Ivorian people. From this positive, or perhaps counter-hegemonic discourse, the Côte d'Ivoire of Houphouët-Boigny is seen as a historical deviation from the right course (the sense of history) which was set by certain former student movements and which the FESCI continues to chart. This, *Marc Dounga* (1 March 2003) expresses aptly when he recounts how he was pursued by the state as a mob leader and an agitator (*meneur de troupes*). 'Yes, we the Fescists,' he says, 'were considered to be *des éclaireurs de conscience* of Côte d'Ivoire.' Read as a military term in the context of *Dounga's* battle with the regime, *éclaireur* (scout) signifies 'precursor' or 'explorer' engaged in reconnaissance. Taken in the more literary or academic sense induced by 'conscience', *éclaireurs* (guides) refers to the intelligentsia (the 'illuminati' in *Dounga's* metaphoric) who, as *Sanga Dogon* (24 May 2003) said before, take it on themselves to 'reinvent the future of the nation'.

In this rhetoric of militant vanguards and intellectual torchbearers, the Fescists reveal the full ambiguity with which they simultaneously identify with the nation or the Ivorian people, and differentiate themselves from it. This ambivalence, I argue, is largely sustained by the metaphors of generation and youth. The latter terms can combine continuity with rupture as well as exclusion with inclusion. In all, youth and generation are powerful discursive instruments for articulating the multi-layered crisis of reproduction that the student youth felt it was entangled in.

---

[11] The controversies of the 1950s mainly centered around (i) the decision by Houphouët-Boigny and the PDCI to break off all ties with the French Communist Party in 1950 (the so-called *désapparentement*), (ii) the acceptance of the *Loi-Cadre* of 1956 which critics felt did not go far enough in the direction of independence, and (iii) the Ivorian leaders' enthusiasm to join the Franco-African community in 1958 – a stance that different student organizations bluntly rejected (de Benoist 1994, Diarra 1997: 56-64, Proteau 2002: 61-98).

In May 1994, the FESCI published a pamphlet containing a poem authored by 'The Voice of 25 Fescists Detained at the National Police School and at the State Security Police (DST)' (Figure 5.2). In two stanzas the poem associates the humiliation and the suffering of 'a youth' with that of 'a country' and 'a people'.

> My *parents*; I have experienced detention and I have been ashamed
> Yes, I have been ashamed and what kind of shame?
> The shame of a country
> The shame of a people
> The shame of a youth.

Towards the end, the poem qualifies the shame as that which is 'armed to the teeth with guns, truncheons, electric whips, and torture chairs', but predicts that some day this shame will only be 'a memory on the triumphant path to real liberty'.

In statements such as those, dramatically voiced from the centres of repression, the geographical, historical and sociological contours of the student movement dissolve into that of an entire country and a whole people, their history and their future. Under critical conditions, FESCI activists speak out in the name of a student population that sees its existence threatened by fierce repression and its reproduction under jeopardy by austerity measures and disqualification. In the above-mentioned poem, as in the entire genealogical discourse of families and ideologies, FESCI seems to put the ultimate hope of its reproduction in the hands of the Ivorian society as a whole. This people, the family narratives illustrate, continued (throughout its history of subjugation and repression) to produce the kind of youth that guarantees its future liberation. This claim is formulated in the mission statement that was published in one of the few official documents that the organization produced – more than three years after its foundation in 1990.

> The autonomous and apolitical movement which we take upon ourselves, expresses the will of a new Ivorian youth to fight for a better life and to assume its *historical role* which consists in taking position in a societal project that takes shape in the popular aspirations. (FESCI 1993, this author's italics)

While both the 1994 poem and the 1993 mission statement tie together the fate of the youth with that of the people, both documents also mark certain ruptures and exclusions. *Parent* (in French), the addressee of the poem, could be wrongly interpreted as any parent or family member but '*parent*' in Fesci-speak signifies 'member of the new (political or union) family' and implies a distancing from the biological family. This rupture finds its political counterpart

<u>Fédération Estudiantine & Scolaire de Côte d'Ivoire</u>
F. E. S. C. I.

Poème

La honte

Mes parents ; j'ai vécu la détention et j'ai connu la honte
oui j'ai connu la honte et quelle honte ?

   la honte d'un pays
   la honte d'un peuple
   la honte d'une jeunesse
   la véritable honte incarnée

Mes amis ; mes camarades de lutte, j'ai vu la honte en personne et

   j'ai mal à mon pays
   j'ai mal à mon peuple
   j'ai mal à ma jeunesse.

Car j'ai vu la honte de sa destinée,
la honte assasine de liberté

   Oui j'ai vécu la honte, et quelle honte ?

Une honte indescriptible. La honte de lendemains incertains parce que obscurcis par
des personnes hélas peu honteuses.

   Et j'ai vu la honte planer comme cherchant une proie et se poser sur mon
   pays.

   Assitôt, j'ai vu une jeunesse prompte et spontanée lutter contre la honte. La
lutte fut âpre. Mais la honte fut vaincue malgré elle.

   Alors mes amis, j'ai vu la honte, une honte méconnaissable s'en aller la
queue entre les pattes, la tête basse, confuse et honteuse
Et une vive lueur d'espoir a pointé à l'horizon éclairant le visage des lutteurs.

Désormais la honte, oui la véritable honte, cette honte qui brutalise des jeunes gens,
traumatise les jeunes lutteurs pour leur arracher des aveux,
Cette honte que j'ai connue ne sera qu'un souvenir sur la voie triomphale de la liberté
véritable qui comme le bien triomphe du mal, triomphera de cette honte armée
jusqu'aux dents de fusils, de matraques, de fouets électriques, de chaises de torture.

   Adieu honte honteuse.

Ecole de Police, le 31 Mai 1994.   La voix des 25 Fescistes détenus
           à l'Ecole Nationale de Police et à la D. S. T.

Figure 5.2: Poem '*La honte*' by 'The Voice of 25 Fescists Detained at the
National Police School and at the State Security Police (DST)'.

in the mission statement which presents the movement as apolitical. By calling itself apolitical, the FESCI maintains its distance from regular party politics and situates its goals at the higher (ideological) level of a societal project. Both ruptures feature in a broader positioning of the student youth as simultaneously acting with and somehow separately from the people. This fundamental ambiguity is examined later as being handled with techniques of populism and crowd management.

Social ruptures: The invention of the new family

By the end of 1989 and in his last year of secondary school (*lycée*) in Abidjan, *Aganda Soul* decided to join FESCI, which was then headed by Ahipeaud Martial. Although he never became a national FESCI leader, *Aganda Soul* was a strong activist and an important recruiter of the student union until 1995. Much later he co-founded the Ivorian Movement for Youth Rights (MIDJ) and is currently directing an internationally operating anti-globalist organization in Abidjan. Looking back on more than a decade of what he calls his 'communist engagement' in the struggle of the Left (*la lutte de gauche*), *Aganda Soul* (24 September 2003) muses:

> Well, at a certain time we did not have the occasion to live with our *natural families* but we had the chance of living with another *political or trade union family* (*famille politique ou syndicale*) [...] What a political friend or a friend from the union (*un ami politique ou syndicale*) has done for me, even a relative (un *parent*) has not done. My studies have been paid by my political friends. My parents said that I was lost. It is only now that some of my kinsfolk speak to me. When I joined the FESCI, my elder brother chased me from the house. (this author's italics)

As was also observed by Konaté (2002: 785) and Proteau (2002: 152-54), the 'parent-talk' of the Fescists is both important and highly significant. In my conversations with former Fescists, 'family' can refer to kin-based ('natural') or activist-based (party, union) socialities but can also function as a metaphor for the educational or the state system, administered by school and university authorities (elders), and ultimately controlled by the president in the figure of the 'Father of the Nation'.

Parental reactions to their sons' and daughters' activism in the FESCI ranged from explicit agreement, to resignation, or to fierce opposition. These reactions often had a direct effect on the living conditions of the students as well as on their academic curriculum. The ill-fated – like *Aganda Soul* who lost all family support because of his activism – either sought alternative funding from the sponsors (elders, professionals) of the wider opposition movement or joined the personal support networks of more privileged students. *Kakou Bi*, currently a colleague of *Aganda Soul* in the anti-globalist movement, was among those fortunate enough to have a father who supported his activism. He recalls that during his time in the FESCI:

> My room was called 'the palace of the people'. I kept my key in a place where everybody knew where it was. You come in, you eat, you sleep. …
> One's natural family had become one's comrades-in-arms *(camarades de lutte)*. Really, it was all about sharing. Hence the word *parent*. Many comrades had been rejected by their parents. For many years they lived with FESCI members. We paid their fees, we put them up, and we fed them, because that was the idea: one must share everything, the misery and the joy. (*Kakou Bi*, 23 September 2003)

While *Aganda Soul* uses 'relative' *(parent)* and 'friend' *(ami)* to distinguish between the 'natural' and the 'new' family, *Kakou Bi* intimates the substitution of the latter by the former and situates this switch in the term *parent*. Indeed, the 'new family' in the fullest sense of the word was given shape in the resignification of the word 'parent'. Very soon after FESCI's foundation in 1990 the word *parent* was used to refer to any fellow activist.[12]

The resignification of *parent* is not so much the change in its meaning, rather its referent. *Parent* can point to any member of the 'union family', but retains its full meaning in terms of material and moral support.[13] Like any 'natural family', the new family also has its relative elders and youngsters. 'Elder' parents are members of the extended 'political family' who are either active in opposition politics (for example, Bernard Zadi Zaourou, Bamba Moriféré and Laurent Gbagbo) or members of the independent unions (SYNARES and SYNESCI) who actively supported the Fescists in general or individual members or small groups of them in particular.

The 'new family' thus constituted, stories about the 'natural family' and the break away from its stifling grip *(embrigadement)* lead us into the realm of repression against the FESCI activists. This repression took the form of open violence by the armed forces, official exclusion from school *(radier)* or from specific departments *(réorienter)*. Moreover, repression also extended into the

---

[12] According to *Bila Foté* (22 September 2003), in the early days of the student movement *parent* was used as a password among student activists. When a student entered a room where a clandestine meeting was being held, one asked him whether he or she was a *parent*. Very soon, however, the password was known by friend and foe alike and was used publicly as an identity label.

[13] *Parent* was sometimes used as a term of reference, such as in the sentence *J'étais le chef des parents à Yopougon* ('I was the head of the student activists at Yopougon'), but also as a term of address, as in the salutation '*hé parent*' ('hey comrade').

private sphere and led to tragic family ruptures and exclusion from home. In a group conversation with former Fescists now living in Germany, *Mandege Louis* (1 March 2003) recalls the conflict he had with his elder brother who was financially responsible for him after their father died at an early age. It was not so much that his brother was against his student activism, *Mandege Louis* explained, but apparatchiks from the PDCI ruling party threatened to sack his brother if he could not persuade his younger relative to abandon the FESCI. The threat was enormous: if his elder brother lost his job as a civil servant, the whole extended family would suffer.

To summarize, the invention of the 'new (FESCI) family' served to create a novel, activist-based sociality that marked a clear rupture with the immediate society. In the way the new family was articulated by the former Fescists one can observe how youngsters, in the words of Eisenstadt (1995/1962: 77) 'rebelled against their elders and the traditional familistic setting with its stress on the latter's authority'. More than that, the metaphor of the 'new family' served to visualize a gerontocratic complex – the interpenetration of the authority of the 'natural family' and that of the state which continued to be ruled by the old PDCI party. However, in contrast to what Eisenstadt indicates, in statements by former Fescists, the despised 'traditional' aspect of the family or the system is not so much identified as cultural in the sense of ethnic or 'tribal' but as political in the sense of political culture or established ways of conducting politics.

Political rupture and the break with 'ancestral politics'

> When Houphouët died and Bédié took over [in December 1993], I was in prison [together with a number of other Fescists]. Within weeks, Bédié sent one of his ministers to come and tell us that 'the Côte d'Ivoire of the grandfather is no more' (*la Côte d'Ivoire du grand-père est dépassé*). We knew what it meant: the system would become even more repressive and [this repression was to be] directed against specific personalities. (*Marc Dounga*, 1 March 2003)

In the above excerpt, *Marc Dounga* recalls that when 'grandfather' Houphouët-Boigny died, Bédié took on the role of the 'father' who more directly supervised, personally manipulated, and (if unsuccessful) mercilessly penalized his disobedient 'children'.[14] According to *Sanga Dogon* (24 May 2003), the

---

[14] Interestingly, the 1993 political transition is presented in terms of alternating generations and hints at the system widely known throughout (West) Africa of joking relationships between grandparents and grandchildren whereby the child-parent rela-

shift from the violent but 'paternalistic' repression by Houphouët-Boigny to the more ruthless methods of Bédié had the effect of rendering the FESCI leadership more mistrustful and rude, and resulted in the movement stepping up, what he calls, its 'logic of rupture' (*la logique de rupture*).[15] This is exemplified by three parallel developments in the post-1993 era: the radicalization of the movement, 'distancing' through expatriation, and the autonomization from politics. Among these three, the latter requires most attention here because it subscribes most forcibly to the overall image of the FESCI as an anti-political, popular movement.

FESCI's radicalization can be measured from new developments in its overt and covert actions. In response to the mounting and more incisive repression of the Bédié regime, the FESCI employed more extreme methods of protest – such as hunger strikes – to its standard range of public demonstrations (Proteau 2002: 158). Simultaneously, it reorganized itself internally and set up shadow command structures such as a substitute national council and underground action groups to ensure it was less vulnerable to government repression against its public agitators.[16]

This internal redeployment of FESCI activism had its outward-bound, geopolitical counterpart in the massive exodus of Fescists from Côte d'Ivoire to Europe. Between 1994 and 1996 an estimated 3,000 Fescists and students left the country: first to London and later to Germany, the Netherlands and Denmark.[17] The expatriation was not only an escape from 'fatherly' repression under Bédié, but was also set up and seen as an astute contribution to the FESCI struggle. None of the Fescists went into exile in France. 'We were all anti-French,' explained *Sanga Dogon* (25 May 2003). 'For us, the Houphouët

---

tionship is seen as more 'serious'. See for example, Griaule (1948) and Drucker-Brown (1982).

[15] The repression against the student movement occurred in a legal vacuum. By June 1991 the student union was publicly outlawed but this ban was never legally formalized by the government. In defiance of its prohibition, the FESCI continued to demonstrate while its members and sympathizers were persecuted. Fescists who fell into the hands of the security forces – whom the Fescists called *les forces du désordre* – were detained in prisons, army camps and police stations around the country, often without being officially charged. There they underwent physical torture and psychological maltreatment (Amnesty International 1994).

[16] Former Fescists are still very discrete about covert action groups and secret operations but none of them denies that they were important and increasingly so in the second half of the 1990s (*Nien Fa* & *Marc Dounga*, 5 August 2003; *Boda Goro*, 15 March 2003).

[17] This exodus more or less came to a standstill in 1996 when all European countries introduced visa requirements for Ivorian visitors.

system only survived because of its neo-colonial relationship with France.' On non-French territory, many student refugees resumed their university studies while organizing themselves in political associations with the explicit goal of continuing the revolutionary struggle.[18] The rupture exemplified in the extraterritorial deployment of the student opposition forces was framed as doubly effective. The student diaspora broke away from neo-colonial Côte d'Ivoire (and its French patrons) and was meant to produce new intellectuals whose dispersion across Europe embodied the awaited multilateral geopolitics of the future Côte d'Ivoire.

If by going underground the FESCI was trying to safeguard its struggle from intervention by a repressive regime, and by going abroad it was avoiding neo-colonial dependency, the FESCI also spelled out its autonomization by 'going ideological' and thereby dissociating itself from established political practice. This needs to be understood in the wider political context of the 1990s.

When in April 1990 the government gave in to the demands of the street and introduced multipartyism, the junior and senior opposition activists organized themselves in almost inverse ways. On the one hand, small anti-government student unions merged into the single FESCI federation that was able to impose a monopoly of student representation on the campus.[19] On the other hand, the left-wing political movement crystallized into four small socialist parties built around former trade unionists: the FPI of Laurent Gbagbo, the PIT of Francis Wodié, the PSI of Bamba Moriféré, and the USD of Zadi Zaourou.[20] The contrast between the monolithic student movement and the fragmented 'democratic left' sharpened even further after 1993.

The death of Houphouët-Boigny heralded a political reshuffling of considerable consequence. In 1994 the ruling PDCI party broke up into a more 'nationalist' fraction represented by President Bédié and a more neo-liberal fraction which, in 1994, converted into the new political party, the RDR (*Rassemblement des Républicains*) of former Prime Minister Alassane Ouattara. In the face of this political rearrangement, the left-wing opposition fragmented

---

[18] In 1994 former FESCI militants set up the MOÍRA (Movement of Ivorian Opponents in Germany) in Cologne. In 1996 this organization was partly replaced by the USP (People's Socialist Union) and the MLTCI (Movement for the Total Liberation of Côte d'Ivoire), both of which had their headquarters in London but regrouped anti-government militants dispersed all over Europe.

[19] This situation of absolute hegemony remained uncontested until very recently (June 2004) when a new student union emerged under the name of AGEECI (*Association Générale des Elèves et Etudiants de Côte d'Ivoire*). Apparently, AGEECI's creation provoked fierce reactions from the FESCI leadership (*Fraternité Matin*, 28 June 2004).

[20] FPI: *Front Populaire Ivoirien*; PIT: *Parti Ivoirien des Travailleurs*; PSI: *Parti Socialiste Ivoirien*; USD: *Union des Socio-Démocrates*.

further. While some old-time opposition figures, such as Bernard Zadi Zaourou and Jean-Marie Adiaffi, joined Bédié's PDCI government, others like former SYNESCI leader Djeny Kobina co-founded the RDR. To make the ideological confusion complete, a number of socialist parties – most notably Laurent Gbagbo's FPI party – formed a strategic alliance with the newly created neo-liberal RDR. This anti-Bédié coalition called the Republican Front (*Front Républicain*) lasted until 1999 when it collapsed in the run-up to the 2000 elections in which Gbagbo and Ouattara both decided to stand as presidential candidates.

The Fescists perceived these rather bewildering reconfigurations of the Ivorian political scene during the 1990s as the result of 'big men' politics and former Fescists often speak in that respect of the post-1990 'multipartisan' instead of 'multiparty' system. The FESCI thus developed a discourse of rupture and autonomy in which it dissociated itself from opportunistic and personalistic party politics (*politique politicienne*) and emphasized its ideological tenacity.

One dramatic event in which FESCI expressed its autonomy from established political practice was the deposition of FESCI Secretary-General Eugène Djué in September 1994. Having been accused of surreptitiously accepting money from President Bédié in return for destabilizing the FESCI from within, Djué was precipitately replaced as the head of the FESCI by Jean Blé Guirao.[21] In a pamphlet on the matter, the new secretary-general put the FESCI leadership's decision in a broader light:

> Beyond the sanctions against Djué, it is the manifest wish of a generation to break with this ancestral past that pursues it relentlessly. (FESCI pamphlet, 12 October 1994)

Here, Blé Guirao denounces the repeated attempts of the system to buy its way into the student movement and calls upon the latter to express its independence and demonstrate its defiance. The tradition of corrupting opponents and dissidents into compliance is also evoked in the 1995 FESCI 'history' brochure in which Secretary-General Soro Guillaume declares:

> Facing the persistent attitude of surrendering, of compromising, and even of betrayal of the People by the intellectuals, there is, for the Present New Generation and in the

---

[21] The list of FESCI leaders who were either accused of collaborating with 'the system' or eventually gave in to pressures from it is long. Accusations of treason were not only spread by Fescists but also by government agents who tried to destabilize the student movement.

Superior interest of the People, a challenge to take up. (FESCI 1995: 11, capitals in original)

What Guirao identifies as 'ancestral', Soro Guillaume qualifies as the 'persisting' political practice of clientelism, corruption and cooptation that emasculates the entire political domain including certain 'elder brothers' of the left-wing opposition parties. In the face of this, both FESCI leaders posited a break and announced the emergence of a 'new generation' of political actors. These actors, it was established in the same 1995 document, saw themselves as 'ideological' in the sense of being led by firm principles, the origins of which were situated in the 1950s and to which they stuck with heroic tenacity. At the same time, the FESCI adopted the image of an anti-political movement that struggled for and with 'the people' as distinct from the restricted group of political elites. Nevertheless, this self-presentation of the FESCI as a popular movement relied on more than the kind of rhetoric illustrated above. It was equally sustained by a comprehensive strategy of popular mobilization and specific populist tactics by which the FESCI imposed itself as the exemplary civil-society organization that voiced the wishes of the Ivorian youth and, by extension, those of the entire Ivorian people.

The organization of popular expression

> There can be no New School without a genuine democracy.
> (*Il ne peut y avoir d'Ecole Nouvelle sans une démocratie véritable.*) (Slogan on FESCI's membership card, see Figure 5.1.)

More than just demanding genuine democracy, the FESCI also put it into practice through a whole range of actions and events that explored and activated alternative ways of political expression. These included mass meetings, sit-ins and marches, sometimes accompanied by street violence. As one former Fescist summarized it, the FESCI was above all an 'organization of mobilization' (*Boda Goro*, 15 March 2003). *Sanga Dogon* explained this as follows:

> In order for the movement to become a societal phenomenon, it is necessary that the students crystallize themselves on FESCI's structure. An organization that does not demonstrate, that does not mobilize, dies. So, whenever there was an occasion we protested but not only by means of declarations, but also with the masses, with meetings. (*Sanga Dogon*, 24 May 2003)

Here, *Sanga Dogon* explains how the FESCI incessantly demonstrated its ability to mobilize crowds of students, whether by assembling them in a car park at the Cocody campus, by bringing them together for a sit-in in front of the town hall, or by having them traverse the city from the Yopougon halls of residence *(cité)* to the Plateau administrative centre in Abidjan. Apart from some sticks and stones and a few charges of the so-called Baule tear gas *(lacrymogène Baule)* that students used to attack government cars or public buildings, they used no weapons other than their own bodies to block the streets, and their slogans and songs that offended the regime and its sym-pathizers.[22] The overall image of FESCI activism that arises from the way the student movement occupied the urban and national public space is one of spontaneous expression and impulsive behaviour that emerged from the revolutionary instinct of its members. In the following quote, *Mandege Louis* connects his own revolutionary feelings and the street violence with FESCI's double demand for educational and political reform.

> I was a rebel *(révolté)*, the system bothered me. While smashing up a car or blocking a street, I felt comfortable because I told myself that it was they who were preventing the school system from developing, it was they who were preventing the people from fully playing their role.

However, like many other former Fescists I spoke to, *Mandege Louis* qualifies the grass-roots view of initiative and achievement and, later in the conversation demanded attention for the way FESCI transformed, channelled and structured the students' discontent.

> The whole issue was to pass from the stage of a rebel *(révolté)* who blocks the streets to that of a revolutionary *(révolutionnaire)* who speaks of the advent of a new society. *(Mandege Louis, 1 March 2003)*

When dealing with the matter of revolutionary practice, former Fescists focus on the command structure and the techniques used by the FESCI leadership to conduct the mobilization it triggered. That mobilization in itself, *Sango Dogon* explained in the opening quote of this section, was the work of the FESCI leadership who were keen to create incidents or ready to respond to any government provocation. For former Secretary-General *Oko Ménéda* (22 September 2003)

> ... that was our method of mobilization, our method of conquest, so to speak; we were toilers *(bosseurs)*, we were robots; we taught the youngsters to sacrifice themselves and to receive nothing in return.

---

[22] 'Lacrymogène Baule' was a self-made tear-gas bomb containing a mixture of kaolin and pepper powder.

For persuading the FESCI membership and the students to participate selflessly in the action, the FESCI leadership used a certain authority that it borrowed, among others, from the military and the school system. As for the former, FESCI gave its active members military ranks such as 'general' for the secretaries-general, 'colonel' or 'captain' for their deputies (*adjoints*), and 'sergeant' for ordinary members.

> That was first of all a question of discipline, but also [meant] to give a bit of courage to all of us who were confronting the police and the army. At the moments when they attacked us grievously we did not have weapons but only our ranks. (*Ramses Séry*, 25 May 2003)

The 'militarization' of the FESCI leadership also resulted in some of them using nicknames with clear military overtones, such as Che, Sankara or Sadam, or in naming their local sections after sites of (past) military conflict such as Kivu, Kosovo or Beirut. By qualifying its struggle as a military one and by associating itself with international revolutionary celebrities, the FESCI leadership can be said to have been 'heroizing' itself.

The second register of authority from which the FESCI leadership extracted power was the school system. For the public distribution of information or instructions, the leadership had recourse to pamphlets or flyers called 'TDs'. In normal university life, TD means *Travaux Dirigés* (guided works) and signifies all sorts of written assignments performed under the supervision of a teacher or lecturer. The FESCI TDs are similar in that they formulate an instruction to be carried out. In most cases, FESCI TDs contain a call (*mot d'ordre*) for a strike, a demonstration or some other impromptu action by which the student leaders who formulate them arrogate the position of an 'academic authority'.

Gathering authority from specific registers of hierarchy and obedience, the FESCI leadership instituted a state of alert on the campus, which required urgent and concerted action such as demanding the liberation of a FESCI leader from prison or the cancellation of a decision by a school authority to expel a group of insubordinate pupils. As a consequence, *Mandege Louis* (1 March 2003) explains, 'there was never much time to reflect on what all this meant'. Apart from the few who brought themselves to read Mao or Marcuse or who received some ideological guidance from 'elder brothers' in the broader opposition movement, there was no other training for the majority of the militants than that which they received 'in the field' (*sur le terrain*) and that was dictated by the pressing needs of the moment. This *modus operandi* could be found back in the relative importance or unimportance of certain posts in the FESCI national council. There, the national secretary responsible for instruction (*formation*) was far less important than the key functions of 'organization' and 'information' – the two pillars on which the student movement rested: the mobilization of students and the direction in which they marched.

If the FESCI leadership employed a number of powerful instruments to guide the movement from above, it equally exercised control over the production of revolutionary ideas and plans that emerged from below.

> During these [mass] meetings students adopted the habit of talking in public and some did very well. There were those who really stirred up the crowd, who guided (*oriente*) the students. Those we got afterwards for a function in the BEN [National Executive Council].

> But we could not have complete confidence in the crowd *(la foule)* because the crowd needed to be organized. Therefore we used the technique of the 'guided synthesis' (*la synthèse orientée*). When everybody had spoken, someone from the [FESCI] leadership provided a synthesis of the debate whereby the conclusion that the leadership favoured was presented as the only feasible one and was then approved by the crowd. (*Sanga Dogon*, 24 May 2003)

This quote provides one of the finest descriptions of what could be called FESCI populist tactics. It reveals a sophisticated combination of student empowerment through free expression and crowd management by which the inflamed student masses were turned into compliant followers of the FESCI leadership. This method of organizing the elicitation of consensus, I believe, is part and parcel of FESCI's search for hegemony among the students and sustains the claim that the students voice 'popular aspirations'.

This examination of how FESCI organized popular expression both from above and below ends this analysis of the FESCI discourse of youth and generation, and how this discourse featured in wider strategies to carve a space of alternative political representation for itself. This claim on representation was based on constructions of continuities and ruptures, inclusions and exclusions. Overall, FESCI inscribed itself in the long battle of the Ivorian people for national emancipation (continuity/inclusion) and positioned itself and was positioned (by the elders of the extended political and union family) as the advance guard in that ongoing struggle that needed constant renewal and a new political morale (rupture). The 'virtual' FESCI hegemony on the campus that resulted from this positioning was sustained by populist mobilization tactics that staged grass-roots spontaneity and student empowerment but resided on an unequal distribution of power and knowledge and resulted in the firm exclusion of possible dissidence.

FESCI discourse in the contemporary political project of autochthony

> Dictatorship is characterized by manifest violence. Mister Gbagbo is inherently violent. His whole political career has been based on violence. In 1990 when he spoke of multipartyism, he sent the students onto the streets to smash traffic lights, burn shops and steal loaves of bread. In 1992, he burned the entire Plateau district of Abidjan, before going to prison in order to pay for it.
> [Journalist:] With the help of the FESCI?
> [Soro Guillaume] (laughing). Let me first finish my answer to your question.[...]
> (*Fraternité Matin*, 2 April 2003)

That is how Soro Guillaume – FESCI's former secretary-general and now leader of the New Forces – presents his erstwhile *parents* as a gang of rascals and pilferers thrown onto the streets by the then opposition leader Laurent Gbagbo. Nevertheless, Soro Guillaume seems to find it difficult to explicitly identify these unruly youngsters as FESCI members. Following the above exchange, the interviewee, indeed, 'first answers the question' but he never comes back to the issue of the FESCI again in the interview. Surely, it is not easy to characterize as instrumentalized the members of an independent union that presented itself (and was at some stage presented by Soro Guillaume himself) as an 'autonomous and apolitical movement'. However, Soro Guillaume sees himself opposed to those many former Fescists who are leading figures in the Young Patriots movement, as well as to the present-day FESCI union that is a prominent member of the Young Patriots' Alliance. Above all, what Soro's statements bring out is that the battle over the FESCI legacy has been won by the Young Patriots and that the New Forces have no option other than to awkwardly dismiss the student movement, even in its past form.

Having won the struggle over FESCI's name and ideology, the Young Patriots took meanings from it which they do not only use themselves but also distribute or insert in the patriotic political discourse of President Laurent Gbagbo and his extensive entourage of supporters in political and civil society. One prominent figure of what opponents would call Gbagbo's civil society is Nyamien Messou, the present leader of the SYNARES teachers' union. When, during a patriotic talk on national television, Nyamien Messou was asked about the apparent success of the Young Patriot movement, he responded by saying that its success was quite normal and explained his answer by situating the new movement in a long tradition of resistance of the Ivorian people that began in the decolonization period. His historical digression is worth quoting *in extenso*.

> The Ivorian people have developed a habit. Before independence there was resistance. [...] Also in 1951 with the break of the RDA away from the Communist

Party; later there was the *Loi-Cadre* [1956] and then the referendum of 1958 to ask the Africans whether they wanted independence or to remain as they were.[23] In 1960 there was also a bit of resistance and all the people of the resistance were thrown into prison around 1963 by Félix Houphouët; but the civil resistance continued to organize itself around the intellectuals, around the universities.

In 1990 the people of Côte d'Ivoire took the opportunity once again to say that they wanted to express themselves. With multipartyism the awareness changed. [...] Then we arrive at the *coup d'état* of 1999. [...] The actors are the same only the scenery has changed. Now it is France who sponsors the new *coup d'etat* [of 2002] by multiplying the resources. [...] Also in 1999 the Ivorians did not understand very well what was going on. Now, however, they are more aware, their analytical abilities have increased. [...] That is why the civil resistance takes this new form different from 1999. (Nyamien Messou on *Radio Télévision Ivoire*, March 2003)

This illustrates the main dimensions of continuity/discontinuity and inclusion/-exclusion that the FESCI developed but that are now inserted in a new political project that could be qualified as autochthony-driven (Dozon 2000; Bayart *et al.* 2001). As far as the issue of 'imagined continuity' is concerned, the parallels with the FESCI discourse are obvious. Messou has constructed a national anti-imperialist tradition that goes back to the earliest moments of decolonization and thus traces a trajectory that coincides with the birth and the coming of age of the nation. Furthermore, this nationalist tradition does not reside in the ideas or interventions of politicians but is presented as the gradual manifestation of the will of the Ivorian people. This gradualness makes for a different approach to the dimension of rupture. Messou segments the national history whereby the different caesura represent moments of renewed and/or heightened awareness and combativeness that have culminated in the present patriotic movement. Finally, considering the inclusive/exclusive character of the movement, it can be seen how, in FESCI fashion, the militant scouts and the torch-bearing guides of this popular ascent to national consciousness are identified as the intelligentsia. Nonetheless, the vanguard qualities of the intellectuals are merely mentioned and their agency is largely overshadowed by that of an emerging 'people'.

Some striking resemblances between the FESCI discourse and that of the patriotic movement in the first few years of the 21st century show certain shifts that signal its insertion into a new-fangled political project. One major shift that allows us to begin to characterize this new project is the one from 'revolution' – indisputably one of the key metaphors of FESCI activism – to 'resistance', the central term indicating patriotic militancy. Read in contrast to the (Fesci)

---

[23] See footnote 11.

'revolution', (patriotic) 'resistance' redefines the different groups of actors engaged in the present struggle, as well as the terrain on which they are operating.

Contrary to revolution and avant-garde ideological struggle, 'resistance' emphasizes continuity over rupture and inclusion over exclusion. Such can be clearly seen in Messou's story of the gradual up-scaling of national awareness among the Ivorian people as a whole. This generalization is of course quite a daring one and throws light on the politics of history that informs it.

In simple historiographic terms, what Messou reconstructs is what Bayart (2003) calls the Ivorian 'nationalist tradition' in the form of an ongoing series of confrontations – first with the French colonizer, then with the France-friendly regime of Houphouët-Boigny, and now with an allegedly French-backed rebellion – concerning genuine national sovereignty against colonial, neo-colonial or contemporary imperialist interference. By equating the history of nationalism with that of the nation and by associating the struggle of the nationalists with that of the Ivorians, Messou operates a virtual collusion of 'the nationalists' with 'the nationals'. In this way, he links up political orientation with citizenship and presents adherence to nationalism not so much as engaging in politics but rather as performing one's civil duty. Redefined in this way, politics and citizenship boil down to the same idealized loyalty to the nation and the ruptures and exclusions in this mystifying unity of history, politics and population are largely defined along these lines.

The ones who are seen as standing out in a positive way by showing exemplary loyalism are the youth. This is poignantly expressed by Charles Groguhet in one of the opening quotes of this chapter. For Groguhet, the 'new youth' and 'the new generation' announce the culmination of the 'nationalist tradition', the advent of genuine sovereignty and of a new nation. The negative equivalent of the Young Patriots are the New Forces and their partisans who are not so much presented as political opponents, for instance as 'anti-nationalists', but as 'non-nationals' or 'anti-nationals' and generally as 'uncivil' people or second-rate (disloyal or untrustworthy) civilians.

Apart from being identified within the temporal framework of national history, the three groups – the young patriots, the patriots/nationals, and the non-patriots/non-nationals – are also positioned in the spatial framework of a hegemonic struggle. Here too, the shift from 'revolution' to 'resistance' is an analytically helpful one. Making use of Gramsci's terminology, it could be said that while revolution is essentially a 'war of manoeuvre' that entails mobility and expedition, 'resistance' has all the makings of a 'war of position' that resolves around entrenchment and staying power. In patriotic discourse, the present war of position is fought on one's own territory with 'the weapons of the weak'.

The 'weapons' that the patriotic movement claims to possess combine physical/military weakness with strength of spirit. Both meanings figure prominently in the quote by Bernard Dadié at the beginning of this chapter. By describing the hands of the new youth as 'unarmed' and with 'no intention of grabbing a portfolio', Dadié invites us to read 'resistance' as combining the sticks-and-stones street violence of youngsters with their tenacity and incurruptibility. Likewise, their opponents are characterized as ideologically spineless and self-seeking political entrepreneurs who, because of their (financial) backing by exterior imperialist forces, possess the kind of superior professional weapons with which they crush the will of the people.

This entire characterization of the warring parties is highly reminiscent of FESCI descriptions of itself as an 'anti-political movement' facing an opportunistic regime that is 'armed to the teeth'. The main difference lies in the space in which this battle unfolds. The discourse of continuity and inclusion that the FESCI developed had a strong horizontal dimension that was articulated through the occupation of public space (demonstrations), geopolitical expansion (expatriation), and claims of expressing the popular 'will'. This spatial dimension was supplemented by a temporal (vertical) one by which the FESCI inscribed itself in the nationalist struggle. What we see happening in the discourse of the Young Patriots, and is attested by Charles Groguhet's quote at the beginning of the chapter, is the extension of this temporal dimension to include 'the ancestors'. In such a way, Groguhet is working towards conditioning patriotic loyalty on Ivorian ancestry.

Conclusion

Most studies of autochthony movements in Africa and far beyond agree that their breeding ground needs to be situated at the conjunction of economic (globalization), political (democratization) and socio-economic (freeing of labour) developments (Bayart *et al.* 2001; Geschiere & Nyamnjoh 2000). I have tried to show elsewhere (Arnaut 2004b) that, in the case of Côte d'Ivoire, autochthony also needs to be situated in a long national history of categorizations of people along different lines (ethnic, religious, political, in terms of nationality) because it rearticulates existing categories into the autochthone-allochthone dichotomy. This chapter may be read as a case study in this broader project that seeks to excavate the layers of older discourses that can be found in the present autochthony rhetoric.

Other authors have noticed the importance of youth and student organizations in the development of autochthony movements, for instance in Cameroon (Konings this volume) and, in the case of Côte d'Ivoire of the FESCI and the Young Patriots in reshaping the political landscape (Konaté 2003, Banégas & Marshall-Fratani 2000). Overall, one can observe in these studies a strong inclination as to how youth and student organizations are instrument-alized by older political leaders. This, of course, is often contradicted by the youth movements themselves, not least by the Young Patriots in Côte d'Ivoire, by stressing their independence as a grass-roots popular movement and claiming ideological autonomy. In its theoretical outlook and its analytical focus and by the choice of its empirical material, this chapter seeks to transcend this divide between instrumentalization and autonomy.

The central argument is that one of the key players in the present-day autochthony movement in Côte d'Ivoire – the Young Patriots – is reclaiming central elements of discourse from the FESCI student union and is inscribing these in a new political project that is being carried by the FPI socialist party and is embodied by current President Laurent Gbagbo. This discursive continuity or stability can in itself be taken as demonstrating the relative 'autonomy' of the student movement since the 1990s. Looking further into which discursive elements are being transferred, we get a better grasp of what, in the way of discursive constructions, the Young Patriots have to offer to the autochthony movement.

The theoretical option taken in this chapter posits a fundamental coevalness between scholars and social actors in their conceptualization of youth and generation.[24] For both groups, it is argued, the latter concepts walk a fine (and often ambiguously vague) line between continuity and rupture, inclusion and exclusion. This is attested by a review of the scholarly literature on youth and generation, and by an in-depth analysis of the FESCI discourse. Turning then to the transfer and contribution (willing or not) of the FESCI to the Young Patriots movement, we can begin to discern that, on essential points, the youngsters are strategic partners of the socialist party and President Gbagbo in the articulation and, above all, the attempted imposition of their new, autochthony-driven political project. It would require more space to sufficiently argue the latter point but my analysis so far leads me to believe that the survival of Gbagbo as the carrier of the hegemonic struggle he currently embodies depends to a large extent on his deep association with the ideas and manifestations of the Young Patriots. Whether Gbagbo and/or the Young Patriots survive or not is another

---

[24] The concept of 'coevalness' was introduced into anthropology by Fabian (1983) when he denounced the anthropologists' denial to 'share time' with their 'subjects' and instead suggested that they engage in a dialectical relationship with them. This idea is taken to heart in this chapter, as well as Kelly's (1999: 264) further elaboration of the challenge of coevalness, namely that anthropologists must 'seek the temporality within the "political confrontations already in place"'.

question altogether, but it is difficult to imagine at this point how any alternative political leader will be able to formulate a new future for Côte d'Ivoire without taking on board the 'youth' that over the last decade and more have so thoroughly inscribed themselves in projects for the regeneration of the Ivorian nation.

References

Akindès, F. 2000, *A Travers les Origines et les Incertitudes des Mutations Politiques Récentes en Côte d'Ivoire: Le Sens de l'Histoire*.
  [http://perso.wanadoo.fr/forum.de.delphes/Forum_de_Delphes_56.html; 3/06/2002].
Akindès, F. 2001, *Dynamique de la Politique Sociale en Côte d'Ivoire*, Geneva: Institut de Recherche des Nations Unies.
Amnesty International 1994, *La Liberté d'Expression et d'Association Menacée*, [http://web.amnesty.org/library/Index/FRAAFR310031994?open&of=FRA-CIV; 10/10/2003]
Arnaut, K. 2004a, 'Re-generating the Nation: Youth, Exile and Violence as Discourses of Renewal in Côte d'Ivoire (1990-2002)', in K. Arnaut, 'Performing Displacements and Rephrasing Attachments: Ethnographic Explorations of Mobility in Art, Ritual, Media, and Politics', forthcoming PhD thesis, Ghent University.
Arnaut, K. 2004b, 'Autochthony and the Postnational Imagination in Côte d'Ivoire (1901-2003)', in K. Arnaut, 'Performing Displacements and Rephrasing Attachments: Ethnographic Explorations of Mobility in Art, Ritual, Media, and Politics', forthcoming PhD thesis, Ghent University.
Bacon, E. 1964, 'Generation', in J. Gould & W. Kolb (eds), *A Dictionary of the Social Sciences*, New York: The Free Press of Glencoe, pp. 284-85.
Bailly, D. 1995, *La Réinstauration du Multipartisme en Côte d'Ivoire ou la Double Mort d'Houphouët-Boigny*, Paris: L'Harmattan.
Banégas, R. & R. Marshall-Fratani 2000, 'Côte d'Ivoire, un Conflit Régional?', *Politique Africaine*, 78: 5-11.
Bathily, A., M. Diouf & M. Mbodj 1995, 'The Senegalese Student Movement from its Origins to 1989', in M. Mamdani & E. Wamba-dia-Wamba (eds), *African Studies in Social Movements and Democracy*, Dakar: CODESRIA, pp. 369-408.
Bayart, J-F. 2003, 'Gbagbo et les "Nouveaux Nationalistes" ', *Nouvel Observateur*, 1996, 6 February 2003.
Bayart, J-F., P. Geschiere & F. Nyamnjoh 2001, 'Autochthonie, Démocratie et Citoyenneté en Afrique', *Critique Internationale*, 10, pp. 177-194.
Blaikie, A. 1999, 'Can There Be a Cultural Sociology of Ageing?' *Education and Ageing*, 14 (2): 127-39.
Bourdieu, P. 1985, 'La "Jeunesse" N'Est Qu'un Mot', in P. Bourdieu, *Questions de Sociologie*,. Paris: Editions de Minuit, pp. 143-54.
Bucholtz, M. 2002, 'Youth and Cultural Practice', *Annual Review of Anthropology*, 31: 323-552.

Bundy, C. 1987, 'Street Sociology and Pavement Politics: Aspects of Youth and Student Resistance in Cape Town', *Journal of Southern African Studies*, 13 (3): 303-29.

Chauveau, J-P. & K.S. Bobo 2003, 'La Situation de Guerre dans l'Arènes Villageoise: Un Example dans le Centre-ouest Ivorien', *Politique Africaine*, 89: 12-32.

Comaroff, J. & J. Comaroff 2000, 'Reflexions sur la Jeunesse: Du Passé à la Post-colonie', *Politique Africaine*, 80: 90-110.

Dadié, B. 2003, 'La Crise Ivoirienne', *Africultures*, 56: 169-74.

de Benoist, J-R. 1994, 'FEANF and the Colonial Authorities', in *The Role of African Student Movements in the Political and Social Evolution of Africa from 1900 to 1975*, Paris: UNESCO Publishing, pp. 108-21.

Diarra, S. 1997, *Les Faux Complots d'Houphouët-Boigny: Fracture dans le Destin d'une Nation*, Paris: Karthala.

Dozon, J-P. 2000, 'La Côte d'Ivoire entre Démocratie, Nationalisme et Ethnonationalisme', *Politique Africaine*, 78: 45-62.

Drucker-Brown, S. 1982, 'Joking at Death: The Mamprusi Grandparent-Grandchild Joking Relationship', *Man* (N.S.), 17: 714-27.

Durham, D. 2000, 'Youth and the Social Imagination in Africa: Introduction', *Anthropological Quarterly*, 73 (3): 113-20.

Eisenstadt, S.N. 1995 (1962), 'Archetypal Patterns of Youth', in S.N. Eisenstadt, *Power, Trust, and Meaning: Essays in Sociological Theory and Analysis*, Chicago: The University of Chicago Press.

Fabian, J. 1983, *Time and the Other: How Anthropology Makes Its Object*, New York: Columbia University Press.

Federici, S. 2000, 'The New African Student Movement', in C.B. Mwaria *et al.* (eds), *African Visions: Literary Images, Political Change, and Social Struggle in Contemporary Africa*, Westport: Praeger, pp. 49-66.

FESCI 1993, *Statuts* [Charter]. Abidjan (26 September 1993).

FESCI 1995, *Le Mouvement Estudantin Ivorien* (with an introduction by Guillaume Soro Kigbafori), Abidjan: Le Bois Sacré.

Gbagbo, L. 1983, *Côte d'Ivoire, Pour une Alternative Démocratique*, Paris: L'Harmattan.

Geschiere, P. & F. Nyamnjoh 2000, 'Capitalism and Autochthony: The Seesaw of Mobility and Belonging', *Public Culture*, 12 (2): 423-52.

Griaule, M. 1948, 'L'Alliance Cathartique', *Africa*, 18 (4): 242-58.

Hall, S. 1990, 'Cultural Identity and Diaspora', in J. Rutherford (ed.), *Identity, Community, Culture, Difference*, London: Lawrence & Wishart, pp. 222-47.

Hugh-Jones, S. & J. Laidlaw (eds) 2000, *The Essential Edmund Leach. vol 1: Anthropology and Society*, New Haven: Yale University Press.

Irwin, S. 1996, 'Age-related Distributive Justice and Claims on Resources', *British Journal of Sociology*, 47 (1): 68-92.

Irwin, S. 1998, 'Age, Generation and Inequality: A Reply to a Reply', *British Journal of Sociology*, 49 (2): 306-10.

Kelly, J. 1999, 'Time and the Global: Against the Homogeneous, Empty Communities in Contemporary Social Theory', in B. Meyer & P. Geschiere (eds), *Globalization and Identity: Dialectics of Flow and Closure*, Oxford: Blackwell, pp. 239-72.

Konaté, Y. 2002, 'Génération Zouglou', *Cahiers d'Etudes Africaines,* 168, 42 (4): 777-96.

Konaté, Y. 2003, 'Les Enfants de la Balle. De la FESCI aux Mouvements de Patriotes', *Politique Africaine*, 89: 49-70.

Le Pape, M. 1986, 'Les Statuts d'une Génération: Les Déscolarisées d'Abidjan entre 1967 et 1986, *Politique Africaine,* 24: 104-12.

Le Pape, M. & C. Vidal 1987, 'L'Ecole à Tout Prix: Stratégies Educatives dans la Petite Bourgeoisie d'Abidjan', *Actes de Recherches en Sciences Sociales,* 70: 64-73.

Loucou, J-N. 1992, *Le Multipartisme en Côte d'Ivoire*, Abidjan: Editions Neter.

Marías, J. 1968, 'Generations', in D. Sillis (ed.), *International Encyclopaedia of the Social Sciences*, New York: Macmillan, pp. 88-92.

Proteau, L. 2002, *Passions Scolaires en Côte d'Ivoire: Ecole, Etat et Société*, Paris: Karthala.

Rintala, M. 1968, 'Political Generations', in D. Sills (ed.), *International Encyclopaedia of the Social Sciences*, New York: Macmillan, pp. 92-96.

Roseberry, W. 1996, 'Hegemony, Power, and Languages of Contention', in E. Wilmsen (ed.), *The Politics of Difference: Ethnic Premises in a World of Power*, Chicago: University of Chicago Press, pp. 71-84.

Seekings, J. 1993, *Heroes or Villains? Youth Politics in the 1980s*, Johannesburg: Raven Press.

Spencer, P. 1990, 'The Riddled Course: Theories of Age and its Transformations', in P. Spencer (ed.), *Anthropology and the Riddle of the Sphinx: Paradoxes of Change in the Life Course,* London: Routledge, pp. 1-34.

Touré, A. 1985, 'La Jeunesse Face à l'Urbanisation Accélérée en Côte d'Ivoire', *Cahiers ORSTOM, Série Sciences Humaines,* 21 (2-3): 275-93.

Turner, B. 1998, 'Ageing and Generational Conflicts: A Reply to Sarah Irwin', *British Journal of Sociology,* 49 (2): 299-304.

Van Dijk, R. 1998, 'Pentecostalism, Cultural Memory and the State: Contested Representations of Time in Postcolonial Malawi', in R. Werbner (ed.), *Memory and the Postcolony: African Anthropology and the Critique of Power*, London: Zed Books, pp. 155-81.

Werbner, R. 1999, 'Bringing Back the Dead in Botswana: Patriarchy and Elderhood Revisited', Paper presented at the African Studies Workshop of the University of Chicago. [http://cas.uchicago.edu/african/papers/werbner.htm; 2/12/2003].

6

War, changing ethics and the position of youth in South Sudan

Jok Madut Jok

This chapter considers the position of youth and children in the context of the on-going war in Sudan, focusing in particular on the war-provoked and growing contradiction between norms held by the Dinka about the importance of children and child-bearing and what young people went through during the second round of the north-south conflict on the other. Three questions are asked. What are the beliefs and values that place children at the centre of people's social and cultural lives? Are the current youth-related issues a result of war or are they ordinary socio-cultural changes that every society must undergo? What do Sudanese communities and humanitarian aid agencies reckon are the main problems facing youth or caused by youth, and what solutions are envisaged? The conclusion arrived at is that violence perpetrated by or exercised against youth is not just the immediate outcome of a prolonged war but is also the sharp end of a long historical process.

Introduction

Much of the literature on wartime violence tends to focus on the use of extreme violence used by the warring parties against civilians under each other's control as a means of fighting the war, i.e. to destabilize the opposing group's support base. But important as it is to document such abuses, equally important and most insidious are the ways in which violence is carried out within the communities by members of armed groups who hail from these same communities. The emergence of sub-cultures of violence during armed conflicts, as seen in Sierra Leone, Sudan, Liberia, northern Uganda and other countries, has to be studied in a historical context. Without condoning it as an ordinary means of communication, and in fact even considering it repugnant, many scholars agree that violence has spatial and temporal meanings attached to it by both the perpetrators and the victims and could be studied 'as a changing form of communication, as a historically developed form of *meaningful* action' (Blok 2000: 26). As Ellis rightly points out, in order to understand why acts of violence are committed, we must situate them in the context in which they occur (Ellis 2003).

In his introduction to a recent special issue of *African Studies Review* on youth in Africa, Mamadou Diouf made the observation that during the years immediately preceding the end of colonialism, when young people were the torch-bearers of anti-colonialism, most colonial societies viewed their youth as the incarnation of the future, with young people representing the promise of restored identity. They had a prestigious status and expected to be treated as a priority group when colonialism ended. However, young people began to lose this 'prestigious status that nationalism gave them in its ascending phase' (Diouf 2003: 4). During the early years of independence, the role of African youth began to change, partly as a result of the economic and political failure of nationalist promises. Expected investment in youth through education and the maintenance of the rites of socialization began to disappear and the immediate outcome of this was a change in the systems of socialization from such methods as training the youth in leadership to efforts to control and repress them. 'Excluded from the arenas of power, work, education, and leisure, young Africans [began to] construct places of socialization and new sociabilities whose function is to show their difference, either on the margins of society or at its heart, simultaneously as victims of active agents, and circulating in a geography that escapes the limits of the national territory' (Diouf 2003).

A discussion of youth and violence in Sudan is faced with two issues that are indirectly raised here by Professor Diouf. The first is that youth violence has to be understood both in terms of the violence carried out by young men against other sectors of the population in response to their marginalization, and the violence perpetrated by the state against young people in response to youth behaviour that is regarded as unacceptable. These two types of violence feed off each other. As youth become frustrated due to a lack of resources, education, jobs and diminished political voice, they engage in activities that challenge the state system. The state then reacts by cracking down on them.

The second issue is the question of who qualifies as youth. It is important to clarify that there is no fixed definition of 'youth' in Sudan, and it is not located within specific chronological parameters. In Sudan, as in many other African nations, especially those with a long history of strife, the term youth is popularly used to refer to young men. But it implies no age limit. Common ages given for the onset of initiation for boys fall between thirteen and twenty. In many instances, people in their late thirties and forties who have not met certain criteria are still considered youth. Therefore 'youth' needs to be seen as a social category with a sliding definition. To be a youth, it seems, is to be single, not to be steadily employed or independent of one's family and, above all, to live under conditions of political conflict where fighting and defending one's family and property is a major preoccupation. So a person as young as ten years of age who takes on the responsibility of protecting his family by joining an army qualifies as a youth rather than coming under the classification of 'child' that would be applied to other people of his age in different circumstances. This is not to suggest that young men who meet certain criteria, such as being married, necessarily graduate from the youth category and cease engaging in violent acts. In fact, many married people continue to be identified as youths and have been observed to perpetrate violence.

While scholars have always problematized politics, identity, religion and economic marginalization as some of the fundamental causes of the war in Sudan, it is equally important to study some of the everyday experiences that keep fanning the flames of war. One of these is that the notion of common motivation cutting through all the youth categories persists. In an attempt to contribute to the work focused on unravelling the complexities of violence associated with this war, this chapter argues that it is within the space of generational conflict that underlying and enduring reasons for the continuation of the current war can be found. Why do young men keep becoming involved in the war considering the suffering and the few obvious benefits it brings them? And once part of a fighting force, why do young men engage in violent activities that do not necessarily serve the cause for which they took up arms? Answers to these questions are hard to come by. The following section presents historical background that might at least paint a partial picture of the local rationalization for wartime violence.

Youth and violence in Sudan: The context

The second round of the civil war between the northern-dominated government of Sudan and the southern opposition Sudan People's Liberation Army (SPLA) was concluded with a provisional peace agreement in early 2004. When it began in 1983, the youth were, just as during the anti-colonial campaigns and during the first civil war, again at the forefront in articulating the grievances of the South. School-children's protests about the crumbling educational system in the early 1980s, the north-south distribution of wealth, and the Jonglei water project were all instrumental in initiating the current round of the war. Two other equally important reasons triggered the youth protests that culminated in the outbreak of the war: the presidential decree to redivide the southern region in contravention of the Addis Ababa Accord that ended the first round of the civil war, and the decision by President Jaafer Nimeiri to transfer some army units from the south to the north, again in violation of the Addis Ababa agreement that promulgated larger numbers of southern soldiers in southern garrisons. The reaction of the Nimeiri government to student protests was to stigmatize the entire southern youth as being anti-government. Sweeping arrests were made and security agents throughout the southern towns embarked on a policy of incessant harassment of young men. A manhunt was unleashed against certain individual youths who were identified as the ringleaders. This propelled many more to join the SPLA. So Diouf's observation is in place: there is a connection between government suppression of young people's desires to participate in governance on the one hand and the violence that is perpetrated by youth on the other. In Sudan, government efforts to suppress the demands of the youth, instead of addressing them, were largely responsible for not only the success of the SPLA in attracting more recruits but also in spreading the ideology behind the southern rebellion to other parts of the country that had been similarly marginalized by the central government.

In reaching back into Sudan's recent history, we can pluck at the threads that are woven into the fabric of the contemporary war to help unearth those ideas and frustrations that have resonated through time and space, and are important factors in the violence perpetrated by and committed against young people in the course of the current war. Sharon Hutchinson (1996) has eloquently portrayed the war in Sudan as one where individuals and communities have grappled with the consequences of a militarized situation by creating new strategies of coping in place of the old norms that governed behaviour in the past. Using this idea of looking at violence at the communal level as an outgrowth of individual efforts to come to grips with the changing political and social environment, it would be helpful to analyze youth violence as the continuation of an ongoing dialogue between people with a shared past who hold common views on gender, power and generational divides.

That the north-south confrontation should result in the use of extreme violence against civilians in the course of executing the war would be a familiar pattern given the nature of the Sudanese conflict. But what defies logic and is the focus of this chapter is the replication of such violence within the communities in both the south and the north, especially against women. There has been extensive documentation of horrific sexual abuse and domestic servitude in some SPLA-controlled areas and, more recently, in Darfur where, since early 2003, government troops and allied Janjawid militias have been unleashing a massive campaign of killing, ethnic cleansing and expulsion of the native Darfur peoples (the Masalit, Zaghawa, Fur, Berti and Daju). The following testimonies were recorded during different research trips to southern Sudan and provide an idea of how members of different population groups understand the realities of violence. In an interview, one young man talked about youth violence as a culmination of feelings of frustration with the state of affairs. He stated:

> To sit at home is boring. To do the sort of activities around the house such as clearing the cultivation fields, grazing cattle or digging a well for drinking water is terribly exhausting and one gets really hungry. That is why I do not like staying around the house and listening to my father distressing about me being lazy. Instead, I hang out at the market where I might run into acquaintances who could buy a meal or cigarette to share. Occasionally, I might go back to the army post where it may be easier to find food, although one also risks being sent to battle. One does not go out with a plan to rob or to fight or to chase girls. You know, it just happens once, and you say that was a mistake and I will not repeat it, but before you know it, you are assaulting another person and everybody begins to talk about you as a bad human being. Once you have been written off and your reputation is gone, you don't care anymore what they say ... you just survive in the best way you know.[1]

Older people and community leaders have contradictory feelings about the place of youth in contemporary societies.

> To have the young men around here is a blessing, but it is also a serious burden. Their presence is vital as we need their physical strength. ... They protect the communities against Arab raids. But having them roaming the villages, especially those among them who are soldiers, is an ordeal. Not only do we have to watch out for our girls, we also have to protect our property against them, and we have to constantly try to talk sense into them. And trying to socialize a young man in the vacuum left by social disruption and in an environment where the wisdom of elders' experience these days meets with disregard or outright violence from the youth is a very difficult task.[2]

We also interviewed SPLA officers about the movement's position on youth violence and about its own use of youth for revolutionary goals. The following is a position shared by many of them.

---

[1] Interview in Akon, Bahr-el-Ghazal, South Sudan in 2002 with Ajang, a young man who had been demobilized and sent to Rumbek by UNICEF. When the programme ended, he had to return home.
[2] Interview in 1999 with Chol Kuol, a community leader in Bahr-el-Ghazal, South Sudan.

SPLA soldiers resting in a tearoom.
Photo: Jok Madut Jok

We sometimes try to prevent them from joining the army because they may be too young, but we are a voluntary army, one that tries to provide as much protection as possible, and we cannot prevent these young men by force from their desire to protect their land. If they decide on occasion to leave the barracks in order to spend time with their families, and commit crimes while away from us, we may punish them … but our measures have not deterred others from embarking on similar paths. What other control measure can we exercise to prevent random violence carried out by these youth? We have partnered with aid organizations such as the United Nations Children's Fund (UNICEF) and Save the Children, UK in an attempt to get these boys back to their families and get them into schools, but there are no good schools, no adequate feeding in the existing schools and at home, and the programme looks like it is failing. Entire communities seem to have failed in their most crucial task, socializing the young into respectful adults.[3]

Contradictions such as those in the above testimonies have always been articulated in Sudan through folklore. There is a wealth of collective memory represented in songs, jokes and stories about the war and its consequences.

---

[3] An interview with Akok, an officer in the Sudan People's Liberation Army (SPLA) in Lokichokio, Kenya in 1999.

Older people continuously compare the behaviour of youth during this war to times past with nostalgia for the old days 'when young men were respectful'.

Youth and children in Sudan: The norms of caring and the realities of the war

For generations of southern Sudanese, children are, first and foremost, 'the reason for human existence'. Dinka people, for example, often say that the power of God manifests itself in granting children and this is one of the reasons why infant mortality, long periods of infertility, and other problems associated with the war are currently regarded as punishment from God for human misconduct. Procreation is, in fact, everyone's paramount goal in life and the only form of immortality universally valued. Every Dinka fears the 'true death', the 'complete death' – which is to say, a death without surviving children to 'stand one's head', remember one's name and more generally revitalize one's influence in the world. For men, the immortality sought is motivated in part by strong collective interests: without heirs a man acquires no permanent position within the patrilineal chain of ancestors from which he emerged. For a woman, childbirth is the threshold to adulthood and to future security and independence in her husband's home.

Owing to the overwhelming centrality of children, Dinka societies have developed highly creative means of overcoming individual experiences of infertility and/or premature death in order to ensure that every adult man and woman has a fighting chance of acquiring heirs. One of the most important of these cultural premises rests on a marked distinction in people's minds between claims of 'social paternity' (based on bridewealth cattle transfers) and those of 'physical genitorship' (based on blood/semen transfers). In situations where these two sets of claims are not held by the same person, 'social paternity' always takes precedence over 'physical paternity' in determining a child's true line of patrilineal descent. In other words, because everyone must have a child, those men who are not capable of having children have to find a way to be fathers. A man deemed infertile could assign his wives to a younger brother who would then father children for him.

The flip side of these cattle-based limitations on the procreative ambitions of individual Dinka men, however, can be profoundly liberating in other ways. Because physical paternity is not a necessary condition of fatherhood as socially defined, it becomes possible, for example, for Nuer and Dinka to marry for the dead. A 'ghost marriage' occurs when a man marries a wife in the name of a deceased male relative in order to provide the latter with posthumous heirs. Any children the wife produces are legally the children of the 'ghost', not those of the 'pro-husband' who sired them. Furthermore, marriages in these societies do not end with the death of the husband. On the contrary, a widow is expected to continue to bear heirs in her late husband's name with the procreative assistance of a brother-in-law, step-son or lover of her choice – an institution known as 'leviratic marriage'. Responsibility for the continued material well-being of the widow and her children rests squarely on the brothers and other close patrilineal relatives of the deceased husband. Like the other Nilotic groups who practice the levirate, Dinka families that have been heavily ravaged by death can potentially regenerate themselves by having surviving members marry wives in the names of deceased older brothers, uncles and fathers, provided that these families retain some access to cattle wealth.

Children are also valued for the future material benefits their parents and families hope to acquire through them. They are, indeed, the only form of social security known in these societies. An elder in the community who needs some work done, for example, will lament publicly that 'there are no young men in this community that I can send to get some work done', and this would come over as a challenge to youth. Dinka elders also say such things when they want the young to go to war. It is thus only when a child matures and begins to develop the unique kin bonds acquired at birth through generosity with his labour and his ability to come forward to protect his people and property that he acquires the status of a real man.

Dinka children are cherished not only for extending specific families and lineages but, more broadly, for preserving valued cultural identities and ways of life. In this sense, 'children are the children of everyone'. Or, at least, this is how most adults viewed each other's children before experiencing this war's full weight. Evidence for this declining attitude is still apparent in some areas. For example, although adult Dinka consider it shameful to mention food or to be seen eating or drinking in the presence of non-relatives, women and men will freely beg food from strangers without fear of losing self-respect provided that the food is destined for the belly of a young child. Similarly, there is a continuing expectation that fellow villagers who are old enough to be parents will freely advise, assist, scold and/or discipline other people's children as the need arises. This important status accorded children is said to have changed as a result of the two-decade-long war. Most Dinka we interviewed declared bluntly that without this continued collective commitment to the raising of the next generation, it is difficult to see how the Dinka will survive as a vibrant and valued ethnic community in the decades ahead. Indeed, it is evident that children's survival prospects in these societies have become increasingly bound up in recent years with changing adult perceptions of children's abilities to take on and extend particular ethnic identities – as distinct from, say, more individualized kinship networks.

Victims or perpetrators: The risks that face wartime youth

The most detrimental effects of this war include: the widespread disruption of family life, the dispersal of communities, the collapse of the regional economy and local administrative structures, the loss of essential health and educational services, accelerated ecological degradation, cultural damage and the psychological consequences of trauma, identity loss and mounting despair. This war has battered every dimension of these societies. Moreover, as people's survival efforts have become more and more individualistic and/or household-oriented, their ability to sustain community-wide institutions, cultural practices and social commitments capable of restraining gross abuses of power have declined dramatically.

These war-time developments have robbed contemporary Dinka children of the opportunity to be children, as their daily lives are swallowed up by rising tides of physical and economic insecurity. Since the beginning of war, rural Dinka civilians have been struggling to cope with an expanding community-wide sub-culture of violence. This sub-cultural force has been both fuelled and characterized by several developments, the most evident of which is a dramatic surge in the scale and frequency of violence against civilians. This is partly a product of the SPLA's policy of militarization and conditioning of youth to identify more with the revolution than with their families. Because young soldiers depend on the leading commanders for patronage, protection and survival, they are used to collecting food taxes from the civilian population, and are told to do so with impunity. They are instructed that this is a people's revolution and everyone must contribute: anyone who attempts to subvert the revolution by refusing to pay their share of the costs of war is swiftly dealt with. This kind of conditioning to violence reached another level in 1991 when the SPLA experienced a debilitating split along Nuer and Dinka ethnic lines. To get the youth to support the war along these new lines and alliances, young people were encouraged to identify more with their ethnic group at the expense of a collective southern identity, which had been the policy of the movement up to that point. This led to an unprecedented unravelling of regional codes of inter-community warfare that had previously condemned the burning of houses, the slashing of crops and the killing of elderly men, women and children of all ages (Jok & Hutchinson 1999). Between 1991 and 1998 when the Dinka-Nuer conflict was at its height, there was increasing public despair about the abilities of the southern leaders in charge of the two SPLA factions, John Garang and Riek Machar, to resolve their personal and political differences peacefully, and so to reduce inter-ethnic violence and mistrust. Young men who were involved in the fighting found themselves increasingly questioning the whole revolution as there was a deepening experiential equation in people's minds between political assertions of the 'right of the south to liberate itself' on the one hand, and militarized demonstrations of people's abilities to kill their own people with impunity on the other. The result has been the birth of an entire generation of younger southern military recruits who have known little but the brutalities of war and who readily translate confrontations at the national level into community and intra-family violence.

Like military movements worldwide, the SPLA and the many splinter militia groups have sought to inculcate a kind of ultra-masculinity in their recruits, equated with demonstrations of aggressiveness, competitiveness and the censure of emotional expression. A growing sense of 'entitlement' to the domestic and sexual services of women also pervades this 'hyper-masculinized world view' (Hutchinson 1999). Just as southern Sudanese men see themselves as being responsible for maintaining the war front, women too, they reason, should be similarly active during the war in keeping up 'the reproductive front'. Pressures on women to disregard the weaning taboo (which prohibits them from having sexual relations during lactation) are steadily mounting as husbands and lovers on short, unpredictable periods of military leave return home determined to conceive another child. Similarly, women are feeling pressured by husbands and their in-laws to reduce the 'fallow period' between pregnancies by weaning their infants earlier. Whereas before this war infants were usually suckled for eighteen months or more, many men now argue that a period of nine months is optimal. And because most southern women do not feel free to refuse their husbands or lovers sexual access on demand for fear of a beating, they are increasingly being forced to make choices that no woman should have to make.

My fieldwork in Bahr-al-Ghazal revealed the agony of the reproductive dilemmas among contemporary Dinka women. To object to sexual demands is to risk being beaten, and to agree to these husbandly rights is to have another unwanted pregnancy. Those who decide to comply with sexual demands and then terminate a pregnancy have to make tough decisions. 'How can I risk another pregnancy and childbirth when I can't even feed the children I already have?' 'Should I attempt to abort my unborn child knowing how many other women have died or become infertile in the process?' 'How would my husband and his family react if they discovered I had aborted "their" child?' 'Who will care for my children if I die?' 'Will God punish me for these thoughts?' These are not societies that have accumulated generations of knowledge or experience in medicinally or physically inducing abortions. It is thus not surprising that the numbers of maternal deaths attributed to 'excessive bleeding' appear to be rising in the region (Jok 1998).

Dinka boys in Aweil East waiting to welcome the Kenyan chief mediator in the Sudanese peace talks, June 2004.
Photo: Jok Madut Jok

To these female hardships must be added the ever-present dangers of rape and the forceful commandeering of scarce household resources by gun-toting men. Nearly every woman in South Sudan has experienced threatening demands by armed men for the immediate provision of cooked or stored food, portage services and/or sexual access. Satisfying these unpredictable and often recurrent demands severely limits the energies and resources these women are able to devote to their children.

In addition to these more obvious war risks, women and children in South Sudan are suffering from the centrifugal forces released by recurrent community displacements and diasporas. Extensive surveys of rural households carried out among the Bahr-el-Ghazal between 1999 and 2002 reveal something of the magnitude of this problem. Nearly a third of all children living in South Sudan today are either orphans or have lost most of their family members to death or abandonment during the war. The child mortality rate, gleaned from the procreative histories of all adult residents and from surveys conducted by aid agencies, is close to 50 per cent. Many houses were occupied by widows who complained of receiving little or no support from their late-husbands' families. With the exception of households headed by men holding positions of leadership in local military and/or administrative organizations or working for foreign-aid agencies, there was very little evidence of food security in any household. In fact during the 'hunger season', many houses lay empty as their members scattered in search of food.

Growing hunger is aggravated in many instances by a gnawing sense of broken promises between husbands and wives, parents and children, and old and young. This is a promise that the society encodes into its norms, that when a man marries or has children he has made a promise to provide for them. For example, Dinka people often say that family networks are cemented by the sharing of food. Currently, however, as resources have become extremely scarce, such norms of generosity and sharing have been compromised and promises to kin groups to aid the weak are undermined. Due to a loss of assets, displacement and death, such promises are now regarded as having been broken. Many women throughout South Sudan complain that their marriages are illusory, since they are so often struggling alone to ensure their own and their children's survival. Sharpening generational cleavages of value and perspective are recognized by just about everyone. Some areas have very few old men and women left, and many of those who are still alive are incredibly malnourished and often blind. What is more, much of the cultural knowledge and historical experience accumulated by the older generation has been deemed irrelevant by disrespectful youth 'who have gone crazy with all the smoke and sound of guns' (Hutchinson 1999). Instead of receiving the retirement support and deference they believe they have earned from their children, many older men and women have been reduced to wearing rags and are openly treated with disdain by members of the younger generation. 'Our children no longer listen to us!' they commonly lament.

Nowhere is this inter-generational breakdown of communication more apparent in contemporary South Sudanese communities than in respect to the surviving remnants of the Red Amy. During the late 1980s, when the hype about the SPLA spread throughout South Sudan, a large number of boys between the ages of six and fourteen, and mainly of Dinka and Nuer origin, went to southwestern Ethiopia for the avowed purpose of enrolling in schools. They were systematically recruited by the SPLA. While some of them were forcibly enlisted on the basis that they could do both military training and attend school, many others were voluntarily released by their parents in the hope that their sons would find both a solid education and refuge from the war. The subsequent plight of these unaccompanied minors is well known. Many hundreds died en route or during their first months in the Ethiopian camps. The vast majority were forcibly inducted into the SPLA army as soon as they grew strong enough to carry a gun. The end result is a socially-isolated community of armed youth who have been brutally trained not only to kill on command but also to torture whoever their military superiors designate. Although some of these heavily traumatized youth eventually made the long journey back to their home areas during the 1990s, they often experienced great difficulty fitting back in again. Some returned only to discover that their parents and siblings were dead or missing. Others bitterly rejected their parents and families, much as they themselves had felt rejected in the past. These and other children who were forced to survive by their wits from an early age are at severe risk of becoming a lost generation – a generation with little faith in the future or in themselves.

A further cause of inter-generational breakdown of communication is the mass conversion to Christianity on the part of thousands upon thousands of younger South Sudanese boys and girls. This has driven an ideological wedge between them and many of their seniors. While bearing a powerful message of hope, communal peace, forgiveness and redemption in a life yet to come, Christianity has undercut the former religious authority of community elders and has splintered, socially and spiritually, numerous families and communities. While there is every reason to believe that the spread of Christianity will continue to attract many more loyal Sudanese converts in the years ahead, there is considerable uncertainty about what position local Christian leaders will eventually adopt with regard to a wide variety of social values and practices, ranging from polygyny and ghost marriages on the one hand, to public dances, animal sacrifices and the powers of indigenous spiritual leaders on the other.

Many of these developments have deepened women and children's vulnerability to social neglect, physical abuse and severe economic destitution. Local military and civilian leaders now monopolize much of the region's wealth, leaving the majority of young men, who are not politically and socially well-connected, with few prospects of a bright future, and propelling them into the further use of violence to secure basic survival. In the Dinka and Nuer areas, for example, cattle wealth has been confiscated from community members through imposed fines and forced contributions to the war effort, leaving young men with few opportunities to raise enough cattle for bridewealth payments. One way young men attempt to rectify this problem is to engage in cattle raids and community attacks, and this has, in turn, fuelled ethnic violence between the Dinka and the Nuer and among many other cattle-keeping groups across southern Sudan. Many of these inter-ethnic raids are carried out for the alleged purpose of recapturing civilian-owned cattle lost in earlier raids. When success-fully recaptured, however, such cattle cannot be reclaimed by their original owners but are claimed as military property to be redistributed as the local commander sees fit. The end result, of course, has been a steady transfer of civilian cattle wealth into the byres of their military 'protectors'.

The present and future well-being of Sudanese youth

The progressive abandonment during this war of former restraints on regional patterns of intra- and inter-ethnic violence constitutes the gravest threat to the present and future well-being of youth and children in South Sudan. Before this war and, indeed, up until the 1991 split in the SPLA, Nuer and Dinka men did not intentionally kill women or children during inter-ethnic confrontations. Acts of homicide within each ethnic group were governed by a complex set of ethics and religious taboos aimed at ensuring the immediate identification of the slayer and the payment of blood-wealth cattle compensation to the family of the deceased. The intentional slaying of a child, woman or elderly person was universally perceived not only as cowardly and reprehensible but, more importantly, as a direct affront to God as the ultimate guardian of human morality. Such acts were expected to provoke manifestations of divine anger in the form of severe illness, death and/or other misfortune visited on the slayer or members of his immediate family. The ethical code of warfare at that time further precluded the burning of houses and the destruction of crops during Nuer-Dinka community confrontations. Cattle, of course, were fair game. And it was not uncommon for raiders to carry off young women and children who would be absorbed as full members of their families.

The gradual unravelling of this regional code of warfare ethics stems in part from the conscious efforts of military strategists, and in part from a technological revolution in local weaponry. For example, Sharon Hutchinson (1999) reports that:

> Western Nuer practices and beliefs in this regard were openly challenged during the late 1980s and early 1990s by leading Nuer members of a then united SPLA. Local SPLA commanders sought to persuade the local citizenry as well as their recruits that homicides carried out under conditions of civil war were entirely devoid of the social, spiritual and material liabilities associated with homicides generated by more localized fighting and feuding. In essence, the military leadership was arguing that the overarching political context of the current war – which it defined as a 'government war' – should take precedence over the personal identities and social interrelations of combatants in people's assessments of the social and spiritual ramifications of homicide. The fact that these arguments were being introduced when the frequency of violent deaths was rising and local cattle stocks were being depleted meant that people's abilities to ensure the 'procreative immortality' of relatives slain in battle were being severely strained.

Furthermore, as guns have become increasingly the sole weapons of choice in the ever-spreading regional patterns of warfare, many people now wonder whether the spiritual and social consequences of intra-ethnic gun slayings are identical to those realized with spears. The older generation of Dinka say that the spear requires a man's strength, while the gun is the weapon of cowards. Unlike individually crafted spears, the source of a bullet lodged deep in someone's body cannot be easily traced. Often a fighter does not know whether or not he has killed someone and, as a result, homicide is becoming more and more depersonalized and secularized in South Sudan. In combination with increased recourse to surprise attacks, night-fighting and the intentional destruction of local food supplies, the premeditated killing of unarmed women and children became standard practice between rival southern military movements between 1991 and 1998. This change in the shared norms governing warfare is currently considered by many civilians as one of the most destructive aspects of the conflict.

These widely lamented trends are also linked to more subtle shifts in people's perceptions of ethnic identities more generally. Violence between ethnic groups has often been portrayed in decontextualized media accounts as the release of ancient tribal hatreds that have allegedly been simmering for years. The historical reality, however, is more fluid and complex. The Nuer and the Dinka have never been organized into neatly circumscribed tribes. On the contrary, they have intermarried regularly for generations and have continued to recognize their common ancestry through a variety of oral traditions and shared cultural practices. During the last round in the north-south civil war, many Nuer families left their original homelands on the west bank of the White Nile in Dinka territories in eastern Bahr-el-Ghazal. They had remained there until the current phase of the war started in 1983 when their security was threatened by the new rivalries between military elites on both sides.

In complex historical relations such as these, one's ethnic identity is always mobile and mutable. The questions that need to be asked then are these: in whose image and whose interests have these ethnic labels been most recently forged? And when and why have southern ethnic groups' politicized sense of their own identity begun to pit their respective ethnic warriors against one another's entire populations?

The key to unlocking these complex issues begins with an appreciation of contemporary differences in people's understandings of the socio-physical bases of their ethnic identifications. For example, one often hears debates about the different perceptions that ethnic groups have of one another. The Nuer consider themselves more open than the Dinka to the assimilation of non-Nuer as full and equal members of their communities. Contemporary Dinka stress the overwhelming importance of human blood lines in their determination of who is and who is not a Dinka, an interpretation that social scientists sometimes dub a 'primordialist' vision of ethnicity. Contemporary Equatorians, in contrast, view their ethnicity as more flexible towards the formation of a strong national identity that groups all southerners together. The Dinka are portrayed by most other groups as having the tendency to dominate and abuse power. For example, the Nuer are quick to say that it is not uncommon for an immigrant Dinka man who demonstrates obvious leadership potential to be elected as a Nuer government chief, and that the Dinka would never do that. These perceptions have been deployed during this war to entice the youth into fighting as a means of challenging Dinka domination.

In many ways, women and girls were less firmly rooted in these ethnic divisions before this war than Nuer and Dinka men were. This is because women and girls can confer potentially any ethnic or lineage identity on their children depending on who marries them. Since 1983, most ethnic groups have witnessed more inter-ethnic marriages than at any other time in the recorded past. Most societies in South Sudan are patrilineal, meaning that under normal circumstances, children take on their lineage affiliations and ethnic identities of their fathers rather than of their mothers' people. These societies are predominantly patrilocal, and wives generally take up residence in their husbands' homes after marriage. This is why women are said to have no permanent ethnic affiliation. A woman may be married to several men during her lifetime and bear heirs for all of them. Because a girl is said to belong to everyone – meaning she is a potential marriage partner for all unrelated men – women and girls have not been killed during the war.

What appears to be happening, however, is a gradual sealing-off of this formerly permeable inter-ethnic divide, a trend with especially disastrous consequences for the women and children on both sides. Whereas during previous periods of inter-ethnic turmoil younger women and children were more likely to be captured than slain by young fighters, the reverse is now true. Although many groups justify their intensifying viciousness in inter-ethnic confrontations as 'retaliation' for abominations experienced earlier, there is much more behind this increasingly conscious targeting of unarmed women and children for elimination. People's concepts of ethnicity are themselves rapidly mutating in ways that bode ill for the future. Dedinga, Nuer and Dinka fighters, in particular, appear to be adopting a more ethnically prejudiced way of thinking about the essence of their ethnicity in recent years. And it is this kind of thinking that can so easily be twisted into military justification for the intentional killing of women and children from other ethnic groups.

Conclusion

This chapter has attempted to summarize the historical process that has culminated in the rise of a sub-culture of violence in Sudan. The role of youth in this sub-culture is a product of the inter-generational gap in communication and a sense among youth that they have lost their political voice, promised protection and future prospects of improving their lives, despite the presence of cultural ethics that should guarantee communal support. A declining sense of communal responsibility for the continued well-being of related and unrelated children is evident everywhere throughout South Sudan. Interviews show that communities attribute much of this apparent shift to the extreme depletion of many people's resources and to a narrowing of their livelihood possibilities. People now feel too poor to share their few remaining assets with those who have even less – including in some cases even hungry young children. Mounting demands on the civilian population to pay for the cost of the war are exacerbating this situation. Add to this the fact that prospects for the situation letting up are zero and the result is a generation of young Sudanese who have lost hope in ever improving their lives. Joining the army, a militia or a gang of robbers is becoming one of the few choices they have.

Additionally, many parents are losing confidence in the material support their children will be able to provide in the future. Not only are children dying during this war in previously unimaginable numbers but parents are often unable to benefit from the labour potential of any surviving children due to critical shortages of livestock, seed, agricultural implements and the collapse of former markets for labour. A badly bruised bridewealth system skewed increasingly towards military monopolization has also meant that fewer and fewer parents are able to secure cattle through marrying off their daughters. Finally, the forced recruitment of under-age boys into the various opposition armies for indefinite periods of time has been a tremendous hardship for many Sudanese parents.

References

Blok, A. 2000, 'The Enigma of Senseless Violence', in G. Aijmer & J. Abbink (eds), *Meanings of Violence: A Cross-Cultural Perspective*, Oxford: Berg, pp. 23-38.

Diouf, M. 2003, 'Engaging Postcolonial Cultures: African Youth and Public Space', *African Studies Review,* 46 (1): 1-12.

Ellis, S. 2003, 'Violence and History: A Response to Thandika Mkandawire', *Journal of Modern African Studies*, 41 (3): 457-75.

Hutchinson, S. 1996, *Nuer Dilemmas: Coping with War, Money and the State*, Los Angeles: University of California Press.

Hutchinson, S. 1999, 'Sacrificing Childhood: The Impact of Sudan's Unresolved Civil War on the Lives of Nuer and Dinka Women and Children', Nairobi: Save the Children Fund, Denmark.

Jok, J.M. 1998, *Militarization, Gender and Reproductive Health in South Sudan*, Lewiston, NY: Edwin Mellen Press.

Jok, J.M. & S. Hutchinson 1999, 'Sudan's Prolonged Second Civil War and Militarization of Nuer and Dinka Ethnic Identities', *African Studies Review*, 42 (2): 125-45.

7

Anglophone university students and Anglophone nationalist struggles in Cameroon

Piet Konings

Although the current generation of Anglophone students in Cameroon feels even more marginalized than their Francophone counterparts because of their Anglophone identity, they have actually displayed a rather ambivalent attitude towards the Francophone-dominated regime that they hold responsible for their predicament. On the one hand, there are students who are seen as rebels and heroes. They have played a vanguard role in the Anglophone protest and, following political liberalization, have formed the leadership of the most militant Anglophone nationalist movement. However on the other hand, there are students who are seen as both predators and victims of the regime. They have been prepared to join the youth militia created by the regime to combat Anglophone organizations in exchange for a share in the ever-diminishing state resources.

Introduction

The dramatic changes that have been affecting the position of university students in African countries since the 1980s are being highlighted in an increasing number of studies (cf. Kpatinde 1991, Cruise O'Brien 1996, Lebeau 1997, Federici *et al.* 2000). Students in the first decades following African independence belonged to the most privileged group in the political system and were assured the desired elite status after graduation, but successive generations have been faced with deteriorating living and study conditions on campuses and bleak prospects after graduating.

African universities are in deep crisis nowadays (cf. Lebeau & Ogunsanya 2000, Nyamnjoh & Jua 2002). Academic standards have been falling rapidly because universities lack the basic infrastructure needed to cope with the massive growth in the student population (Mbembe 1985, Tedga 1988, Lebeau 1997, Konings 2002) and the severe economic crisis and the implementation of Structural Adjustment Programmes (SAPs) are aggravating the situation further. The increasing withdrawal of state support for universities, university students and university graduates is seen in the drastic cuts in university budgets, the imposition of tuition fees and additional levies on the student population, and a virtual halt in the recruitment of new graduates into already over-sized state bureaucracies (Caffentzis 2000). Many graduates are finding themselves obliged to defer their entry into adulthood indefinitely as they are unable to achieve economic independence, to marry and start a family of their own. They are also being forced to abandon their aspirations for elite status.

Given these conditions, the question to be posed is: how is the current generation of African university students reacting to their growing marginaliza-tion? Most of the existing studies (cf. Kpatinde 1991, Federici 2000, Amutabi 2002) claim that these students have refused to become a 'lost' or 'abandoned' generation (Cruise O'Brien 1996: 56). To bring about the needed reforms in the university system and society at large they have instead become engaged in struggles against the corrupt and authoritarian political elite whom they hold responsible for their predicament and have received the support of other groups including secondary school students, their teachers and organized labour, all of whom feel equally marginalized by the state (Bratton & Van de Walle 1992, Albert 1995). In a few countries they have been at the forefront of struggles for political liberalization (Smith 1997) but in most they have increased the intensity of their struggles after the introduction of political liberalization. It has created more space for students to voice their multiple grievances, to organize and to establish alliances with newly founded opposition parties and civil-society organizations. While in the past, with few exceptions, African student protest was sporadic, today it has become endemic in many countries, continuing year after year in spite of frequent university closures in what appears to have become protracted warfare. Federici and Caffentzis (2000: 115-50) have published a chronology of African university students' struggles between 1985 and 1998 that provides an impressive list of the violent confront-ations between students and the forces of law and order in African states.

Some of the existing studies also attempt to explain why both parties appear to prefer violence to dialogue and negotiations in solving student problems. They emphasize that government authorities continue to look upon students as 'minors' or 'cadets' who, according to African tradition, should listen to their elders and simply obey orders. These officials therefore often fail to take students and their grievances seriously and usually refuse to create channels of regular communication or to enter into peaceful negotiations. They continue to present students as a privileged and unproductive minority group that, on the basis of state largesse, is being offered the opportunity to prepare itself for its future leading role in national reconstruction. Consequently, students are expected to express their gratitude to the state through 'responsible' behaviour, devoting their time to study and not to politics (Mbembe 1985: 53).[1] In these circumstances, the use of violence has different meanings for the different actors. For students, it is often the only means of pressing home their demands to the government authorities. For government officials, it serves as a deterrent to the cadets from engaging in any similar 'irresponsible' behaviour in the future. As a result of increasing student activism, African governments have been inclined to treat students as if they were their countries' major enemies, turning campuses into war zones. Police intervention and the occupation of campuses by security forces are becoming routine in many places and so is the presence of intelligence officers and police informants in classrooms (Felici 2000, Amutabi 2002, Konings 2002).

While the existing body of literature has helped to underscore the growing importance of student politics in Africa, it nevertheless tends to present a one-sided picture, usually considering students as a homogeneous group, notably rebels and heroes. The situation is obviously more complex. Besides the rebels, there are students who tend to conform to the state model of student behaviour which the President of Cameroon, Paul Biya, defined in 1991 as follows: '*La politique aux politiciens, l'école aux écoliers*' (Konings 2002). They usually project themselves as responsible students who refuse to participate in any form of student activism, claiming that they have no other interest than advancing their academic careers. In addition, there are students who are designated as victims and predators alike. Unlike the rebels, they still appear to have faith in the state as a vehicle for upward mobility. They belong to the group of citizens that, as Bratton (1989: 414-15) has acutely observed, 'remains drawn to the state, because, even in diminished circumstances, it remains a major source of spoils and one of the available channels for getting what little there is to get'. They are eager to seek favours from the state in exchange for their expressed loyalty to the regime and its ideology and their offers of rendering services to the state. This is a group of clients that can be easily manipulated by the ruling regime to do any 'dirty work', especially in recruiting for the militia that were

---

[1] Although they have often warned students that the university is a temple of learning and not a haven of politics, one-party and military regimes have never discouraged student motions and demonstrations of support. They have often even encouraged the creation of a youth wing at universities.

created by the state to combat student rebels and other opponents of the regime.

In this chapter, I focus on Anglophone students in Cameroon, who feel even more marginalized than their Francophone counterparts because of the allegedly second-class citizenship of Anglophones in the post-colonial Francophone-dominated state. In the first section I briefly describe the development of the Anglophone identity, nationalism and organization. This serves as a background for my subsequent discussion of the role of Anglophone students in their current struggles against Francophone dominance. In the second section, I argue that Anglophone students have played a vanguard role in Anglophone protest actions in the wake of Paul Biya's accession to power in 1982. In the third section, I show that two new Anglophone youth organizations have emerged during political liberalization, in which students are playing a leading role. These organizations clearly differ in their attitude towards the Francophone-dominated state.

On the one hand, there is the Southern Cameroons Youth League (SCYL) that has identified itself with the Anglophone struggle to such an extent that its members are even prepared to defer their entry into adulthood and elite status until the 'Anglophone problem' has been solved. It agrees with the leadership of the newly created Anglophone movements on the main aim of the Anglophone struggles – namely the creation of an independent Anglophone state – but it disagrees with their strategy of realizing this objective. In sharp contrast to the Anglophone elite who have continued to pursue independence through peaceful negotiations, the SCYL opted for armed struggle after Paul Biya's persistent refusal to enter into any meaningful negotiations with the Anglophone movements.

On the other hand, the President Biya's Youths (PRESBY) has claimed to be opposed to the Anglophone struggle, having expressed its undivided loyalty to President Biya and his 'New Deal' ideals in exchange for a share in the ever-diminishing pool of state resources, thus facilitating their entry into adulthood and elite status. PRESBY has been transformed by the regime into a militia that intimidates and terrorizes the SCYL and other Anglophone organizations.

The development of Anglophone nationalism and organization

The emergence and development of what has come to be called the 'Anglophone problem' has been explained by several authors (cf. Konings & Nyamnjoh 1997, 2000, 2003, Nkoum-Me-Ntseny 1996, Eyoh 1998). Most agree that its roots can be traced back to the partitioning after the First World war of the erstwhile German Kamerun Protectorate (1884-1916) between the

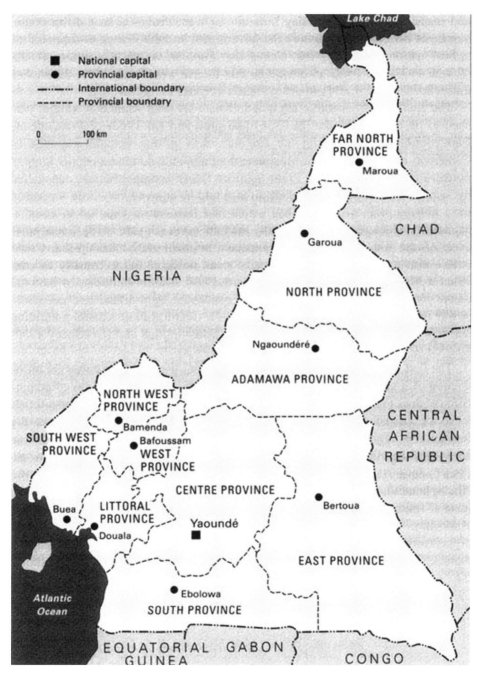

Map 7.1: Cameroon

French and English victors, first as mandates under the League of Nations and later as trusts under the United Nations. Following this partitioning, the British acquired two narrow and non-contiguous regions bordering Nigeria in the western part of the country. The southern part, and the focus of this chapter, was christened Southern Cameroons, while the northern part became known as Northern Cameroons.[2] Significantly, the British territory was much smaller than the French, comprising only about one fifth of the total area and population of the former German colony.

The partitioning of the territory into English and French spheres had some significant consequences for future political developments. Importantly, it laid the foundation for the construction of Anglophone and Francophone identities in the territory and the populations of each sphere came to see themselves as a distinct community, defined by differences in language and inherited colonial traditions of education, law, public administration and worldview. Second, while French Cameroon was incorporated into the French colonial empire as a distinct administrative unit separate from neighbouring French Equatorial Africa, the British Cameroons was administered as part of Nigeria, leading to a blatant neglect of its socio-economic development and an increasing migration of Nigerians, notably Igbos, to the Southern Cameroons where they came to dominate the regional economy.

With the approaching independence of Nigeria in 1960, the population of the British Trust Territory had to decide on its own political future. It soon became evident that the majority of the Southern Cameroonians would opt for the creation of an independent state. That their expressed wish was eventually not honoured must be attributed to two main factors. First, internal divisions among the Anglophone political elite prevented them from rallying behind the majority option in the territory. Second, and maybe even more importantly, the United Nations refused, with the complicity of the British, to put the option of an independent Southern Cameroons state to the voters in the UN-organized plebiscite of 11 February 1961 on the grounds that the creation of another tiny state was politically undesirable (and likely to contribute to a further 'Balkanization' of Africa) and economically unviable. Being deprived of this preferred option, Southern Cameroonians were given what amounted to Hobson's choice: independence by joining Nigeria or reunification with Franco-phone Cameroon, which had become independent in 1960 under the new name of the Republic of Cameroon. In the end, they chose the lesser of the two evils

---

[2]   During the 1961 UN-organized plebiscite on the political future of the British Trust Territory, the Northern Cameroons voted for integration into Nigeria. For the history of the Northern Cameroons, see, for instance, Le Vine (1964) and Welch (1966).

but their vote in favour of reunification appeared to be more a rejection of continuous ties with Nigeria, which had proved to be harmful to Southern Cameroonian development, than a vote for union with Francophone Cameroon, a territory with a different cultural heritage and that at the time was involved in a violent civil war (Joseph 1977).

By reuniting with the former French Cameroon, the Anglophone political elite had hoped to enter into a loose federal union as a way of protecting their territory's minority status and cultural heritage. Instead, it soon became evident that the Francophone political elite preferred a highly centralized, unitary state as a means of promoting national unity and economic development. While the Francophone elite received strong support from the French during constitutional negotiations, the Anglophone elite was virtually abandoned by the British who deeply resented the Southern Cameroons option for reunification with Francophone Cameroon (Awasom 2000). As a result, rumours quickly spread through the region that Charles de Gaulle looked upon the Southern Cameroons as 'a small gift of the Queen of England to France' (Jua & Konings forthcoming). In the end, during constitutional talks at Foumban in July 1961, the Francophone elite was only prepared to accept a highly centralized federation, regarding it as merely a transitional phase to a unitary state. Such a federation demanded relatively few amendments to the 1960 constitution of the Republic of Cameroon. In his recent book, Pierre Messmer (1998: 134-35), one of the last French high commissioners in Cameroon and a close advisor of President Ahmadou Ahidjo, admitted that he and others knew at the time that the so-called federal constitution provided merely a 'sham federation', which was 'save for appearance, an annexation of West Cameroon (the new name of the Southern Cameroons after reunification)'.[3] Under the new constitution, West Cameroon lost most of the limited autonomy it had enjoyed as part of the Nigerian federation (Ardener 1967, Stark 1976). When Ahidjo created a unitary state in 1972 in blatant disregard for constitutional provisions, there was in reality little left of the federation, except perhaps in name (Benjamin 1972). To reduce the danger of any future united Anglophone action, Ahidjo then decided to divide the erstwhile federated state of West Cameroon into two provinces, albeit well aware of the internal contradictions within the Anglophone community between the coastal-forest people in South West Province and the Grassfields people in North West Province (Konings & Nyamnjoh 1997: 211-13). What many regarded as one of the last visible symbols of the 1961 union

---

[3] Following reunification, the Federal Republic of Cameroon consisted of the federated state of East Cameroon (formerly French Cameroon) and the federated state of West Cameroon (formerly Southern Cameroons).

was removed in 1984 when Ahidjo's successor, Paul Biya, abolished the appellation 'United Republic of Cameroon' and replaced it with 'Republic of Cameroon', which was, significantly, the name of the Francophone part of the country when it became independent in 1960.

An even more decisive factor in the development of the Anglophone problem, however, was the nation-state project after reunification. For the Anglophone population, nation-building has been driven by the firm determination of the Francophone political elite to dominate the Anglophone minority in the post-colonial state and to erase the cultural and institutional foundations of Anglophone identity. Anglophones have regularly been relegated to inferior positions in the national decision-making process and have been constantly underrepresented in ministerial as well as senior and middle-ranking positions in the administration, the military and parastatals (cf. Kofele-Kale 1986, Takougang & Krieger 1998). There is general agreement that Anglophones have been exposed to a carefully considered policy aimed at eroding their language and institutions even though Francophone political leaders had assured their Anglophone counterparts during the constitutional talks on reunification that the inherited colonial differences in language and institutions would be respected in the bilingual union. And, last but not least, the relative underdevelopment of the Anglophone region shows that it has not benefited substantially from its rich resources, particularly oil. Gradually this created an Anglophone consciousness: the feeling of being recolonized and marginalized in all spheres of public life and thus of being second-class citizens in their own country. The co-optation of the Anglophone elite into the 'hegemonic alliance' (Bayart 1979) and the autocratic nature of the post-colonial regimes prevented Anglophones from openly organizing in defence of their interests until political liberalization in the early 1990s.

Given the deep resentment in the Anglophone region of Francophone dominance in the post-colonial state, it is not surprising that the country's first opposition party emerged in Anglophone Cameroon. In 1990 the Social Democratic Front (SDF) was formed in Bamenda, the capital of the North West Province, demanding liberalization of public space and capitalizing on popular frustrations among Anglophones after three decades of marginalization. Its chairman was John Fru Ndi, who was to enjoy widespread popularity among the urban masses because of his courage and populist style of leadership. After a massive rally to launch the SDF on 26 May 1990 ended in the death of six young Anglophones, the state-controlled media tried to deny government responsibility for this bloody event and to distort the facts. Leading members of the ruling party, the Cameroon People's Democratic Movement (CPDM), strongly condemned the Anglophones for this 'treacherous action' and what they considered the premature birth of multipartyism in the post-colonial state.

Their reaction to this peaceful demonstration shocked many people. Anglophone Cameroonians were termed 'Biafrans', referred to as 'enemies in the house' and were asked by the then Minister of Territorial Administration, Ibrahim Mbombo Njoya, 'to go elsewhere' if they were dissatisfied with national unity.

The leaders of the SDF helped to turn the Anglophone region into a veritable hotbed of rebellion leading to fierce confrontations with the regime in power, especially during the 1991-92 'ghost town' campaign, which was essentially a prolonged demonstration of civil disobedience organized by the SDF and the allied opposition parties to force the Biya government to hold a sovereign national conference (Mbu 1993). The impact of this on the Anglophone community was particularly visible during the ensuing presidential elections when Fru Ndi received 86.3 per cent and 51.6 per cent of the votes cast in the North West and South West Provinces respectively. It is hardly surprising that Biya's declared victory in these fraudulent elections was a traumatic experience in Anglophone Cameroon that sparked off violent protests throughout the North West against his 'theft of Fru Ndi's victory'.

Paradoxically, although the SDF and Fru Ndi contributed immensely to Anglophone consciousness and action, the party increasingly presented itself as a national rather than an Anglophone party as evidenced by its growing membership in Francophone Cameroon, notably among the neighbouring Bamileke, who are closely related to the ethnic groups in the North West Province and are inclined to see the SDF as a springboard to political power (Socpa 2002). Subsequently, Anglophone interests came to be first and foremost represented and defended by associations and pressure groups that had been created by the Anglophone elite in the aftermath of political liberalization in December 1990.

The newly created Anglophone movements were able to place the Anglophone problem on the national and international agenda. In April 1993, they organized the First All Anglophone Conference (AAC I) in Buea, the former capital of West Cameroon. It turned out to be a landmark in the history of Anglophone Cameroon, bringing together over 5,000 members of the Anglophone elite. Significantly, some leading members of the old-guard politicians or 'Foumban generation', like John Ngu Foncha and Solomon Tandeng Muna (the Anglophone architects of reunification), expressed their satisfaction with the meeting and apologized for their shortcomings in representing Anglophone interests, especially during the federation era, and handed over the relay baton to a new generation of Anglophone technocrats, the leaders of the newly created Anglophone movements (Wache & Fualefeh 1993). The Buea Declaration, which was issued after this historic meeting, listed the numerous Anglophone grievances about Francophone domination, assimilation and exploitation, and called for the return to a two-state (Anglophone-Francophone) federation (All Anglophone Conference 1993).

The Biya government's persistent refusal to enter into any negotiations caused a growing radicalization among Anglophone movements. In the so-called Bamenda Proclamation, adopted by the Second All Anglophone Conference (AAC II) held in Bamenda from 29 April-1 May 1994, it was stipulated that 'should the government either persist in its refusal to engage in meaningful constitutional talks or fail to engage in such talks *within a reasonable time,* the Anglophone leadership would proclaim the revival of the independence and sovereignty of the Anglophone territory and take all measures necessary to secure, defend and preserve the independence, sovereignty and integrity of the said country' (Konings & Nyamnjoh 1997: 218-20).

Following the AAC II, the Anglophone movements provocatively re-intro-duced the name of Southern Cameroons to refer to the Anglophone territory in an attempt to 'make it clear that our struggles are neither of an essentially linguistic character nor in defence of an alien colonial culture. ... but are aimed at the restoration of the autonomy of the former Southern Cameroons which has been annexed by the Republic of Cameroon'.[4] The umbrella organization of all the Anglophone movements was subsequently named the Southern Cameroons National Council (SCNC). Its leadership soon adopted a secessionist stand, striving for an independent Southern Cameroons state through peaceful negotiations with the regime, the 'sensitization' of the regional population and a diplomatic offensive. A sense of euphoria spread through Anglophone Cameroon when a SCNC delegation returned from a mission to the United Nations in 1995. During rallies attended by huge crowds in several Anglophone towns, the delegation displayed a huge UN flag, claiming it had received it from the United Nations to show that the Southern Cameroons was still a UN trust territory and that independence was only a matter of time.[5]

From 1996 onwards, however, Anglophone movements appeared to lose their initial momentum. Two factors were primarily responsible for this development. First, the Biya government was able to neutralize the Anglophone

---

[4] SCNC press release reprinted in *Cameroon Post,* 16-23 August 1994, p. 3.
[5] The SCNC leaders alleged that the proper procedures for the enactment and amendment of the federal constitution had not been followed by Ahidjo and that Francophone Cameroon had seceded from the union in 1984 when the Biya government unilaterally changed the country's name from the United Republic of Cameroon to the Republic of Cameroon, the name of independent Francophone Cameroon prior to reunification. From this perspective, they claimed that the Trust Territory of Southern Cameroons had never really ceased to exist or had been revived. They therefore still believed in continued UN responsibility for the Southern Cameroons.

movements to a large extent by employing a number of well-known tactics including divide-and-rule, co-opting Anglophone leaders into the regime, and severe repression. Second, there was the problem of leadership. With the resignation of its founding fathers, the SCNC lacked competent and committed leadership. Given the leadership problem and the government's reluctance to enter into any negotiations, a generational conflict developed within the Anglophone movements between the new generation of Anglophone leaders, who continued to adhere to a negotiated separation from *La République du Cameroun,*[6] and the youths, who had concluded that the independence of Southern Cameroons would only be achieved through armed struggle. The Southern Cameroons Youth League (SCYL) in particular opted for the latter strategy.

However, it would be a grave error to assume that the Anglophone movements became fully paralyzed or even defeated by divisive and repressive government tactics and their own organizational and strategic shortcomings. Of late, Anglophone struggles appear to have acquired new impetus. On 30 December 1999, Justice Frederick Alobwede Ebong, an SCNC activist with close ties to the SCYL, took over the Cameroon Radio and Television (CRTV) station in Buea proclaiming the restoration of the independence of the former Bristish Southern Cameroons. This was followed by the nomination of a provisional government and the announcement of a coat of arms, a flag and a national anthem.

Significantly, due to these and past events, an increasing number of the pro-government Anglophone and Francophone elite now acknowledge, after long years of public denial, that there is indeed an Anglophone problem. In January 1999, even President Biya admitted for the first time, albeit in a dismissive fashion, that such a problem existed, even if he perceived it as one created by a handful of hotheads and vandals. Still, he has not yet shown any interest in negotiating with Anglophone movements in spite of regular appeals by Anglophone, Francophone and international dignitaries for dialogue to find a solution to the Anglophone problem.[7]

---

[6]   Reference to the incumbent regime as the government of *La République du Cameroun,* the name adopted by Francophone Cameroon at independence, has become a key signifier in the replotting of the country's constitutional history as a progressive consolidation of the recolonization and annexation of Anglophone Cameroon by the post-colonial Francophone-dominated state. See Eyoh (1998: 264).

[7]   For example, during his visit to Cameroon in May 2000, the UN Secretary-General Kofi Annan pleaded for dialogue between Anglophone and Francophone leaders.

The vanguard role of Anglophone students in Anglophone nationalist struggles

In the wake of the limited degree of liberalization that Paul Biya introduced after assuming power in November 1982 (Takougang & Krieger 1998: 76-78), Anglophone students at the University of Yaoundé were the first to voice long-standing Anglophone grievances. Their initiative can be explained by the many hardships they experienced at the University of Yaoundé – the only university in Cameroon until the 1993 university reforms (Konings 2002). Though officially a bilingual institution, the University of Yaoundé has clearly remained a Francophone institute. Not only is it based on the French university system but courses are mostly given in French, thus putting English-speaking students at a disadvantage.

Government announcements of educational reforms in 1983 fuelled discontent among Anglophone students, which eventually led to their spontaneous organization. In September of that year, the Minister of National Education promulgated an order modifying the Anglophone General Certificate of Education (GCE) examination by making it similar to the *Baccalauréat*. The order was apparently intended to facilitate the entry of Anglophone students into professional and technical institutes in Cameroon, which were exclusively based on the French system. Anglophone students, however, interpreted the proposed reform as a subtle attempt by the Francophone-dominated state to absorb the Anglophone educational system. They maintained that the problem of Anglophone exclusion from the country's professional and technical institutes could not be resolved by assimilation but rather by the creation of institutes based on the English system.

The students used the unpopular educational reform issue to express some of their other grievances, including the dismissal of Dr Bisong, an Anglophone lecturer in the Faculty of Law and Economics, simply because he refused to yield to pressure by Francophone students to teach in French. In a petition addressed to the Minister of National Education, they took up the matter as follows:

> With regard to the University of Yaoundé, we strongly condemn the discrimination in the teaching languages as glaringly exemplified by the ignominious suppression of the accountancy courses offered in English by Dr Bisong for the sole reason that such courses were offered in English. The Francophone students of the department had protested to the Chancellor of the University that such important courses could not be delivered in English. Immediately Dr Bisong was accused of inefficient delivery of his lessons and they were handed over to a Francophone lecturer. The

inefficiency was surely the use of the wrong language and not the substance of academic stuff delivered.[8]

They demanded his immediate and unconditional reinstatement, and called for a more rigorous policy of bilingualism based on justice, equality and academic honesty.

They then began to demonstrate and boycott classes. Instead of looking for ways to solve their grievances, government and university authorities initially tried to crush the students' actions by using extreme police brutality. This strengthened the students' belief that the authorities had no genuine concern for their plight. The situation did not calm down until eleven days later when students were informed that the Anglophone president of the National Assembly, Solomon Tandeng Muna, along with other Anglophone political elites, was to transmit an important message to them from the head of state. During the meeting, Muna said that the head of state was requesting that the students go back to class and pursue their studies while their grievances and other matters affecting their education received appropriate attention. He stressed that none of them would be allowed to raise any questions about the president's message because no parliamentarian would ever dare to do so. Expecting the students' respect either as the president of parliament where their parents met to discuss important issues, or at least as their 'white-haired grandfather', he asked them to applaud the president's message and to go back to class calmly and quietly, adding that 'a word to the wise is enough'. But the most radical students were not yet willing to listen to their elders and questioned the authenticity of the message since no written statement signed by the president had been handed over to the students during the meeting. They only agreed to call off the strike when the full presidential message was broadcast nationwide in the evening, announcing the installation of a commission of highly qualified and experienced Anglophones and Francophones to look into the students' grievances. It is striking that no report has ever been published by this commission and that Anglophone struggles for the preservation of the GCE have continued to the present day (Nyamnjoh 1996: 19-39).

In an open letter in 1985, Anglophone students urgently appealed to their parents 'to assume squarely their responsibilities before history concerning the grave [Anglophone] identity situation and help solve the problem'. They summed up the Anglophone population's multitude of grievances and those of the Anglophone students in particular and requested their parents take imme-

---

[8] Petition of English-speaking students from the University of Yaoundé to the Minister of National Education, dated 19 November 1983, reproduced in Mukong (1990: 26).

diate action: 'apart from drawing up a new constitution, justice also requires the establishment of a fully-fledged English-speaking university based on the educational principles we cherish'. Should their parents fail to solve the Anglophone problem, they threatened to resort to violent action in the future.[9] Apparently, this letter was not supported by the entire Anglophone student population. A group calling itself 'The Anglophone Students of the New Deal'[10] strongly protested against the behaviour of students 'who falsely claim that the Anglophone community is being oppressed and threaten to disturb the scarcity and peace of our United Kingdom'. These 'subversive' elements should instead 'take stock of the achievements of the Man of the New Deal [Paul Biya] towards better integration of all ethnic and linguistic communities'. Most probably, this protest action had been organized by the then single party that used some Anglophone students to discredit their colleagues and the Anglophone cause in exchange for immediate or future rewards.[11]

Relations between Anglophone students, the government and the university authorities rapidly deteriorated from the early 1990s onwards. On 26 May 1990, a group of students, most of them Anglophones, marched in support of launching the SDF in Bamenda and the introduction of multipartyism in the country. The government press accused them of singing the Nigerian national anthem (Kamto 1993). The implication of this false claim was that Anglophones did not see themselves as Cameroonians but rather as Nigerians or – even more common in government discourse – secessionist Biafrans. Subsequently, the gendarmes harassed and brutalized the demonstrators, looted their property and arrested about three hundred of them. This march by Anglophone students incited disaffection and resentment among the autochthonous Beti population on and off campus, which tended to support the ruling CPDM party led by President Biya, who was himself a Beti.[12] Some Beti landlords even threatened to remove Anglophone students from their houses. To forestall any

---

[9] Open letter to all English-speaking parents of Cameroon from the English-speaking students of the North West and South West Provinces, dated 20 August 1985, reproduced in Mukong (1990: 109-19).

[10] After assuming power in 1982, Paul Biya promised the Cameroonian people a New Deal.

[11] The Anglophone Students of the New Deal, 'Open Letter to the Cameroonian Patriotic Students of the North West and South West', reproduced in Nyamnjoh (1996: 64-68).

[12] It is important to emphasize here that the name 'Beti' as an ethnic label is a historically circumscribed construct and subject to constant change. Since the 1980s, the term has come to cover a number of ethnic groups in the Centre and South Provinces of Cameroon, in particular the Bulu and Eton or Ewondo. President Biya belongs to the Bulu group. See Socpa (2002).

further student protests, the regime stationed gendarmes permanently on campuses.

As I have shown elsewhere (Konings 2002), the political liberalization process that started in December 1990 not only created space for students to organize in defence of their interests but also tended to encourage a further polarization among student factions along party and ethno-regional lines. On the one hand, there emerged what was initially called the National Coordination of Cameroon Students that later changed its name to the Students' Parliament or simply 'Parliament'. It was by far the largest student union on campus. The core of its membership and leadership was formed by Anglophone and Bamileke students who in common parlance are often referred to as 'Anglo-Bami' students. Parliament soon came under the influence of the opposition parties, notably the SDF. It agreed with the opposition that the regime had to be overthrown in order to bring about real change in society at large and within the university in particular. Anglophone members also participated in the Anglophone struggles. Following AAC I and the Buea Declaration in 1993, they created the Cameroon Anglophone Students' Association (CANSA), which operated under the umbrella of the SCNC and participated in various actions undertaken by the SCNC. Parliament members often presented themselves as revolutionaries who were prepared to use all the means at their disposal, including demonstrations, strikes and acts of vandalism, should the regime and the university authorities fail to listen to or give in to their demands.

On the other hand, a Committee for Self-Defence, a vigilante group or militia, was set up by the regime to counteract the actions of Parliament. Its membership and leadership was mainly made up of Beti students. Nevertheless, some students from other ethnic groups were also part of the Self-Defence group, for example, a few of its leaders were Anglophone and Bamileke students. They and other non-Beti members were recruited by the regime to give the public the impression that the Self-Defence group was not an exclusively Beti affair but an organization of responsible students who were prevented from peacefully continuing their studies by the political actions of Parliament 'rebels' and 'vandals'. The Self-Defence group was well rewarded for its services: its members were given cash and, in some cases, free accommo-dation. A few leaders were even given lucrative jobs after graduation despite the freeze on public-sector employment. Since the Committee for Self-Defence was made up of only a small minority of students, they were allowed to carry weapons – clubs, knives and pistols – to attack Parliament members and sympathizers. It usually worked closely with other, even more extremist, Beti vigilante groups on campus, particularly the self-styled Direct Action group that openly declared that the University of Yaoundé was on Beti land and thus should fall under Beti control. It claimed that the Anglo-Bami students should either recognize Beti control or 'go home'. Following the formation of the Committee for Self-Defence and the Beti vigilante groups, which received logistic support from the forces of law and order, Parliament created its own commandos to fight these hostile groups and to protect its members.

The University of Yaoundé barely functioned from 1990 to 1996, with university life being repeatedly paralyzed by student protests and unprecedented violent confrontations between the two camps. I mention here only the three most important confrontations. The first was in 1991 when Parliament members marched in support of the opposition parties' call for the holding of a sovereign national conference and an unconditional general amnesty for political prisoners and exiles. The second took place in 1993 after Parliament's protest against the introduction of university tuition fees and the third occurred in 1996 following Parliament's resistance to the university authorities' imposition of special levies on students in addition to tuition fees (Konings 2002).

Interestingly, from the mid-1990s Parliament and the Self-Defence group became the cradle of two new Anglophone youth groups which turned out to be fierce opponents in the on-going Anglophone struggle: on the one hand, the Southern Cameroons Youth League (SCYL) and on the other, President Biya's Youths (PRESBY). Both groups sought to strengthen their positions by extending their membership from the Anglophone university student population to other sectors of well-educated Anglophone youths who were facing similar educational and employment problems. These included university graduates, university dropouts and other sections of the educated youth, many being either unemployed or scraping together a meagre existence in the informal sector.

The Southern Cameroons Youth League (SCYL)

The SCYL was founded in Buea on 28 May 1995 to reinforce the role of the educated Anglophone youth in the Anglophone struggle. It vowed to 'revive, defend, protect and preserve the independence and sovereignty of the once nation, the Southern Cameroons' and to serve as the militant youth wing of the SCNC.[13] Its original leadership was largely made up of Anglophone members of Parliament and its membership was composed of 'young people who do not see any future for themselves and who would prefer to die fighting than continue to submit to the fate imposed on Southern Cameroons by *La République du Cameroun*'.[14] SCYL members perceived the creation of an independent

---

[13] SCYL, 'Seventh Anniversary of the SCYL', *BSCNation*, 27 May 2002.

[14] See Mr Fidelis Chiabi, chairman of the former Anglophone Youth Council, in

Southern Cameroons state as the only avenue to a better future for themselves and the Anglophone population as a whole. They were even in the habit of swearing under oath to make the necessary sacrifices for the achievement of this goal and to never betray the Anglophone cause. Their fanatical commitment to the Anglophone struggle actually gave them a new feeling of self-esteem.

In 1996, soon after its foundation, the SCYL began to express its discontent with the Anglophone movements' rapid loss of momentum. It blamed the new SCNC leadership chaired by Henry Fossung, a retired ambassador, for its armchair approach to Southern Cameroons' independence as evidenced by its failure to mobilize the Anglophone population in the face of increasing government repression and its continued advocacy of dialogue with the Francophone-dominated state in spite of the Biya government's persistent failure to enter into meaningful negotiation with the SCNC. Having learnt from their Parliament days that violence was the only means of pressing home their demands with the autocratic Biya regime, the SCYL leaders declined to adhere to the SCNC motto of 'the force of argument' any longer. They instead adopted a new motto, namely 'the argument of force', which expressed their determination to achieve the independence of Southern Cameroons through armed struggle. Little wonder then that the relationship between the SCYL and the SCNC became even more strained.

While preparing for action in both Anglophone provinces, the SCYL was unexpectedly faced with the detention of its chairman, Mr Ebenezer Akwanga, following the failure of its members to steal explosives from the Razel Company in Jakiri in the North West Province during the night of 23-24 March 1997. It immediately reacted by attacking some military and civil establishments in the North West Province between 27-31 March. According to official reports, three gendarmes and seven unidentified assailants were killed in these operations. The government paper, the *Cameroon Tribune,* claimed that 'nearly 500 people had been trained to enable that part of the country to secede' and another newspaper, the pro-government *Le Patriote* went even further, claiming that '2000 gangsters had been trained to effect the liberation of Southern Cameroons'.[15] Not even the passage of time has enabled the truth of these charges to be ascertained. Government repression of this ill-planned revolt was out of all proportion. It ruthlessly killed, tortured, raped and arrested hundreds of local men and women, and forced many others to go into exile. Above all, it seized the opportunity to clamp down on the SDF and the SCNC, accusing both

---

Cameroon Post, 1-2 February 1994, p. 7.
[15] Cited in *L'Expression,* no. 107, 8 April 1997, p. 8.

organizations of being responsible for the uprising.[16] A considerable number of SCNC and SCYL members were arrested and imprisoned in Yaoundé. Some died while in prison and others were not brought to trial until 1999 when they were not treated as political prisoners but were charged with criminal offences (Ball Maps 2002).

The SCNC chairman, Henry Fossung, who had gone into hiding after the revolt, publicly denied any SCNC involvement insisting 'that the SCNC motto "the force of argument and not the argument of force" has remained today as valid as yesterday'.[17] He instead claimed that the incident had been orchestrated by a desperate government in an attempt to frustrate the legitimate struggles of the Southern Cameroons people to restore their independence. Strikingly, following the revolt, the SCNC leadership appeared to be even less inclined to sensitize and mobilize the Anglophone population. It was only after the proclamation of independence by Justice Frederick Ebong on 30 December 1999 that a more committed and radical leadership seized power in the SCNC.

There is sufficient proof that state brutality and torture have failed to dampen the SCYL tenacity and fervour to achieve its objectives. One indication is the following submission of SCYL President Ebenezer Akwanga before the military tribunal in Yaoundé in 1999:

> I am the National President of the SCYL. Our fathers who took us into reunification have told us that its terms are being grossly and flagrantly disrespected. I believe in the SCNC which is fighting a just cause, to see how the violation of the terms of reunification can be corrected. (*The Post*, 19 July 1999)

Another indication is the publication by the SCYL of a document entitled 'The Southern Cameroons Independence is Here and Now' in which the SCYL champions a 'people's war' which 'has to be aggressive, not cool and cautious, bold and audacious, violent, and an expression of icy, disdainful hatred'. In furtherance of this goal, it reaffirms its commitment to the Anglophone cause: Nothing can stop us, we are not intimidated by the spectre of repression; today it is me, tomorrow it would be you.'[18]

---

[16] In a report that was full of factual errors and based on spurious evidence, *Jeune Afrique Economie* supported the Biya government's allegation that the SCNC was responsible for the revolt. See *Jeune Afrique Economie*, no. 239, 14 April 1997, p. 8. The journal's support of the Biya government's allegation is not altogether surprising. Professor Titus Edzoa, a former Secretary-General at the Presidency, once revealed that the journal was used for public relations purposes by the regime. To this end, the regime had funded the journal to the tune of FCFA 1.5 billion (or US$ 3 million).

[17] *Le Messager*, 23 April 1997, p. 8.

[18] *The Post*, 15 May 2000, p. 3. For a reiteration of this position, see *The Post*, 24

Confronted with severe repression in Cameroon, the SCYL was forced underground. Like the *Mouvement des Forces Démocratiques de la Casamance* (MFDC*)* in Senegal (De Jong 2001: 211-15), it has almost become a secret society for security purposes. During my fieldwork I only succeeded in meeting some of its leaders through the intermediary of a high-ranking SCNC leader and even during the actual interviews I received little information about the size, organizational set-up, weapons and plans of the SCYL. I discovered later that most SCYL members lack this knowledge themselves and simply wait for instructions from their local leaders. Having become painfully aware that their organization still lacked the necessary weapons and training to engage in regular guerrilla warfare against the large and well-equipped Cameroonian armed forces,[19] the SCYL leaders apparently decided after the dismal failure of the 1997 revolt to temporarily resort to less controllable forms of action.

The SCYL leadership in exile has discovered the importance of the Internet, using it to raise Anglophone consciousness and promote the visibility of the Anglophone cause in the Cameroonian and international community, thus frustrating the regular attempts of the Francophone-dominated state to control information to the outside world and cover up its frequently brutal repression of SCNC and SCYL actions. Strikingly, they have also become deeply concerned with naming and flagging. Although such activities may initially appear as somewhat 'banal' (Billig 1995), they turn out to be closely connected with the symbolic construction and preservation of the Anglophone identity and heritage and to be instrumental in raising Anglophone consciousness (Jua & Konings forthcoming).

Like other Anglophone movements, the SCYL refuses to recognize the government's designation of 20 May – the date of the inauguration of the unitary state in 1972 – as the country's National Day. It has continued to boycott its celebrations, declaring 20 May as a 'Day of Mourning' and a 'Day of Shame'. It also indicts the regime for declaring 11 February – the day of the 1961 plebiscite – as Youth Day. It sees the persistent failure of the government to highlight the historical significance of this day as a conscious attempt to reconfigure national history. It has thus called upon the Anglophone population to mark 11 February as the 'Day of the Plebiscite' and 1 October as the 'Day of Independence' as alternative days of national celebration. On these days, it has frequently attempted to hoist the Southern Cameroons flag; attempts that were often brutally challenged by the security forces.

February 2001, p. 3.
[19] Although government authorities regularly allege that Anglophone leaders have imported large quantities of weapons, the 1997 SCYL revolt was carried out with bows and arrows, hunting guns and a few pistols captured from gendarmes.

Road signs also became a focus of SCYL protest action during the millennium year when the regime decided to put up French-only road signs on the Douala-Victoria (Limbe) road, the so-called reunification road linking Francophone and Anglophone Cameroon. Irked by what it perceived as signs of recolonization, the SCYL then sprayed black paint on all the French road signs. The use of black paint was significant as it is the colour of mourning.

A few years later, in May 2002, the SCYL, together with 'SCNC North America', undertook a spectacular action called 'Operation Stamp Your Identity'. Eighteen thousand bumper stickers calling for the creation of a federal republic in Anglophone Cameroon were printed in the United States and sent to Anglophone Cameroon. They were symbolically flagged in Anglophone towns on 20 May 2002, the day that Cameroon celebrated its 30th anniversary of being a unitary state. On 1 October of the same year when Southern Cameroonians were celebrating their independence day, the Secretary-General of the SCYL, Lucas Cho Ayaba, who is living in exile in Germany, together with other SCYL members and sympathizers, took over the Cameroonian embassy in Bonn and hoisted the Southern Cameroonian flag on top of the building.[20]

The Cameroonian government still sees the SCYL as the most dangerous Anglophone movement. It has therefore become the main target not only of the security forces but also of the newly created youth militia.

President Biya's Youths (PRESBY)

PRESBY was founded in Yaoundé in 1996 as the successor of the Committee for Self-Defence that had been operating at the University of Yaoundé. It was an attempt by the regime to transform a local, almost exclusively Beti, militia into a nationwide militia to fight opponents of the regime, including the SCYL. To attract a nationwide membership, it shifted the objective of the new group from the protection of Beti interests to the promotion of President Biya's New Deal policies, which became the regime's ideological basis after Biya's accession to power.

Soon after Paul Biya succeeded Ahmadou Ahidjo as president on 6 November 1982, he proposed a New Deal to the Cameroonian people. The New Deal policy guidelines were political liberalization, rigour and moralization, and national integration. They were intended to bring about a state characterized by a larger degree of individual liberty and a freer exchange of ideas, the judicious and stringent management of public affairs, transparency and public account-

---

[20]　SCYL, 'Today is Independence Day', *BSCNation*, 1 October 2002.

ability by government officials, as well as a total absence of ethno-regional particularism and favouritism (Biya 1987, Krieger & Takougang 1998). It quickly became evident, however, that the New Deal policy guidelines were mere slogans, probably used by Biya to distance himself from Ahidjo's shadow (Konings 1996: 250). Political liberalization proved to be limited. Corruption and mismanagement in public life reached unprecedented levels, and Transparency International designated Cameroon as the most corrupt country in the world in 1998. National integration turned out to be an ideological justification for effacing and assimilating the Anglophone cultural legacy. Moreover, there was a growing monopolization of economic and political power by the Beti, the president's ethnic group. The ruling CPDM party has nevertheless continued to present Paul Biya as the 'Man of the New Deal' and to praise his wonderful achievements.

Since its foundation, PRESBY has indeed extended its influence to all regions in Cameroon, recruiting members among similar youth groups such as the SCYL. In 2001, it was estimated that the new organization comprised 120,000 members and 7,900 officials (Fokwang 2002: 13). Despite its national claims, it should not be forgotten that the Beti still continue to control the organization to a large extent and Beti members residing in various regions of the country have been used as vectors for expanding its sphere of influence, mostly initiating the launch of local chapters in their areas of residence. While autochthonous youths have adopted leadership roles at the local level, Beti youths still occupy most leadership positions at the national level. PRESBY's founder and self-imposed president, Philomon Ntyam Ntyam, is a Beti and other members of this ethnic group occupy three-quarters of the seats in PRESBY's National Bureau.

Far from being an apolitical organization as it has continued to claim, PRESBY is clearly affiliated to the ruling party. Not only is Philomon Ntyam Ntyam a member of the Central Committee of the CPDM but members of the group are also sooner or later expected to obtain CPDM membership cards. It enjoys widespread support and patronage from the CPDM elite. CPDM bigwigs openly attend and fund elections in the various local organs of PRESBY and when PRESBY in the South West Province organized a seminar in Mutengene in September 2001, Prime Minister Peter Mafany Musonge, a South Westerner himself, requested that all the heads of regional ministries contribute to its funding. In Cameroon, where officials owe their appointments to the president or prime minister, such a request is tantamount to an order (Jua forthcoming).

PRESBY members appear not to have lost faith in the neo-patrimonial state, the essence of which two leading Anglophone government members, Prime

Minister Simon Achidi Achu (1992-96) and his successor Peter Mafany Musonge (1996-present),[21] have defined as follows: 'politics *na njangi*[22] and 'the politics of you scratch my back, I'll scratch yours', both meaning *quid pro quo* or 'one good turn deserves another' (Konings & Nyamnjoh 1997: 214). Unlike SCYL members, the Anglophone members of PRESBY publicly declare that they are being prepared to support and forcibly defend the Francophone-dominated unitary state in exchange for favours, including admission to the prestigious *grand écoles* like the *Ecole Nationale Supérieure* (ENS) and *Ecole Nationale d'Administration et de Magistrature* (ENAM), employment in the civil service and public sector, and assistance in the setting up or expansion of business – favours which are often denied to non-members nowadays. They tend to look upon PRESBY as a vehicle through which they can lobby for a share in the national cake and thus obtain access to adulthood and even elite status. PRESBY leaders have constantly emphasized reciprocal exchange. For example, during a trip to Bui Division in the North West Province in September 2001, Mr Roger Penandjo, one of PRESBY's leaders responsible for national missions, is said to have promised government favours to youths of the division who joined the organization. He then presented thirty forms to PRESBY members who had the minimum qualification of GCE Advanced Level to apply for Bangladeshi scholarships. After the presentation, he told his audience: 'So you see that it is only when you join PRESBY that you can have these opportunities' (Fokwang 2002: 12).

It should, however, be noted that, compared to SCYL members, PRESBY members tend to show less commitment to their organization's objectives. During my interviews, some confessed that they 'support the Anglophone cause with their hearts in private, but pretend to speak against it in public to protect their positions'.[23] They claimed that they had joined PRESBY for no other reason than to get sinecures, pointing out that even their elders in power, including the Man of the New Deal, Paul Biya, did not live up to the lofty ideals

---

[21] Their appointment in the 1990s shows that the Anglophone problem has, paradoxically, enhanced the chances of pro-government Anglophone elites being appointed to government posts which used to be reserved for Francophones only. Obviously the decision to improve the position of Anglophones in the state apparatus is designed to belie charges that they only play second fiddle in the Francophone-dominated unitary state, and simultaneously to attract new members of the Anglophone elite into the hegemonic alliance.

[22] This is a Pidgin-English expression meaning 'politics is like a rotating credit association'.

[23] More and more Anglophone CPDM members are making similar confessions nowadays. See *The Post,* 7 February 2000, p. 3.

of the New Deal. In their view, the latter only displayed 'rigour in corruption', perceiving the state as a source of spoils to be plundered without remorse.

Moreover, a considerable number of PRESBY members were disappointed when they discovered that the number and range of prebends offered by their organization were limited. This largely explains the fluid nature of the organization's membership, the continuous struggles for power among its leadership, and the emergence of new youth groups – with objectives similar to those of PRESBY – eager to gain access to state resources by any means possible.

Although the PRESBY leadership often created the illusion that all the members would be rewarded for their services, the reality was, to paraphrase the Bible, that, in the end, many were called but few were chosen. This situation had an ambivalent effect on the organization's membership: on the one hand, a number of the existing membership decided to resign from the organization, their hopes never having been fulfilled, but on the other, the relatively few success stories attracted new members.

Unsurprisingly, access to the state was guaranteed mostly to the group's leadership. Due to PRESBY's strategic position as a militia in the patron-client networks in Cameroon, its leaders tend to be regarded as power brokers who can hold people to ransom and are feared even by provincial governors. Leadership positions are highly contested as was demonstrated by the power struggles in the South West Province in 2000. The Regional Secretary, Enow Charles Eseme, accused the Regional Coordinator, Mayengi Thomas Kendi, of being involved in criminal activities. He alleged that Kendi was in the habit of extorting money from young people who wanted to migrate to Europe and the United States in search of greener pastures, promising them that he would use his influence to obtain visas for them. Eventually, Eseme was able to replace him at the helm of the organization, but once in power he embarked on similar activities. Exploiting his supposed connections with the regime, he extorted money from the various parastatals in the South West Province as well as from state employees by either threatening them with punitive transfers or by promising them promotions. In 2000, the North West chapter of PRESBY spent the entire year fighting over leadership positions, which eventually resulted in the resignation of its president (Jua forthcoming).

Similarly, a group of leaders who had been working closely with the National President of PRESBY blamed him for 'eating' alone and decided to form an organization of their own, the so-called Youths for the Support of Those in Power (YOSUPO). The objective of this new group, they claimed, was to extend youth support from President Paul Biya to the entire leadership of the ruling regime. The initiative was followed by the creation of other youth groups such as *L'Association des Camerounais Biyaristes* (ACB), the Movement for

Youths of the Presidential Majority (MYPM) and the *Jeunesse Active pour Chantal Biya* (JACHABI) (Fokwang 2002).[24] Against this background, one can begin to understand the lack of cooperation between these organizations in spite of their similar objectives. Evidently, cooperation would reduce the political space of these organizations and the leverage of their leaders.

Since its foundation, PRESBY has been used by the Francophone-dominated state to counteract the activities of Anglophone movements and parties such as the SDF, the SCNC and particularly the SCYL. It has been regularly engaged in using violence to disrupt their meetings, rallies and demonstrations and to terrorize their individual members. Like the former Committee for Self-Defence, PRESBY members are armed and receive active and open support from the security forces. One of their actions in early January 2001 received a lot of publicity, occurring as it did just a few days before the Franco-African Summit in Yaoundé. On that occasion, PRESBY members disturbed a peaceful SDF rally and attacked participants in the presence of security forces.[25] Since the declaration of Southern Cameroons' independence by Justice Frederick Ebong on 30 December 1999 and the subsequent revival of SCNC and SCYL activities, PRESBY members have been openly requested by CPDM and government officials to clamp down on Anglophone secessionists – a request they have promised to carry out religiously.

Conclusion

The importance of student politics in Africa during economic and political liberalization cannot be underestimated. The present generation of African students is not only being confronted with growing marginalization during economic liberalization but has also acquired more space during political liberalization to articulate its grievances and to organize in defence of its interests against the ruling political elite whom it holds responsible for its predicament.

My case study of Anglophone students, however, cautions against treating students as a homogeneous category. Although the Anglophone students of today feel even more marginalized because of their Anglophone identity than their Francophone counterparts, they have actually displayed a rather ambi-valent attitude towards the Francophone-dominated state. On the one hand, there are students who are seen as rebels by the regime and as heroes by the

---

[24] Chantal Biya is the president's wife.
[25] See *The Post,* 15 January 2001, p. 3; and *Le Messager,* 15 January 2001, p. 5.

Anglophone population. They first played a vanguard role in Anglophone protests and later, during the political liberalization era, joined the Anglophone struggle for an independent Anglophone state, which they saw as a precondition for a better future for themselves and the Anglophone community as a whole. Having learnt during the heyday of 'Parliament' at the University of Yaoundé that violence is a more effective weapon than dialogue to press home demands with the autocratic state, the leaders of the most militant Anglophone organization, the SCYL, soon opted for armed struggle to achieve the desired independence. This caused a generational conflict within the Anglophone movement itself, the Anglophone elite clinging to a strategy of achieving independence through dialogue with the regime in spite of the Biya government's persistent refusal to enter into any meaningful negotiation with the Anglophone movements.

On the other hand, there are students who are seen by the Anglophone population as both predators and victims of the regime. They are prepared to support and defend the Francophone-dominated unitary state in exchange for a share in the ever-diminishing state resources. The regime, in turn, expects them to join the newly created militia organizations such as the Committee for Self-Defence and PRESBY, with a view to challenging the Anglophone associations and parties.

Studies of student politics in other African countries such as Ethiopia (Tiruneh 1990), Nigeria (Lebeau & Ogunsanya 2000), South Africa (Seekings 1993) and Senegal and Mali (Wigram 1993) provide evidence that the ambiguity of student politics is not restricted to Cameroon alone.

While PRESBY has greatly expanded its membership among the educated Anglophone youth in recent years, the role of the SCYL instead appears to have been drastically reduced. Following the government's brutal repression of the SCYL's ill-planned 1997 revolt, most of its leaders have either been imprisoned or have fled the country. Of course, this does not mean that the government has finally defeated the SCYL. It is still operating underground and is engaged in a variety of Internet and boycott activities. One of its actions was the spectacular liberation in 1993 of its chairman, Mr Ebenezer Akwanga, from the Kondengui maximum security prison in Yaoundé where he was serving a 20-year jail sentence for secessionist activities. Nevertheless, severe government repression of SCYL activities has discouraged the educated Anglophone youth from joining the organization. The SCYL will, therefore, inevitably continue to occupy a minority position within the Anglophone movements that are predominantly trying to solve the 'Anglophone problem' through peaceful negotiations.

References

Albert, I.O. 1995, 'University Students and the Politics of Structural Adjustment in Nigeria', in T. Mkandawire & A. Olukoshi (eds), *Between Liberalisation and Oppression: The Politics of Structural Adjustment in Africa*, Dakar: CODESRIA, pp. 374-92.

All Anglophone Congress 1993, *The Buea Declaration*, Limbe: Nooremac Press.

Amutabi, M.N. 2002, 'Crisis and Student Protest in Universities in Kenya: Examining the Role of Students in National Leadership and the Democratization Process', *African Studies Review*, 45 (2): 157-78.

Ardener, E. 1967, 'The Nature of the Reunification of Cameroon', in A. Hazlewood (ed.), *African Integration and Disintegration*, Oxford: Oxford University Press, pp. 285-337.

Awasom, N.F. 2000, 'The Reunification Question in Cameroon History: Was the Bride an Enthusiastic or a Reluctant One?', *Africa Today*, 47 (2): 91-119.

Ball Maps, O. 2002, *Every Morning, Just Like Coffee: Torture in Cameroon*, London: Medical Foundation for the Care of Victims of Torture.

Bayart, J-F. 1979, *L'Etat au Cameroun*, Paris: Presses de la Fondation Nationale des Sciences Politiques.

Benjamin, J. 1972, *Les Camerounais Occidentaux: La Minorité dans un Etat Bicommunautaire*, Montréal: Les Presses de l'Université de Montréal.

Billig, M. 1995, *Banal Nationalism*, London: SAGE Publications.

Biya, P. 1987, *Communal Liberalism*, London/Basingstoke: Macmillan.

Bratton, M. 1989, 'Beyond the State: Civil Society and Associational Life in Africa', *World Politics*, 41 (3): 407-29.

Bratton, M. & N. van de Walle 1992, 'Popular Protest and Political Reform in Africa', *Comparative Politics*, 24: 419-42.

Buijtenhuijs, R. & C. Thiriot 1995, *Democratization in Sub-Saharan Africa, 1992-1995: An Overview of the Literature*, Leiden/Bordeaux: ASC/CEAN.

Caffentzis, G. 2000, 'The World Bank and Education in Africa', in S. Federici, G. Caffentzis & O. Alidou (eds), *A Thousand Flowers: Social Struggles against Structural Adjustment in African Universities*, Trenton/Asmara: Africa World Press, pp. 3-18.

Cruise O'Brien, D.B. 1996, 'A Lost Generation?: Youth Identity and State Decay in West Africa', in R. Werbner & T. Ranger (eds), *Postcolonial Identities in Africa*, London: Zed Books, pp. 54-74.

Eyoh, D. 1998, 'Conflicting Narratives of Anglophone Protest and the Politics of Identity in Cameroon', *Journal of Contemporary African Studies*, 16 (2): 249-76.

Federici, S. 2000, 'The New African Student Movement', in C.B. Mwara, S. Federici & J. McLaren (eds), *African Visions: Literary Images, Political Change and Social Struggle in Contemporary Africa*, Westport: Greenwood Press, pp. 49-66.

Federici, S. & G. Caffentzis 2000, 'Chronology of African University Students' Struggles: 1985-1998', in S. Federici, G. Caffentzis & O. Alidou (eds), *A Thousand Flowers: Social Struggles against Structural Adjustment in African Universities*, Trenton/Asmara: Africa World Press, pp. 115-50.

Federici, S., G. Caffentzis & O. Alidou (eds) 2000, *A Thousand Flowers: Social Struggles against Structural Adjustment in African Universities,* Trenton/Asmara: Africa World Press.

Fokwang, J. 2002, '"An Unlimited Generation?": Youth, Intersubjectivity and the State in Cameroon', Paper presented at the conference on 'Understanding Exclusion, Creating Value: African Youth in a Global Age', Dakar: Codesria, 7-10 June (mimeo).

Jong, F. de 2001, 'Modern Secrets: The Power of Locality in Casamance, Senegal', University of Amsterdam, PhD thesis.

Joseph, R.1977, *Radical Nationalism in Cameroon: Social Origins of the UPC Rebellion,* Oxford: Oxford University Press.

Jua, N. (forthcoming), 'Of Spaces, Morality and Social Integration of Youths in Cameroon under Structural Adjustment'.

Jua, N. & P. Konings (forthcoming), 'Occupation of Public Space: Anglophone Nationalism in Cameroon', *Cahiers d'Etudes Africaines.*

Kamto, M. 1993, 'Quelques Réflexions sur la Transition vers le Pluralisme Politique au Cameroun', in G. Conac (ed.), *L'Afrique en Transition vers le Pluralisme Politique,* Paris: Economica, pp. 209-36.

Kofele-Kale, N. 1986, 'Ethnicity, Regionalism, and Political Power: A Post-Mortem of Ahidjo's Cameroon', in M.G. Schatzberg & I.W. Zartman (eds), *The Political Economy of Cameroon,* New York: Praeger Publishers, pp. 53-82.

Konings, P. 1996, 'The Post-Colonial State and Economic and Political Reforms in Cameroon', in A.E. Fernández Jilberto & A. Mommen (eds), *Liberalization in the Developing World: Institutional and Economic Changes in Latin America, Africa and Asia,* London: Routledge, pp. 244-65.

Konings, P. 2002, 'University Students' Revolt, Ethnic Militia and Violence during Political Liberalization in Cameroon', *African Studies Review*, 45 (2): 179-204.

Konings, P. & F.B. Nyamnjoh 1997, 'The Anglophone Problem in Cameroon', *The Journal of Modern African Studies*, 35 (2): 207-29.

Konings, P. & F.B. Nyamnjoh 2000, 'Construction and Deconstruction: Anglophones or Autochtones?', *The African Anthropologist*, 7 (1): 207-29.

Konings, P. & F.B. Nyamnjoh 2003, *Negotiating an Anglophone Identity: A Study of the Politics of Recognition and Representation in Cameroon,* Leiden: Brill, Afrika-Studiecentrum Series, Vol. 1.

Kpatinde, F. 1991, 'Que Veulent les Etudiants?', *Jeune Afrique*, 1593 (11-16 July): 22-24.

Lebeau, Y. 1997, *Etudiants et Campus du Nigéria,* Paris: Karthala.

Lebeau, Y. & M. Ogunsanya (eds) 2000, *The Dilemma of Post-Colonial Universities,* Ibadan: IFRA/Africa BookBuilders.

Le Vine, V.T. 1964, *The Cameroons: From Mandate to Independence,* Berkeley/Los Angeles: University of California Press.

Mbembe, A. 1985, *Les Jeunes et l'Ordre Politique en Afrique Noire,* Paris: L'Harmattan.

Mbu, A.N.T. 1993, *Civil Disobedience in Cameroon,* Douala: Imprimerie Georges Freres.

Messmer, P. 1998, *Les Blancs S'en Vont: Récits de Décolonisation,* Paris: Albin Michel.

Mukong, A. (ed.) 1990, *The Case for the Southern Cameroons,* Uwani-Enugu: Chuka Printing Company.

Nkoum-Me-Ntseny, L-M.M. 1996, 'Dynamique de Positionnement Anglophone et Libéralisation Politique au Cameroun: De l'Identité à l'Identification', *Polis: Cameroonian Political Science Review,* 1: 68-100.

Nyamnjoh, F.B. 1996, *The Cameroon GCE Crisis: A Test of Anglophone Solidarity,* Limbe: Nooremac.

Nyamnjoh, F.B. & N.B. Jua 2002, 'African Universities in Crisis and the Promotion of a Democratic Culture: The Political Economy of Violence in African Educational Systems', *African Studies Review,* 45 (2): 1-26.

Seekings, J. 1993, *Heroes or Villains: Youth Politics in the 1980s,* Johannesburg: Ravan Press.

Smith, Z.K. 1997, 'From Demons to Democrats: Mali's Student Movement 1991-1996', *Review of African Political Economy,* 72: 249-63.

Socpa, A. 2002, 'Démocratisation et Autochtonie au Cameroun: Trajectoires Régionales Divergentes', University of Leiden, PhD thesis.

Stark, F.M. 1976, 'Federalism in Cameroon: The Shadow and the Reality', *Canadian Journal of African Studies,* 10 (3): 423-42.

Takougang, J. & M. Krieger 1998, *African State in the 1990s: Cameroon's Political Crossroads,* Boulder: Westview Press.

Tedga, A.J.M. 1988, *L'Enseignement Supérieur en Afrique Noire Francophone: La Catastrophe?,* Paris: L'Harmattan.

Tiruneh, F. 1990, *The Ethiopian Students: Their Struggle to Articulate the Ethiopian Revolution,* Chicago: Nyala Type.

Wache, F.K. & V.A. Fualefeh 1993, 'The Untold Story of the All Anglophone Conference: Anglophones, Fed Up with their Marginalisation and Second-class Status, Meet in Buea and Map Strategies for Survival', *Cameroon Life,* 2 (8): 8-31.

Welch, C.E. 1966, *Dreams of Unity: Pan-Africanism and Political Unification in West Africa,* Ithaca, NY: Cornell University Press.

Wigram, S. 1994, 'Elites, Vanguards and Vandals: The Political Role of Students in Senegal and Mali, 1968-1993', London School of Oriental and African Studies, MSc thesis.

8

Past the Kalashnikov: Youth, politics and the state in Eritrea

Sara Rich Dorman

Since 1991, Eritrea has faced certain specific challenges in the process of nation-building: how to transform a war-stricken economy and how to relate the former liberation movement to the citizens of the new state. This chapter examines the ways in which the youth of the independent state have become central to conceptions of Eritrean statehood and nationalism. The chapter proposes that since independence the relationship between youth and the state has been typified by mobilization and limited pluralism. The liberation war that brought independence also incurred obligations to the older generations of fighters, which the youth have to 'pay back'. Education and employment opportunities are administered and allocated in a top-down fashion. In return, youth are expected to follow the paths set out for them, contribute to development and serve in the military. Especially since 2001 however, Eritrean youth have questioned and rejected these expectations and obligations – challenging the conditions under which students provide voluntary work, and fleeing national service. In doing so, the youth fundamentally challenge the nature of the post-liberation state, its definitions of citizenship, and the post-1991 regime itself.

The spirit of youth is just incredible ... almost every *tegadelai* [fighter] accepts martyrdom as an inevitable outcome of his or her love and loyalty to country and cause. But, our youth go far beyond that ... especially now that they are about to go to the place of their dreams, the frontline ....

> ... kids in their late teens and early twenties have turned courage into a norm. Death is being defied as it is just a hurdle to jump over, as if it is not the end of a person's journey ... they have this unflinching conviction that they will live on in their

surviving comrades, in the realization of the dream they are dying for. (Alemseged
Tesfai 2002: 46-47, 50)

Introduction

The war diary of veteran EPLF member and author Alemseged Tesfai captures
the ethos of both the Eritrean liberation war and of the young fighters he was
observing in 1985. Six years later, the Eritrean People's Liberation Front
(EPLF) fought the last battle of the independence struggle and marched into
Asmara, the capital of Eritrea. Given the iconic nature of the thirty-year struggle
to liberate Eritrea, the post-liberation state has been marked by the ethos of
youthful sacrifice, captured above. 'Martyrdom' was an inevitable outcome of
liberation (Tesfai 2002: 46): no one died; they simply became a martyr
(Bereketeab 2000: 232). Eritrea's current generation of youth bears much of the
weight of this inheritance, but under very different circumstances than previous
generations.

Like other post-liberation states, such as Zimbabwe, South Africa, Namibia,
Mozambique and Uganda, Eritrea has faced the challenges of how to transform
a war-stricken economy, and how the former liberation movement should relate
to the citizens of the new state. While Eritrea's solutions have been similar to
those of other newly independent African states, they have also had distinctive
features. The goal of this chapter is to consider the particular dynamics of
Eritrean politics through an examination of the relationship between youth and
the state, which is not merely typical of state-society relations but constitutive
of Eritrean identity and nationalism. Since the summer of 2001, Eritrean youth
have been at the centre of interlinked political crises. The rejection of the notion
– by some youth – of societal and state expectations that they will 'serve the
nation' challenges the post-liberation political culture and institutions.

Youth and the state 1991-2001

The politics of Eritrea's youth has so far been described mainly in unpublished
material by students and recent graduates of the University of Asmara (for
example, Ahmed 2000, Gebregiorgis *et al.* 2001). In a recent paper, I
investigated how post-liberation shifts have obligated the National Union of
Eritrean Youths and Students (NUEYS), previously a party-affiliated mass
movement, to function like an NGO (Dorman 2002). Little other sector-specific
research has been carried out, with the exceptions of gender (Bernal 2000,

forthcoming), literature (Negash 1999), language (Hailemariam 2002, Wolde-mikael 2003), and education (Gottesman 1998, Bjorndal 2003).

In 1994, the victorious EPLF transformed itself into the avowedly civilian People's Front for Democracy and Justice (PFDJ). Since then, academic research on the topic of state-society relations in Eritrea has emphasized debates about development policy, political parties and the constitution, and tended, at least until 1998, to be 'cautiously optimistic' (Iyob 1997). Fouad Makki's 'reasoned optimism' (1996: 496) led him to predict that the 'juridical and political framework' designed under the new constitution would subject the PFDJ to 'a healthy contestation for hegemony' which would create 'national political pluralism' (ibid: 1996: 490). In a short but detailed consideration of the post-independence regime, Dan Connell (2000) argued in some detail that it is not anti-pluralist, but rather open to societal participation. Sadly, this optimism, based on the emergent independent press and the enthusiasm of social movements, seems to have been misplaced. As is discussed in more detail below, since the 1998-2000 war between Eritrea and Ethiopia, democratization has gone seriously off-track.

Nevertheless, some preliminary comments can be made on the state and nation-building process, and how it has affected the formation and development of social organizations. Ruth Iyob described the post-independence politics as representing a 'politics of inclusion' because of the regime's willingness to re-incorporate old rivals into government (Iyob 1997: 665). We can extend this idea of 'inclusion' to reflect also the politicians' approach to 'non-political' associations, which are expected to work cooperatively with the state, as they did with the nationalist movement (Dorman 2003).

As Fouad Makki (1996: 477) noted, in Eritrea the 'political and cultural project' of nationalism 'found practical embodiment primarily within the liberation movements. … In the absence of a civil society that could monitor and steer their dynamics, the liberation movements developed an autonomous and somewhat substitutionist political culture.' The implications of this are obvious: 'the hierarchical organizational frames encouraged a compliant culture in which the ideal of a self-empowering citizenry was somewhat restricted' (ibid). In practice, this has meant that 'after liberation many people, long accustomed to strict controls under Ethiopian occupation or to the highly centralized war-time structures of the EPLF, appeared hesitant to start new organizations outside the control of the liberation movement' (Connell 1997: 152). While Eritrea is best known for its restrictions on international NGOs, the restraints on local NGOs are at least as constricting. There are presently only fourteen local NGOs operating in Eritrea, three of which are the former EPLF mass organizations (interview with Habte Abraham, Eritrean Relief and

Rehabilitation Commission, 3 September 2002). Eleven years after *de-facto* independence, Eritrea is arguably Africa's least plural society.[1]

Limited pluralism and youth organization

One legacy of the liberation war for state-society relations has been the close relationship between the former mass organizations and the new state. Young people and students were at the heart of early uprisings in Asmara against the Ethiopian regime. Members of the Eritrean Liberation Front (ELF) and EPLF, including Isaias Afewerki, emerged out of the students' movements in Asmara, Addis Ababa and Cairo (Ammar 1997). As the struggle went on, youth associations formed in Egypt, Sudan and further afield to recruit supporters and raise funds for the struggle. In 1978 the youth movement became a formal part of the EPLF, along with associations of women and workers.

Most liberation movements attempted to subsume societal bases under them. The EPLF seems to have succeeded to an unusual degree, perhaps because of the particularly unpromising conditions of their struggle. This contrasts with the situation in Zimbabwe and South Africa, where the multiplicity of liberation forces meant that internal and diaspora groups supported 'liberation' rather than being formally part of particular parties. In Namibia, the youth movement affiliated with SWAPO only very late in the process, just before independence, and disaffiliated shortly thereafter (Maseko 1995: 115-16, 126-27).

In Eritrea, not only did the mass organizations come under the jurisdiction of the liberation movement during the struggle, but they also resisted disengagement after independence was achieved. In 1992, the EPLF declared that the mass organizations had to become independent. This declaration was unexpected and proved difficult to implement for NUEYS. As one long-time member said, 'We are [were] proud to be members of EPLF, but after the independence the government declared that the organization would be non-governmental, so for me this was strange' (interview with Luul Fessehaye, NUEYS Executive Committee Member, 8 August 2002). At their 1994 congress, NUEYS members voiced their bewilderment. As the press reported,

> As far as the Union's links with the PFDJ were concerned, there was some debate as to the extent of close political ties. Union chairman, Muheiddin Shengeb, said that free association is not a matter of choice. In 1992 the government decreed that mass organizations have to be independent... (*Eritrea Profile*, 3 September 1994)

---

[1] While Eritrea's 'front-led government' can be usefully compared to the NRM in Uganda, it lacks the latter's mitigating decentralization, pluralism and independent press. On the importance of decentralization in Uganda, see Doornbos (2000: 99-121).

Although the official line is clear: 'It certainly is an independent union ... If we have close relations with PFDJ it is because we have unity of aim' (*Eritrea Profile*, 24 January 1998), NUEYS staff and senior leadership recognize and admit the ambiguity of their relationship with the party. As the chairman said, shaking his head in amusement:

> We always talk to them and still they are not clear ... we share history and culture and there should be values in common ... we are not yet clear ... this is the question that always remains without a full answer. (Interview with Moheiden Shengeb, NUEYS chairman, 19 August 2002)

Despite this candour, his reference to 'them' is somewhat misleading, as he himself is a member of the PFDJ's executive committee.

Whatever the actual status and relationship between NUEYS and the ruling party, it is important to note that NUEYS is one of the most significant NGOs in Eritrea. Dan Connell, who has written extensively about the EPLF and the mass organizations, described NUEYS as 'the fastest growing, the feistiest, and the most campaign oriented of the sectoral associations' (Connell 1997: 151). NUEYS is also the only group apparently working with young people in Eritrea – all school-based groups, including Scouts, are subsumed into their structures.

Pluralism in Eritrea, fairly limited since independence, became more constricted after the 1998-2000 war with Ethiopia. In 2001, Eritrea was convulsed by a political debate in which high-profile members of the ruling PFDJ called for internal party reform, the implementation of the 1997 constitution and the holding of national elections (Sherifo 2001). Discussion percolated briefly in government and independent newspapers (including those of the youth movement) until September 2001, when the leading critics and journalists were detained and newspapers were closed down (Plaut 2002). Two and a half years later, no charges have been laid against those detained, no national elections have been held and the constitution remains unimplemented.

Mobilization and the role of youth
A second legacy of the liberation war has been an emphasis on social mobilization. Drawing on the traditions of the fighters, many of whom continued to work as volunteers after independence in 1991, national service for all was introduced in 1994 (*Eritrea Profile*, 4 June 1994) and written into the 1997 constitution (Constitution of Eritrea 1997: article 25.3). It was designed to create a trained reserve army, connect young people to the older liberation-war generation, and to develop cross-cultural understanding by integrating the different ethnic groups and religions (Bereketeab 2004). Although Eritreans see these concerns as particularly important for Eritrea's ethnically, religiously and

linguistically plural society, similar concerns were voiced by other newly independent African states when launching their prototypical national service schemes in the 1960s (Callaway 1963).

The programme involved all 'youth' between the ages of 18 and 40 training at the Sawa Military Camp for six months (military service), followed by twelve months working in various ministries (national service) on a nominal wage. Young people on national service were being paid Nakfa 145 (US$ 10), which was recently increased to Nakfa 500 (US$ 30) per month. Although Bereketeab (2004) has noted that this small amount of money may have a profound transformative effect in rural areas, it is not a salary that one can live on in urban areas, especially if one has a family, or needs to pay rent. National Service employees at the university referred to it derisorily as 'pocket money'. Rural families are, of course, also affected by the loss of manpower, especially for ploughing and at harvest time.

In 1998, a National Development Campaign was briefly implemented, which called upon all of those who had participated in National Service since 1994 to remobilize for one month and carry out development projects. The programme, designed to mobilize 50,000-60,000 Eritreans, was scheduled to start at the end of April and to continue through May *(Eritrea Profile*, 21 March 1998, 14 March 1998). When the border war started in mid-May, the development projects were abandoned but the already mobilized youth were transferred to the front, along with remobilized veterans *(Eritrea Profile*, 13 June 1998, 10 October 1998). Since then national service has become a permanent condition for the nation's 'youth'. With those who have turned 40 since 1998 not yet excused, multiple generations of families are serving together. The *warsai-yikealo*[2] initiative, launched in 2002, is thought to extend national service commitments for at least another two years, as conscripts are mobilized to rebuild Eritrea's shattered economy *(Eritrea Profile*, 11 May 2002; *Hadas Ertra*, 16 July 2002).

Although these campaigns are thought of as 'voluntary' and encouraging 'self-sacrifice', in practice they are tightly controlled. In an interview, President Isaias emphasized:

> Everybody recruited for national service has to go. As for those who create lame excuses for not going, let them know that there is no way one can evade it. (*Eritrea Profile*, 7 March 1998)

---

[2] *Warsai-yikealo* is usually translated as 'old and new fighters'. It is intended to symbolize the continuity between the older generation of fighters from the liberation war and those who fought from 1998 onwards.

The 'Kalashnikov Boom' at the National Union of Youths' and Students'
Exhibition, December 2002.
Photo: W. Dorman

The irony is that in 1994, during a public meeting called in response to fears
that the N[ational] S[ervice] P[rogramme] would not end in 18 months,
President Isaias said:

> We are going to replace the demobilized army. There is no *derg* here (during the
> *derg* conscripts were forced to serve for an indefinite period) the NSP lasts for 18
> months and not a day longer. The Ministry of Defence has a separate programme for
> recruiting a standing army. (*Eritrea Profile*, 4 June 1994)

Youth, the military, service and sacrifice are symbolically linked in Eritrea's
political culture. Alemseged Tesfai's memoirs, quoted at the start of this
chapter, give a sense of how youth was portrayed in the liberation struggle.
These images are also imprinted on the urban fabric in murals, shop-front
displays and public monuments. Since the 1998-2000 war, similar images have
appeared depicting the new young generation of fighters. In 2002, an exhibition
of artwork and inventions by Eritrean youth was opened by President Afewerki
ceremonially raising a boom modelled to resemble a giant Kalashnikov. Like
the youth, who must shoulder the Kalashnikov to become part of the nation,

participants passed under the symbolic reminder of a state created through and by military force.

Two political crises[3]

In the summer of 2001, Eritrea moved slowly into a political crisis which coalesced around the notion of 'service', linked to, but also distinct from, the internal PFDJ crisis that emerged when fifteen leading EPLF/PFDJ members and old comrades of President Isaias Afewerqi registered their protest against his policies and style of rule. This group, later known as the G-15, was ignored, sidelined and arrested in September 2001 (except for three who were outside the country).

Crisis 1: Summer work programmes
In 1994, when military service was introduced for high-school graduates, a student work programme for secondary-school students was also initiated under the auspices of the Ministry of Education (*Eritrea Profile*, 25 June 1994, 28 July 1997). These have become a staple part of student life – each year the media reports how many seedlings have been planted, how many metres of terraces constructed, how many irrigation canals dug over the summer break. From 1999 to 2001, university students were also expected to spend their summer vacations in work programmes.

In July 2001 the president of the University of Asmara student union, Semere Kesete, used the well-publicized occasion of graduation to criticize the expectation that university students would spend their summers on the work programme, and the conditions of those programmes. The university, for its part, suggested that the summer programmes were expected because the university had waived national service for students and that they were willing to

---

[3]   Conducting research in Eritrea is subject to numerous constraints. I was able to interview many NUEYS members and staff as part of another research project in the summer of 2002. In discussing the issues of national service and the events of August 2001 with students, colleagues and acquaintances, I avoided formal interviews and have maintained the confidentiality of all my contacts. *Eritrea Profile* and *Hadas Ertra* are publications of the Ministry of Information, and much of their content can be taken to be formal statements of government policy. In the interests of transparency, I have attempted to provide sources for other allegations and statements, many of which circulated widely within and outside Eritrea, even where those sources may be biased or politically-influenced.

negotiate over the conditions and type of work *(Eritrea Profile*, 25 August 2001).

Soon after this speech, Semere was detained and imprisoned in solitary confinement. Student protesters outside the court were arrested and detained in the National Stadium. Parents who demonstrated against the detention of their children were dispersed (*Chronicle*, 21 August 2001). The students – including those who had been arrested – were sent to a forced work camp in the area bordering the Red Sea, near the Danakil depression which is barely habitable in the summer months. Two students died of heatstroke, and the rest were only allowed to return to studies in Asmara after the intervention of the university president (*Awate.com*, 1 August 2001, 20 August 2001).

Semere Kesete remained in solitary confinement, with no access to his family or lawyers until almost exactly a year after his detention, when he and one of his guards – a young ex-fighter – apparently escaped and fled to Ethiopia (*BBC*, 9 August 2002).

Throughout these events, the association of youths and students was either silent, or intervened on the side of the government. This has been interpreted as a political move. One former student leader said, 'they are merely interested in signalling to the executive that they are prepared to succeed them'. Yet, from a less cynical perspective, we can see this situation as capturing the central dilemma of NUEYS. Existing firmly within Eritrea's nationalist culture which reifies 'sacrifice', NUEYS appeals to youth to provide volunteer service is one of its defining characteristics: 'Eritrean youth is the bearer of responsibility' (NUEYS 2000: 10), As a university student said to me:

> As members of NUEYS we believe we should do things for free. Members of the student union at the university claimed that if you do service, you should be paid.

NUEYS leadership actually claims that the 'volunteer' initiatives, which so dominate current Eritrean life, were originated by them. As the chairman reported in an interview on ERI-TV, and was later transcribed in the press:

> ... programs which involve the youth such as the National Service Program, the Summer Work Program, and the National Development Campaign are basically initiated by NUEYS. The National Service Program was proclaimed by the union in its 1981 congress. The Summer Work Program was initiated in the 1980s. Eritrean youths used to serve the revolution during their spare time in summer. The youth have participated in collecting cotton ... and constructing building complexes ... before the National Service Program was launched in 1992-93. (*Eritrea Profile*, 10 October 1998)

NUEYS has chosen to portray the students' resistance to engaging in the summer work programme as the machinations of 'an enemy' rather than as an independently derived rejection of national policy.

NUEYS has seen the university student union as a rival for some time because the university had refused to allow NUEYS to organize a branch or open an office on campus. NUEYS thinks that it was discouraged from organizing university youth because it is too strong, suggesting that the university wanted a more easily influenced group of students, in an autonomous union, which would not have outside sources of strength.[4] Nevertheless, NUEYS sees it as a direct challenge to their representation of youths:

> They see NUEYS as structured from outside. Allowing us to have a branch within the university would have interfered ... they said you can work in the university but you cannot have a branch. Maybe they think, if you have a branch, the university administration might feel not at ease. I think that the main reason it is about power. We are seen as too powerful, in contrast with university... (interview with Moheiden Shengeb, NUEYS chairman, 19 August 2002)

In contrast, university administrators, although extremely reluctant to discuss the case, suggest that it is because NUEYS is 'too political': 'Maybe we don't want to have these political associations on campus.' Or as another former administrator said, emphasizing that this was a personal, and not an official, opinion:

> If there is only one party, how can we let this group influence the students? Under the *Derg*, there was a similar union that was always interfering in our activities, so when this group comes, we think, we don't want them interfering in our activities.

In its 2001 annual report, NUEYS vented its frustrations over being blocked from the campus:

> NUEYS was kept at a distance, only to watch, instead of working with the university to cultivate the youth and to solve their problems. In contrast, the campus was a convenient forum for religious and other political activists to spread their out-dated ideas. (NUEYS 2002)

The University of Asmara students are represented as being manipulated by the G-15:

---

[4] Ironically, one university staff member suggested to me that the students' union had in fact been created as a balance to faculty demands for a staff union.

... all this was a political movement by a few students with a hidden political mission, trying to exploit the economic problems of the student masses ... as it carefully watched this destructive and anti-national interest movement, the Union condemned it. (NUEYS 2002)

In contrast, opposition websites report that NUEYS's own antagonism to the G-15 has more to do with business deals than ideology. According to *Awate.com*:

NUEYS officials considered the G-15 as obstacles to their career goals and at least two, Brigadier General Estifanos Seyoum the former chief of the Inland Revenue Service; and Petros Solomon, former Minister of Fisheries, had objected to NUEYS refusal to pay taxes and port fees. *(Awate.com*, 23 January 2002)

NUEYS was widely seen as more dogmatic and set against the reformers than many other groups in society. It was noted by many that when even state-owned newspapers avoided taking sides in what was seen as an intra-party struggle, NUEYS came out publicly against the G-15. Or, as they say themselves:

Our newspapers worked hard in challenging the false allegations that used to be issued in the private media discourses and in preserving national unity. (NUEYS 2002)

Since 2001, NUEYS has opened a university branch, with an office near the campus, but not on it. The branch hopes to provide access to computers and subsidized photocopiers, in addition to social and sporting activities. It has proved very popular, with 800 members joining.

Crisis 2: Draft-dodging
In the years since the ceasefire agreement with Ethiopia, there has been resistance to military-service recruitment, with young people fleeing the country illegally, hiding from soldiers, and resisting capture. Cities are surrounded by army roadblocks where the identification papers of all passengers are checked. Those who have not 'served' cannot get exit-visas. During the annual *gffa* (in Tigrinya) or 'round-up' of draft-dodgers there are young military police on street corners, walking up and down every street, checking the documents of passers-by. The streets often appear unusually quiet, with few young people visible. In 2002, the *gffa* was particularly severe, with unconfirmed reports of several deaths from exchanges between parents and soldiers (*Awate.com*, 9 July 2002, 17 July 2002).

Resistance to national service centres on reports of sexual abuse of female conscripts by senior army officers who act with impunity. Although these allegations appear to be widely believed, little evidence and few first-hand accounts have emerged. Two foreign journalists have reported interviewing women who claim to be rape victims from Sawa (*Sette, Corriere della Sera*, 26 September 2002, *The Age*, 5 December 2002), but their information has not been verified by other sources. Young women are reported to seek consensual sexual relationships with their peers, in the hope that they will become pregnant, get married, and avoid potential rape. This may also be their best chance of marriage, as young men say that they will not consider marrying women who have attended Sawa Military Camp because of the 'damage' done to them there.

University graduates resent being paid only Nakfa 500, and having little choice in their post-graduate employment or training. In 2003, the previous year's university graduates were sent to Sawa to teach in the new *Warsai-Yikealo* high school offering final-year courses for all students, prior to attending university or entering the National Service programme (UN IRIN news service, 13 November 2002). Graduates sent abroad to study complain that they were given little information concerning their destination and no choice about their degree programme (Mekonnen *et al.* 2004).

In August and September 2002, there were also frequent reports of Eritreans deserting to neighbouring countries. For example, it was reported in August that 122 Eritreans had fled to Ethiopia. In a typical report, compiled from the Ethiopian press (which is virulently critical of the Eritrean regime), it was claimed that fourteen students and three soldiers had arrived in Meqelle, the capital of Tigray Province (*AGP*, 29 August 2002). Or, that on 2 October, 39 members of the navy had fled to Yemen (*Walta*, 2 October 2002). While these reports must be read with caution – emanating as they do from hostile sources – interviews on Ethiopian radio and television (received on satellite in Eritrea) with these escapees do add veracity. Even more intriguing was a report from UNHCR that a refugee camp in Ethiopia, set up to accommodate ethnic Kunama refugees from the border war, was sheltering 960 non-Kunama refugees who all arrived in 2002 – over 200 in October and November 2002 alone. These new refugees were described by camp officials as 'mostly young men' – draft-dodgers and army deserters (IRIN, 22 November 2002).

Conclusion

Despite this recent, and limited, resistance, Eritrea's ability to allocate workers, to generate compliance with regulations and to restrict exit visas must place it among the strongest states in Africa. While the state's strength has historically been derived from the remarkable legitimacy of the liberation movement, the brief moment of opening in 2001 revealed dissension in the ranks. President Isaias's ability to re-assert control, thereby stifling prominent opponents, revealed a willingness to use the state's coercive apparatus against those who reject the consensus.

These two factors – limited pluralism and a strong state – distinguish Eritrea from other African states. If we conceptualize interaction of state and society in Africa as a continuum, Eritrea appears to be at the extreme end of both societal mobilization and state-led organization. Even in contrast to other countries that have fought liberation wars, Eritrea stands out. Most African post-independence states have been characterized by 'demobilization', not only of ex-soldiers but also of societal groups. Proposals to 'remobilize' the youth have also been problematic, and often of limited effectiveness. In Zimbabwe, oft-voiced intentions of creating national service did not become reality until 2001. In Namibia, when students were recruited for a National Youth Service Scheme in 2002, they mutinied in reaction to the poor conditions and marched into Windhoek, demanding to see the president (*The Namibian*, 19 August 2002).

In Eritrea, the expectation that the youth will defend the nation, and also serve the nation in peacetime, has been much more widespread. The culture of martyrdom (Tesfai 2002: 49) has proved pervasive and influential in the years since independence, reinforced by annual events, ceremonies and remembrance. The 1998-2000 war with Ethiopia, rather than denting the enthusiasm of youth, seemed to enhance it. But the delayed demobilization of the military and the extension of national service through the *warsai-yikealo* programme have enabled youth to exercise both an exit option and their voice in criticizing the top-down determination of service.

The linking of citizenship and 'service' is particularly distinctive in Eritrea. The refusal of Jehovah's Witnesses to participate in national service led the state to revoke their citizenship rights (Government of Eritrea 1994). Similarly, in August 2001, the University of Asmara declared that '… no citizen is above the law and that students cannot change the law of the land by any sort of intimidation' (*Eritrea Profile*, 25 August 2001). Eritrean youth are told that they *owe* their service because of the debts they have incurred to older generations of fighters. Their obligations are not costed in terms of education or healthcare expenses but in terms of a contract they have entered into upon birth as Eritrean citizens. The Eritrean diaspora is also drawn into this 'national project'.

Ruth Iyob's analysis of Eritrea as a diasporic state is pertinent here:

> The identity of diaspora populations is forged in struggles for political, economic and social survival… At times, it risks whatever democratic credentials it had built up as a champion of a victimised people as it eliminates opponents to its survival. At other times it attempts to unilaterally redefine the normative and conventional rules embedded in the international system. (Iyob 2000: 661)

Iyob is concerned with how the diasporic state impacts on foreign policy. But its impact on domestic policy is at least as significant. Alemseged Tesfai captures this dynamic in a recent reflection, describing how during the liberation an attitude may have developed among combatants that 'he or she knew best for the country and the people'. And as he further noted, after a protracted liberation struggle, 'a population that is thankful to its liberator is often ready to submit to his or her direction. The problem always arises when the people begin to assert their views' (Tesfai 2003: 252). In 2003, President Isaias called on Eritreans to pay tribute to the martyrs through a 'relentless commitment to the development of Eritrea' (*Eritrea Profile*, 21 June 2003). But the youth are increasingly seeking to exercise voice and choice for themselves. The Australia-based Eritrean Youth Action Network said, 'The youth are not just war machines ... they are demanding education and development, not war and slavery' (*Awate.com*, 8 January 2003). The issues contested are the policies of limited pluralism and social mobilization which dominate Eritrea's political landscape. Youth are not unwilling to pass through military and national service, to participate in the commemoration of martyrs and celebrate independence, but they are increasingly unwilling to be simply foot-soldiers in the development of the nation.

References

Ahmed, M.M.O. 2000, 'NUEYS and its Role in Eritrean Politics', Senior research paper, Dept. of Political Science, University of Asmara.

Ammar, W-Y. 1997, 'The Role of Asmara Students in the Eritrean Nationalist Movement', *Eritrean Studies Review*, 2: 159-84.

Bereketeab, R. 2000, *Eritrea: The Making of a Nation 1890-1991*, Uppsala: Uppsala University.

Bereketeab, R. 2004, 'Dynamics of National Service in Eritrea', *News from the Nordic Africa Institute*, 2004/1: 9-11.

Bernal, V. 2000, 'Equality to Die For? Women Guerrilla Fighters and Eritrea's Cultural Revolution', *Political and Legal Anthropology Review*, 23 (2): 61-76.

Bernal, V. forthcoming, 'From Warriors to Wives: Contradictions of Liberation and Development in Eritrea', *Northeast African Studies*.

Bjorndal, I.K.M. 2003, *"We Never Felt Like Soldiers!" Education in Eritrea: From EPLF and Education to a National Culture of Education – A Hermeneutic Conversation*, Oslo: University College.

Callaway, A.C. 1963, 'Inter-governmental Symposium on Unemployed Youth', *Journal of Modern African Studies*, 1 (1): 108-109.

Connell, D. 1997, 'New Challenges in Post-War Eritrea', *Eritrean Studies Review*, 1 (2): 129-59.

Connell, D. 2000, 'The Importance of Self-reliance: NGOs and Democracy-Building in Eritrea', *Middle East Report*, 214 (Spring): 28-32.

Constitution of Eritrea 1997.

Doornbos, M. 2000, 'African Multipartyism and the Quest for Democratic Alternatives', in J. Abbink & G. Hesseling (eds), *Election Observation and Democratization in Africa*, London: Macmillan, pp. 99-121.

Dorman, S.R. 2002, 'National Union of Eritrean Youth and Students: Constraints and Opportunities for Organizational Development', NUEYS conference on 'Eritrean Youths: Post-War Challenges and Expectations', Asmara, Eritrea.

Dorman, S.R. 2003, 'From the Politics of Inclusion to the Politics of Exclusion: NGOs and the Constitutional Debate in Zimbabwe', *Journal of Southern African Studies* 29(4): 845-63.

Gebregiorgis, I., S. Tesfayohannes & D. Gebretensae 2001, 'Emerging Civil Society in an Emerging State: The Case of the National Union of Eritrean Youth and Students', Eritrean Studies Association, First International Conference, Asmara, Eritrea.

Gottesman, L. 1998, *To Fight and Learn: The Praxis and Promise of Literacy in Eritrea's Independence War*, Lawrenceville, NJ: Red Sea Press.

Government of Eritrea 1994, *A Presidential Directive on Jehovah's Witnesses*, Asmara.

Hailemariam, C. 2002, *Language and Education in Eritrea: A Case Study of Language Diversity, Policy and Practice*, Amsterdam: Aksant Academic Publishers.

Iyob, R. 1997, 'The Eritrean Experiment: A Cautious Pragmatism?', *Journal of Modern African Studies*, 35 (4): 647-73.

Iyob, R. 2000, 'The Ethiopian-Eritrean Conflict: Diasporic vs. Hegemonic States in the Horn of Africa, 1991-2000', *Journal of Modern African Studies*, 38 (4): 659-82.

Makki, F. 1996, 'Nationalism, State Formation and the Public Sphere: Eritrea 1991-96', *Review of African Political Economy*, 70: 465-97.

Maseko, S.S. 1995, 'The Namibian Student Movement: Its Role and Effects', in C. Leys, J.S. Saul & S. Brown (eds), *Namibia's Liberation Struggle: The Two-Edged Sword*, Oxford: James Currey.

Mekonnen, D.R. & S.B. Abraha 2004, 'The Plight of Eritrean Students in South Africa', http://ajn.rti.org/index.cfm?fuseaction=listing&l=fr.

Negash, G. 1999, A History of Tigrinya Literature in Eritrea: The Oral and the Written 1890-1991, University of Leiden, PhD thesis.

NUEYS 2000, *Major Undertakings of NUEYS, 1992-2000*, Asmara.

NUEYS 2002, *NUEYS Activities of 2001*. Asmara.

Plaut, M. 2002, 'The Birth of the Eritrean Reform Movement', *Review of African Political Economy*, 91: 119-24.

Sherifo, Mahmoud Ahmed, Haile Woldensae, Mesfin Hagos, Ogbe Abrha, Hamid Hmd, Saleh Kekya, Estifanos Seyoum, Berhane Ghebreeghzabiher, Astier Fehatsion, Mohammed Berhan Blata, Petros Solomon, Germano Nati, Beraki Gebreslassie, Adhanom Ghebremariam, Haile Menkarios 2001, 'Open Letter to EPLF Members', http://news.asmarino.com/PFDJ_Membership/Introduction.asp.

Tesfai, A. 2002, *Two Weeks in the Trenches: Reminiscences of Childhood and War in Eritrea*, Lawrenceville, NJ: Red Sea Press.

Tesfai, A. 2003, 'Land and Liberation in Eritrea: Reflecting on the Work of Lionel Cliffe', *Review of African Political Economy*, 96: 249-54.

Woldemikael, T. 2003, 'Language, Education and Public Policy in Eritrea', *African Studies Review*, 46 (1): 117-36.

PART III:
Interventions: Dealing with youth in crisis

9

From generational conflict to renewed dialogue: Winning the trust of street children in Lomé, Togo[1]

Yves Marguerat

The problem of street children is basically one of conflict between the generations. Irresponsible adults and crisis within the nuclear family result in some children running away or them being be thrown out of their homes to fend for themselves on the streets of urban centres. Lomé is a particularly significant example as it is a city dominated by a traditional trading middle-class. During the 1970s and 1980s, in a then still wealthy country, most of the street children came from well-established and prestigious urban families. The children's fundamental problem was a lack of emotional support. This, in fact, provides the key to the solution – establishing, with an adult, friendly contact that is based on mutual respect and freedom. Youngsters can then resume a normal school life or train for jobs since their strongest wish is to be like other children again. This chapter recounts the author's experiences with such children in Lomé.

Introduction

Scientific studies on the reasons for the existence of street children – those youngsters left to fend for themselves in the public spaces in central urban areas – all confirm that this phenomenon is not due to poverty, as the local authorities and the media usually maintain. Nor is it due to the unruliness or the depravity

---

[1] Translated from French by Ann Reeves and Judith Herbertson.

of the child,[2] as the families involved often claim. It is always the direct consequence of conflict between the child's generation and that of the adults who ought to be taking care of him, as parents or guardians depending on the local traditions, and who do not properly live up to that responsibility.[3] It is the duty of parents to meet the child's material needs – to ensure the child has enough to eat and can develop properly. Even more importantly, the parents have an emotional duty of care, to provide the parental love, both before and after birth, which alone can ensure that the child feels psychologically secure. These basic truths of human existence are unconnected with socio-economic status. Frequently families living in a precarious state of poverty prove to be both supportive and affectionate[4] and equally often better-off families fail to assume their responsibilities – as will be seen in the examples cited in this chapter.

The break-up between the child and family is sometimes involuntary, for example in the case of the *talibé*, West African boys sent to Koranic schools to raise their social status. They are entrusted to a *marabout*, a religious scholar, who in fact often turns out to be interested only in exploiting their ability to beg. Another example would be young people from rural areas who imagine that they will find a better future in town but have no means to access this. Children whose parents have died or have become disabled are clearly in the first instance victims of bad fortune, but all societies have a duty to support them and help them to fulfil their potential.[5] The biggest problem for these children is that whether the family has broken up due to the death or the departure of one of the parents, the family unit usually reconstitutes, and in the process the relationship between the child and the new stepfather or stepmother becomes strained. A suffocating family atmosphere is the most common reason for a child to run away or to be thrown out of the home. Street children are often the product of crisis in the family unit and for this reason they are often emotionally distressed and in conflict with the adult generation.

---

[2] A child is defined as a young person between the ages of 5 and 15 approximately.

[3] See also Marguerat (2000).

[4] See, for example, Peltre-Wurtz (1998). But of course the economic collapse of a society (older and more pressurized in Latin America than in Sub-Saharan Africa and where a more serious situation for street children exists) is a factor in the breakdown of families.

[5] A completely new problem is, of course, the AIDS epidemic that is killing parents in vast numbers and leaving behind children and older relatives who are having to provide for the orphans. A new phenomenon is the appearance of families entirely made up of children, with the 'head of the family' being often only 13-15 years of age, sometimes even younger. I know of no good descriptions of the functioning and evolution of households deprived of adults.

This lack of good personal relationships broadly shapes their behaviour on the street, after the initial need to survive has been met through adaptability, bravery, energy and intelligence. Gangs and drugs are two ways of responding to the despair caused by loneliness; prostitution can be another. Although not always an enemy or a threat, adults are seen essentially as a potential source of benefit, someone in the first instance to be exploited through their own pity or by a smile, through cunning or by force. Through mutual fear and give-and-take with adults, street children try to survive on a day-to-day basis by any means possible, even if this seems to be suicidal in the short or long term, and moreover, not without danger for society as a whole. It is possible to foresee the endpoint of the natural development of this phenomenon: when marginalized children get together in gangs and as the increasing numbers of girls begin to have children of their own, the urban centres start to see the formation of a youthful anti-society at war with the adult world (cf. Marguerat 2002).

To avoid this happening, action is needed to allow children marginalized by adults to reintegrate into society. The cause of the problem can also provide a long-term solution: the re-establishing of a new and trusting relationship between the isolated child and another adult who can act as a substitute for the sorely missed parent. This adult, not for a moment posing as a Pygmalion character moulding them to his wishes, must quite simply offer them the means to become children again, like others, by giving them back what they have lost: trust in the present and the sense of having a future. It is not only possible but is, in fact, quite straightforward.

It is not common practice in scientific studies to use personal experience as a source of evidence. However, my experience over the last 25 years with street children in the capital of Togo seems to me to be relevant to the questions and answers raised by the existence of these marginalized children both in Africa and elsewhere.

Discovering the lost children of Lomé

The phenomenon of large numbers of children living alone on city streets in nearly every country in Africa emerged in the mid-1980s. The first meeting between representatives from social services and NGOs dedicated to marginalized children, at the Grand-Bassam Forum in Côte d'Ivoire[6] in 1985, saw the decision to break with the old stigmatizing terminology such as 'young delinquents' or 'pre-delinquents' and to retain only the more neutral and direct

---

[6] See also Marguerat & Poitou (1994).

name of 'street children' to designate those young people who escape the responsibility of any particular adult and live day and night in public urban spaces, either on main thoroughfares such as streets, crossroads and squares, or in 'non-places', those undeveloped areas used by them only as places of shelter to sleep or curl up out of the public eye, such as beside canals, under bridges, in ravines or on beaches. The problems facing these street children (in the strict sense of the word) are very different from those of children who work in public places but who remain more or less in contact with their families, and who are exploited in secret either by their families or by workshops. They pose specific questions, as much for the scientific analysis of the problem they present as for the solutions to their difficulties.

It might seem that the easiest way to meet and establish a dialogue with these children would be to go and find them directly on the streets. But this approach tends to incite considerable mistrust on their part, particularly when the approach basically only corresponds to the personal interests of the researcher. The children pick this up very quickly and it does not encourage honesty on their part: a good number of the studies carried out on the streets have, for this reason, only obtained results quite far removed from reality.[7]

My entry into the world of the street children in Lomé was very different; it was the children who first approached me. It was only much later, after I had started to help them, that I began to undertake scientific studies and to use them as a subject for research. This was a source of unexpected and very fertile material that helped me to understand the social mechanisms operating within the city I was studying. It was a unique and largely unplanned journey from which a number of clear conclusions emerged, as many concerning the peculiarities of the case of Lomé as those relating to general conclusions also valid elsewhere in cases of marginalized young people.

The starting point for a story that turned me into someone strongly committed both personally and professionally to the problem of street children is to be found in 1977 in France where I was engaged in two assignments. Various events had led to my being elected to the advisory board of a municipal association for the prevention of juvenile delinquency in the suburbs of Paris. I knew nothing about the subject and I had no other philosophy than that of upholding human rights and an aversion to what could be called social exclusion. Our administrative role was purely technical – to implement new statutes, to formulate a budget and justify it to the prefecture, and to formalize

---

[7] I would advise anyone planning to do such research first to go to the institutions where similar children, who are already reintegrated and have learnt to trust adults again, are living.

teaching projects, without ever seeing any of the youngsters concerned. Through discussions with the educational specialists, I discovered to my astonishment that in order to respond to their problems, it was not enough just to wait for global changes in society: these children with significant family problems wanted first of all a personal commitment from adults, a sincere and friendly relationship with them and not abstract promises for the future. Our main achievement was the opening of a drop-in centre for young 8 to 12 year olds to provide a safe haven, where someone would listen, away from both the home where the family atmosphere was often very tense, and the violence that already blighted the public areas around the tower blocks in poorer neighbourhoods. It was the only way to help these pre-adolescents avoid an apparently inevitable slide into juvenile delinquency. This was just a short experience for me but, as a wake-up call, essential in making me aware of the problems.

On arriving at ORSTOM [8] in Lomé in March 1978 for a research programme on the developments in urban networks in Togo, I met a sociology student who the Ministry for Social Affairs had asked to undertake a study of juvenile delinquency in Lomé. This young colleague was struggling because, in order to adopt modern methods, he was looking above all to gather statistics, which proved to be either non-existent or hopelessly unpredictable, but which he felt would be indispensable in demonstrating what were, in fact, simply assumptions he had imported from Europe. Aware that he needed some first-hand accounts, he was making use of the policemen working with young people as interpreters for youngsters in prison, which was not perhaps the best means of obtaining their trust. His theory – which to be fair was shared by all at the time – was that these street children came from the rural areas, attracted by the bright lights of the city and that on failing to integrate, they stole in order to survive. In fact, with hindsight, the situation in Lomé, a city of well-established bourgeois traders with a high rate of marital break-up, had a number of peculiarities: it is the oldest city families, including the most socially presti-gious, who started to produce street children at war with adults, beginning as far back as 1945.[9] In Lomé, those actually from the rural areas accounted for less than 10 per cent of the population living on the streets. Hence the thesis this young sociologist brilliantly defended at a French university in front of a jury that scarcely had any understanding of African cities in general – and no

---

[8] L'Institut Français de Recherche Scientifique en Coopération pour le Développement (now IRD).

[9] See, in particular, Marguerat & Poitou (1994).

Two of Lomé's current street children: Marc (top) aged 13 who is a gang leader
and 15-year-old Joseph (bottom) who has been living on the streets for the last
five years. (The boys' names have been changed to protect their true identity.)
Photos: Yves Marguerat (2004)

knowledge at all of this particular subject – was completely removed from reality.

But this young colleague's real problem – and he has since sensibly abandoned sociology – was quite simply a fear of the research terrain, a fear of the young people. With my limited experience in Paris, he asked me to accompany him to the juvenile police bureau to see what it was doing. I went there with him several times, getting to know the place and the people who would later play such a large part in my life. I met a French nun who was running the social services part of the bureau with great energy and passion. The youngsters also immediately identified me as someone who was interested in them. Initially pigeonholed as a policeman, I later became known as a missionary.[10]

In the centre of Lomé, the children, who had broken family ties and were mainly between 12 and 15 years old, lived in well-defined areas close to one another; during the day in the car park of the main supermarket and on the pavements of the Rue du Commerce with its big shops, banks and smart boutiques, or around the main market. In the evenings they would hang around outside the cinemas and the nightclubs a short distance away. They used to lie in wait for the whites, who were more compassionate and generous (and much richer too) than the locals. Moreover, if problems arose, there was less to fear from foreigners who were incapable of recognizing the instigator of the misfortune among all the only half-glimpsed black faces. Officially the children's task was to guard the cars, in fact to guard against one sole danger: the one which they themselves posed, since rejection of their services often resulted in a flat tyre or scratched bodywork. Whenever you parked, there were always four or five of them who would run up shouting their name, or their nickname: 'It's Kossi!'....'It's Jojo!' so that you would recognize them when you returned and not give the coin to the wrong child. Unfortunately the bigger ones had the irritating habit of pushing away the younger one who had actually been keeping an eye on the car.[11]

In this way I quickly got to know several by name. As I was not afraid of them, I greeted them pleasantly and had a quick chat before slipping them a little present. (If I had no change on me, it was forgiven with a smile: 'You'll give it to us next time.') They had been so used to the mistrust and hostility of adults that these very modest gestures of kindness encouraged some of them to trust me and to ask me to help them.

---

[10] At the police stations I was often called 'Monsieur le Pasteur'.
[11] There were no close ties of friendship among the street children in Lomé, only temporary groups where relations between the younger and older ones were volatile: without protection, the weaker children were bullied and had no form of redress.

It was the start of the rainy season in June 1978 and one of the children from the Rue du Commerce, F, who was around 14 years old, both funny and mistrustful, full of banter and yet quite introverted, showed me that all his limited belongings were soaked from being left outside. Would I allow him to leave them at my house? I lived alone in a three-roomed house scarcely a kilometre from the town centre. I didn't refuse. A little while later, he asked me in a begging tone that appeared genuine if he could occasionally come to take a shower in my bathroom.[12] I didn't refuse. Others did the same: G, D and O – in total about six of them. They would come at any time, but particularly in the evening after their day's work on the Rue du Commerce. Some time afterwards, they asked me if, when it was late and they were tired and had to walk a long way to their corner of the pavement, they could perhaps from time to time sleep at my house. I didn't refuse and I bought some mats.

My car began to provide a taxi service between my district and the town centre, or on Sundays to the beach. In the Rue du Commerce, one boy, R, stood out. He was the youngest, having just turned ten, and was always to stay small physically. He had the most terrifying character. He was a bundle of aggression and, at the least provocation, was capable of yelling at the top of his voice, with tears welling up in his eyes: 'Why do you give it to him and not to me?', 'Why don't you take me in your car?', 'Why don't you take me home?'. His imperious tone did little to engender compassion, but it was obvious that this vehemence had only one meaning: 'Why don't you love me?'.

Living together

My mother came to visit me for Christmas in 1978. I had to clear everything away and make the boys promise not to show their faces for two weeks. Among those who came to my home from time to time, there was one bigger boy, M, who was in fact no longer a minor and whom I mistrusted because I did not like his aggressive manner with the younger ones. He was not allowed to sleep at my place. But he had stolen a key to the back door[13] and took advantage of our absence on a trip to the countryside to let himself in and go through our things, stealing a sizeable sum of French money from my mother's bedroom.

---

[12] For washing the street children only had the filthy puddles on the beach, the effluence of sewers blocked by the moving sands or the hardly any less polluted water in the lagoon.

[13] In those days I still locked up my house. Later, until the time when I left Togo it was always open, except for my own room.

The next day I came across O and G in the street. There was a brief exchange: 'Hi, Yves. Are you OK?' Me: 'No, I'm not.' 'Why?' 'I was burgled.' 'No! What was taken?' 'Money.' 'Yes? French money?' 'Yes, French money.' 'Don't worry. We'll sort it out!' And they disappeared. Within a few hours they had pieced together the whole situation – on the streets nothing remains secret. It was indeed M who had broken into my house in my absence. He had wanted to exchange the French francs in a shop in town but they had asked him where he had stolen the money. He had fled and found another less curious assistant.[14] With his CFA francs he had bought himself some nice shoes and a pile of clothes. The money had vanished in no time as always happens on the street where people live for the moment: they know that they cannot hang onto anything for themselves and so can spend a fortune in a flash. On the insistence of my cook – since servants are always automatically suspected when there is a theft at a foreigner's house and their honour is in doubt[15] – we went to register a complaint at the juvenile police bureau and spoke to the commissioner, a remarkable man who later became a good friend. The matter was quickly solved: with the assistance of O and G, the police officers located both the thief and his booty.[16]

Suddenly, O, G and the others were not just my friends: they were my allies. They had rendered me a service and were proud of this. Once my mother had left, they returned triumphantly to my home. Faced with R's obvious distress, I offered this very difficult child a permanent place in my home for as long as he wanted it. And so that he was not alone, I made the same offer to C, who was a little older at 12 but more fragile, quite soft and visibly unhappy on the streets where he had been living. R had been sent out to beg by his vixen of a grandmother at the age of five.[17]

---

[14] I asked her if she had not thought it strange when M said that he had been given the money by a European. Her response was even more surprising: 'One never knows what white people will do!' It was true that those were times when large amounts of money were won and just as quickly lost by foreigners.

[15] It is evident that he was not very pleased to see all these dreadful street children in his master's house. But, before long, he knew well enough how to delegate the household cleaning tasks amongst those living with me. These would traditionally be the children's tasks in most homes, so boys knew what was expected of them.

[16] These were returned to me and I divided them up amongst the children.

[17] This, however, did not stop him loving her from the bottom of his heart. One day when we were discussing the national lottery and I asked him what he would do with the money if he won it, his immediate reply was that he would give it to his grandmother. And then after a moment's thought, he added that he would give some to me too.

My house increasingly became home to this little group, and they came when they wanted. I discovered to my great surprise that these outwardly tough children were starved of friendship, of trust and of tenderness: fortunately I had enough for all of them. For a time several asked me to help them to become shoeshine boys. I gave them what they needed to buy shoe polish and I acted as banker for their savings, organized the money in little piles in my wardrobe – a few coins that disappeared as soon as they felt the urge, which was often. This phase of street work was never going to last: real street children are usually too unstable to carry out tasks that allow others, who are still able to depend upon the psychological security provided by their family links, to survive.

On the whole, things were going well for us; we were leading our own lives without wondering about the future. At that time I worked at home in the evenings on a large table covered in books, which they accepted they were not to touch. They amused themselves as they wished, but this entailed an irritating number of arguments, particularly fights over money caused by their love of gambling. (Money is always an obsession with street children.) R in particular had his fists ready at all times even when faced with a much bigger youngster. A passing friend, who had much more experience of children than I had, made the excellent suggestion of giving them coloured crayons, which were very popular. Later I discovered their enthusiasm for Monopoly, a game that one might automatically consider to be too far removed from the lives of African street children. In fact, nothing connected with money was foreign to them. I enjoyed long peaceful evenings as a result. However to ensure harmony I sometimes had to resort to emotional blackmail. I remember one evening when R and C were playing with their crayons while I was reading. I do not know why but R flew into a rage and threw his crayons on the floor. I told him sharply that if he was my child, it was impossible for him to behave in that way. Without a word but with tears rolling down his face, he sulkily picked up his crayons and I returned to my book. A few moments later, he threw his arms round my neck for a cuddle. This did not prevent further outbursts but they became less frequent. Our life together unfolded smoothly. When I had to go away for a week at one point I left the house and its occupants in the charge of a colleague, Suzanne Lallemand, a well-known specialist in the anthropology of African families. When I returned, I asked her how she had found my little monsters: 'Frighteningly normal,' she replied laughingly.

I had no idea where I was going with them. If I had known the place these children would later have in my life – I who so treasured my freedom – I would no doubt have fled. And I would have been very wrong to do so: they have brought me immense happiness and, professionally, have given me an incredible insight into African city life with all its ups and downs. This has led me little by little to alter the depth of my scientific studies and to focus my research on the marginalization of young people within the urban context. I therefore owe them a great deal.

Freedom and mutual respect: The route to social reintegration

At the start of the new school year in September 1979, I was told to enrol or re-enrol the children in school. This was not a request, it was an order. At that time, primary education in Lomé was almost universal, at least for boys. But little interest was taken in the quality of the education provided. The children had all been to school for varying lengths of time and G had never really stopped going; he went every day for a few hours and spent the rest of his time guarding cars outside the main supermarket. He was intelligent, willing and ambitious and my help allowed him to start his studies at secondary school, which he finished without difficulty, becoming the first street child in Lomé to sit his baccalaureate and go to university. The others were less successful. But when I saw them in those first days of the new term leaving for school in their new khaki uniforms and with their schoolbags full of books, radiating joy and pride, I began to understand something fundamental: the passionate desire of marginalized youngsters to become children again like other children. This desire is a means of influencing them and not much is possible without it.

The nun at the juvenile bureau, who had become a friend, admitted to me that she had a problem. Among the imprisoned children there was one – whom she assured me was well behaved and quiet – who could not be released quite simply because he came originally from Benin and had no family to take care of him. How could he be released and returned to school? 'One more won't make much difference. Give him to me,' I replied. No sooner said than done. As always in such cases, the first few days were idyllic and he was impeccably behaved. But B was not living with me by choice and, as could have been predicted, he soon let it show. He began to test all the possible limits to his independence and my patience. But I am patient and stubborn, even if he made me fly off the handle on occasions. Finally, after a few months, B calmed down and gave in to his own emotional needs. I worked out how to bring us closer and we were able to live together without problems after that. But this episode showed that even when faced with an opportunity to change things for the better, the child's desire to do so is essential for success.

Another case allowed me to understand better what freedom means to street children. K used to be a regular on the Rue du Commerce and had been taken in by a Belgian couple who later became good friends of mine. In the beginning K seemed to be adapting easily to life with this family, which had to be well organized since they had four boys between 6 and 12 years old. Domestic chores were divided up equally between them all and K was given his fair share. Pretty soon he refused to do anything. Was this in reaction to the irritating levels of freedom enjoyed by the boys staying with me? Whatever the reason, he became less and less willing to play his part and shouting and threats were required to make him comply. Once he finished his chores he would come straight round to my home a few streets away and, without a word, pick up a broom and start sweeping to show that he could do it of his own free will. Moreover, his relationship with the four brothers, who were all gentle, hard-working and great readers, deteriorated rapidly. K only knew how to fight, not to play, and would send them hurtling to the bottom of the garden with his blows. They had to be separated as much as possible. The father's contract finished sooner than had been expected and before leaving he sent K back to his own father. Inevitably this did not work out and I soon took K in to live with us without further difficulties. I should stress that K remained very attached to the Belgian family, both to the adults and children, and still writes to them 25 years later. Sincere warmth and love is never wasted. But as for taking in street children, I concluded that it is better to avoid putting them into a family with children of the same age as the street child. There are no problems with a baby or grown-up children, but among adolescents with very different backgrounds a real sense of brotherhood is impossible and jealousy is inevitable.

I can offer here another example from a few years later. A high-ranking police officer asked me one day to go and see him in his office at the central police station. He explained all the problems he was having with his own 16-year-old son with whom relations had become extremely tense and who was currently locked up on remand in that very same building. We considered all the options as to how his son could rebuild his life at some distance from his father and came to the conclusion that the only possible solution was for him to come and live with me. He brought in E who was a big, clumsy youth and asked him outright: 'What do you want to do, stay locked up or go with this man?' It was not exactly a free and rational choice that E made when he said he wanted to come with me. He did not know me, as he was a young delinquent not a street child. His apprenticeship was particularly hard work since he persisted in getting into trouble, not missing a chance to get into a fight, to steal – but not from my home – and to get locked up again.[18] I had to go and fetch him from all

---

[18]   This appeared to be to gain revenge on his father. If I understood the situation properly, their problems had started a few years earlier. E's father had surprised him one day when he was smoking cannabis (which was a common pastime among the youth of Lomé) and had reacted with excessive violence, turning his son against him, while still showing love and affection to his other older children. It is often the case that people who are used to unlimited power at work have pedagogical problems with their

over the city from places where the authorities were allowed to detain people – the furthest-flung police stations, the railway station, the main market… But I can confirm that in spite of the number of crimes that he committed and workplaces he was asked to leave, he never did anything to me. He did not show me any particular affection but he always treated me with a respect and deference which I believed to be sincere.[19] It is certainly therefore the adult's attitude that determines the quality of the relationship, but it is the child who has to choose freely whether or not to get off the streets. Even with a period of transition when slippage can occur, but should if possible be overlooked, patience tends to win out in the end.

At the start of the academic year in 1979 most of 'my' children simply had to pick up where they had left off regarding school. Finding a school for R and B was less easy. I went first of all to the Catholic school close to my home. They replied firmly, but with some awkwardness, that taking in children with such backgrounds created too many problems for them. I went next to the local state school and asked to speak to the headmaster who listened carefully to my request and agreed to take the two little ones, relieved me of the need to pay fees, congratulated me on what I was doing and asked me to keep in contact – which I did. I thus discovered, little by little, an exceptional man with a broad background in both politics and trade unions and a sincere commitment to a humanist lifestyle. He quickly became one of my closest friends in Togo. Naturally I involved him from the very start in the organization that we established in 1981 to create a centre for street children. He has been president for the last dozen or so years and demonstrates the same devotion, sensitivity and wisdom as ever. Meeting street children in Lomé also brought me into contact with many adults of outstanding personal qualities without whom none of my work would have lasted and whose friendship I value deeply.

However, while the others took to their studies with great application, it soon become clear that F could not choose between school and the streets and continued to spend all his free time (or at least that which he decided was free) guarding cars on the Rue du Commerce. This ran contrary to our agreement and put him in disloyal competition with the little ones still on the streets who had no guaranteed food or shelter. I told him to make the choice. I tried to involve the others in the decision-making process with the aim of instilling a sense of collective responsibility for our communal life, but in vain. They refused point blank to associate themselves with him and he remained my responsibility

---

offspring. This is one reason for many of their children living on the streets, the other major cause being the 'Don Juan' effect of their wearing a uniform.

[19]   After a long period of being involved in drugs, his life finally stabilized and he became a wood sculptor. He recently died of AIDS.

alone. F preferred life on the streets.[20] So six students and I spent the remainder of that school year and the next together: R, C – easy, but so laid-back he was frankly lazy, G – endearing despite his irritating qualities, O – always funny and nice although not to be trusted, D – kind, serious and devoted and a bit older so he played the big brother a bit, and B who was making progress. I had asked a neighbour to provide food for the boys for a monthly payment. However fairly soon, using the excuse that she came from a different ethnic background and therefore did not provide the food they liked, the youngsters asked to be given the money themselves so that they could sort it out as they preferred, as they had always done – a practice we maintained. This was the easiest period during our life together, despite the relatively frequent fights. With only six of them, I could keep an eye on their educational and medical well-being and the financial burden was not as great then as it would later become, and still remains.

From 1981, numbers began to increase with the arrival of older youngsters, including the three older brothers of some of the first group, which immediately led to clashes over seniority and age. Then in the late 1980s problems arose linked to drug use that meant building new links with local medical contacts – but that is another story.

Discovering an unusual urban problem

The need for documents to register the children in school forced me to take a step I had not yet found necessary: to get in contact with the boys' families. R, who was 11 at the time, asked me to go with him to his home in Aneho, a town about 50 kilometres from Lomé. This had been the main economic centre on the coast from the beginning of the 18th century but was financially ruined through competition with Lomé when the latter became, first, the political capital of Togo in 1897 and then, more importantly, its economic capital following the construction of marine and rail infrastructure in 1904-05. This gave it a monopoly over foreign trade and hence a permanently dominant position in the urban framework of the country. At the start of the 20th century, the old, established families in Aneho came to work in Lomé whilst retaining a place in their home town for their families and their own retirement.

I was completely unaware of the unusual social history of Togo, although it would later become a focus for my research, and so I expected to find R's family in some poverty-stricken slum area. When we arrived in the old quarter I

---

[20] He finally – much later – managed to find work as a security guard. He never fails to greet me when our paths cross.

parked the car where he suggested. We walked through a magnificent gateway and entered a vast compound, passing a three-storey building, then older, lower houses and then still more. We were finally received in a huge drawing room hung with large photos of distinguished gentlemen in dark suits with wing collars. This was a family of the highest Togolese social class, which comprised, among others, numerous academics, doctors and senior civil servants, and even a juvenile-court judge. We were received very amicably by R's great-grandfather, a charming man who explained that after R's parents split up to go their own ways, R had broken away from under his grandmother's guardianship.[21] She had been a midwife but decided, along with many other Togolese women, to go into the textile trade. Several times they had brought R home and fed him, but he always quickly took off again, not hesitating to cover the fifty kilometres to Lomé to get back to his life on the streets. Had anyone ever shown that they loved him and that he mattered? Obviously not. Throughout the whole visit, R never left my side: he hung onto my hand until we got back to the car, turning a deaf ear to any suggestion from his aunts that he spend a few days with them. It was a year before he agreed to go back on his own and I suspect that he has never spent a single night there, except for his great-grandfather's wake, when I could only be there on the following day.

This was not my only surprise. If D was from a modest background, the son of a former soldier from Ghana whose pension had been eroded by inflation and whose successive wives had left him with a string of children, the others came from what used to be called 'excellent family backgrounds'. G was also from a well-known family in Aneho: his father was an accountant with a large company.[22] His mother was separated from his father and when her textile business had gone up in flames no-one in this respectable family had seen fit to come to help, even though G's uncle was deputy manager of the supermarket in whose car park G used to beg. C was the great-nephew of a Minister from the time of independence: his father, a teacher, had fathered half a dozen children around the place (notably even with some of his pupils), and had abandoned them all to get married in France and carry on peacefully with his own career. As for O, he was descended from one of Lomé's founding businessmen of a century earlier, and one of his paternal uncles was professor of medicine at the CHU in Lomé and married to a European. He had clearly made his choice between his own family and his origins – although he agreed to treat O for free

---

[21] His mother got remarried in a village; his father became a mechanic in Côte d'Ivoire, where I once met him. He was one of the very few parents to give me a present for his child. He then went to Gabon and I have never heard any more of him.

[22] It was G's bitter desire for revenge that pushed him to succeed in becoming an accountant: hate can be just as strong a motive as love.

when his health problems were beyond my means, except that I obviously had to pay for any medicine he might need.

I thus discovered a model completely different from the classic theory of street children resulting either from urban poverty or from an exodus from the rural areas. This strange version challenged me as a scientist. Later on, in order to rebuild the spatial dynamics of the city, I was led to explore the past and clarify the role of these old urban families, a fairly rare case in Africa. On reflection, there is little reason to be surprised: each city has its own social history, its own individual multifaceted evolution and the shape of its marginalized peoples is bound to be a specific product of this history. Even if the living conditions and the impact on the children are broadly similar, the causes of their marginalization are not the same in Dakar as in Nairobi or in Abidjan or Johannesburg.[23] This may also mean that solutions that have proved effective in one of these cities may be quite inappropriate in another.

In the case of Lomé, we are dealing with a true city society that was founded on international trade in the 19th – or even the 18th – century. It was African traders from the old merchant cities on what was known as the Slave Coast who founded Lomé in 1880 to allow them to carry out their business beyond the reach of the British customs and who, in 1884, formally called upon the German Protectorate to defend their prosperity.[24] It is a very modern population, with all that entails in the way of dynamism and being outward-looking. But it has also led to a loss of traditional solidarity, an 'each man for himself' mentality in the race for riches and power, and the gradual break-up and distancing of the social classes, even if polygamy – which is just as widespread among the rich with Christianity having changed nothing – means that among almost all the longstanding urban families everyone is related to everyone else. It was these oldest families in the town – those most affected by marital break-up – those producing Ministers and the upper middle classes that also produced the first street children in Togo.[25]

Lomé has seen its population multiply by a factor of 2.5 in 20 years. Today the old families are hidden beneath the wave of new arrivals but the mechanism

---

[23] See Marguerat (1998).

[24] See Marguerat (1993).

[25] Another interesting anecdote here – in the years 1985-1990 I used to work at my desk most evenings and the children often joined me, just for the pleasure of my company. One day when I was sorting out documents about land and properties in the German period (to understand a city it is necessary to know who it belonged to), one of the children asked me why I was making notes about them. I was not, but the child had seen his own name in the papers and wanted to know why it was there. It was in fact the name of his great-grandfather and namesake, one of the city's founding fathers.

is the same. Lomé's street children remain fundamentally a product of the city because the more recently urbanized families have quickly adopted the same habits as the older and more established ones, especially regarding marital and household instability. There is a particularly unusual social factor here: the importance of the role of women in trade, at every level,[26] which has given them considerable financial independence, with men and women running separate accounts. These women also demonstrate a degree of migrational autonomy, for example, when they leave their husbands in the fields to go and attend to their own business in town. That is not of course the cause of marital instability but it certainly makes it more likely and more commonplace. The early disappearance of the dowry, which impacts so strongly upon relations between families elsewhere in Africa, has meant that couples set up life together with very little ceremony and split up equally easily. The outcome according to the 1981 general census, the most recent in Togo, shows that only 43 per cent of households in Lomé are made up of a couple with children, and perhaps with other close relations too. Only two-thirds of children in the city live with both their parents.[27]

The mapping of these children's movements, and those of many others whom I met later,[28] prove that it is not single-parent families that are the basic problem – if that were the case there would be many more street children. It is the reconfiguring of the family unit, which leads to conflict with the stepfather or even more often with the stepmother, which then causes some boys to leave and to live on the streets.[29] This is the picture the children also have of

---

[26] The famous *mama-benz* had the top positions in the huge pyramid of cloth traders.

[27] According to *Enquête Démographique et de Santé 1998* (Direction de la Statistique, 1999, Lomé, 287 p.), this figure has decreased: only 53.8% of children in Lomé (from 0 to 14 years) live with both their parents (63.9% in the rural areas where migration is strong), 19.5% live with just their mother, 8.4% with their father, 18.3% with neither parent (10% have lost one of their parents, 1.4% have lost both). Across the country as a whole, the number of children living with both parents naturally decreases with age (from 77.9% for those aged 0-2 years to 47.6% for those in the 10-12 age range). The sex of the child does not appear to play a role (for all ages the figures are boys: 60.5%, girls: 59.8%). I have never come across a case where the problem for the child was to have been fostered out by the parents to another member of the family, as so often happens in Africa.

[28] In March 2003 we managed to open a refuge for children aged between 9 and 12 years of age who were surviving by working as porters along the Togo-Ghana border. Out of the 82 I surveyed, 76 had parents who were separated for one reason or another.

[29] Girls, on the contrary, who can help in the house and with selling things, are never abandoned, but often exploited. This too is a serious problem but totally different and much less visible. For any girl that leaves her family, the female world of the markets offers the chance to earn some money by selling goods. It is necessary to be very well

themselves. I think of the Christmas celebrations organized with the children locked up in the juvenile prison. They used to choose to put on little sketches demonstrating admirable acting skills – a very useful skill when living on the street – which always told the same story: that of their life: 'My father is good but my stepmother mistreats me as soon as he turns his back: that's why I do stupid things'…

In recent years, during the deepest of economic recessions, the problem of poverty has been the primary cause of family breakdown, especially when there were already difficulties of one sort or another, for example the loss of adult support to the family through death, illness, unemployment or departure. The way followed by the street children of Lomé is always the same, except that nowadays the young city dwellers from the longest established urban families – of which some members held well-regarded jobs – have decreased proportionally, submerged beneath those from the lower classes. The disfunctionality of the adult generation has thus become more commonplace or perhaps even 'democratized'.

The frequency of this more psychological rather than economic reason for boys leaving home to live on the streets explains why the emotional relationship is so important for them, and critical to their reintegration into society. They have a great need for love and tenderness, even though this may often be hidden beneath ostentatious displays of provocative and aggressive behaviour. This is why the personal relationship that I nurtured with the street children I came into contact with, without knowing where it would lead us, was so effective. It is not simply the best solution, it is the only one possible.[30]

Conclusion

I can only sketch briefly here the latest developments in a project which now spans 25 years. In 1980 the nun attached to the juvenile section of the police station in Lomé asked a planning expert and me to establish a hostel for young people. She was seeing more and more youngsters arriving who had no family to take them back home and for whom a solution had to be found. The experience I had had with my small tribe showed that offering a liberal 'family' framework created an acceptable solution. In August 1981 we set up a local NGO, *L'Association pour la Promotion de l'Enfance à Lomé* (APPEL) with a deliberately neutral and non-political name, involving as many of our Togolese

---

informed to pick out these cases.

[30] Of course, this conclusion is not only true for Lomé.

friends as possible. (European people are useful but one day they have to go back home.) We were finally able to open a temporary hostel for 12 youngsters in June 1982. Forewarned weeks earlier, the children from the Rue du Commerce came on foot every day to the bureau to remind us that we should not forget them.

Then we made a big mistake due to our lack of adequate knowledge of the rules of the streets. We took as our starting point the supposedly ideal set up in a normal family by grouping together children of different ages. I had not yet understood that on the streets the real curse for the little ones is the bigger children who mercilessly bully and extort money from them. These exploitative relationships were, therefore, recreated in the hostel. The older ones had ultimately to be told to leave.[31]

In 1983 we built a permanent building with 20 beds that grew to 40 in 1986,[32] which represents a maximum not to be exceeded for fear of creating a barracks requiring unavoidably repressive disciplinary measures. For several years we were able to help all the children who wanted to be off the Rue du Commerce – not all of them did – and visibly reduce the numbers there, which gained us plenty of official support. However at the end of the 1980s the economic situation worsened rapidly, and more and more children started to leave home but not to head for the centre of the city. They tended to seek shelter in the markets and bus stations on the outskirts of town where they were less visible to the untrained eye.

Since then the hostel has continued to take in the smallest children. Overwhelmed with requests for help from older children, I had to turn many away but inevitably I took in some from time to time and I found myself father to a huge family: 150 youngsters whom I helped, to the best of my ability, to earn their living.

I had to leave Lomé at the beginning of 1994 following the breakdown of relations between France and Togo, but fortunately I was able later to start up two development projects. One helps to finance around 30 school pupils and students who could not carry on with their studies without the support of our Committee to Help Children of Lomé.[33] The other is more original as it was aimed at the older youths – the 18 to 22 year olds – whom nobody wanted to look after. This lack of help is a mistake as they are much more aware than the

---

[31] It was me who took them back later.

[32] This was thanks to 17 different financial sponsors. It can only be imaged what efforts were put into fundraising and organization.

[33] *Le Comité de Soutien aux Enfamts de Lomé*, set up in 1982, finances the shelter and has helped me enormously as costs rose. It is this organization in the Paris region that entirely funds this group of students.

younger ones that the streets represent a dead-end from which they cannot escape on their own. The programme offers them the chance of an apprenticeship in the informal sector and it works – thanks to good supervision on the ground, mostly from former street children who know exactly what it means to be in such a situation. Our only real problems are financial because the older ones on the streets do not interest donors. We have had to find the means to set up workshops so that those who finish their training can earn a living from the skills they have learned – which is their deepest wish.[34] As always, it is more difficult to negotiate with adults than with the street kids themselves.

What has happened to my former children? G has done the best – with his baccalaureate and three further years of studies, he went to France to study accountancy. He now has a good job in Paris, a wife and children. He sends as much help as he can to the members of his family who stayed in Togo, where he is hoping to invest once the political situation is more stable. B is a taxi driver in Cotonou. O is a tailor and, more profitably, does work for a funeral chapel. D is a designer, with a business that mirrors the economic situation in Lomé, which is very difficult at present. After abandoning numerous apprenticeships, C now sells second-hand tyres in the port. K, who learned to cook, has become a factory worker in Abidjan. Despite his meagre salary he has undertaken to pay the school fees of a young Ivorian neighbour – a bright but poor pupil.[35]

As for R, it took him a long time to sort himself out – he had such a long way to come. He completed several years at secondary school then tried several apprenticeships without finding one that suited him. He had a deep sense of anxiety that made him fearful of the adult world. Over the last few years he has learned to do batik; he is quite talented in this direction, but we had to recognize that he will never be able to run his own workshop. Thanks to a donation received for the apprentices, I was able to buy him a motorbike that he uses, like many young people in Togo, to run a taxi service and he is proud of the freedom that this gives him. As for many former street children, the discipline needed to run a workshop is too much for him. These youngsters have to be helped to find a future in jobs that offer them more freedom such as trade or driving taxis.

In R's case it will have taken 20 years for him to 'settle'. I was lucky enough to be able to give him those 20 years. It is always worth responding to a child in distress. It is quite easy to do because if you are able to bring an unselfish affection to the child, he will seek you out much more than you seek him. On the other hand, the experience shows that, apart from exceptional cases, street

---

[34] Currently this is the case for 85 of our former street children (with 19 failures).

[35] However because of the current economic crisis in Côte d'Ivoire and his poor health he had to return to Lomé, where he died of AIDS in 2003.

children cannot honestly escape their situation on their own. Leaving these young people to their own devices in the big public spaces is bound to lead to the formation of a anti-society in the urban centres whose relations with the 'normal' adult world can only become increasingly fraught and dangerous for all concerned, as can be seen all over Africa and Latin America. To intervene and help build links between the generations in order to give these young people the chance of getting off the streets is therefore vital to everybody's safety and well-being. When an argument between a child and his parents ends up with the child running away to live on the streets it is up to other adults to overcome the conflict between the generations and to repair the damage. My practical experience – and that of many others – proves it can work remarkably well.

It is not the best method, it is the only one that works.

References

Marguerat, Y. 1993, *La Naissance du Togo Selon les Documents de l'Epoque (1874-84)*, Lomé: Haho & Karthala.

Marguerat, Y. 1998, 'Jeunes, Cultures de la Rue et Violence Urbaine', *Cahier de Marjuvia*, 7: 43-66.

Marguerat, Y. 2000, 'Les Chemins de la Rue: Essai de Synthèse sur les Processus de Production d'Enfants de la Rue en Afrique', in C. Pairault (ed.), *Citadins et Ruraux en Afrique Subsaharienne*, Paris: Karthala-Université Catholique d'Afrique Centrale, pp. 387-403.

Marguerat, Y. 2002, 'Woe to Thee, O City, When Thy King is a (Street) Child!', in B. Trudell, K. King, S. McGrath & P. Nugent (eds), *Africa's Young Majority*, Centre of African Studies, University of Edinburgh, pp. 229-54.

Marguerat Y. & D. Poitou (eds) 1994, *A l'Ecoute des Enfants de la Rue en Afrique Noire*, Paris: Fayard.

Peltre-Wurtz, J. 1998, 'Pauvreté, Famille et Enfance à Quito (Equateur)', *Cahier de Marjuvia*, 7: 14-33.

10

Children as conflict stakeholders: Towards a new discourse on young combatants

Angela McIntyre

The emergence of child soldiers as a high-profile international policy issue has brought a particular understanding to the role of young people in conflict; one that has served the needs of advocacy against the use of children as combatants. While this victim-definition has lent itself successfully to mobilizing support for the international ban, it has perhaps restricted understandings of the role of young people in conflict. The ubiquitous involvement of young people in both peaceful and violent political transformation suggests that conflicts might be better informed by a more varied discourse on children involved in war, one that recognizes them as actors in a conflict rather than as collateral damage.

Introduction

The phenomenon of children participating in violent conflicts has generally been viewed as a by-product of clashes between real conflict stakeholders (governments and armed insurgents, for example), much in the same way as happy, healthy, educated children are seen as a collateral benefit of peaceful, functional and prosperous states. Children have most often appeared as secondary stakeholders in armed conflict, where they come to public attention only when agencies such as national and international non-governmental organizations, human-rights monitoring groups and various United Nations branches act on their behalf in the humanitarian interest of protecting civilians in armed conflict. The problem of child soldiers, of which there are an estimated 300,000 serving in militaries worldwide (Coalition to Stop the Use of Child Soldiers 2001), has received special international attention in this regard and culminated in early 2002 in the Optional Protocol to the United Nations

Convention on the Rights of the Child on the involvement of children in armed conflict.

Strong arguments have been made for peace negotiation processes to raise the standards of adherence to humanitarian and, specifically, child-rights instruments in the interests of protecting children. Cohn (1999) argues that formal peace processes must explicitly include child-oriented elements such as the disarmament, demobilization and reintegration of child combatants, family tracing and reunification to assist unaccompanied children in locating their families, and specialized training for peacekeeping forces to combat, among others, the ubiquitous problem of child prostitution by troops. Formal peace processes, she also argues, present an opportunity to address longer-term and systemic policy problems that have historically affected children even before the outbreak of hostilities. While the prioritization of children has received attention in the context of broader efforts to protect civilians in armed conflict, much of this work is directed towards the reform of humanitarian law and advocacy (see Kuper 1997). Cohn (1999: 137) argues that child advocates

… must creatively characterize child rights policy concerns in the language of economic incentives and imagine ways of bringing certain child protection issues out of the typically 'private' domain into the realm of public regulation and programmatic response.

Few analysts have actually treated children as conflict stakeholders, that is, by recognizing how they become political and military agents and influence the nature and trajectories of armed conflicts. The need for discourse on children that lends itself to conflict analysis has a number of possible motivations.

Firstly, demographic transitions may be worthy of attention. An estimated half of the African population is under the age of 15. Bloom, Canning and Sevilla (2003: 61-66) suggest that Africa's relatively high fertility rates coupled with the negative growth of the workforce due to AIDS deaths among adults have resulted in an overall rise in dependency ratios. The problems of economic hardship, political exclusion, competition for resources, and ethnic and religious intolerance are experienced by majorities who are relatively young. Data from most Sub-Saharan African countries suggest that over half of the population is under the age of 18 (UNAIDS 2000). National policies aimed not only at education, health and social services but also broader development planning and governance have an impact on the young majorities and their caregivers, those who manage the child-adult transition in the interests of perpetuating families and communities.

Collier et al. (2003) shed light on the political and economic motivators of war; their line of argument might be extended to include factors such as age structure, perceived exclusion or marginalization based on the generational aspects of power structures and the proportion of child workers and child household heads participating in the economy. Without pursuing this in any depth, it is probably safe to say that the collective agency of children, as a group that makes up over half the population of Sub-Saharan Africa, must surely be more than the sum of its parts, and this has some interplay with the causes, trajectories and recurrences of conflict. While such a study is beyond the scope of this chapter, I suggest that it is kept on the horizon when taking a closer look at the circumstances in which children make the decision to take up arms.

The second motivation arises from the belief that advocacy should not constrain the parameters of understanding by becoming hypothesis, method and conclusion, as it so often does in this age of fierce competition between civil-society organizations whose survival often relies quite rigidly on paying homage to international policy frameworks and those who fund their implementation, normally Northern donor governments. Although advocating compliance with human-rights instruments, human-rights monitoring and policy research are of importance, they cannot replace an accurate analysis of conflicts. Unfortunately, in the case of children involved in armed conflict, there is relatively little informative analysis of young people as conflict stakeholders. Detailed accounts only of the physical and mental suffering of children do not enrich our understanding of their agency, just as discourse on women in war that revolves exclusively around sexual abuse and reproductive health is sure to distance strategists and analysts and fails to deepen understandings of their stakeholdership. While human-rights standards are important benchmarks for advocacy, descriptions of violations present a somewhat linear picture of the causes and consequences of conflict.

A third motivation for exploring the agency of young people, and the one on which this chapter dwells, arises from the reality that children and youth have unfailingly been the targets of the campaigns of liberation movements, electioneers and insurgents – an indication of the widespread recognition of their strategic value in political change. There is no doubt that recruitment strategies from the brutal and coercive to the more subtle and ideological have entailed efforts to capture the loyalty of young people, boys and girls, from young children to young adults, and that incentives are crafted in ways that capitalize on the characteristics and circumstances of these population groups.

Although there are many forms of military and non-military child and youth recruitment of historical importance that are worthy of discussion, this chapter looks mainly at military recruitment, drawing on case studies gathered in Mozambique, Uganda, Ethiopia, Angola and Sierra Leone between 2001 and 2003.

First a word on definitions: this discussion asks for a certain flexibility on the international definition of under-18s (contained in the UN Convention on the Rights of the Child and its Optional Protocols) as the delimitation of childhood, and rather situates the discussion within a framework that is assumed to be more universal: the transition of under-18s from childhood to adulthood. The terms 'children and youth' and 'young people' are used to describe the people who contributed to the case studies, most of whom – for the record – were recruited and participated in armed conflicts whilst under the age of 18.

While chronological definitions of childhood can be problematic, the notion of an adult-child transition entails not only the passing of years but also changes in roles, responsibilities, expectations and, to varying extents, physical and developmental characteristics. The responsibilities and privileges that come with adulthood are sometimes unattainable by young people because of economic and social constraints, yet this vulnerability is not recognized in the (low, in this case, if soldiering is to be the exclusive domain of adults) 18-standard of international law. Conversely, children under 18 often assume what could be called adult responsibilities, also because of the constraints and opportunities of their societies. It is interesting to note here that the term 'youth' has become an important political construct that does not adhere to any particular chronological age but has been successfully used in rallying those members of societies who perceive themselves to be in states of transition. Though youth generally includes young people, the upper limitations can be stretched to rally the disenfranchised, sometimes up to the age of 35 and even beyond. The United Nations definition of youth includes 15-24 year-olds and thus overlaps with the definition of children.

Critical to this discussion is the idea that the roles, responsibilities and expectations that accompany growing up are capitalized upon by political and military actors to recruit and to secure the allegiance of young people. In this respect, recruiters often present themselves as 'surrogates' for civilian life, offering – or at least seeming to offer – security, education, employment, social status, livelihood and avenues for political expression.

Security, insurgency and advocacy: Children as instruments

The response of moral outrage to images of children in ill-fitting scraps of camouflage clothing carrying assault rifles has been a double-edged sword. Graça Machel (2001) draws attention to cases where 'in the effort to publicise a relief programme or organisation, or even to make a political point, ex-child soldiers have been asked to pose with guns'. Similarly, she points out that humanitarian organisations have been known to comply with requests from film-makers and journalists to talk to 'younger girls' who have been raped or children with 'more traumatic' stories. She goes on to warn of the danger of distorting the reality of conflict situations through inaccurate representations of the involvement of children in conflict.

Child soldiers have become media shorthand for all that is seemingly irrational and brutal in African warfare, violating that most precious of human institutions – childhood – at least insofar as it is defined by the Convention on the Rights of the Child. The images used by the media and advocates have successfully moved people from the most cynical Northern taxpayers to the most fatigued international aid agencies. Recruiting children under the age of 15 has become a war crime under the Rome Statute of the International Criminal Court and punishable under several other highly specialized legal instruments designed to preserve a particular notion of the integrity of childhood.

Yet there are conflicting attitudes towards the presence of children in fighting forces, and the issue of accountability for the 'crime' is fraught with ambiguity. Those apparently most responsible for turning children into cannon fodder are a handful of heinous human-rights abusers who abduct children, rather than those officially accountable for the welfare and protection of what, in many cases, constitutes over half of the nation's population. It is unlikely that creating accessible recruitment pools, through neglect, mismanagement or corruption, will be acknowledged as a war crime any time soon.

For military commanders and wartime politicians, the welfare of children is a distant collateral benefit of victory, future peace, and stability. In the heat of transition, children and youth constitute a critical recruitment pool, one that has been tapped into by regimes and rebels alike, for agendas that have ranged from colonial liberation struggles to election campaigns to armed insurgencies, using recruitment tactics that correspond to the urgency of battle.

To truly understand the role of young people in change, we need to consider the environments that shape their agency, and accept that children do make decisions in the interest of their own survival and advancement. Even a decision to fight rather than die at the hands of rebel abductors can be a rational decision – one that certainly carries with it military or political consequences at some level.

The mobilization of African governments to sign on to the Optional Protocol by advocacy groups may have been effective in part because it takes the problem of child and youth involvement in armed violence out of the immediate military/political context and into one circumscribed by international legal and moral concern. Governments that both employ and fight under-18s have signed and ratified the Optional Protocol, perhaps because at the time there was adequate distance between an internationally lauded commitment to protect the 'most vulnerable' and the reality that fighting a civil war might require one's own young people.

While national commitments to high-profile international processes such as the Optional Protocol are hailed as an advance, the progress of humanitarian agencies operating in conflict settings, by contrast, tends to be incremental and dictated by emergency prioritization, limitations on infrastructure, concerns for the security of workers, the ability to engage with hostile belligerents and perhaps most importantly, by funding from outside. Given these limitations, there have been remarkable achievements on the part of humanitarian workers carrying with them the legal and moral imperative of child protection. Vaccination campaigns, basic education provided to internally displaced and refugee children, the release of child abductees, and family tracing and reunification efforts have taken place in the most impossible of circumstances. The United Nations Children's Fund (UNICEF), for example, has succeeded in negotiating 'days of tranquillity', brief periods of ceasefire during which emergency humanitarian activities are allowed to take place with guarantees of relative security. Direct negotiations with Uganda's Lord's Resistance Army (LRA) and Sierra Leone's Revolutionary United Front (RUF) have resulted in the release of abducted children.

These small victories might be viewed cynically as attempts by insurgents to establish credibility or to create proximity to humanitarian agencies for the purpose of procuring essential supplies such as food and medicines. On the other hand, perhaps any opportunity to hold belligerents to a higher standard of conduct should not be lost (Cohn 1999).

In any case, the common certainty of the political leverage of children, among conflict actors, cynical or otherwise, periodically displays itself. It is exercised not only in the battles-within-battles fought by churches and charities rather than militaries, but by states, the United Nations, insurgents, the media and international aid donors. This agency-by-proxy offers only a vague glimpse of children and youth through the lenses of those who profess to act on their behalf.

Children act on their own behalf – however small or insecure their spheres of influence – within the larger parameters set by humanitarians, belligerents and governments. The choices children make in what they perceive at the time as their own best interests have political and military consequences, evidence of which has been all but obscured in portrayals of suffering child victims. Boys and girls helped bring down the Derg regime in Ethiopia, liberated Mozambique from colonial occupation only to later bring formidable opposition to a Marxist-Leninist regime over a sixteen-year civil war; they participated politically and

Youth recruits in the Democratic Republic of the Congo in 2003.
Photos courtesy of Guy Tillim

militarily in Angola's seemingly intractable conflict until the death of Jonas Savimbi in 2002, and sustain an ongoing war between the Ugandan government and the rebel Lord's Resistance Army in the north of Uganda.

The recruitment spectrum: Enticement, ruses and coercion

Joining fighting forces means different things to different children. The alleged incoherence of the political agendas of armed insurgents such as Sierra Leone's Revolutionary United Front and Uganda's Lord's Resistance Army may be a moot point, since appeals to young people need not always lie in the long-term promise of a better future. On the contrary, they sometimes appeal to immediate survival. In this sense, mobilization strategies present something of a continuum, populated by incentives given in various contexts of dissent, nationalist fervour, hunger, instability, threats of danger and so forth.

Mobilization strategies serve the changing needs of warfare by targeting different geographical areas or populations. And in cases of forced recruitment, some populations are rendered more vulnerable in the course of violence as a result of displacement and community and familial fragmentation, presenting easier targets than stable, more protected communities. Children often become separated from their families in these instances; in others, adults have actually been killed while children are spared for the purpose of co-option by the group. As is reportedly the case in forced recruitment by the LRA and previously by the RUF, mass abductions appear to be most successful when conducted amidst the chaos of attacks on communities of civilians or when targeting people who have strayed from the safety of their communities, driven by food shortages to take risks.

At the other end of the spectrum, governments have equally effective, if sometimes less immediately violent, means at their disposal to make joining up an attractive prospect for potential young recruits. The use and abuse of patrimony (Chabal & Daloz 1999) includes party youth leagues that dole out privileges to loyal young people, control educational and employment opportunities and manipulate criminal justice systems in order to channel 'delinquent' youth into military service.

Mozambique offers an example within this diversity of recruitment strategies. Mozambique's civil war was one of the first African conflicts in which the child soldier phenomenon first received widespread international publicity. Analyses of the Mozambique conflict over the years refer to the use of children by the Mozambique National Resistance (RENAMO), while frequently overlooking the fact that the Mozambique Liberation Front (FRELIMO) did the same, sometimes using forced recruitment but commonly more sophisticated ruses employing mechanisms of the state to draw on the loyalty of young people. These enticements often landed children and youth on the front lines rather than in the classroom, a clear example of the duplicitous use of the state apparatus to co-opt young people.

One account, given by a boy recruited at the age of 14, describes how his family received a letter from the government in 1988 announcing that he would receive a scholarship to study in the German Democratic Republic. On presenting himself at the Ministry of Education, he was promptly shipped off, along with dozens of other letter recipients, to a military base for training where he and the rest of the new batch that had swallowed the bait were mocked by their captors for harbouring the silly expectation of studying abroad. The fact that FRELIMO did, at the time, sponsor young people to study in Cuba, East Germany and other Eastern bloc states was widely known. Studying abroad was a common aspiration of young people habituated to the loss of family members to the cause of fighting the 'armed bandits' and anxious to avoid recruitment.[1]

---

[1]   This account was given by a former FRELIMO child soldier interviewed in Chimoio

During Angola's civil war, both UNITA (the Movement for the Total Independence of Angola) and the MPLA (Popular Movement for the Liberation of Angola) engaged systems of co-option that have been described as both 'bottom up' and 'top down' (Parsons 2003). Forming a part of UNITA's political and military machinery were Alvorada (Dawn), a compulsory group for pre-adolescent children living in UNITA areas, and JURA, a youth military wing.

> Children were taught songs and dances that illustrated celebrated UNITA heroes and victories. Alvorada in particular then entertained visiting troops with these when they came to the villages. JURA went further in separating youth from their families so that they could work for UNITA troops, transporting food and weapons to the front lines, growing food or even fighting. It also had an additional element, however, of explicit political sensibilization and preparation. This was a recurrent theme of education in UNITA, which 'bought' their loyalty by offering them a concrete opportunity and a form of normalization of life. (Parsons 2003)

Youth combatants underwent education covering UNITA's version of the political history of Angola and the necessity of the struggle:

> I joined the armed forces of UNITA in 1992 ... I did not begin fighting immediately. In 1992 we were still in political preparation. We were given material. The reason why we were fighting, who we were fighting against, why we had to fight. This was the politics of the party. ... We had to learn all this. So that when I fought I would understand.[2]

The MPLA's answer to this was the JMPLA (Youth of the Popular Movement for the Liberation of Angola) and the Agostinho Neto Organization of Pioneers (OPA), both of which engaged in the education and mobilization of children. A 1996 proclamation of 'the end of corruption' by President dos Santos was accompanied by the creation of the National Spontaneous Movement, a youth organization without apparent affiliation to the party. Parsons (2003) sees this as:

> an attempt to draw youth into clientelistic relations of power, centred on Dos Santos, and also to capitalise on existing social tensions to divert attention away from the country's economic problems and towards his opposition, UNITA. ... Youth who may have had no desire to participate directly in the war were thus inadvertently incorporated into its dynamics.

---

in 2003.

[2] Interview with a 21-year-old ex-UNITA soldier in Uamba Gathering Area, January 2002.

The ruses of the Mozambican and Angolan states and UNITA appear benign in comparison with the methods adopted by Uganda's Lord's Resistance Army. Clearly, the question of choice becomes moot in the face of the kinds of life-or-death decisions offered to child abductees, as illustrated in the following interview with a former LRA child combatant.

> Youth: My friend was beaten to death, stoned to death, after knowing he wanted to escape.
> Interviewer: How did they find out he was trying to escape?
> Youth: We had been talking – one among us had been talking – go and tell the secret to the army man; and they called the man. You, you want to escape, we want you to be an army man, we take the government but we have no prison to keep you here, the only thing is dying. You are going to die. And they called four or five and they stoned that man to death.[3]

This is an example of 'recruitment potential' perpetuated during armed conflict by insurgents who, with apparent nihilism and the use of terror tactics, destroy infrastructure and the social fabric, in itself a way of facilitating coerced recruitment. In razing all that is anthropogenic, they are then able to present their group as the only entity representing survival. This has been a prominently featured recruitment style in child-soldier advocacy for obvious reasons: it represents the grossest violations of human rights and clearly traumatizes not only children but also whole communities. In context, however, the recruitability of Acholi children is better understood as being sustained by the activities of the LRA itself but exacerbated by the heightened insecurity brought on by the periodic up-scaling of the military efforts of the Ugandan government. Stavrou (2003) understands the relation of the LRA to the Acholi community as one of plunder:

> ... the LRA is not at war with the community, but utilises the community as a resource base for both food and human capital – and uses terror as a mechanism to wield control and power.

The ongoing positioning of Acholi children to make the decision to fight or die is inextricable from the dynamic of conflict in northern Uganda and critical to the survival of the LRA. Although estimates vary, most would suggest that, by the end of 2000, over 15,500 children had been abducted since the beginning of the war. Fewer than 6,000 of these children had managed to escape or have been liberated from captivity (United Nations 2001).

---

[3] Interviews with former child fighters of the Lord's Resistance Army were conducted in Gulu District in northern Uganda in 2002 by the Institute for Security Studies (ISS).

Collective agency from individual motives

Ethiopia's Tigrayan People's Liberation Front (TPLF) was founded in 1975 in opposition to Mengistu's Derg military dictatorship. Combined with the forces of a number of other regional resistance movements that formed the Ethiopian People's Revolutionary Democratic Front (EPRDF), a third of which consisted of female fighters, they brought about the overthrow of the dictatorship in 1991. Accounts by individual women of how they joined the fighters, in which abduction was notably absent, show a remarkable range of motivations: [4]

> I knew nothing about the TPLF but then one of my classmates told me about TPLF liberators, and about people being oppressed by the Derg. I withdrew from my family and went to the army. My family were not happy about it because it was difficult for my family to tell others that I had joined the TPLF.

> I became a fighter because my best friend went to the fighters and I went with her because I liked it more than staying.

> … because my family members joined the army. There was drought, migration and other problems at that time. The reaction of my family was not good because they did not think I would be coming back.

> There were my three brothers who joined the army before. I didn't know why they had joined the fighters but I expected that I would meet them and join them there. At that time, many people were joining, even girls. My parents were not happy because my brothers had disappeared and they thought the same might happen to me.

> When I was 11 years old, I became involved with the fighters because of the Goila. Goila is the fighters' dance. It implies if anyone joins that Goila and dances with them, he or she has already entered the fighters and is ready to become a fighter. Therefore I joined the Goila when I was 11 years old, and I was taken to the training programme.

> I joined the fighters to escape marriage. I was married when I was 12 years old and the only option to escape was to go join the fighters.

A budding political awareness interspersed with decidedly social motivations and a sense of impending insecurity, met by the mobilization strategies of the

---

[4] Interviews with a group of former TPLF fighters were conducted in Addis Ababa in 2002 by a team of researchers headed by Dr Angela Veale as part of a collection of case studies on recruitment and reintegration undertaken by the Institute for Security Studies project on children in armed conflict (see Veale 2003).

TPLF, turned many young women with arguably different motivations into a force to be reckoned with.

The significance of co-option

The numbers of children and youth who have served as combatants and their supporting political and military contingencies are rough estimates (see Coalition to Stop the Use of Child Soldiers 2001). Statistical accuracy is difficult and definitions accommodate children who work in subsidiary roles, such as cooks or porters, spies, messengers and concubines. More difficult still would be an estimate of the number of children and youth whose agency has been absorbed into the momentum of change, peaceful or violent. An interesting question revolves around proportion: do the proportions of children serving in military and political movements reflect the structure of the population? Are youth really 'excluded' as has often been assessed? More likely a case can be made for selective inclusion, carried out with a great degree of opportunism.

A second question revolves around what can only be called the human resources of war. The availability of young people to be actors in conflicts has clearly been a critical strategic consideration. Although only the recruitment methods have been discussed here, it is likely that training, preferred weaponry, and discipline – the very pillars of military culture – have adapted to some extent to accommodate the available recruitment pools. Assuming that children's social, developmental and physical needs and capabilities differ from those of adults, their motivations and behaviour in situations of combat would also differ. Hence, the means of securing their loyalty and cooperation and ensuring their effectiveness must correspond. It has been argued that children make good soldiers due to their pliability, loyalty that stems from emotional immaturity, under-developed moral and ethical substance, a fearlessness akin to that of children at play, and a lack of appreciation of the value of human life (Machel 2001). Others have suggested the opposite, that these features are liabilities in combat and that higher principles, or notions thereof, such as nationalism, honour and valour have a necessary place in effective forces (Carlton 2001). The important point here is that the strengths and limitations of young people are somehow accommodated in African warfare.

Then of course there is the cyclical nature of co-option. While revolutions are often about young people challenging old orders, as regimes solidify and age, youth can once again develop the perception of being excluded, and discontent foments (see Dorman this volume). In contrast to western societies, where youth have avenues of expression such as educational institutions and other social and economic incentives that offer safe and even productive arenas for rebellion, the lot of African children and youth seems to add to the already fertile ground for turbulent transitions.

Conclusion

There is nothing particularly new in observing the roles that youth occupy in the context of global trends: colonialism and liberation struggles, structural adjustment programmes and economic globalization. What is relatively new is the emergence of child soldiers as a high-profile international policy issue and an accompanying tendency for advocates to decontextualize the phenomenon, thus making it less relevant not only to the rest of the international research and policy community but also for parties in conflict resolution for whom an accurate understanding of stakeholders is critical. This brief examination of recruitment suggests that there are still debates to be had on the issue of child soldiers stimulated by better understandings of the causes and dynamics of conflict from their perspectives. Defining the stakeholdership of young people by proxy, that is, as a beneficiary group with 'protectors' acting on their behalf, ensures their marginality in discussions of conflict when their agency should arguably be considered more central. If anything, this should give more leverage to advocates.

References

Bloom, D.E., D. Canning & J. Sevilla 2003, *The Demographic Dividend: A New Perspective on the Economic Consequences of Population Change*, Santa Monica: RAND.

Carlton, E. 2001, *Militarism: Rule Without Law*, Aldershot: Ashgate Publishing.

Chabal, P. & J. Daloz 1999, *Africa Works: Disorder as a Political Instrument*, Oxford: James Currey.

Coalition to Stop the Use of Child Soldiers 2001, http://www.child-soldiers.org.

Cohn, I. 1999, 'The Protection of Children in Peacemaking and Peacekeeping Processes', *Harvard Human Rights Journal*, 12: 129-96.

Collier, P., V.L. Elliot, H. Hegre, A. Hoeffler, M. Reynal Querol & N. Sambanis 2003, Breaking the Conflict Trap: Civil War and Development Policy, http://econ.worldbank.org/ prr/CivilWarPRR/text-26671/

Kuper, J. 1997, *International Law Concerning Child Civilians in Armed Conflict*, Oxford: Oxford University Press.

Machel, G. 2001, *The Impact of War on Children*, Cape Town: David Philip Publishers.

Parsons, I, 2003, 'Youth, Conflict and Identity: Political Mobilisation and Subjection in Angola', in A. McIntyre (ed.), forthcoming in 2004, *The Impact of Children on War: Young People as Conflict Stakeholders in Africa*, Pretoria: Institute for Security Studies.

Stavrou, A. 2003, 'Youth Mobilization in Uganda', in A. McIntyre (ed.), forthcoming in 2004, *The Impact of Children on War: Young People as Conflict Stakeholders in Africa*, Pretoria: Institute for Security Studies.

UNAIDS 2000, http://www.UNAIDS.org.

United Nations Commission on Human Rights 2001, Fifty-eighth session, Item 13 of the provisional agenda, E/CN.4/2002/86, 9 November, p. 9.

Veale, A. 2003, 'From Child Soldier to Ex-fighter: Female Fighter, Demobilization and Reintegration in Ethiopia', Institute for Security Studies Monograph no. 85, Pretoria: Institute for Security Studies.

11

Warriors, hooligans and mercenaries: Failed statehood and the violence of young male pastoralists in the Horn of Africa

Simon Simonse

The decline in the effectiveness of the state in the Horn of Africa is matched by an upswing in the importance of local, community-based, military actors. This tendency is particularly marked in the pastoralist areas that have always remained marginal to state control. It boosts the martial role of young herdsmen as providers of security for their communities and also offers them opportunities for violent adventures, cattle-raiding and highway banditry. This chapter presents a case study of the role of young men in endemic pastoral conflict in Karamoja, Uganda to illustrate this point. Recent government measures to bring these young men under control – by disarming them or by co-opting them into the state's security forces – only seem to have deepened the failure of the state. It is suggested that governmental and civil-society actors should make a concerted effort to recognize the warrior herdsmen as a major stakeholder in peace, security and development.

Introduction

This chapter deals with a category of contemporary young African men who lead very violent lives: the warrior herdsmen of northeastern Africa. In contrast to the young rebels and religious converts that form the subjects of other chapters in this book, these are people whose primary ambitions are not to replace or to conserve a particular political regime. Nor are they recruits of political entrepreneurs or of economic adventurers. Their cultural pedigree shows little admixture with the political values associated with the post-colonial state or with the religious values of world religions.[1]

While the owners and managers of livestock are usually aged patriarchs, the actual herding of the cattle is done by young male adults. Boys under 14 years of age take care of small livestock that stay in the vicinity of the homestead, and adolescents and young adults lead the cattle to dry-season pastures a considerable distance from the village. Most African herdsmen occupy an ecological niche that requires cattle to move away from the permanent settlements to wetter areas where temporary camps, the so-called 'cattle camps' are established. The ecological duality of the existence of the pastoralists is emphasized by cultural forms. Life away from the village and beyond the control of elders is more sportsmanlike, youthful and martial (Zanen & Van den Hoek 1987: 170-96). In the cattle camps the herdsmen meet and mix not only with herdsmen from different villages of their own ethnic communities but also with herdsmen from communities that are culturally different. Relations with some of these strangers are friendly, a friendliness that may be institutionalized by the mutual loaning of cattle so that both friends become 'bond partners'. With other strangers relations are hostile. They are likely to be suspected of cattle theft and their proximity requires a permanent state of alertness. They are also a legitimate target for raids. The dry-season pastures are not only associated with the youthful joys of freedom from authority but also with the dangers of war. Herdsmen need to be well armed in the cattle camps. In the past, most northeastern African herdsmen used spears but nowadays they have automatic rifles. The wars in Congo, Sudan, Ethiopia and Somalia have brought millions of guns to the region.

The heavy armament of the pastoralists of northeastern Africa is the result of three complementary trends. Since the Congo rebellion of 1965 huge numbers of small arms have been pouring into the region where war has been intermittent. For over 40 years the superpowers and regional governments have supplied their varying allies – be they rebels or governments – with small arms and many, if not most, of these arms have now ended up in civilian hands.[2]

Another trend is the relentless weakening of the state in the region, especially in its capacity to provide security for its citizens. While most state armies have grown in size, the effectiveness of their control of state subjects has

---

[1] This chapter is based on my experiences as a project leader and research coordinator for Pax Christi Netherlands, one of the international civil-society organizations that contributes to the United Nations Agenda to Combat Small-Arms Proliferation.

[2] According to an official estimate by the Inter-Governmental Authority on Development (IGAD) that links Ethiopia, Eritrea, Sudan, Kenya, Uganda, Somalia, and Djibouti, the figure could be as high as 5 million.

dramatically decreased. Compared to the colonial state with its relatively small armies, the post-colonial state is far less effective in extending its protection to the marginal areas inhabited by pastoralists. But even the colonial state never fully succeeded in establishing a monopoly on the legitimate use of force in the marginal pastoral areas. Despite harsh punishments (for example, hanging) and scheduled cross-border meetings between local administrators of different colonial territories, the practice of cattle-raiding persisted until independence. Post-independence civil wars sucked the army and police away from the marginal areas where the pastoralists live, redeploying them to areas of strategic interest.

A third factor that has increased the potential for conflict in pastoral areas is the pressure on resources. As a result of the population increase, many of the better and wetter grazing areas were occupied by farmers or were allocated to development projects. With arms always readily available and state security absent, conflicts between pastoral communities have acquired a violent dynamic of their own and have become endemic.

Self-help security in the context of state failure

In most of the Horn of Africa gun ownership remained the prerogative of chiefs and big men until the 1960s. These were guns that could shoot at most 10 rounds at a time. The wars in Congo and Sudan brought in automatic rifles, and the ownership of such weapons was soon within reach of pastoralists of average wealth. At a price of 20 head of cattle per gun, a weapon was – for owners of large herds – a worthwhile investment in their personal security. For adventurers it meant a shortcut to wealth. From the early 1980s onwards, as a result of abundant supplies, the value gradually dropped to present levels: one head of cattle (or less depending on the firearm's state of maintenance) close to the source (war-torn areas of Sudan, Somalia), or up to 10 head of cattle at the ends of the supply lines (in Tanzania for example).

Of the estimated five million small arms in the IGAD countries, the overwhelming majority are used illegally at the grass-roots level, many, if not most of them, by the pastoralists.

Purchase is not the only way of procuring a gun. Many private guns have been acquired by enrolment in rebel groups or militias. Depending on the fortunes of war, soldiers desert and keep their guns. For example, there was large-scale desertion after the split in the Sudan People's Liberation Army

At a borehole in Buya-Didinga County, South Sudan. Before reaching the age
of *karacuna*, boys are thoroughly familiar with guns.
Photo courtesy of E. Kurimoto

(SPLA) in 1991. In an attempt to 'buy' their support, communities were armed
by rebel groups and/or states. Groups changing sides more than once were able
to build up huge arsenals. The Toposa of South Sudan are a case in point.

As a result of the proliferation of arms, there has been a gradual shift in the
character of intra-state conflict. In the 1970s and 1980s the adversaries of the
regime in power snatched portions of territory from the control of the state step
by step, and established their own system of control. The communities remained
more or less passive during a change of guard. To use the famous metaphor, the
communities were like 'the grass trampled by the fighting elephants'. Once the
non-state actors take control, their exercise of authority is modelled on that of a
top-down state.

This pattern changed in the 1990s when many communities acquired
sufficient stocks of arms to be reckoned with as a military entity. The nature of
the relationship between the protagonists in the war and local communities
tilted. From subjects to be liberated or to be brought under control, grass-roots

communities were now being approached and integrated in the war as allies. In exchange for their support, they received a measure of military protection, supplies of guns and ammunition, and access to humanitarian relief supplies and services. Gradually the top-down structure of the beginning of the war acquired a bottom-up dimension, making the state or non-state actor vulnerable to defections. A large part of the current intra-state conflict focuses on this vulnerability. Snatching allies away from one another has become an important strategy of war.

For the local communities this means a widening of their scope of initiative. The state or non-state actors to which they are linked have an interest in keeping them on their side. They are encouraged to attack communities belonging to the adversary. When communities who enjoy protection from the same state or non-state actor raid one another, the lack of mechanisms of adjudication only leaves two options: either to adopt a *laissez-faire* attitude or to display a show of strength, usually in the form of a punitive expedition. Any booty taken is confiscated by the actor meting out the punishment. In this context of lawlessness local communities are thrown back on themselves and are forced to set their own security objectives, build their own defence capacity, secure regular supplies of arms and ammunition, and forge defensive alliances with other communities, militias, rebels or state armies. Partial or complete self-reliance in security matters characterizes the condition in which many of the pastoralist communities in the Horn now find themselves. While the situation in the various countries of the Greater Horn is the outcome of specific trajectories, the end result is strikingly similar.

In the Kenya of the 1990s the arming of local communities was a strategy in the struggle between the incumbent government and the political opposition. The government, wanting to maintain its hold on the centre at all costs, instigated the constituencies supporting the government party to use violence to intimidate the mostly ethnic constituencies of the opposition. This localized violence was in turn used as a propaganda argument against multipartyism, proving the importance of the central government's unifying role.

In Somalia the state collapsed under the pressure of clan-based factional fighting and the country now consists of rival and, as far as security is concerned, self-reliant clans and factions. As the slow progress of the peace process shows, the clan factions are reluctant to surrender their military independence to a jointly approved monopolist of physical force.

There is a similar shift in southern Sudan. When the strong centralism that characterized the SPLA collapsed in the split of 1991, the SPLA was forced to regain its control of the south by forging deals with local factional leaders, militias and communities.

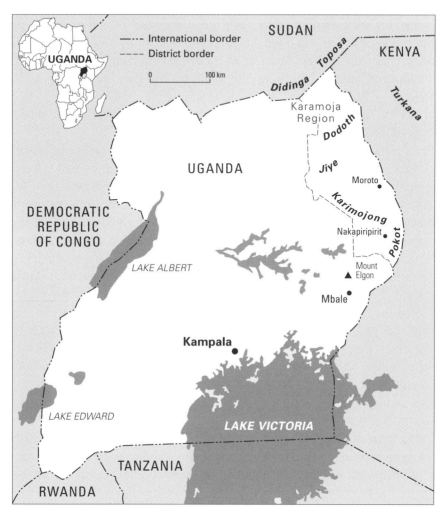

Map 11.1 Uganda and the Karamoja region

After the ruthless centralism of the Ethiopian *derg*, there is now a situation where the regime's survival depends on the continuation of existing divisions between nationalities that do not support the regime. State measures touching on local control of security, such as attempts to reduce the possession of illegal arms, are therefore viewed as a threat to the fragile status quo. While the armed communities fear the establishment of a genuine monopoly of the use of violence by the state, the regime fears the destabilizing consequences of an escalating confrontation.[1]

In Uganda, the largest pastoralist group, the Karimojong, became allies with the young Museveni regime to repress the Teso rebellion. Since then, the government has been opportunistic in its dealings with the Karimojong. In times of stress they are called upon to put their military capacity to the service of the state. At other times, they are treated as rivals to the state's ambition to monopolize the legitimate use of physical force.

The shared picture for the IGAD countries at the beginning of new millennium is that of a decline in the effectiveness of the state and of state-like actors in providing security to the subjects under their protection. Parallel and complementary to this, there is an upswing in the importance of dispersed, community-based military capacities. The superiority of the centre is to a large extent dependent on its capacity to win over these dispersed military actors, or to neutralize their effectiveness by fomenting rivalry between them. From a claim to integral control over a bounded territory, state power has turned into the cumulative effect of a network of alliances. It is in this context of a weak state glad to shed the burden of patrolling vast and thinly populated territories that pastoralist communities are reverting to self-help security mechanisms.

There is a striking parallel here with a typological distinction introduced by the anthropologist Aidan Southall in his study of the state systems of pre-colonial East Africa. He distinguished the 'hierarchical state model' of Buganda and Rwanda from the 'pyramidal state model' of the Alur. In the pyramidal case, the power of the centre is the sum of its constituent units. The power varies with the strength of the appeal of the centre or, in other words, with the massiveness of the response from the periphery (Southall 1970).

Generational dynamics and conflict in the Karimojong cluster

In this context of military self-reliance in the midst of generalized insecurity, the fit and able-bodied male members of pastoral communities are gaining a renewed social importance. This sets the scene for a specific kind of association between youth and violence in present-day Africa. To highlight this association, this chapter presents the case of the warriors of Karamoja in northeastern Uganda. Karamoja is home to a dozen ethnic groups, the majority of which speak languages of the Karimojong cluster. These are the Karimojong them-

---

[1] For western Ethiopia these tendencies have been analyzed in detail by Abbink (1994, 2004), Feyissa (2003), Kurimoto (1997), Masuda (2001) and Matsuda (1997).

selves (who have now broken up into three groups which act as independent units: the Bokora, Matheniko and Pian), the Dodoth and the Jie. Karimojong speakers also include the Turkana of Kenya, the Toposa and the Jiye of Sudan and the Nyangatom of Sudan and Ethiopia. The peoples of the Karimojong cluster are also referred to as Ateker or Ngitunga. Some of the neighbouring non-Karimojong peoples, the Ethur and the Tepeth in Karamoja, the Pokot in Uganda and Kenya and the Didinga in Sudan show considerable assimilation into the Ngitunga way of life.

These peoples broadly share the same principles of socio-political organization: central is the generational and age system. The 'Fathers' have sovereign, if not divine, powers and are the addressees of their sons' sacrifices. When they have lived their span, their Sons as a collectivity succeed them and become the Fathers of the Land. Recruitment to these generational groupings is by age-set. Young men of the same age join in the activities associated with the cattle camp and in war. An age-set passes through successive age-grades: from that of young boy to that of elder. The age-grade of the men between 15 and 30 years of age is that of the *karacuna*, the warriors.[2]

Central to the culture of the Karimojong cluster is what could be called the 'enemy complex'.[3] Unity of identity is primarily expressed in opposition to the enemy. Violence aimed at an enemy is not only socially approved, it also marks the progression to full membership of the society. In the past, a man proudly showed the scarification marks cut into his upper arm as part of the purification ceremony following homicide. He also acquired a praise name derived from the circumstances in which 'his' enemy had been killed. While the killer-marks and praise songs have become rare because of the impact of the church and the police, the battlefield continues to be an arena where a man can gain distinction, not only in the eyes of his fellow warriors but also in those of the Fathers and nubile women.

In the public debate on the causes of conflict and arms proliferation, the *karacuna*, who are said to be beyond the control of their Fathers, carry much of

---

[2] I cannot enter here into the problem the Ngitunga have in delimiting the span of a generation. It is obvious that unless each generation strictly limits the period during which a man procreates, generation spans will get larger with each successive generation. The Ngitunga do not have such rules and, as such, they contrast with the peoples practicing the *gada* system (the Boran-Oromo and the Konso, for instance). For a deeper analysis of the age and generation systems, see Baxter & Almagor (1978) and Kurimoto & Simonse (1998). Well-known monographs of the peoples of the Karimojong cluster include Gulliver (1955), Marshall-Thomas (1966), Dyson-Hudson (1966), Lamphear (1976, 1992), Müller (1989) and Tornay (2001).
[3] This concept has been developed as an anthropological model in Simonse (1992: 24-28).

the blame. The gun has made them independent of their Fathers, who are afraid to carry out old-time sanctions against their disobedient sons. Among the Karimojong proper, very few representatives are left of the Mountains (*Ngimoru*), the generation of Fathers, and this may help to explain their weakness. The Mountains, who assumed their responsibilities in 1956, represent less than 1 per cent of the population, live in different places and are often too old to move around.[4]

Others emphasize the marginality of the *karacuna* in decision-making. Because they are not involved in community decisions they have no commitment to the common interest and feel free to indulge in their sport of cattle-raiding. By living dangerously, they win the admiration of young ladies and their peers.

Recent research, however, indicates that there is more collusion between elders and young men than these observations would suggest (De Koning 2004: 11-16). In the midst of the present insecurity, the elderly men depend on the young men to protect their cattle. Raiders normally ask a blessing from their father and, after a successful raid, the elders usually happily accept part of the raided cattle. A successful raider not only gains credit for his courage but also for his generosity after the raid. Some of the raided cattle are sold to the slaughterhouses in the south of the country before the young men reach home, with the money being used for conspicuous consumption and the buying of bullets.

The raids also allow for long-term investments that will make the young men more independent of their elders. Bridewealth is paid from the family herd and each son or younger brother has to wait his turn before he can marry. This is a father's main lever of power over his sons. Raided cattle allow a young man to circumvent this power. He chooses a girl, who then becomes pregnant, and provides her with milking cows. He then gives his in-laws a first instalment of bridewealth to ensure that the girl's father does not marry her off to someone else. If the young man is lucky in raiding, he can start his own family at the age of 20 whereas following the time-honoured procedure would take him on average a further fifteen years to do so. A successful young raider may start two or three marriages in this way. If they are not lucky and cannot pay the first bridewealth instalments they may lose all of these 'half-wives' (De Koning 2004: 25-28).

Interestingly De Koning's findings among the Jie of Kotido District, the northernmost district of Karamoja, suggest that poverty is not a prime causal factor in raiding. Sons of rich families engage as much, if not more, in raiding

---

[4] This is based on the number of Ngimoru still alive in Bokora (Gomes 2002: 271).

than their peers from poorer households. An important trigger for raiding is the experience of vulnerability and loss. Being the victim of a raid puts both poor and rich on the war path. Since the rich have more to lose they may raid more frequently. De Koning's findings would suggest that the cattle warlordism that is found among the Pokot of western Kenya – where military entrepreneurs recruit young men (in groups of up to 500 or more) for raids and sell the booty off to slaughterhouses and markets in order to buy commodities for the shops they own – has not developed in Kotido District. However, it does exist among the Matheniko of Central Karamoja. In an interview, young Matheniko warriors admitted that they raided to get money for food (Mkutu & Gomes 2004: 24-27) and they acknowledged that many raids were organized by well-known kraal-leaders with the express purpose of selling the raided animals. Cattle war-lordism was first reported among the Pokot of Kenya in the early 1980s (Osamba 2000) and it is clear that the system is spreading in Karamoja. It can be seen as a logical response to the increased inequality in cattle ownership (Mkutu & Gomes 2004: 27-29). No reliable data are available on the extent of cattle warlordism or on the speed with which it is spreading.

Warrior herdsmen as hooligans

Automatic rifles were acquired by the Karimojong in large numbers in 1979 after the fall of Idi Amin. The Matheniko, on whose territory the army barracks were located, opened the arms store and looted it. Estimates of the number of rifles taken vary from 12,000 to 60,000.[5] The arms were immediately used by the Matheniko to settle outstanding scores with the Bokora. The scale on which this happened set in motion a cycle of revenge and an arms race that continues to the present day. It has undermined the reunification of the Karimojong into a single group and ingrained the division among Pian, Bokora and Matheniko, a case of ethnogenesis in our time.[6] Idi Amin's government was the last to have

---

[5] Wangoola (1999) mentions the number of 12,000 guns (mainly G3s) while Muhereza (1997), an authority on Karamoja affairs, has come up with the figure of 60,000.

[6] When Dyson-Hudson (1966: 104-54) carried out research in the 1950s, the Karimo-jong had ten territorial sections that formed a single political unit in the sense that there was no warfare between the different groups. While these divisions are still recognized for ritual purposes, they have, as a result of processes of segmentary balancing of military force, divided into three large clusters centred on the numerically and militarily stronger groups of Pian, Matheniko and Bokora. There is no reason why in future the three groups should not recognize their common identity. In a sense they still do: the ethnonym Karimojong is used for all the Akarimojong-speaking peoples of Karamoja,

clear military superiority over the Karimojong – a superiority that manifested itself in excessive brutality. Since 1980 successive civil wars have absorbed most of the available military capacity. Attempts to create a semblance of state control have never got very far. Over the same period, the military capacity of the Karimojong – in terms of armaments, coordination and fighting skills – have improved. Numbers and equipment being equal, the average soldier in the national army is considered to be no match for the Karimojong warrior.

Due to a steady flow of arms since the outbreak of the civil war in Sudan there is an over-supply of different sorts of guns (ADOL 2001: 97-110, Adwok Nyaba 2001: 7-96). Ammunition, however, is often in short supply, with a negative correlation in the fluctuation of the prices of bullets and guns. If ammunition is expensive or difficult to come by, the price of guns falls. Estimates of the number of guns vary but a conservative estimate puts the number at 40,000. This is the figure used by the government, which has an interest in keeping the figure low in order to be able to boost the percentage of guns it collected (in 2002) or may collect in future. A round figure that is often mentioned is 100,000, a number that corresponds to the assumption that every nuclear family owns at least one gun except for marginal groups (for example, the Ik), agriculturists (the Ethur of Labwor) and the poorest sectors of the population. The main pressure for disarmament is coming from the constituencies bordering Karamoja.

As a result of the omnipresence of arms, conflicts have become more deadly and more difficult to solve. Traditional mechanisms of conflict resolution, indigenous punitive sanctions as well as state-based judiciary procedures are not able to cope with the increasing number of cases. The extent of the violence can be illustrated by relating one sequence of internal conflicts that culminated in September 1999. After a battle between the Matheniko and the Jie, the army dispatched an expedition to recover the cattle stolen from the Matheniko. The Ugandan army confiscated the wrong cattle, which then prompted an attack by the Jie on the army in which six soldiers and seven Matheniko auxiliaries were killed. This led to a retaliatory operation by the army and the deaths of two more soldiers and a policeman. In the same week, the Bokora, allies of the Jie, revenged an attack by Matheniko which had taken place in July on the village of Turutuko in which 110 Bokora had been killed. In the counterattack, 240

---

including the Jie, Dodoth and Tepeth but sometimes excluding the Pokot (southern Nilotes of the Kalenjin cluster), Ethur (western Nilotes of the Lwo cluster), Ik and Ngikadam (Kuliak-speakers), etc. The distinction introduced by some intellectuals between the term Karamojong for the peoples of Karamoja in this last sense, and Karimojong for the members of the above-mentioned ten territorial sections has not (yet) sunk in.

Bokora warriors were killed. Again the army intervened, using a helicopter gunship to stop the counterattack by the Jie-Bokora alliance. While aiming at the Bokora, many Matheniko, who were being helped in their pursuit of the Bokora by Turkana warriors, were shot by the government helicopter. According to a newspaper report, the death toll amounted to 600. This was not the total extent of warfare in September. The Pian, the southern group of the Karimojong, were at that time involved in raiding the Sabiny, their southern neighbours living on the lower slopes of Mount Elgon. During one attack they lost 42 men, killing three soldiers and injuring twelve others (*New Vision*, 23 September 1999). In late September 1999 the whole of Karamoja was up in arms. The insecurity in northeastern Uganda acquired an international dimension and the Kenyan government deployed its army, police, police reservists and home guard all the way along its border with Karamoja to ward off an attack by the Karimojong on the Pokot (*Monitor*, 1 October 1999; *East African*, 12 October 1999).

This account shows how easily the government can become entangled in these conflicts and end up as just another warring party in a cycle of revenge, being allied to some groups and fighting others. The most common scenario for government involvement in the general chaos is when it confiscates cattle, either on behalf of a raided group or as a punishment. When recovering cattle, the chances that it will identify the right animals are minimal. The rightful owners will then seek ways to get their cattle back. If the government confiscates cattle as a collective punishment, the whole community may rise up in arms. Such situations are aggravated when the confiscated cattle are sold or eaten by the soldiers – a fairly common occurrence.

The small-arms violence has not only increased quantitatively, in terms of the number of victims of violence, but also qualitatively, in terms of the choice of targets. Social categories that used to be taboo as targets of war – women, children and old men – are now killed and there has been an enormous increase in highway violence, which has made Karamoja a very dangerous place for any car to venture. Cars are frequently attacked after a failed raid when the returning raiders vent their frustrations on a soft target. But hijackings and car theft do not depend only on the frustrations of raiders: the headmaster of Moroto High School casually informed me that he had found out that some of his pupils had collected their school fees by staging ambushes on the road. The same arbitrariness in killing is found in South Sudan, where a man may be killed for his rifle or his bicycle without any prior warning. Such cold-blooded killings are considered a major challenge to post-conflict peace-building.

The reduction in the availability of grazing land is popularly stated as the root cause of this violence and brutality being carried out by young men. And it is true that sizeable tracts of good grazing land have been commandeered for national parks and game reserves, and that, despite large numbers of men being killed in fighting and low life-expectancy rates, the population is growing. Yet, the violence is also a cause of reduced resources. Grazing areas in the no-man's land between communities have become no-go areas as a result of the insecurity. For reasons of safety, the herdsmen now live in larger groups than in the past. In addition, the cattle brought home from raids on neighbouring districts (Teso, Acholi) may have increased the total number of cattle owned by the people of Karamoja, as Table 11.1 suggests.

The impact of this violence is now being widely felt. Estimates of the sex ratio in Karamoja give a figure of 4 women to every 3 men, and it is not exceptional to find women who have lost two or three husbands in succession to violence. In Sudan, I heard a woman testifying during peace negotiations that she had lost five husbands; she had been passed down from one brother to the next, all five of whom had been killed in raiding and local warfare.

Table 11.1 Livestock trends 1980-1998

District	1980	1989	1998	Loss/Gain
Apac	183,725	46,000	83,054	-100,671
Lira	244,442	10,000	41,000	-203,442
Gulu	101,786	11,000	4,700	-97,086
Kitgum	155,106	5,000	4,263	-150,843
Kotido*	**226,000**	**400,000**	**420,000**	**+194,000**
Moroto*	**282,000**	**600,000**	**450,000**	**+168,000**
Soroti	317,563	20,000	92,424	-225,139
Kumi	135,000	150,000	53,169	-81,831
Total	1,330,622	1,104,000	1,148,610	

* The districts in bold form Karamoja.
Source: C. Ocan (1992) 'Pastoral Crisis in North-Eastern Uganda: The Changing Significance of Cattle Raids', Working Paper, Centre for Basic Research (CBR), Kampala.

Life expectancy in Karamoja is the lowest in Uganda, lower even than in the Acholi districts affected by the war between the government and the Lord's Resistance Army (LRA).[7] According to the Uganda Bureau of Statistics in 2003, the Human Poverty Index and the Human Development Index in Karamoja are the lowest in Uganda.

---

[7] The Lord's Resistance Army is a rebel movement that is currently fighting the Uganda government in northern Uganda.

The failure of state-driven disarmament

As the ambition to control all of its territory and its subjects is the very motor of state power, the government has repeatedly tried to disarm the Karimojong. During his second term in office (1980-1985), President Milton Obote made two attempts, both of which ended in failure. In 1987, soon after Museveni had come to power, he also failed to achieve disarmament. The Karimojong warriors offered fierce resistance and hundreds of government soldiers died in the process. Halfway through the operation the government made an about-turn: they engaged the Karimojong to fight the Teso rebels and provided them with more arms. Since the Karimojong did not pose a direct threat to the sovereignty of the Ugandan state, which had more pressing problems at hand, the arms were tolerated.

This changed in the late 1990s when the violence in Karamoja reached dramatic levels. The crisis coincided with a build-up of international attention on the issue of small-arms proliferation that resulted in the Nairobi Declaration on Small Arms and Light Weapons of 15 March 2000 and the United Nations 'Conference on the Illicit Trade in Small Arms and Light Weapons in All Its Aspects'.[8] Karamoja parliamentarians pleaded for a non-violent approach to the disarmament of their people and welcomed this international attention. There was wide support, in Karamoja and in the country at large, in favour of measures to stop the proliferation of small arms. Since the population of Karamoja was considered to be generally pro-government, Karamoja seemed to be an ideal place for an exercise to improve controls of the use and transfer of small arms at the grass-roots level. Except in Tanzania and Kenya, opportunities for civil-society action against small arms in other countries in the region are limited. In countries at war (Congo, Sudan, Burundi), small arms illegally held by civilians are needed for protection. In other countries (Ethiopia, Somalia), arms are part of the political equation between different regions, ethnic groups and clans. Any appeal for arms reduction triggers suspicions as to who the beneficiaries will be.

---

[8] For details of 'The Nairobi Declaration on the Problem of the Proliferation of Illicit Small Arms and Light Weapons in the Great Lakes Region and the Horn Of Africa', see http://www.saligad.org/declarations/declaraition_nairobi.html. The report of the United Nations 'Conference on the Illicit Trade in Small Arms and Light Weapons in All Its Aspects' (9-20 July 2001) is available on the UN website http://disarmament2.un.org/cab/smallarms/files/aconf192_15.pdf, along with other documents relating to the UN-led 'International Programme of Action to Prevent, Combat and Eradicate the Illicit Trade in Small Arms and Light Weapons in All Its Aspects'.

Western peace organizations saw the opportunity offered by the Karamoja situation and developed, in consultation with politicians, high-ranking government officials and academics from the Karamoja region, a scenario for a step-by-step voluntary disarmament based on community participation (Karamoja Parliamentary Group 1999, Limlim 2000, Pax Christi 2000). In view of the continuing war situation in Sudan to the north and in the Acholi districts to the west of Karamoja, it was unrealistic to advocate immediate disarmament, even if that had been an option. Action would have to concentrate initially on resolving existing inter-communal conflicts and, secondly, on the strengthening of mechanisms of conflict resolution and the establishment of judicial institutions. Next there would have to be an awareness campaign reaching out at the grass-roots levels. As a third step, communities would be able to assume responsibility for the arms in their possession as part of their security arrangements. This should happen in a transparent way both internally and externally, for example by establishing a public register of the guns owned by the community and by setting up a procedure that would submit the use of guns to approval by a committee accountable to the community. By the time a degree of peace and internal security had been achieved in the area, many of the guns would have become redundant. The document proposed that they could then be exchanged at an advantageous rate against developmental inputs through a fund managed by the communities at the sub-county level.[9] This scenario received support from civil-society forums and organizations in Karamoja, from the Karamoja Parliamentary Group, from the elected authorities at the district level, from ministers and civil servants who originated from Karamoja, and from the main coordination body of donors. When the two ministers of state responsible for Karamoja affairs and for the reconstruction of the north submitted it to the security committee of the Cabinet, it was rejected. It was later leaked that the main objection came from the army, which did not approve of the idea of the collected guns being destroyed. There may have been other, unreported, objections against donor involvement in issues that touched directly on security.

In the meantime, parliament's recommendations resulted in the Disarmament Act issued in December 2000.[10] The policy guidelines accommodated the views

---

[9] Reckoning from the bottom level (the parish), the sub-county is the political and administrative unit at the third level comprising several villages (second level). Each sub-county in Karamoja has between 15,000 and 20,000 inhabitants.

[10] The Disarmament Act of December 2002 had the following stated objectives: (i) to stop armed Karimojong from terrorizing their neighbours in Uganda, Kenya and Sudan; (ii) to stop inter-clan terrorism within Karamoja and the infiltration of arms; (iii) to deploy the Uganda People's Defence Forces (UPDF), Local Defence Units (LDUs) and vigilantes in strategic areas within Karamoja and along the boarders to ensure protection

of the Karamoja parliamentarians as well as those of the parliamentarians of Teso and Acholi, the main victims of Karimojong small-arms violence. However, the government never translated the Act into a plan of action. Finally, on 24-25 January 2001, a whole year later, the date of disarmament was divulged to be 7 February 2001 (i.e. in two weeks' time). This decision was in immediate response to pressure from Teso leaders speaking on behalf of their constituencies who were angered by new Karimojong incursions. The Karamoja parliamentarians protested, fearing a punitive approach by the army. They demanded that the operation be postponed until a plan of action and a methodology were developed (*New Vision*, 7 February 2001). The motion was accepted.

The plan was never made because the government was playing for time. With the elections in sight, the president did not want to antagonize the Teso and Acholi electorate by being seen to pamper the Karimojong with a 'soft' disarmament package, nor did he want to lose support among the generally pro-government Karimojong. For six months, disarmament disappeared from the front pages of the press. On 14 September 2001, a group of Pian warriors attacked the market in the Ngariam Internally Displaced Persons' Camp and killed around twenty inhabitants, injuring another ten. In revenge, seven Bokora and two Teso – having been mistaken for Karimojong – were lynched by an angry mob. The bloodbath prompted a general outcry for the effective and immediate disarmament of the Karimojong. The president was now under real pressure to be seen to be acting on the issue.

The disarmament campaign was launched on 2 December 2001. It was to consist of a voluntary period of one month to be followed by the forced disarmament of those who had not yet handed in their guns. Again there was no overall plan. On the eve of the campaign the president announced that no compensation would be offered for any arms surrendered since the owners of the guns were law-breakers. A certificate would be all they would receive. Later, however, corrugated-iron sheets and ox ploughs were offered but supplies were exhausted after only a few days. Certificates were not ready. The donors who had initially taken an interest in the disarmament process were not

---

of life and property; (iv) to enlist support for the peaceful disarmament of people at the grass-roots level through rigorous sensitization programmes; (v) to cooperate with Kenya and Sudan in a concurrent disarmament of the Turkana and Didinga; (vi) to stop the illegal trafficking of guns from Sudan and Kenya into Uganda; (vii) to resettle and rehabilitate those who surrendered guns and ensure the socio-economic transformation of Karamoja; (viii) to improve radio communication to allow the effective dissemination of information and education; and (ix) to strengthen the police and the judiciary to ensure peace and the administration of justice.

consulted beforehand so they were not ready when the president called upon them to supply the incentives and to help build security roads along the Ugandan border to intercept arms traffickers and offer protection against cattle raids from across the Sudanese and Kenyan borders. The voluntary period was extended by an extra month, which ended on 2 February 2002.

There was no systematic peace-building to prepare the ground for disarmament. Awareness-raising only happened in a top-down method during the first phase of the campaign. There was no consensus building in the villages and no special attempts were made to explain the disarmament to those who were carrying guns. The calculation seemed to be that fear of the use of force would be sufficient to win everyone, or almost everyone, over. The most significant campaigner was the president himself and it was largely due to his popularity that, in a two-month period, almost 8,000 guns were collected. In view of the continued insecurity and the hurried preparations of the campaign this was an impressive number and showed, more than anything else, the good will of the Karimojong and the popularity of the president.

The difficulties started with the second phase of disarmament when the army was allowed to use force to collect arms. The amnesty period for those holding illegal guns was over and in response to resistance from gun owners, the army acted in ways that prompted accusations of human-rights violations. A donor team, which was ready to identify development inputs that would make the disarmament sustainable, had to cancel its visit when informed of the accusations. The Civil Military Operation Centres, which had been established under the Uganda Human Rights Commission at the start of the disarmament operation, lacked the necessary experience and support among the local population to deal effectively with these human-rights violations (Uganda Human Rights Commission 2002).

Forced collections turned into a debacle. In the four months from February to July 2002 only 2,000 guns were collected, just a quarter of the number that had previously been turned in on a voluntary basis in half of the time. Armed groups of *karacuna* raided communities that had surrendered their guns and by August 2002 the situation was back to where it had been before disarmament began. However there were two differences now: the illusion that disarmament could be a quick process was gone, and arms were no longer being carried in public. Otherwise, cattle-raiding was still a serious problem, communities and households that had disarmed were reported to be re-arming, and trafficking in arms was booming.

Warrior herdsmen as mercenaries

To address the antagonism between the communities and the government, the army responded with a recruitment campaign among warriors – with preference being given to those with a reputation in raiding – in order to form new paramilitary units. This was not a new strategy as the idea had originated in the mid-1990s among local politicians who were helped by the church. The 'vigilantes' as the paramilitaries were then called were initially very successful in reducing the numbers of raids, but by 1999 they had lost their independence and had become mixed up in inter-sectional warfare and cattle-raiding politics. Some of the vigilante commanders were *de-facto* generals of ethnic or sectional warrior bands. At the time this was the reason for the government to replace the old force with a new paramilitary formula: the Anti-Stock Theft Unit (ASTU). They incorporated some of the old-time vigilantes while excluding others. Like the vigilantes, the ASTUs lived in their own communities, enjoyed a modest monthly allowance and were legally allowed to carry guns.

However, because of the close relations between ASTUs and their communities of origin, they were considered incapable of completing the disarmament process. In accordance with the Disarmament Act, they were therefore replaced by Local Defence Units (LDUs), a paramilitary structure that already existed in other parts of Uganda. These consisted of *karacuna*, former ASTUs and former vigilantes. The plan was to locate them in strategic places, for instance the no-man's land that had been vacated as a result of the insecurity, in units in which rival sections and ethnic groups would be mixed. Each of Karamoja's eight counties would have 600 of them. In addition to disarmament, their tasks would include the sealing-off of Karamajo's external borders against attacks from outside and against arms traffickers. Vigilantes and ASTUs who had not been incorporated into the LDU structure continued as armed home guards guarding cattle camps – a role recognized by the government. The arms surrendered by aspiring LDUs who received new ones from the army were sometimes handed to these home guards. On the basis of the quality of the arms, one could distinguish two classes of paramilitaries: those working with the army and those working for the communities.

Unlike the ASTUs and vigilantes, the LDUs were stationed in the army barracks. During their first period of operation their primary role was not to disarm their communities but to act as an auxiliary force to the UPDF in the war against the Lord's Resistance Army. They were enrolled as second-rank soldiers, a reason for a number of them to desert and return to their communities of origin. This again led to fighting between loyal LDUs and those who had deserted. Despite the attachment of the LDUs to the army, their loyalty to their communities of origin came first. This was the other major reason for the defection of so many LDUs. During a workshop on community security in Karamoja in 2003, the LDU participants took a clear stand, declaring that they should be accountable to their communities rather than to the army (Recommendation 4.1 in the Community Security Workshop 2003).

The force that was designed to create a bridge between the army and the community has made the interface between the two only more opaque. What is clear and unchanged, however, is that communities – with or without LDUs, ASTUs, vigilantes or home guards – continue to rely on their own devices and strategies for security and survival.

The situation depicted above is not just one of failed statehood with communities being left to their own devices with an absent or powerless state standing by. It is worse. 'Messed-up statehood' might be a more appropriate term. The fundamental relationship defined by the concept of state is that of an authority having superior (sovereign) power offering protection to groups or individuals who submit to its authority. This submission first of all implies forsaking the use of arms against the authority pretending sovereignty, if not surrendering the arms. In the Karamoja situation there is a state that does not have the capacity to protect its subjects. Yet it is demanding the surrender of their arms, while simultaneously giving arms to local fighters recruited to compensate for the state's inability to protect them. To add insult to injury, these fighters are being forced to help protect the state against the LRA – just as they helped the regime against the Teso rebels in 1987.

In the present situation, the state's monopoly of the legitimate use of physical force exists in name only. In Karamoja its implementation depends on the willingness of *karacuna* to enrol in paramilitary units in exchange for a new gun and a meagre payment. Since the LDUs lack legal status according to the Ugandan constitution, the connection between the state's sources of legitimation and the actual use of force is flimsy at best. Wars are started and ended with the government standing by. If the state army interferes in local fighting, it is, because of its reliance on local auxiliaries, bound to become involved on one side or the other. It is not able to maintain its position as a third party standing above the antagonists.

The creation of paramilitary groups has added a new level of complexity to the relationship between community and state. In many parts of Karamoja there are now two kinds of paramilitaries: the LDUs who are expected to help the army, and the home guards who are supposed to protect the communities. Whether attached to the army or to the communities, the LDUs and home guards have their own loyalties and their own agendas. LDUs leave the army and merge back into the communities if their expectations are not met. From this perspective, the distinction between the legal guns of the paramilitaries and the illegal ones of their brothers in the communities is purely theoretical, and so is the state's claim to a monopoly on the legitimate use of force.

Betting on the warrior herdsmen

The *karacuna* find themselves in the middle of the confusion and are playing a key role in the perpetration of all kinds of violence. They are the raiders admired for their bravery and the cowardly hooligans who attack the vehicles of aid agencies. They are also a vast reservoir of support for the army in its operations inside and outside Karamoja. The *karacuna* embody the key cultural values of the societies of Karamoja and offer a man the opportunity to become a hero in his lifetime. Yet, within the decision-making process they have no say, the *karacuna* are minors when it comes to community affairs. As long as they keep their fathers happy with gifts of raided cattle or the booty won by violence, they will get away with it. It is not only animals they come home with. The money they receive from the sale of cattle and loot is used to impress their entourage with newfangled commodities: bottled beer, watches and radios. Their exclusion from long-term responsibilities is counterbalanced by the prestige generated by their defiance, bravery and generosity. As long as they manage to impress, their violence will continue to be glorious.

The disarmament campaign was met with defiance by the *karacuna*. In 2000 the Action for the Development of Local Communities (ADOL), a local NGO, carried out a survey of attitudes towards disarmament. They compared 1,600 respondents belonging to four social categories: elders and adult women, girls, the elite (officials, businessmen, the educated class) and *karacuna* (see Table 11.2, also ADOL 2001). Among the first three groups, the scores in favour of disarmament were 88 per cent (elders and women), 82 per cent (girls), 89 per cent (the elite). The *karacuna* scored 32 per cent in favour of disarmament.

The *karacuna*'s central role in both socially approved and socially condemned violence, combined with their exclusion from real responsibilities in their communities of belonging, poses an interesting challenge. If the *karacuna* take responsibility for their communities, they could be a powerful force promoting peace and law and order in Karamoja. Therefore, among the various actors able to move the situation of general insecurity and lawlessness in a positive direction, the *karacuna* offer great potential. They may be the key to a home-grown strategy amid Karamoja's chaos.

I do not underestimate the importance of efforts to improve governance by building the capacity of civil servants or the urgency of a reform of the security apparatus. But these measures only target one side of the problem of the failed state. The state is primarily a relationship, a relationship between two agents:

the government in the dominating role and the communities in the role of subject. In this unequal relationship, democratic controls are grafted, turning the subjects into citizens and the ruler into a law-bound system of ad-'ministration' implemented by a civil 'service'. If this primary relationship is bedevilled with 'double binds', the ruler will behave as a military ally today and as a bully tomorrow. The citizens will treat the government as an enemy today, but allow themselves to be recruited by that same government to patrol their own brothers the next day. In such a situation there is no basis on which sustainable governance and security can be built.

Table 11.2 Disarmament in Karamoja

	Respondents		Pro-disarmament		Against disarmament		No opinion	
Group	No.	%	No.	%	No.	%	No.	%
Pastoralist	1,280	80	807	63	358	28	115	9
Non-pastoralist	320	20	301	94	6	2	13	4
Total	1,600	100	1,108	69	364	23	128	8
Ethnicity								
Jie	200	12.5	110	55	70	35	20	10
Dodoth	200	12,5	138	69	42	21	20	10
Labwor	200	12.5	196	98	2	1	2	1
Matheniko	200	12.5	118	59	62	31	20	10
Bokora	200	12.5	152	76	38	19	10	5
Pian	200	12.5	130	65	42	21	28	14
Tepeth	200	12.5	122	61	54	27	24	12
Pokot	200	12.5	142	71	54	27	4	2
Total	1,600	100	1,108		364		128	
Elders/women	656	41	577	88	31	5	48	7
Karacunas (youth)	512	32	163	32	297	58	52	10
Girls	240	15	197	82	25	10	19	8
Others*	192	12	171	89	11	6	9	5
Total	1,600	100	1,108		364		128	

Response to disarmament (spanning header over Pro-disarmament, Against disarmament, No opinion)

* This category includes businessmen, the elite and government representatives.
Source: ADOL (2000) 'Report of the Workshop on Participatory Disarmament in Karamoja', held in Kotide 18-19 December 2000, p. 5.

To normalize the relationship of statehood, both partners in the relationship have a role to play. The government should build its capacity to protect all its subjects effectively, and the subjects should actively promote a government they can trust. If, for historical reasons, the government is not able to provide full protection, and even shifts that burden onto civilians, this fact should be openly acknowledged. In such situations, government and civilians should coordinate their respective contributions to overall security through consultation. Militias deployed in their home areas are bound to have double loyalties. If this fact is not openly recognized it will only confuse communication, especially when they are recruited from communities that are on a war footing, as is the case in Karamoja.

In the civil-society workshop on community security in Karamoja in Moroto in November 2003 this was the gist of many of recommendations. Both government officials and *karacuna* groups demanded openness in communication, joint consultations on security, more community involvement in the Civil Military Operation Centres, and accountability of LDUs to the communities rather than to the army.[11] It was a unique meeting because of the active participation of a good number of *karacuna*. (*Karacuna* do not usually participate in public meetings but if they do, they often remain silent, sometimes grumble or only make occasional defiant remarks.) Here they participated actively in their own working group and most of their input at the meeting related to their exclusion from society at large. Their primary demand was recognition of the contributions that they made to community security on a daily basis.[12] In the final session of the meeting, the *karacuna* decided to establish their own 'Karamoja Association of *Karacuna*', and plan to start by setting up a communication office as a focal point for *karacuna* from different communities.

Peace organizations like to believe that this initiative means important progress towards the emergence of a new type of *karacuna*. If this is true, much will have been achieved: the chance to break the cycles of retaliatory violence and the possibility of an end to marginalization. There will also be losses. Nobody will miss the hooligans. No one will yearn for the paramilitaries. What African nomad-watchers will miss, however, is the heroism and defiance, the noble pastoralist dying for his cows, or standing up to the Leviathan of the state. For them, and for the memory of today's pastoralists, it is to be hoped that the grandsons of today's warriors will revere their grandfathers as models of heroism, rather than the cowboys of Western movies who are the models of the ascending generation.

---

[11] Community Security Workshop (2003). Recommendations: B7 – *karacuna* demanded frankness with the government; B9 appointed leaders demanded open communication with *karacuna,* and prompt and correct reporting; C3 *karacuna* wanted joint security meetings with the government and more community involvement in Civil-Military Coordination Centres; 4.1 LDUs should be made accountable to communities.

[12] Community Security Workshop (2003). Recommendations A3, A10, E7 in the same report.

References

Abbink, J. 1994, 'Changing Pattern of "Ethnic" Violence: Peasant-Pastoralist Confrontation in Southern Ethiopia and its Implications for a Theory of Violence', *Sociologus*, 44 (1): 66-78.

Abbink, J. 2004, 'Ritual and Political Forms of Violence Practice among the Suri of Southern Ethiopia', in T. Young (ed.), *Readings in African Politics*, Oxford: James Currey, pp. 80-89.

ADOL 2000, 'Report of the Workshop on Participatory Disarmament in Karamoja', held in Kotide 18-19 December 2000.

ADOL 2001, 'Arms Trafficking in the Border Regions of Uganda', International Conference on Small Arms Trafficking in the Border Regions of Sudan, Uganda and Kenya: Determining the Issues and Setting the Strategies, Jinja (Uganda), 9-13 November, pp. 97-110; also available on www.paxchristi.nl.

Adwok Nyaba, P. 2001, 'The Disarmament of the Gel-Weng of Bahr-el-Ghazal and the Consolidation of the Nuer-Dinka Peace Agreement', Utrecht: Pax Christi Netherlands, available on www.paxchristi.nl.

Baxter, P.T.W. & U. Almagor (eds) 1978, *Age, Generation, and Time: Some Features of East African Age Organisations*, London: C. Hurst & Co.

Community Security Workshop, Moroto, 20-21 November 2003 'Recommendations', available on www.paxchristi.nl.

Dyson-Hudson, N. 1966, *Karimojong Politics*, Oxford: Clarendon Press.

Feyissa, D. 2003, 'Evaluation Report on the EECMY's Gambela Peace Initiative', Report submitted to Pax Christi, Utrecht.

Gomes, N. 2002, 'Intra and Inter-ethnic Conflicts in Southern Karamoja, Uganda', *L'Afrique Orientale: Annuaire 2002*, Paris: L'Harmattan.

Gulliver, P.H. 1955, *The Family Herds, A Study of Two Pastoral Tribes in East Africa: The Jie and the Turkana*, London: Routledge & Kegan Paul.

Karamoja Parliamentary Group 1999, 'Report on the Consultative Process on Insecurity in the Region', Kampala, 18-30 October.

Koning, R. de 2004, '"What Warriors Want", Young Men's Perspectives on Armed Violence, Peace and Development in Najie, Karamoja', Utrecht: Pax Christi Netherlands.

Kurimoto, E. 1997, 'Politicization of Ethnicity in Gambella Region', in K. Fukui, E. Kurimoto & M. Shigeta (eds), *Ethiopia in Broader Perspective: Papers of the XIIIth International Conference of Ethiopian Studies,*, Kyoto: Shokado Book Sellers, Vol. II, pp. 798-815.

Kurimoto, E. & S. Simonse (eds) 1998, *Conflict, Age and Power in North East Africa*, London: James Currey.

Lamphear, J. 1976, *The Traditional History of the Jie of Uganda*, Oxford: Clarendon Press.

Lamphear, J. 1992, *The Scattering Time: Turkana Responses to Colonial Rule*, Oxford: Clarendon Press.

Limlim, R. 2000, 'Confronting the Current Crisis and Future Challenges of Karamoja and its Neighbourhood', Discussion paper submitted to the President, Kampala.

Marshall-Thomas, E. 1966, *Warrior Herdsmen*, London: Secker & Warburg. (Second edition: New York: W.W. Norton, 1981).

Masuda, K. 2001, 'The Armed Periphery, Memories of Guns and Warfare among the Banna in Southern Ethiopia', Research paper, Kanagawa University. (Also in: *Minzokugaku Kenkyuu* (The Japanese Journal of Ethnology), 65(4):313-340.)

Matsuda, H. 1997, 'How Guns Change the Muguji: Ethnic Identity and Armament the Periphery', in K. Fukui, E. Kurimoto & M. Shigeta (eds), *Ethiopia in Broader Perspective: Papers of the XIIIth International Conference of Ethiopian Studies*, Kyoto: Shokado Book Sellers, vol. II, pp. 471-78.

Mkutu, K. & N. Gomes 2004, 'Breaking the Cycle of Violence: Building Capacity for Peace and Development in Karamoja, Uganda', Research report, Kampala/Utrecht: SNV/Pax Christi.

Muhereza, E.F. 1997, 'Cross-border Grazing and the Challenges for Development in the Dryland Areas of Eastern Africa: The Case of Karamoja', Paper for the International Conference on Economic Integration and Trans-boundary Resources, Ethiopian Institute for Peace and Development, Addis Ababa, 7-13 September.

Müller, H.K. 1989, *Changing Generations: Dynamics of Generations and Age-Sets in Southeastern Sudan (Toposa) and Nortwestern Kenya (Turkana)*, Saarbrücken & Fort Lauderdale: Breitenbach.

Ocan, C. 1992, *Pastoral Crisis in North-Eastern Uganda: The Changing Significance of Cattle Raids*, Kampala: Center for Basic Research (CBR), Working paper.

Osamba, J.O. 2000, 'The Sociology of Insecurity: Cattle Rustling and Banditry in North-Western Kenya', *African Journal on Conflict Resolution*, 1 (2): 11-38.

Pax Christi Netherlands 2000, 'Voluntary Disarmament of Pastoralists: An Integrated, Phased, Community-based Approach, Pilot Project Karamoja', available on www.paxchristi.nl.

Simonse, S. 1992, *Kings of Disaster. Dualism, Centralism and the Scapegoat King in Southeastern Sudan.* Leiden: Brill.

Southall, A.W. 1970, *Alur Society, A Study in Processes and Types of Domination*, Oxford: Oxford University Press.

Tornay, S. 2001, *Les Fusils Jaunes. Générations et Politique en Pays Nyangatom (Éthiopie)*, Nanterre: Société d'Ethnologie.

Uganda Human Rights Commission 2002, 'Civil Military Operation Centres, Karamoja: Joint Lessons Learnt, Evaluation Report', Kampala.

Wangoola, P. 1999, 'Cattle Rustling and Conflicts in N.E. Uganda: Views and Perspectives Reported by Ugandan Papers, 1989-1999', Paper for the Brainstorming Workshop on Cattle Rustling and Conflicts in North Eastern Uganda, Yiga Ngokola Folk Institute, 25-28 October.

Zanen, Sj. M. & A.W. van den Hoek 1987, 'Dinka Dualism and the Nilotic Hierarchy of Values', in R. de Ridder & J.A.J. Karremans (eds), *The Leiden Tradition in Structural Anthropology*, Leiden: Brill, pp. 170-96.

12

Reintegrating young ex-combatants in Sierra Leone: Accommodating indigenous and wartime value systems

Krijn Peters

Present-day tensions in Sierra Leone between the older generation on the one hand and youngsters who participated in the conflict on the other cannot be explained solely in terms of generational conflict between different age-groups. The vast majority of fighters in the Sierra Leonean conflict have grown ucp inside a faction and been socialized by the dominant struture of an armed group. Differences between the various factions in the challenges and threats to survival led to differences in their organizational principles regarding the articulation of the social structure, which in turn led to different value systems. To lessen the gap between faction life and civilian life and make the process of reintegration for ex-combatants easier, it is necessary to try to identify socio-economic structures in post-war Sierra Leonean society that operate on similar, but peaceful, organizational principles.

Introduction

One of the first phases in the rehabilitation of post-war countries is the implementation of a so-called 'Disarmament, Demobilization and Reintegration' programme for government forces and guerrilla groups. There is considerable knowledge about best practices in and lessons learnt from these programmes but in practice they remain dogged by failures. These failures have many causes – lack of funds, poor timing, excessive haste, corruption and inefficiency, and a lack of specific knowledge about the conflict.

However, these programmes fail to acknowledge the existence of different war-generated value systems that ex-combatants have internalized, often subconsciously. These determine to a considerable extent whether one is able to accept, adapt and function in a specific civilian setting. If someone has been part of a hierarchically structured armed faction during a war and adopted new values as his own, it is likely that he will adapt more quickly to civilian life in a hierarchically structured setting. For those who have operated in a much more egalitarian faction, reintegration into a setting operating predominately according to hierarchical values will be more difficult. They should instead look for niches in society that operate according to egalitarian principles.

Factions differ in the way they are organized. This is as much the result of differences in the origin and background of a faction and its conscripts as the different challenges and constraints for survival that the faction faces during war. These organizational principles create different group-generated modes of thought or value systems.

One's beliefs and values are to a large extent shaped during adolescence – although ongoing life experiences will result in some adaptations. The social environments people find themselves in and their dominant mode of thought are decisive. To most older ex-combatants – or those who spent only a limited time in an armed faction – this environment is the pre-war or prior-to-conscription period. Many contemporary African conflicts, however, show high numbers of youthful conscripts growing up within armed factions.

After a short overview of the war in Sierra Leone and details about the factions involved in it, this chapter discusses the cultural differences between the main factions in the conflict and considers their effect on the social and economic reintegration process of ex-combatants. It concludes with a case study that shows how complete a faction's socialization process was for some of these ex-combatants and the impact it had on the reintegration process after peace was established.

The conflict in Sierra Leone and its recruits

In March 1991 a small group of about a hundred guerrilla fighters entered eastern Sierra Leone from Liberia. The majority of the group were Sierra Leoneans. This vanguard can be divided into two: Sierra Leoneans who had received guerrilla training in Libya in 1987/88 and those who were recruited in Liberia just before the incursion. Some had fighting experiences from the war in Liberia (Abdullah 1997) and most had an urban background or had previously lived in an urban centre.

Besides Sierra Leoneans, the initial insurgents included some Liberian fighters, special forces who were on loan from Charles Taylor's National Patriotic Front of Liberia (NPFL) and a few mercenaries from Burkina Faso. The guerrilla forces called themselves the Revolutionary United Front of Sierra Leone (henceforth RUF). Its proclaimed aim was to overthrow President Major

General Joseph Momoh of the All People's Congress (henceforth APC), whose previous leader and president, Siaka Stevens, had declared Sierra Leone a one-party state in 1978.

The ranks of the guerrilla forces swelled rapidly due to a mixture of coerced and voluntary recruitment among primary-school pupils and secondary-school dropouts in the Sierra Leone/Liberia border region, many of whom found themselves working in small-scale alluvial diamond mining in eastern Sierra Leone. Some joined the RUF because they saw it as a Mende uprising[1] against the Temne-dominated APC party. Many youths however just considered it a good opportunity to escape from the political, social and economic marginaliza-tion of youth at a national as well as a village level in Sierra Leone (Peters & Richards 1998a, Peters 2004).

The Sierra Leonean army was ill-prepared to challenge the incursion. With a total of no more than 3,000 troops with out-dated weaponry[2] and most senior officers residing in Freetown, the government forces lost ground rapidly. The RUF met its first serious resistance when it tried to take over the eastern town of Daru, the home of the 3rd army battalion. Lacking the support of Freetown and with insufficient logistics, front-line army officers realized they were fighting the battle virtually alone, and changed tactics. In response to the threat by the RUF's youthful combatants, army officers at the front started to recruit and train youths as fighters and personal bodyguards, tapping into the same pool of local patron-less war-zone youngsters as the RUF (Richards 1996). These young fighters, loyal to their recruiting commander and with no official army number, were referred to as 'irregulars'.

A new phase in the conflict started in April 1992 when Captain Valentine Strasser became the new Head of State after a successful military coup. Together with other young soldiers – Strasser was 27 years of age at the time of the coup – most of whom came from the Daru battalion, he established the National Provisional Ruling Council (NPRC). This not only removed the RUF's proclaimed reason for fighting – to overthrow the APC government – but threatened to deprive the RUF of its main source of recruits, namely marginalized and excluded youths. The NPRC's youthful leaders were successfully recruiting in the capital and provincial towns among unemployed youth, street children and petty criminals. Having access to this vast reservoir of

---

[1] In the east and south of the country, people were ordered by the RUF to cut palm leaves, the symbol of the Mende-dominated Sierra Leone People's Party, to decorate their villages and towns.

[2] According to an informant: 'whenever you had fired 10 bullets you had to drop the gun, open your zipper and pee on the gun to cool it down before you could use it again'.

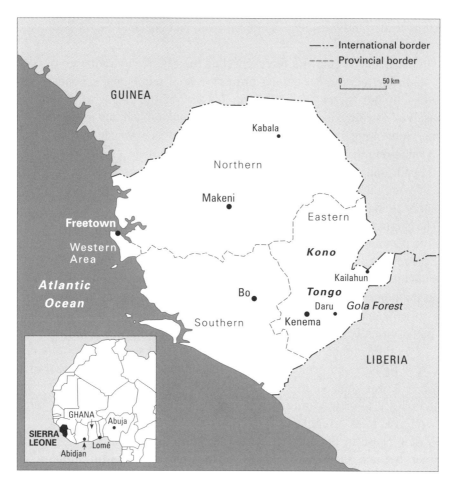

Map 12.1: Sierra Leone

young people, the NPRC was able to expand the army from a pre-war figure of 3,000-4,000 to a 1993-94 total of around 15,000-20,000 (Fithen & Richards 2002). Many of these new recruits received only limited military training, and serious discipline problems arose with large groups being involved in looting. They became known as *sobels* – soldiers by day, rebels by night. However, the expanded army succeeded in driving back the RUF which, by the time of the coup, had been able to take over most of the country's eastern region. The RUF saw its routes of retreat into Liberia blocked by hostile ULIMO[3] forces and

---

[3] The United Liberian Movement for Democracy (ULIMO) was established in Sierra Leone by political refugees who had fled Charles Taylor's NPFL. It started to assist the

decided to withdraw into the jungle of the Gola Forest on the Liberian/Sierra Leonean border at the end of 1993 to regroup, abandoning the little heavy military equipment it had.

With the war apparently coming to an end and as a result of international pressure from NGOs, the NPRC began to demobilize their considerable number of under-age combatants. However from 1994 onwards, the RUF started a new campaign, not only in the eastern part of the country. It established jungle camps[4] all over the country and used the narrow bush paths to launch quick hit-and-run attacks before disappearing into the forest. Isolated from society at large, it was cut off from the vast reservoir of potential youthful conscripts. The RUF not only changed its military tactics but was also faced with the need to raid villages in search of food, medicines and, above all, new conscripts.[5]

As early as 1991/92, government forces started to make use of local game-hunters as scouts during their patrols. From 1993 onwards, in response to continued RUF attacks and the inadequate protection offered by the rapidly expanded but increasingly badly disciplined army, local communities started to organize citizen civil-defence groups to protect their villages. Drawing organi-

---

Sierra Leonean government forces fighting the RUF (the ally of the NPFL) and later entered Liberia to fight Taylor's forces directly.

[4] According to an RUF informant, after near defeat at the end of 1993, the RUF leadership held a crucial meeting at Pumpudu in Kailahun to decide on its new strategy. Foday Sankoh and his group, after their retreat through the Gola Forest, held Nomo-Faama for a week and went back into the Gola Forest where the cadres built their first *bafa* (shelter) for Sankoh, before establishing the Zogoda Camp in the Kambui Hills in Kenema District. His lieutenants – Samuel Bockarie, Issa Sesay, Mohamed Tarawalie, Dennis Mingo and Morris Kallon – were ordered to set up other forest bases – Camp Burkina at Ngiyema in Kailahun (Tarawalie), Peyeima Camp adjacent to Tongo Field (Bockarie), Camp Bokor in the Kangari Hills (Kallon), and a camp on the ridge of the Malal Hills in Northern Province (Mingo). Tarawalie was ordered to leave Camp Burkina to found Camp Bokor and then the Malal Hills base, before becoming commander of the Zogoda Camp. After the Zogoda Camp was ransacked in 1996, RUF survivors made their way through the Gola Forest to the safety of Camp Burkina in northern Kailahun.

[5] An ex-RUF commander explained how the RUF viewed this new way of operating: 'Some of the civilians who stayed in the RUF camps decided to join the movement as combatants. Some prisoners of war also decided to join after we explained our ideology. Then, if we attacked a village or town, we assembled some civilians who had to carry the captured items to the base. Those we could not release afterwards because of security reasons. So they joined us to go to the base and received training there. … It was not by force. We captured the civilians and then later we started to sensitize them and after that they joined us. But if you did not want to join us you stayed with the RUF as a civilian. What helped us was that the people were afraid to go back to the SLA-controlled area.'

zational modalities from the hunting tradition known in the south and east as *kamajo* and in the north as *tamaboro* and *kapra*, these local defence forces consisted of a leader or initiator, a *kami*, and a small group of apprentices. Although coming from rural communities like many of the RUF conscripts and army irregulars, most of the Kamajor youth fighters were not alienated from their villages and differed greatly from the RUF and NPRC recruits in that they were still largely under the control of the village or town chief who played a key role in their recruitment.[6] According to Muana (1997), the Kamajor movement was more or less organized as a guild.

The combined forces of the army and the Kamajors were not able to prevent the RUF from getting close to the capital city, Freetown, in early 1995. Not able to take the capital and claim total victory but strong enough not to be defeated by the combined power of the military forces and rapidly expanding Kamajor militia, peace negotiations were initiated. A provisional ceasefire was agreed upon in January 1996. In February 1996 the first democratic elections in decades were held and Captain Julius Maada Bio (who was installed after a palace coup the previous month) saw himself handing over power to Ahmad Tejan-Kabbah of the Sierra Leone People's Party (SLPP). The government's new policy was to continue peace negotiations with the RUF and to sideline the army, whose loyalty was uncertain, and to depend increasingly on the Kamajor Movement for defence.

While the 1996 peace negotiations continued, key RUF bases were attacked by Kamajor militias, with the support of mercenaries of the South Africa-based security-cum-mining company Executive Outcomes. The government argued that it was not in control of the Kamajor Movement and thus unable to stop them. In November 1996 the Abidjan Peace Accord was signed between the Sierra Leonean government and the Revolutionary United Front of Sierra Leone. Officially the war was over but mutual suspicion between the former enemies resulted in neither of them disarming or demobilizing their fighters to any significant extent.

In May 1997 a third coup took place because the army was disgruntled at being sidelined by the government. Most of the demobilized child combatants joined their former comrades and re-enlisted. The new regime, the Armed Forces Revolutionary Council (AFRC) headed by Major Johnny-Paul Koroma, invited the RUF to join the military junta. For more than eight months the AFRC and the RUF were in control of Freetown and the major towns in Sierra

---

[6] Most of the young people who joined the Kamajor movement were still at school or had seen their education disrupted as a direct result of the war (cf. Peters & Richards 1998b).

Leone. In February 1998 the West-African peacekeeping force ECOMOG,[7] together with Kamajor fighters and a few hundred loyal government soldiers, launched an attack aimed at driving the junta out of the capital.

The Kabbah government reassumed power in Freetown in March 1998. Although some 5,000 AFRC troops had surrendered, many AFRC soldiers and most of the RUF units did not, and retreated to areas where the civil-defence movement was at its weakest. Contrary to claims by the newly installed government that the rebels were now on their last legs, the RUF started to regroup and expand. Major towns were taken over by the RUF and, by the end of 1998, AFRC and rebel fighters had infiltrated the capital. On 6 January 1999 the battle for Freetown started. More than two weeks of street fighting resulted in 5,000-6,000 people being killed, countless others being mutilated by machete attacks and hundreds of houses being destroyed. The AFRC and the RUF were pushed back into the hinterland and many civilians were forced to join them in retreat to carry loads and/or join as new recruits. Again it became clear that a military victory was not possible for either side.

New peace negotiations started in May 1999 in the Togolese capital Lomé. After two months of talks a peace accord was signed offering the rebels a blanket amnesty, the RUF leader Foday Sankoh a status equal to that of vice-president, and the deployment of a UN peacekeeping force to Sierra Leone. Disarmament and demobilization as outlined in the peace accord started to take shape, but painfully slowly. The RUF's second-in-command, Sam 'Maskito' Bockarie who was unwilling to disarm, fled to Liberia with a group of hard-core fighters. After a dispute between UN military observers and RUF commanders over the return of disarmed combatants to the RUF, the RUF captured about 500 UN peacekeepers. Protests by women in front of Sankoh's residence in May 2000 led to gunshots and the subsequent fleeing of the former rebel leader, before his capture a few days later. With Sankoh in custody and tensions rising, the UN expanded their peacekeeping force from 9,250 to 13,000 and later to about 17,500, with it thus becoming the largest UN mission in the world. RUF commander Issa Sessay took over command. Meanwhile special commando forces from the UK showed their readiness to fight in a hostage-freeing operation in September 2000 against a splinter group of the former AFRC called the West Side Boys. To prevent the very real prospect of annihilation, the RUF had few options other than to continue the disarmament process.

After the signing of another ceasefire accord on 10 November 2000, the Disarmament, Demobilization and Reintegration (DDR) process finally commenced in May 2001. But it was only at the end of 2001 that disarmament

---

[7] ECOMOG: Economic Community of West African States Monitoring Group.

started in RUF strongholds such as Kailahun, Kono and Kenema Districts. President Kabbah declared the war at an end in February 2002. The reintegration process of ex-combatants into civilian life was continuing at that time and in many parts of the country it had only just started. The process, as commissioned by the National Commission on Disarmament, Demobilization and Reintegration, finished at the end of December 2003.

Different factions, different social worlds

The conflict in Sierra Leone defies simple explanations. One is that the war was solely about control of the lucrative Kono and Tongo diamond fields. During the first part of the war, the RUF attacked the diamond areas but was never in control for any substantial period of time.[8] Furthermore, the geographical location of most of its forest camps and the targets of its military actions refute any suggestion that the RUF was a movement primarily interested in controlling the country's diamond-producing areas. Sierra Leonean governments, however, have heavily depended on revenues from diamond sales, making these areas an obvious military target for any insurgent group trying to undermine the ruling government.

Another explanation is that the Sierra Leone conflict offers a preview of what is about to happen in the Third World, and specifically on the African continent – senseless and barbaric violence committed by uneducated youths who are, as 'loose molecules', rapidly destroying the social fabric of our planet (Kaplan 1994). The extreme and apparently random violence, mostly committed by RUF cadres, is considered clear evidence of this but questions remain unanswered. Why, for instance, if the RUF was no more than a loose group of mindless bandits, murderers and rapists, did it prove so difficult to defeat it with the combined forces of the army, ECOMOG troops, civil-defence units and the support of mercenaries? Why did it continue to operate as a coherent group even during long periods of absence of its leader? And why did the RUF, at least in some areas, try to put into practice its proclaimed revolutionary agenda of free education and medical care, and the promotion of food production?[9]

---

[8] This changed in the second half of the conflict (particularly during 1999 and afterwards) when the RUF controlled and mined heavily in Tongo and Kono.

[9] According to Abdullah (1997: 71), '...actions such as the redistribution of "food, drugs, clothes and shoes from 'liberated' government sources" (as mentioned in Richards 1996) ... should be seen as populist propaganda'. But why should 'lumpens' – as Abdullah labels the RUF combatants – put any effort into making propaganda? If self-enrichment was their sole agenda, inflicting fear on the people would be much

Others aspects, such as the collaboration between the junta forces and the RUF and later the massive voluntary RUF conscription of youths in Makeni[10] – many of whom had fought with the Civil Defence Forces (CDF) for several years – challenge explanations of the 'good guys' versus the 'bad guys'.

To fully understand the political violence in Sierra Leone, a cultural analysis is required of the different fighting forces. According to Richards (1999), political violence expresses beliefs and is shaped by social orientation. He uses the neo-Durkheimian cultural theory[11] that builds on the legacy of the French sociologist Emile Durkheim and focuses on group-generated modes of thought. It argues that there are only a limited number of ways in which groups can organize themselves to manage the constraints and regulations imposed by others. Mary Douglas (1982, 1993) distinguishes four distinctive patterns or systems of claims that can produce a potentially stable cultural type. These principal distinctive cultural types can be defined along two dimensions, one based on concern with the outside boundary, the other on the articulation of social structure. The first cultural bias is the hierarchy with a strong boundary around its population and a strongly articulated, self-repeating structure. The next type – the sectarian or egalitarian culture – is also concerned with its boundary but it has a weakly articulated social structure. Thirdly, a culture of competitive individualism can be distinguished in which group membership is not important and no group boundary can thus be found. Here the individual is expected to negotiate for his own status, unconstrained by group allegiance or prescriptive rules. However, some individuals experience the constraining effect of strong social structures made by others but, similar to the individualists, they do not form a group together and therefore there is no concern about a group boundary. This is the culture of the isolate (sometimes also referred to as fatalist).

The above scheme has been used by Richards[12] to gain insight into the war in Sierra Leone, a war that has been considered by outside commentators to be barbaric, bizarre and pointless. It makes clear many of the patterns and turns the conflict has taken since 1991. In 'Making War, Crafting Peace: Militia

---

more effective.

[10] According to Arthy (2003), 'there is a general misconception that the majority of youth were "forced" to take up arms by the RUF. Whilst this is true for many, many more joined voluntarily or were actively encouraged by their parents to join. Indeed, as late 1999, a recruitment drive by the RUF in Makeni led to far more youth volunteering to join than the RUF had the capacity to take on.'

[11] On neo-Durkheimian theory, see Douglas (1993) and Douglas & Ney (1998).

[12] See, for example, Richards (1999, 2001), Fithen & Richards (2002) and Archibald & Richards (2002).

Solidarities and Demobilization in Sierra Leone', Fithen and Richards (2002) elaborate on how four cultural outcomes cover the different fighting factions.

- The RUF, sequestered in high forest, with fragile communications, and highly dependent on the self-organizing capacities of its ultra-youthful captive converts, manifests some of the social features and values associated with an enclave or sect (otiose leadership, flat hierarchy of command, egalitarian distribution of available resources, steep entry and exit cost).[13]

- Soldiers in the government army began under conventional hierarchical command and control. Some still respected orders (one of the basic hierarchical values). Others, abandoned by the state, became classic freebooting bandits, with value systems typical of individualists in the cultural theory scheme.

- Civil-defence fighters draw on the organizational modalities and value systems of specialist craft hunters. Hunters operate in the bush alone, or with a small group of apprentices, and are strongly individualistic in orientation. Organisers within the Kabbah government later attempted to mould hunter-led civil defence into a national militia capability. The resulting ethnically based quasi-army faced increasing problems of command and control as the individualism of hunter social organization reasserted itself.

- The remaining group, the culture of the isolate, is of less relevance here. Richards has argued that the various mercenary groups operating in Sierra Leone show characteristics of this.

One of the above cultures – that of the government army – is discussed in more detail here in an attempt to elaborate on the specific circumstances that resulted in these characteristic organizational principles and to clarify how this influenced the soldiers' value system. A better understanding of this process will not only provide insight into the conflict and how it developed but will also show the reintegration opportunities and difficulties of ex-combatants. The case study of an army irregular (later in this chapter) illustrates the difficulties he experienced, after long years of being socialized in the army, on returning to his village to live in an environment that required another set of values and operated according to different organizational principles.

---

[13] There is a constant danger that those RUF fighters who escaped or were expelled from the movement, but who cannot or prefer not to return to civilian society due to fear, will become isolates or, more negatively, fatalists. Reintegration into society will then be much more difficult.

The military culture of irregulars

To gain more insight into the war in Sierra Leone, the widespread violence and looting, and the recurring coups, it is important to take into account the role and culture of army irregulars.

In 1991, an ill-equipped government army, the Republic of Sierra Leone Military Force (RSLMF), had to confront the invasion of a quickly expanding rebel force. Without sufficient logistical back-up and manpower support by the Freetown government, the inexperienced front-line junior officers quickly learnt to survive by copying RUF/SL guerrilla tactics, including the recruitment and training of under-age irregulars. Much of the fighting was done by these locally recruited irregulars who were less daunted than RSLMF soldiers by the RUF/SL cadres prepared for combat with fear-inhibiting drugs. Many of the army irregulars were under-age, both male and female, and were highly rated by the commanding officers: under-age irregulars fight with no inhibitions and kill without compunction. They are good in ambush situations, one of the main combat tactics, and – separated from their kin – are fiercely loyal to their *bra* (*Krio*, literally 'big brother'), the officer responsible for recruiting and training them (Peters & Richards 1998a, 1998b). Whenever an officer is transferred to another location, he will bring his 'boys' with him.

If an officer, who might be personally responsible for up to twenty or thirty irregulars, is for some reason cut off from the support of military headquarters (often for political reasons), he has to find other ways of providing for his boys. One option was to pack them off to areas where there were still signs of RUF activity, ostensibly to defend outlying villages but in reality to fend for themselves from the rich local pickings of cocoa, coffee and diamonds (Richards 1996).

The Sierra Leonean army, which was supposed to function on hierarchical principles (like most standing armies), began to operate differently. The anonymous character, in which ranks and not individuals were important, was replaced by personalized links between officers and their irregulars. Irregulars were loyal to their *bra*, more so than to other (sometimes higher-ranking) officers or the army in general. A patrimonial system, present in so many other sectors in Sierra Leone, started to operate on the front line. So whenever a commander changed sides, joining the RUF or later the AFRC, all his boys went with him.

If for some reason the relationship between the irregular and his officer ended, for example if the officer died or a dispute arose, the irregular faced serious problems. Without an official army number he was not entitled to any military provisions and, excluded and alienated from his village and family, the irregular had few options other than to search for another commander who would be his *bra*.

Many of the irregulars faced problems when the war was coming to an end. The military resources available to their commanders dried up, making it hard for them to cater for all their boys. At the same time, there was less need for a commander to have a large group of loyal boys around him as bodyguards. Rather than dividing up the capital some of these commanders had been able to accumulate during the war, commanders choose to abandon most of their boys. Obviously this was to the disappointment and anger of the irregulars who considered the ties as ever-lasting, having fought together and survived for many years. Many expected to be employed by their commanders in any commercial venture they would be undertaking. Others expected to be taken along if their *bra* travelled overseas to study or live in England or America.[14] But rather than learning a lesson from this deception, most irregulars found it difficult to change their way of thinking, going in search of another, this time civilian, *bra*. Others returned to the most familiar world they knew and re-enlisted in the army.

The challenges of reintegration

After several attempts, the final Disarmament, Demobilization and Reintegration (DDR) programme for government and guerrilla forces started in May 2001, after the signing of the Abuja Ceasefire Accord on 10 November 2000. In general, DDR programmes aim to collect the arms and ammunition of combatants, break command structures, and support and promote the peaceful rehabilitation of the demobilized ex-fighters into civilian society.

The disarmament and demobilization components of the Sierra Leone DDR programme have been labelled successful. Although in some areas disarmament started as late as November or December 2002, most weapons were finally collected. Furthermore, there is no evidence that the command structures are still in place or that ex-combatants are living together in high concentrations.[15]

---

[14] A considerable number of commanders travelled overseas to study or to live. For some it was a reward for their loyalty to the government, others have 'done well' out of the war and financed their own travels.

[15] The case of Tongo, a diamond-producing area, was one of the few exceptions. Under RUF control in the latter stages of the war, Tongo was one of the last places to see disarmament. Instead of returning to their places of origin, ex-RUF combatants remained in Tongo, continuing to occupy the labour camp of a former diamond-mining plant. This was much to the disdain of the original inhabitants of Tongo who had seen most of their houses destroyed during the war and ex-RUF combatants now living in relatively undamaged houses. Moreover, the large concentration of ex-combatants was considered a security threat. Contrary to the rest of Tongo, the traditional authorities, such as the town chief, did not operate in 'Labour Camp' and the chiefdom authorities

However, small groups of ex-combatants might be doing so, partly because of ongoing ex-combatant reintegration programmes or because their former comrades have become a substitute family for them.

But not all combatants have been able to register as ex-combatants. Large groups saw their weapons confiscated by their commanders before the actual disarmament process began. Not being able to present a weapon meant that they were unable to prove they were a combatant. Others, mainly ex-RUF combatants, feared repercussions if they identified themselves. When the Special Court – with its mandate to try those who bore the greatest responsibility for crimes against humanity – and the Truth and Reconciliation Commission started work, this fear rose to sometimes paranoid levels.

The reintegration part of the DDR programme proved to be less straight-forward. The programme for ex-combatants was characterized by relatively long and extensive support for the beneficiaries contrary to, for instance, the 1997 disarmament process in Liberia where ex-combatants only received a small financial payment and a few items upon disarmament. In Sierra Leone, combatants received Le 300,000 (approx. US$ 150) upon disarmament. Then they could choose between financial support for three years[16] of formal education, an agricultural reintegration package, or six to nine months of vocational training including a monthly allowance of about Le 60,000 and a tool-kit upon completion of the training. The rationale behind this extensive reintegration programme was to make it attractive for combatants to give up their life as a fighter by offering them an opportunity to become economically independent without the use of a gun. It was also assumed that it offered a necessary cooling-off period to facilitate the transition from a fighter's life to civilian life.

The reintegration programme in Sierra Leone is already being quoted as an example for other countries as to how to move from war to peace. But there were major shortcomings. These included (i) the slow implementation of the reintegration programmes, resulting in many ex-combatants waiting for more than a year after disarmament before starting their skills training; (ii) high levels of corruption that meant low-quality training programmes and combatants not receiving their monthly allowances and graduation tool-kits on time (or not at all); and (iii) the relatively short period of vocational training – you cannot

---

were unaware of what was going on there. After a series of negotiations, the ex-RUF combatants finally abandoned the camp and became assimilated into the wider Tongo community.

[16] The length of funding decreased over the years, so those demobilizing last received a shorter period of sponsorship.

become a carpenter in six months. This limited the chances of establishing oneself as an artisan and making a living out of it.

The ex-combatants reintegration programme attached great value to the beneficiaries acquiring skills to become economically self-sufficient. One might question whether this was enough to prepare them for re-entry into civilian life and it is doubtful whether ex-combatants were aware of the extent to which their lives inside a faction had shaped their ways of thinking and how far these might differ from civilian values. More specifically, one could question how far the ex-combatants were aware that their choice for a certain skill, or to go back to farming, to school or to re-settle in their community of origin, required a certain compatible attitude and cultural norms that differed from skill to skill and from place to place.

The DDR programme in Sierra Leone finished at the end of December 2003. It is therefore difficult to evaluate its impact on the actual economic and social reintegration process of ex combatants. However, some cohorts of ex-combatants who benefited from the training they were offered immediately after disarmament finished their skills training at least a year ago. A World Bank Assessment of Reintegration Programmes of NCDDR in September/October 2002 found that only 28 per cent of those who opted for skills training subsequently proved able to earn a livelihood through the skills they had been provided with (Arthy 2003).[17] A more recent quantitative study by the World Bank found that slightly more than 70 per cent of the ex-combatants interviewed felt that the skills training they received related to at least one of the jobs they had. However, this figure reflects the responses of those who are in employment. Almost half of the total number of interviewees stated that they had not been employed since completing their training (Stavrou *et al.* 2003).

This is not surprising if one looks at the general macroeconomic situation in Sierra Leone. Simon Arthy (2003) states that: 'In a country where over 85 per cent of the population rely on agriculture for their economic livelihood, the relative unattractiveness of the NCDDR agricultural reintegration package offered, compared for example to the vocational training package (with its associated financial benefits), meant that only 16 per cent of the ex-combatants opted for agriculture, in comparison to 60 per cent for skills training and short-term artisan apprenticeships.' The near impossibility of finding work in a

---

[17] This figure is likely to be even lower if one deducts the many ex-combatants who are temporarily employed by the same organization that provided their skills training, some as new trainers but the vast majority as workers on short-term contracts such as the rebuilding of schools and clinics.

specific area of training forced many ex-combatants to become involved in agricultural activities after all, purely as a means of survival.[18]

There is also a sociological aspect here. As explained earlier, the different challenges and threats faced by the various armed factions resulted in variations in the way they organized themselves to overcome both external and internal difficulties. According to the neo-Durkheimian theory, specific organizational principles or modalities foster specific values and norms. Those ex-combatants who spent a long time inside an armed faction are likely to have internalized its dominant organizational culture – be it hierarchical, egalitarian, individualistic or the culture of the isolates – and to have adopted the values that go with it. In their post-war civilian life, therefore, it is likely that they will feel more comfortable in an environment that operates more or less according to the same structuring principles and values.

To clarify this, let me give some examples.

- The government army is a system of hierarchical command and control but vast numbers of soldiers in Sierra Leone were recruited and started to operate under the less-stratified and more-personalized system of *bra*s and their irregulars. In return for loyalty and protection, irregulars expected benefits from their commander. Systems organized according to the same principles are, for example, the business and trade sector or the transport sector, where a businessman or vehicle owner (the *bra*) employs several workers who are paid with some regularity.

- The civil-defence fighters have more individualistic value systems and operated during the war (and particularly prior to 1997) according to the master-apprentice model.[19] Trades organized in the same way include carpentry, masonry and tailoring, with a master teaching the apprentice a specific skill. The apprentice will not receive any payment for his work but is expected to open his own artisan shop after he is a fully skilled artisan (postponed benefits).

---

[18] In Makeni in the northern part of Sierra Leone, I came upon an agricultural project set up by ex-combatants. Most of the 75 ex-combatants who were taking part in the project had been trained as part of their reintegration process in skills such as carpentry, masonry and computer skills. However, none had been able to find a job that offered enough income to live on.

[19] An important difference between the *bra*-irregular system in the army and the master-apprentice system in the CDF is that in the first it is not the commander's aim to train the irregular to become a *bra* himself. It is, in other words, a static system. The CDF master-apprentice system aimed to train the apprentice up to a level where he (the CDF was almost exclusively male) could become a master or initiator himself and start to train his own group of apprentices.

- The RUF was to some extent organized according to sectarian principles,[20] with a flat hierarchy and the equal distribution of available resources. Small-scale alluvial diamond mining in Sierra Leone is organized in more or less the same way. A group of no more than fifteen (less than five is the most common size) young males dig for diamonds in pits and the leader of the group – usually a more experienced diamond digger – is responsible for providing food and medical needs for his workers[21] but also takes part in the back-breaking work. If a diamond is found it will be sold to the leader, after which the money is shared equally among the miners. Many miners use such money to start small-scale mining operations themselves, hiring diggers and so becoming leaders themselves. Because alluvial diamond mining is nothing less than a lottery,[22] a leader can run out of money and become an ordinary digger again.

There are other examples in post-war Sierra Leone of the tendency of ex-combatants to look for, and function better, in socio-economic structures that are organized along similar lines to those they became used to during the war. An obvious example is the fact that the majority of those who opted to re-enter the military were ex-soldiers. Many ex-CDF fighters, in particular the older ones (who had only spent a relatively short part of their lives in an armed faction), chose to go into agriculture, which in many cases meant returning to their villages and continuing the work they had done before the war in an environment structured along principles still familiar to them. A considerable number of ex-RUF fighters who had joined the rebel movement early on in the conflict also opted for agriculture.[23] However, collected data suggest that ex-CDF fighters seem to have been more involved in individual farming,

---

[20] The exact extent to which the RUF was organized along sectarian principles is not yet known. It may therefore be useful to make a distinction between the period the movement spent in isolated bush camps (1994-1997) and the latter part (1997-2001) when they were less isolated.

[21] Sometimes in small-scale mining operations the diggers bring their own food and equipment. But they can still select a leader among themselves. If the workers consider their leader incapable, they can vote on whether he should be replaced and subsequently select a new leader from among themselves.

[22] After the removal of the sand, the diamond-rich gravel is divided into three piles. One pile is for the miners, one for the master who provides equipment and fuel for the pumps that drain the water from the pits, and one pile is for the landowner. The piles are allocated by means of a lottery.

[23] In particular ex-RUF fighters who joined the movement in the first years (and held relatively higher positions) were involved in agriculture activities. When asked why they had chosen agriculture, they stated that agriculture was 'the backbone of every country' and that it was an integral part of RUF ideology to involve oneself in agriculture.

cultivating their own plots of land, while ex-RUF fighters appear to prefer communal farming, cultivating larger areas and working in groups.

Obviously there are other factors of importance in the reintegration process of ex-combatants. Training someone in computers skills (when there is so little demand) or not giving him or her the promised tool-kit after graduation definitely limits the chances of a smooth economic reintegration process. Whether or not the community accepts an ex-combatant is greatly influenced by the person's behaviour and whether or not he or she respects the local authorities. Clearly, if someone committed atrocities in a community during the war it is unlikely that he will return straightaway after demobilization. But in many cases where ex-combatants are not able to function economically and socially as expected and with no clear reason why not, it is likely that this is related to differences between faction life and civilian life and the structuring principles guiding day-to-day matters and the fundamental differences in the values and norms these entail.

Taking into account the organizational modalities and value systems that ex-combatants became used to during the war can give useful insights into the specific future possibilities and limitations ex-combatants will experience during socio-economic reintegration. Instead of increasing the amount of DDR support given to ex-combatants or extending its duration in an overall attempt to increase the number of ex-combatants successfully[24] reintegrated, an assessment should be made as to what skills are most needed and in demand. The different organizational modalities that accompany these skills should also be identified. If the various armed factions are classified according to their organizational modality and values, it should be possible to offer a more tailor-made reintegration package to the ex-combatant, one that is sensitive to the sociological aspects of the reintegration process. If one matches this reintegration package with structures already present in civilian life, it would then be possible to limit the period of reintegration assistance and minimize the creation of special vocational training institutes for ex-combatants. This is particularly important in the context of a weak state and poorly functioning institutions, as is the case in so many post-war African countries. One should accept that the role of the state in the reintegration process is limited and instead look for opportunities in the damaged, but often still functioning, civilian society. In this way, supporting ex-combatants in their reintegration process can go hand in hand with the rebuilding of civilian society.

---

[24] What is 'successful' reintegration? The most commonly used but clearly limited yardstick is whether or not an ex-combatant is employed and has returned to his or her place of origin.

Samuel: An irregular's case

Samuel is a young Sierra Leonean irregular[25] whose story clearly illustrates the issues discussed above. The many clashes between him and his father are an indication of strong generational tensions, but the values Samuel holds are to such a large extent shaped by his many years in the army that it is not possible to label the problems between him and his father solely as a conflict between generations.

Samuel joined the army in 1993 at the age of twelve but was demobilized in 1995 as part of a larger demobilization programme for under-age combatants during the military regime of President Strasser. In 1997, after the overthrow of the newly elected democratic government of President Kabbah by renegade soldiers, he rejoined the forces, like the vast majority of other demobilized former-child combatants. As part of the loyal troops which helped ECOMOG to overthrow the military junta of the AFRC, this was the beginning of a new period of fighting for Samuel that culminated in the defence of Freetown in the 6 January 1999 attack on the combined forces of the ex-junta soldiers and RUF forces during their notorious operation 'No Living Thing'.

According to the 1999 Lomé Peace Accord, the Sierra Leonean army would be restructured and absorb fighters from all different factions. It was then to be trained by British troops. Our interviewee – who by now was a young adult – received this training but, not feeling secure in the new army that had enrolled so many of his former enemies, decided to desert and go to Ghana. In 2002 he returned to Sierra Leone. After a failed attempt to settle in his native village, he joined the LURD (Liberians United for Reconciliation and Democracy) rebels in Liberia just before the Liberian president Charles Taylor stepped down.

His army years

Samuel grew up in a village in the eastern district of Kailahun where the majority of villagers depend on agriculture, combining rice farming (mainly for their own consumption) with the commercial exploitation of crops such as coffee, palm oil and cocoa. Children and youth have always been expected to contribute their labour. Authority is in the hands of a village chief, advised by the elders of the community: young people have little or no say in the decision-

---

[25]   I first interviewed this young man (Samuel is not his real name) in 1996 and he has since become a close friend. Over the following years we kept in contact by telephone, e-mail and letters. A second interview took place in 2000 and in 2002/03, during a long period of fieldwork, he became a key informant and accompanied me on some of my field trips.

making process.[26] A mixture of a collapsing patrimonial system and a worsening economic situation leading to increasing numbers of young people dropping out of school in combination with their heavy social and cultural obligations and the extraordinary punishment of youths in local courts has resulted in the exclusion and alienation of many of the area's young people. Those who were living as outcasts from their villages and likely to be involved in small-scale diamond mining for survival were among the first to join the RUF. Young people still living in the village because they were too young to leave came either under RUF control or were lucky enough to be able to make their way to the government-controlled area, as our interviewee did.

Samuel voluntarily joined the army when he was twelve. He had fled his village close to the Liberian border during a rebel attack in the early stages of the war and went to the town of Kenema where he stayed with a relative.[27] Without his parents around and with his relative unable to pay his school fees, he decided to join the army. After two weeks of military training he was sent to Daru, close to the front line. Here he became the personal bodyguard of Colonel M.

> All the young men around Daru had joined together to fight the rebels in the bush. We all were boys, but there was a big leader, the commander. That is where I met this man, Colonel M. So I was with Colonel M. and took part in patrols.

Without an official army number Samuel was not entitled to receive a salary. He was solely dependent on what his commanders gave him and what he was able to get at the front. Later, Samuel was able to take the army number of a soldier who died in action, and then received a small monthly allowance. At some stage, Samuel got wounded and was treated in hospital.

> So from there I wanted to find where my colonel was, Colonel M. At that time he was in this place Cockerill (military HQ, Wilkinson Rd, Freetown). Right now [1996] he is in Bo, as a brigade commander. His wife is here in Freetown ... everyday I can go to her. But now we are here in Freetown.

At the time of his first demobilization Samuel visited his former commander's house on a regular basis. When the 1997 coup took place, he immediately rushed there.

> We heard Corporal B. on the SLBS radio announcing that they had overthrown the SLPP government. But I did not know the Corporal. I was still in the house with my

---

[26] For a detailed discussion on justice in rural Sierra Leone, see Archibald & Richards (2002).

[27] See interview in Peters & Richards (1998a).

guardian[28] for about one hour more. Then I decided to contact my commander, Commander M. I went to him to hear more about it. They said that it was a coup and that I should join. So I did not waste time, there was a reserve weapon and a reserve uniform. I took it and wore it.

The following part clearly shows the dilemma these irregular forces faced. Although Samuel seems to have had some sense of a wider loyalty towards the country and the president, his feelings were more with the army. However, his real loyalty lay with the person who was directly responsible for him and taking care of him.

After that I came back to my guardian. I was in a different mood now. When he saw me he said very angrily: 'What is that?' I said to him that it was not my fault because they said that I should join them and it is a military order that I should not refuse.

Q. So you joined the coup?
A. *Well, not actively. But I participate. Well, I should not lie, I joined.*
Q. You said that it was a military order but you must also be loyal to the president?
A. *Yes, but ... I was not directly under his ... But yes, he is our Commander in Chief but by then I was not enlisted as a numbered soldier because I had my own commander.*
Q. So you are more loyal to your commander than to your president?
A. *Yes, because I do not have direct contact with the president. They do not even know me.*

In 1998, after his long-time commander was accused of collaboration with the junta forces, Samuel built up a relationship with a new officer. During the 6 January attack on Freetown in 1999, Samuel personally safeguarded the properties of this other officer.

My commander was already out of the city but I was still in his house. Then he phoned me and told me to check if his bag was still there. He told me that I just had to take that bag and bring it to him. So I found the bag, jumped on my bike and managed to reach the safe area where I handed the bag over to him. He opened the bag and inside were millions of Leones in it. You know what he did? He counted the money two times to see if there was anything missing! All the money was there, I had not taken a single cent, but he never gave me even 500 Leones.

---

[28] The former child combatants in this particular programme spent at least six months in a demobilization camp. After that, if no relative could be traced, foster families were found for them.

Samuel became even more disappointed in his new *bra*. At some point his officer went to England to study, leaving Samuel behind. Not being protected by a high-ranking officer anymore and with the new Sierra Leonean army containing soldiers who formerly belonged to the various opposing factions, it became a dangerous place for Samuel since some of his new colleagues considered him a traitor and one-time enemy. He decided to go to Ghana to wait for calmer times.

Reintegration attempts

By the end of 2002, Samuel was living in Freetown. Without a job, he managed to live by linking up with friends who were better off. This is common practice in Sierra Leone for many youths who are looking for a senior person who is able and willing to support them in their education, to help them find a job or give them a little money. These persons are also referred to as *bra*.

A friend of Samuel's, a former child soldier himself, had recently arrived from London and was staying in one of the city's top hotels.[29] On arriving in Sierra Leone he found out that Samuel had been arrested, together with some other soldiers, and had been in prison for the previous two months. His friend immediately paid for his release. Then Samuel stayed with him – his new *bra* – and enjoyed expensive meals, drinks and female company, all in large quantities. Not having a cent to his name, he was totally dependent on his friend. Without doubt, Samuel would have preferred to have had the cash rather than the meals.

> You know, I am really confused by his behaviour. How he can spend so much money on staying in this hotel and these expensive meals. I wish I had that money, I would make better use of it.

His loyalty to his well-off friend became clear during an incident (an argument about an empty chair that escalated into a fight) at a bar, where Samuel was eager to protect '*my captain* with my life', if necessary. The luxurious lifestyle was short-lived and came to an end with the sudden departure of his friend, leaving Samuel empty-handed.

Samuel had to make a choice. One possibility was to go back to the army, the life that was most familiar to him. But he stated:

---

[29] This young man became the spokesman for former child combatants during the first under-age demobilization programme. Later, he became close to ECOMOG's Chief Commander Maxwell Kobbie. Known by NGO workers, business people and various scholars, he was able to get a British visa.

I do no want to go back to the army because I really decided to leave that life behind. And I know that if I stay here in Freetown I will not do a better thing. I can survive but I will probably run into problems and life is very expensive here and all these goods they have here make you to want to have a lot of money.

Without doubt, with his contacts and street wisdom he would have managed to survive in Freetown. His other option was to return to his village and start a new life. Samuel returned to his village in early 2003 and after a preliminary visit decided to settle there. Since he had not taken part in the final disarmament process and therefore not profited from reintegration support, I decided to assist him with US$ 150, an amount equivalent to the financial support combatants received upon their disarmament under the official DDR programme. He bought a bundle of second-hand clothes and a few marketable items such as medicines and salt to set up a small business in his village. Almost everybody in the village depended on farming but he did not yet see himself as a full-time farmer.

About a month later, I visited Samuel during a field trip. He had finally decided to settle in the village and had even started to build a house. Most of the houses in the village had been badly damaged or totally destroyed during the war. The remaining houses were already occupied, while internally displaced people and refugees were still returning to the village, putting even more pressure on the limited facilities. Samuel's mother, the first of his father's three wives, was not even living in his father's house.

You know, I am living with my mother in her brother's house. But we should really live with my father in his house. When my mother returned to the village after the war, the family of my father's second wife was already living in my father's house, so there was no place for my mother. If it was not for my mother who convinced me otherwise I would have driven them away. I was really angry with my father.

And he told his father so. In pre-war Sierra Leonean society, children rarely argued with their fathers. But times have changed.

Although part of the labour required for building the house was 'donated' by his family members (mainly his relatives on his mother's side), some of the labour had to be paid for. Some of the clothes were used to pay people off. In general, the rate at which he was able to market his second-hand clothes was much slower than he had expected, and he found himself walking miles to nearby villages to sell just a few. The need might be high but the necessary cash to buy clothes was not yet available for the village people. This is probably one of the biggest problems the villagers face. Before the war most of them earned the cash they needed by selling their cash crops – cocoa, coffee and palm kernels. As a result of the conflict and the long displacement of most of the people, cash-crop plantations had become seriously overgrown. Before any real income could be made out of the plantations, considerable cleaning of the undergrowth had to take place. To do this heavy work, a group of young people could be hired, if the money was available.[30] Before the war, parents – like Samuel's father – could easily mobilize their children to work on their plantations, but not anymore.

> Before the war you were supposed to work for your father for nothing. You were working for him until he died. It was only after that that you would start to profit for yourself. But now, everything has changed. I am not going to help my father for nothing. But he still expects me to help him for nothing. He even expects my older brother to come all the way from Freetown to help him on the farm. But my brother is following a course over there and the amount of money he needs for the journey, he just does not have it. And it is not only me, every youth in the village is focusing on his own garden or farm, for his own profit.

The power of the chief and the elders over the young people has also decreased. This becomes clear from the difficulties the authorities have in mobilizing the youth for community work, such as the repair of the *barré* or collective brushing on community-owned land.

> When they rang the bell the first time to gather the youths, I did not even know what it was meant for. Later my father told me that all the youths were supposed to come to start to work for the community. The next time I heard the call for community labour, I just ignored it, although my father was annoyed with me. You know, as long as you are single and not yet married you can easily escape community labour. You can even go to another village for one or two days. They just do not have grips on you yet. That is why they want you to marry at an early age in the village.

Nowadays, young people are present at village meetings and important community decisions are not taken without youth representation. Most of the elders have realized that the social, political and economic marginalization of youth was one of the root causes of the conflict. Afraid of creating another pool of disgruntled and excluded youths, they know that they should not discourage them. Moreover, villagers need young people's labour to rebuild villages and recover their plantations.

Business was going too slowly to make a living so Samuel decided to start farming. His father owned 25 acres of improved oil palms and another 30 acres

---

[30] One financial injection of cash seems to be enough to break this post-war cycle of lack of cash-generating possibilities. A few months later a project was implemented in the area to help farmers with the brushing of their plantations. After registration, the project paid people – mainly village youths – to clear the plantations of the registered farmers.

of cocoa and coffee trees. Enough land to give a part to Samuel, one might think.

> My father did not give me anything. He said that I should help him on the land and that we later would share the profit, but I know that he will keep it all for himself. So now my mother gave me 8 acres with coffee trees. Her uncle was the owner of the land and even had a court case about it because the village people said that the land was part of the Poro Society.[31] But nobody will take this land from me, nobody will scare me with any threats or devils. You know, my blood is too bitter for their witchcraft.

Samuel's almost complete lack of respect for traditional belief is interesting. In general there is a strong belief in things such as witchcraft, devils and spells among rural people in Sierra Leone and the power and control of the secret societies over daily life in rural Sierra Leone is still considerable.

> Now, the Sande Society has just started in our village. The little rice my father had, he has used it all to send his daughter of his second wife to the society. This society is just about eating food. Everyday they are carrying food to the women who are leading the initiation.

Although born and raised for the first part of his life in the village, Samuel clearly is now rooted in a different world and reality. He survived ten years of active service during the war that took him to various parts of the country, and even abroad. He experienced life in the city and has been exposed to its novelties. Listening daily to the BBC World Service and accessing the Internet whenever he is in Freetown, he is as much part of today's 'global village' as his youthful counterparts in the West.

Another factor sets him apart from the other villagers. During the time of his first demobilization in 1995 in Freetown, he became a Christian, much to the disapproval of his father who is a respected Hajji and who has visited Mecca three times. Now he finds himself in a village where 99 per cent of the population is Muslim.

> When my father found out that I was going to church he almost cried. He just could not believe it. But that will not stop me. I told him that if he had not spent all his money before the war on these useless trips to Mecca we would not be suffering now. The only thing I do not want him to know is that I drink alcohol. If he finds out

---

[31] The Poro Society for males and the Sande Society for females are part of the so-called secret societies in Sierra Leone. These societies regulate the initiation rites for boys and girls in Sierra Leonean society.

he will never forgive me. My mother knows but will not accept it. She refused to wash the cup I always take when I am going to drink the local wine.

During the following months Samuel stayed in his village, occasionally going to the regional capital for a few days. It seemed that he was going to settle down in the village, slowly leaving his former way of life behind. In fact, he stated that he liked his new life and the village. The only setback seemed to be the almost complete lack of entertainment.

> You know, after all, this is my home. This is the place where I was born. And here you do not need money. Even 1,000 Leones is enough for a day. … After seven or eight o'clock it becomes quiet in the village. Only if it is full moon do the people stay up longer. It is only my radio which helps me through the long evenings.

Compared to the city and larger towns where youths have access to clubs, bars and video centres and which are livelier in general, life in this small village must have seemed boring. During the war many people lived for a period of time in the displaced-persons' camps that were located close to the major towns and there they came in contact with a more modern lifestyle. And of course those who had been involved in active fighting had experienced a much more 'lively' life than village life could ever offer. However, there were quite a number of ex-combatants living (temporarily) in the village. Some had been born in the same area and considered it their home. Others were based in the village during the war when it was an RUF stronghold. These ex-RUF fighters did not yet consider it the right time to return to their own places of birth. Some were afraid to return to their homes, either because of the atrocities they had committed in their home area or because their hometown was located in a former CDF stronghold. Another group felt that after so many years of being away from home, it would be embarrassing to return to their family with nothing. An ex-RUF commander commented:

> My family is living in Freetown and they are doing fine. But how can I go back to them after all these years without anything. If I had some money, I am sure that my brothers would help me to start up a business by adding some of their own capital. But if I do not have anything, the first day they will be happy to see me, but the next day they will start to grumble.

So this interviewee decided to stay for the time being in the village and is raising some money by farming. According to Samuel, this ex-RUF fighter had secretly cultivated a large marijuana farm and was planning to use the profit to buy his ticket home.

Another ex-RUF commander, who was in control of a part of the diamond production in the latter part of the conflict, was also residing in Samuel's village. Born in a nearby village he was using Samuel's village as a temporary base. During the war he owned two nightclubs and he currently had a music-set with him that people could hire for discos and parties. A few of his former boys lived with him. Upon his arrival Samuel immediately started to build up a relationship with him, although he was the former enemy against whom he had fought so long. Clearly, Samuel was using the same survival mechanisms as he used during the war.

> I just must make friendship. He has a complete music-set so he will be doing fine. If you have a friendship with him, it may help you in the future.

Samuel's relationship with his father might be best described as one of mutual annoyance. They had many arguments, varying from his father neglecting Samuel's advice in matters where Samuel feared that his father would be fooled by business people[32] to the more general grumbling about his father's many wives.

> My father just does not care about us. He cannot give us anything, not even the smallest support. He never helped my brother with his education in Freetown, but if he succeeds in finding a job my father will be so proud and the next thing he will do is ask for assistance from my brother. I told him that if he had not married so many wives and had not had so many children, he would have been able to assist his children properly. But he says that I must be quiet because that is not my business.

> You know, now he has raised a little money he wants to marry another wife, can you imagine?

Obviously, his father was annoyed with Samuel because of his rebellious behaviour and the lack of respect he displayed for his father's orders. But many people in the village, in particular the youth, liked Samuel for his outspoken character, although fearing him at the same time.

---

[32] For instance, many plantation owners had trees on their land which could be sold for timber production. Small groups of youths, equipped with a chain-saw, went around doing this job. Urgently in need of cash, the land owners saw themselves agreeing to extremely unfavourable terms with the chain-saw operators, as was the case with Samuel's father.

Back to his old life?

Samuel spent several months in his village. Unfortunately, during a next visit to the regional capital an incident happened which influenced our relationship and, to some extent, the support I was giving him. A quick calculation of the new situation was enough to change his mind. He would leave the village, at least for the time being because he obviously did not have the patience to accumulate wealth step by step. He told me that he would be going to Liberia to see what the situation was like.

> If I live in the village I just keep on waiting. We, the young people, we just have to wait until our fathers die. I am going there [to Liberia] to check up on the situation. If I am able to link up with a big commander of the LURD rebels,[33] I am sure that as soon as they are in power, I will get a good job. And when they take Monrovia there will be a lot of loot.

After a few weeks I got a phone call from Samuel. He enthusiastically told me that he had succeeded and was now staying with an important LURD rebel commander.

Discussion

Samuel has been shaped by his long years in the army. Irregulars like him had typical patron-client relationships with their commanders, whereby the commander would provide food, protection and military training, while the irregulars worked as part of his personal and loyal force, protecting him and handing over loot from the front line. For both parties this was, under the given circumstances, a profitable relationship. To the younger irregulars, the commander was probably considered as a substitute for lost family, but the older and more experienced ones consciously evaluated whether or not the relationship was beneficial to them. If not, they would try to look for another *bra*. In this way it would be wrong to consider irregulars, together with so many other youthful combatants, as victims. They were used by their commanders but at the same time they used their commanders to get scarce but necessary resources such as protection, food and shelter. They also got a substitute for their disrupted education or vocational training, namely the deadly – but highly useful and relevant – skill of how to handle a weapon and fight a war.

---

[33] The Liberians United for Reconciliation and Democracy (LURD) fought against the former warlord, but later democratically elected president, Charles Taylor.

When Samuel returned to his village without the backing of a *bra*,[34] he immediately identified a potential new 'big brother' (the ex-RUF commander with the music-set). The relationship was short-lived because the ex-commander, afraid of the Special Court, decided to move further into Kailahun District (the former stronghold of the RUF close to the Liberian border).

With most of the people in the village, including his father, being poor farmers recovering from the war, Samuel was forced to build his life without the support of a patron –something he had never learned to do before. If he had been determined, hard-working and patient, he would have stood a good chance of accumulating some wealth in a few years' time. With his contacts, experience, and skills in English, he could have played an important role in the village. However, his years in the army had made too big an impact on him. The gap between his father and the more traditional way of life on the one hand and Samuel's army life and ways of surviving on the other hand was too big.[35]

What is clear from the above case study is that there was considerable generational tension between Samuel and his father. His father felt that, now the war had ended, everything would return to how it was in the pre-war days, including the absolute authority of parents over their children. Samuel clearly had a different opinion.

But to consider the post-war tensions between elders and youth solely in terms of generational conflict only partly explains the situation as it is in Sierra Leone today. The war catalyzed already existing organizational modalities and value systems in Sierra Leone. Samuel grew up in a totally different culture with its own specific social features. To understand fully the social dynamics in post-war Sierra Leone, and more specifically the difficulties and constraints youth ex-combatants experience during their reintegration process, the neo-Durkheimian theory can be useful. Once fully aware of the different value systems of the various factions and those present in post-war Sierra Leone, careful consideration of these different types of cultural biases, as predicted by the model, should enable policy-makers to link those which correspond. This

---

[34] It became clear to me that my friendship with Samuel might not have been on as equal a basis as I had assumed it to be. Helping Samuel financially to return to his village, he probably considered me not only as a friend but also as a *bra*. This reminded me of some former child soldiers who I had interviewed at the end of 2001 and who had been in the same reintegration programme as Samuel in 1994/95. These former army combatants still felt that the programme should assist them in their education and daily life six years later, considering this programme almost as a *bra* in itself.

[35] An ex-CDF combatant might have been more patient under the same circumstances. The apprentice system (the CDF mode of operation) is based on benefits in the future, after graduation. Farming does not bring immediate rewards and an ex-CDF fighter might even patiently wait to inherit his father's land.

should ease the reintegration process and make it more sustainable. It could forecast many of the problems a DDR programme and post-programme reintegration process might face, and offer improvements in the programme's design.

It is perhaps important to stress that the value systems of armed factions do not need to be violent. They are rooted in the specific way a group manages restrictions and regulations, often imposed by others, or by environmental constraints. They could be considered as the subjects' social capital, in this case that of the ex-combatants. Rather than trying to break down these modalities during the demobilization process, they should be considered as valuable social capital that can be put to peaceful use in the right circumstances and environment. Post-war Sierra Leonean society offers, and should offer, scope for a wide variety of modalities and values in an effort to incorporate as many people as possible. After all, one of the main underlying causes of the conflict in Sierra Leone was the dominant character of just one such system: the hierarchical patrimonial system.

References

Abdullah, I. 1997, 'Bush Path to Destruction: The Origin and Character of the Revolutionary United Front (RUF/SL)', *Africa Development*, 22 (3/4): 45-76 (Special Issue: 'Lumpen Culture and Political Violence: The Sierra Leone Civil War').

Archibald, S. & P. Richards 2002, 'Converts to Human Rights? Popular Debate about War and Justice in Rural Central Sierra Leone', *Africa,* 72 (3): 339-367.

Arthy, S. 2003, 'Ex-combatant Reintegration. Key Issues for Policy Makers and Practitioners Based on Lessons from Sierra Leone', London: DFID (unpublished).

Douglas, M. 1982 (1970), *Natural Symbols: Explorations in Cosmology*, New York: Pantheon Books.

Douglas, M. 1993, *In the Wilderness: The Doctrine of Defilement in the Book of Numbers*, Sheffield: JSOT Press.

Douglas, M. & S. Ney 1998, *Missing Persons*, Berkeley, Los Angeles/London & New York: University of California Press/Russell Sage Foundation.

Fithen, C. & P. Richards 2002, 'Making War, Crafting Peace: Militia Solidarities and Demobilization in Sierra Leone', in P. Richards (ed.), *No Peace No War: Learning to Live Beyond Violent Conflict* (forthcoming).

Kaplan, R.D. 1994, 'The Coming Anarchy: How Scarcity, Crime, Overpopulation, and Disease Are Rapidly Destroying the Social Fabric of our Planet', *Atlantic Monthly*, February, 44-76.

Muana, P.K. 1997, 'The Kamajoi Militia: Civil War, Internal Displacement and the Politics of Counter-Insurgency', *Africa Development*, 22 (3/4): 77-100.

Peters, K. 2004, 'Re-examining Voluntarism. Youth Combatants in Sierra Leone', Pretoria: Institute for Security Studies (ISS monograph series, 100, 4/2004).

Peters, K. & P. Richards 1998a, '"When They Say Soldiers Are Rebels, It's a Lie": Young Fighters Talk about War and Peace in Sierra Leone', *Cahiers d'Etudes Africaines*, 150-152 (38): 581-617.

Peters, K. & P. Richards 1998b, 'Why We Fight: Voices of Under-Age Youth Combatants in Sierra Leone', *Africa*, 68 (2): 183-210.

Richards, P. 1996, *Fighting for the Rain Forest: War, Youth and Resources in Sierra Leone*, Oxford: James Currey (reprinted with additional material 1998).

Richards, P. 1999, 'New Political Violence in Africa: Secular Sectarianism in Sierra Leone', *GeoJournal*, 47: 433-44.

Richards, P. 2001, 'Green Book Millenarians? The Sierra Leone War from the Perspective of an Anthropology of Religion', in N. Kastfelt (ed.), *Religion and Civil War in Africa*, London: C. Hurst.

Stavrou, A., P. Burton, S. Johnson, K. Peters & J. Vincent 2003, 'NCDDR Ex-combatants 2003 Tracer Study', Sierra Leone Multi-Donor Trust Fund, Unpublished report.

List of authors

Jon Abbink is head of the Culture, Politics and Inequality theme group at the African Studies Centre in Leiden and has a professorial chair at the Vrije Universiteit in Amsterdam. His research interests include ethnicity in Africa, developments in the political cultures of Northeast Africa, Ethio-Eritrean relations, and the ethno-history and social organization of the Wolayta region in Ethiopia. He is involved in the ongoing *Encyclopedia Aethiopica* project for which he acts as a specialist on Ethiopian ethnology and history. In 2003 he published papers in the journals *Journal of Contemporary African Studies*, *Africa*(Roma) and *Ethnos*. He is currently working on a book on Southern Ethiopia.
abbink@fsw.leidenuniv.nl

Karel Arnaut is a lecturer in the Department of African Languages and Cultures at Ghent University in Belgium. Public performances in Côte d'Ivoire, ranging from masquerades and processions over political demonstrations to media and publicity, are the central focus of his research. He is currently completing his PhD on mobility and mobilization and is the author of numerous articles, for example, 'Islam and Its Others: Sakaraboutou as Masquerade in Bondoukou (Côte d'Ivoire)' in *Etnofoor* (2001), and "Out of the Race": The Poiesis of Genocide in Mass Media Discourses in Côte d'Ivoire' in G. Baumann & A. Gingrich (eds) *Grammars of Identity/Alterity* (Berghahn 2004).
karel.arnaut@UGent.be

G. Thomas Burgess is assistant professor of history at Hampton University in the United States where he is researching the relationships between the Zanzibari Revolution, generation, nationalism and discipline. His work has appeared in the *International Journal of African Historical Studies* and *Africa Today*, and he is currently completing two book projects. The first is a revision of his dissertation, and the second, which he is editing with Ali Sultan Issa, has the working title *Walk on Two Legs: An Oral Memoir of the Zanzibari Revolution*.
kennedybyu@yahoo.com

Sara Rich Dorman is a lecturer in politics at the University of Edinburgh. She has also taught at the University of Asmara, Eritrea, and the University of

Oxford. Her research interests include the politics of NGOs, churches, elections and election observation, and state-society relations in post-liberation societies. Her recent publications include: 'Democrats and Donors: Studying Democratization in Africa' in T. Kelsall & J. Igoe (eds), *Donors, NGOs, and the Liberal Agenda in Africa* (2004), 'NGOs and the Constitutional Debate in Zimbabwe: from Inclusion to Exclusion' in the *Journal of Southern African Studies* (2003), and 'Rocking the Boat? Church NGOs and Democratization in Zimbabwe' in *African Affairs* (2002).

sara.dorman@ed.ac.uk

Jok Madut Jok studied anthropology in Egypt and the United States. He is now associate professor of history at Loyola Marymount University in Los Angeles and a fellow of the Rift Valley Institute. With John Ryle, he recently completed a UK government-funded project investigating abduction and enslavement in the course of the ongoing conflict in Sudan. He is the author of *War and Slavery in Sudan* (University of Pennsylvania Press, 2001), 'Militarism, Gender and Reproductive Suffering: The Case of Abortion in Western Dinka' in *Africa* (1999), and, with Sharon Hutchinson, 'Gendered Violence and the Militarization of Ethnicity: A Case from South Sudan' in *African Studies Review* (1999).

jjok@lmu.edu

Peter Mwangi Kagwanja is the director of the International Crisis Group Southern Africa Project and a research associate with the Centre for International Political Studies at the University of Pretoria. Prior to joining the ICG, he was a senior researcher on peace, security and governance with SaferAfrica, a lecturer in political science and history at Moi University, and a research associate with the Kenya Human Rights Commission. He has published numerous articles, book chapters and commissioned reports on human rights, forced migration, governance, (violent) conflict, globalization and citizenship with a special focus on women, youth and refugees. He is a member of the editorial board of *African Affairs*.

Pkagwanja@hotmail.com

Ineke van Kessel is a historian at the African Studies Centre in Leiden whose work focuses mainly on contemporary South Africa. She is, however, currently working on the history of Dutch-Ghanaian relations and doing research into the

African soldiers enlisted in the Netherlands East Indies army in the 19th century.
kessel@fsw.leidenuniv.nl

Piet Konings is a senior researcher at the African Studies Centre in Leiden. He has published widely on the political economy and labour in Africa, especially in Ghana and Cameroon. His current research focuses on political change and regionalism in Cameroon and the role of civil society in Africa. His most recent publications include *Unilever Estates in Crisis and the Power of Organizations in Cameroon* (Lit Verlag, 1998), *Trajectoires de Libération en Afrique Contemporaine* (Karthala, 2000), and *Negotiating an Anglophone Identity: A Study of the Politics of Recognition and Representation in Cameroon* (Brill, 2003).
konings@fsw.leidenuniv.nl

Murray Last, now professor emeritus in the Department of Anthropology at University College London, first went to Nigeria in 1961 and was Professor of History at Bayero University, Kano from 1978-1980. His 1967 book, *The Sokoto Caliphate* (Longmans) has also been published in Arabic and is currently being translated into Hausa. He has published extensively on the anthropology of traditional medicine, and his recent publications include 'Notes on the Implementation of Shari'a in Northern Nigeria' in *FAIS Journal of Humanities*, and 'Hausa' in C. & M. Ember (eds) *Encyclopaedia of Medical Anthropology: Health and Illness in the World's Cultures* (Kluwer Academic Publishers, 2004).
m.last@ucl.ac.uk

Yves Marguerat is director of research in social sciences at the Institut de Recherche pour le Développement (IRD), (formerly ORSTOM). He has worked in Cameroon, Côte d'Ivoire and Togo where, in addition to researching the political history of Togo, he has worked with marginalized street children. He has written extensively on the topic, for example, 'Woe to Thee, O City, When Thy King is a (Street) Child', in B. Trudell *et al.* (eds) *Africa's Young Majority* (University of Edinburgh, 2002). In Paris he heads GREJEM (*Groupe de Recherche et d'Echanges sur les Jeunesses Marginalisées*) at the Centre d'Etudes Africaines at the EHESS and he is also working at the Institute of Criminology at the University of Abidjan.
yves.marguerat@bondy.ird.fr

Angela McIntyre coordinates Interact, a research project on children in armed conflict at the Institute for Security Studies in Pretoria, South Africa. She contributes regularly to the *African Security Review*, has co-written a number of ISS occasional papers, edited a series of monographs on children in armed conflict and is currently editing a book entitled *The Impact of Children on War: Young People as Stakeholders in African Conflicts*.
angela@iss.org.za

Krijn Peters has a background in rural development sociology and has been involved in research on the disarmament, demobilization and reintegration process of under-age combatants in Sierra Leone and Liberia since 1996. He is currently working on his PhD on the war experiences and reintegration process of youthful ex-combatants in Sierra Leone's Revolutionary United Front. His recent publications include *Re-examining Voluntarism. Youth Combatants in Sierra Leone* (Pretoria, ISS monograph series 2004) and a report published in 2003 for Save the Children Fund entitled *When Children Affected by War Go Home: Lessons Learned from Liberia* (with S. Laws).
krijn.peters@alg.tao.wau.nl

Simon Simonse is an anthropologist with an interest in warfare and kingship as institutions capable of generating social consensus. He has done field research in South Sudan but for the past ten years, while working as a UN staff member and for various NGOs, his research has focused on the humanitarian response to the complex political emergencies in the Great Lakes Region and in the Horn of Africa. He is the author of a study of sacred kingship in South Sudan entitled *Kings of Disaster* (Brill, 1992), and, with Eisei Kurimoto, he edited *Conflict, Age and Power in North East Africa* (James Currey 1998).
simonse@paxchristi.nl

AFRICAN DYNAMICS

ISSN 1568-1777

1. Bruijn, M. de, R. van Dijk and D. Foeken (eds.) *Mobile Africa*. Changing Patterns of Movement in Africa and Beyond. 2001. ISBN 90 04 12072 6
2. Abbink, J., M. de Bruijn and K. van Walraven. *Rethinking Resistance*. Revolt and Violence in African History. 2003. ISBN 90 04 12624 4
3. Van Binsbergen, W. and R. van Dijk. *Situating Globality*. African Agency in the Appropriation of Global Culture. 2004. ISBN 90 04 13133 7
4. Abbink, J. and I. van Kessel. *Vanguard or Vandals*. Youth, Politics and Conflict in Africa. 2005. ISBN 90 04 14275 4